D0081176

THE
EGYPTIAN HERMES

THE
EGYPTIAN HERMES

A HISTORICAL APPROACH TO
THE LATE PAGAN MIND

GARTH FOWDEN

Center for Greek and Roman Antiquity
National Research Foundation, Athens

PRINCETON UNIVERSITY PRESS
PRINCETON, NEW JERSEY

Published by Princeton University Press, 41 William Street,
Princeton, New Jersey 08540
In the United Kingdom: Princeton University Press, Chichester,
West Sussex

Library of Congress Cataloging-in-Publication Data

Fowden, Garth.
The Egyptian Hermes: a historical approach to the late pagan
mind / Garth Fowden.
p.   cm.—(Mythos)
Originally published: Cambridge, Cambridgeshire; New York:
Cambridge University Press, 1986. With new pref.
Includes bibliographical references and index.
ISBN 0-691-02498-7 (pbk.)
1. Hermetism.   2. Hermes, Trismegistus.   3. Egypt—Religion.
4. Paganism—History.   I. Title.   II. Series: Mythos
(Princeton, N.J.)
BF1591.F75   1993
135'.4—dc20   92-37534

First Princeton Paperback printing, with corrections and
a new preface, 1993

Reprinted by arrangement with Cambridge University Press

Princeton University Press books are printed on acid-free paper
and meet the guidelines for permanence and durability of the
Committee on Production Guidelines for Book Longevity of the
Council on Library Resources

10 9 8 7 6 5 4 3

Printed in the United States of America

ΠΟΛΥΜΝΙΑΙ

παιδεύουσιν ἡμῶν αἱ Μοῦσαι σὺν Ἑρμῇ λογίῳ τὰς ψυχάς

Contents

Contents

Abbreviations

The conventions of *L'année philologique* have been followed for periodical titles, and those of J. F. Oates *et al.*, *Checklist of editions of Greek papyri and ostraca* (Chico, Ca. 1985³), for papyrological collections. Note also the following:

Aeg. I. Berl.	*Aegyptische Inschriften aus den Königlichen Museen zu Berlin* (Leipzig 1913–14)
A.E.H.E.G.	*Annales de l'Ecole des Hautes-Etudes de Gand* (Gent)
Alch. gr.	M. Berthelot and C.-E. Ruelle (eds.), *Collection des anciens alchimistes grecs: texte grec* (Paris 1888)
A.R.B.S.H.	*Académie Roumaine. Bulletin de la Section Historique* (Bucharest)
Ascl.	*Asclepius*, ed. N.F. 2
B.S.F.E.	*Bulletin de la Société Française d'Egyptologie* (Paris)
C.C.A.G.	F. Cumont *et al.* (eds.), *Catalogus codicum astrologorum graecorum* (Brussels 1898–1936)
C.C.S.L.	*Corpus christianorum, series latina* (Turnhout)
C.H.	*Corpus Hermeticum*, ed. N.F. 1–2
C.M.A.G.	J. Bidez *et al.* (eds.), *Catalogue des manuscrits alchimiques grecs* (Brussels 1924–32)
C.P.G.	M. Geerard (ed.), *Clavis patrum graecorum* (Turnhout 1974–)
C.S.E.L.	*Corpus scriptorum ecclesiasticorum latinorum* (Vienna)
Cyr. H.	*Cyrilli [Alexandrini] Hermetica*, ed. N.F. 4.125–43
D.H.	*Definitions of Hermes Trismegistus to Asclepius*, ed. Mahé 2
D.S.B.	C. C. Gillispie (ed.), *Dictionary of scientific biography* (New York 1970–6)
E.A.C.	*Entretiens sur l'antiquité classique* (*Fondation Hardt*) (Geneva)

E.R.E.	J. Hastings *et al.* (eds.), *Encyclopaedia of religion and ethics* (Edinburgh 1908–26)
Festugière	A.-J. Festugière, *La révélation d'Hermès Trismégiste* (Paris 1944–54; 1², 1950)
F. Gr. H.	F. Jacoby (ed.), *Die Fragmente der griechischen Historiker* (Berlin, Leiden 1923–58)
F. Gr. Th.	H. Erbse (ed.), *Fragmente griechischer Theosophien* (Hamburg 1941)
Fraser	P. M. Fraser, *Ptolemaic Alexandria* (Oxford 1972)
G.C.S.	*Die griechischen christlichen Schriftsteller der ersten drei Jahrhunderte* (Leipzig, Berlin)
Gr. D. Fr.	E. Heitsch (ed.), *Die griechischen Dichterfragmente der römischen Kaiserzeit* (Göttingen 1963–4²)
Gundel	W. G. and H. G. Gundel, *Astrologumena. Die astrologische Literatur in der Antike und ihre Geschichte* (Wiesbaden 1966)
I. Cyme	H. Engelmann (ed.), *Die Inschriften von Kyme* (Bonn 1976)
I.G.L.P.	A. and E. Bernand (eds.), *Les inscriptions grecques [et latines] de Philae* (Paris 1969)
I. L. Alg.	S. Gsell *et al.* (eds.), *Inscriptions latines de l'Algérie* (Paris 1922–)
I. mét. Eg.	E. Bernand (ed.), *Inscriptions métriques de l'Egypte gréco-romaine. Recherches sur la poésie épigrammatique des grecs en Egypte* (Paris 1969)
Kl. Pauly	K. Ziegler and W. Sontheimer (eds.), *Der kleine Pauly: Lexikon der Antike* (Munich 1975)
Lex. Äg.	W. Helck *et al.* (eds.), *Lexikon der Ägyptologie* (Wiesbaden 1975–)
L.S.J.	H. G. Liddell, R. Scott, H. S. Jones (eds.), *A Greek–English lexicon* (Oxford 1940⁹; Suppl. 1968)
Mahé	J.-P. Mahé, *Hermès en Haute-Egypte* (Quebec 1978–82)
N.F.	A. D. Nock and A. J. Festugière (eds.), *Corpus Hermeticum* (Paris 1946–54)
N.G.G.	*Nachrichten von der Königlichen Gesellschaft der Wissenschaften zu Göttingen, Philologisch-historische Klasse* (Göttingen, Berlin)
N.H.C.	*Nag Hammadi codices*

N.H.S.	*Nag Hammadi studies* (Leiden):

7. J.-E. Ménard (ed.), *Les textes de Nag Hammadi. Colloque du Centre d'Histoire des Religions (Strasbourg, 23–25 octobre 1974)* (1975)

11. D. M. Parrott (ed.), *Nag Hammadi codices V, 2–5 and VI, with Papyrus Berolinensis 8502,1 and 4* (1979)

13. C. Schmidt (ed.), *The Books of Jeu and the Untitled Text in the Bruce Codex* (1978)

15. B. A. Pearson (ed.), *Nag Hammadi codices IX and X* (1981)

16. J. W. B. Barns, G. M. Browne and J. C. Shelton (eds.), *Nag Hammadi codices: Greek and Coptic papyri from the cartonnage of the covers* (1981)

17. M. Krause (ed.), *Gnosis and Gnosticism. Papers read at the Eighth International Conference on Patristic Studies (Oxford, September 3rd–8th 1979)* (1981)

O.C.A.	*Orientalia christiana analecta* (Rome)
O.G.I.S.	W. Dittenberger (ed.), *Orientis graeci inscriptiones selectae* (Leipzig 1903–5)
Orph. fr.	O. Kern (ed.), *Orphicorum fragmenta* (Berlin 1922)
P.D.	*Perfect discourse.*
P.G.	J.-P. Migne (ed.), *Patrologia graeca* (Paris)
Philae	F.Ll. Griffith (ed.), *Catalogue of the demotic graffiti of the Dodecaschoenus* 1 (Oxford 1937) 42–130 (Philae)
Phys. med. gr.	I. L. Ideler (ed.), *Physici et medici graeci minores* (Berlin 1841–2)
P. Insinger	(1) F. Lexa (ed.), *Papyrus Insinger. Les enseignements moraux d'un scribe égyptien du premier siècle après J.-C.* (Paris 1926). (2) A. Volten (ed.), *Kopenhagener Texte zum demotischen Weisheitsbuch (Pap. Carlsberg II, III verso, IV verso und V)* (Copenhagen 1940)
P.L.R.E.	A. H. M. Jones (1), J. R. Martindale (1 + 2) and J. Morris (1) (eds.), *The prosopography of the later Roman empire* (Cambridge 1971–80)
R.I.P.B.	*Revue de l'instruction publique en Belgique* (Brussels)

Abbreviations

S.A.O.C.	*Studies in ancient oriental civilization* (Chicago)
S.C.	*Sources chrétiennes* (Paris)
Scott	W. Scott, *Hermetica. The ancient Greek and Latin writings which contain religious or philosophic teachings ascribed to Hermes Trismegistus* (Oxford 1924–36)
S.H.	*Stobaei Hermetica*, ed. N.F. 3–4
S.M.S.R.	*Studi e materiali di storia delle religioni* (Rome)
S. Or.	*Sources orientales* (Paris)
S.P.A.	*Sitzungsberichte der Königlich Preussischen Akademie der Wissenschaften* (Berlin)
Stud. Aeg.	*Studia Aegyptiaca* (Budapest)
W.A.	*World archaeology* (Henley-on-Thames)

Preface to the 1993 edition

By way of introduction to this paperback edition of a book first published in 1986, it seems appropriate to add some remarks about the place of *The Egyptian Hermes* in the general context of current work on cultural interaction in the ancient Mediterranean world.

Hard on the heels of *The Egyptian Hermes* came *Black Athena* in 1987.[1] Martin Bernal had a good deal to say about Hermetism in the first volume of this now-notorious work. While we both emphasize Egyptian elements in the teachings of Hermes Trismegistus, I do so in order to describe cultural interaction in late antique Egypt, whereas Bernal's aim is to establish Egypt's chronological priority and preeminence. To this end he revives Flinders Petrie's long-forgotten dating of parts of the Hermetic literature as early as the sixth century B.C., so that it antedates Plato and even Pythagoras. The originality of the Greeks is in this way undermined, and the long pedigree of early modern Europe's Egyptocentric and often explicitly Hermetic view of the past is forcefully recalled.

Black Athena is in general highly political, and so in particular is its view of Hermetism. Although Bernal pushes the evidence very hard in order to make his point, I do not in principle dissent from his political approach to the Hermetica and to the wider question of Hellenism's identity and influence. The classical Greek ideal remains, after all, a political force as we celebrate the 2500th anniversary of the inauguration of democracy, and those who aspire to impose a new world order invoke democracy as their slogan. But the ancient Greeks had much more than democracy to offer, and even their democracy was not much like ours. While the ancient Greeks were Hellenism's beginning, they were certainly not its end. It would be a sad diminution of Hellenism's historical range and spiritual depth if it were to be monopolized by classicists, not to

---

[1] M. Bernal, *Black Athena: The Afroasiatic roots of classical civilization* 1 (London 1987), especially 134–45 on the Hermetica.

mention "democrats." A useful corrective is to investigate the Hellenic tradition's interaction with the ancient, mediaeval, and modern cultures that provide its context in Eastern Mediterranean lands. In a stimulating essay, Glen Bowersock has recently shown the way by tackling Hellenism's role as lingua franca among the various ethnic traditions of late polytheist antiquity, and noting its influence on early Islam.[2]

What Bowersock does not do is carry his argument very far into the Christian world. In my *Empire to commonwealth: Consequences of monotheism in late antiquity* (Princeton 1993), I have broached a related theme from the history of Christian Rome, namely the formation of a Byzantine Commonwealth in the Monophysite world of the eastern provinces and beyond, whose culture owed much to Greek Christianity but was deemed heretical by Constantinople. *The Egyptian Hermes* deals with an earlier phase in this relationship between Hellenism and the East; and because it is narrowly focused on the Hermetic milieu, it does not bring out fully the relevance of its subject-matter to later developments. This is now perhaps best perceived if we read *The Egyptian Hermes* in conjunction with Rowan Williams's excellent monograph on Arius.[3]

Williams's Arius is a typical product of that same Alexandrian philosophical milieu in which the Hermetists were at home. He was a sage with his study-circle and a doctrine that grew from a tradition but was in significant part his own individual creation. Seen from this perspective, the world of the late Platonists can be clearly understood by the student of Christianity to be neither pure antithesis nor merely a backdrop, but a context in the fullest sense. The Christian counterpart of the "pagan" philosopher is, in other words, not necessarily the monk, and to label both "holy men" can be misleading. The monastic way of life came, it is true, to be called the Christian "philosophy," but monks were not encouraged to be independent minds in the manner of Origen and Arius, who were much closer to the traditional ideal of the philosopher. Both these teachers were to be condemned by a Church that valued conformity to conciliar decisions, episcopally and even imperially enforced, above the personal authority of the sage.

From Constantine onward, belief was centrally dictated and a highly political issue—necessarily so, if institutional Christianity

---

[2] G. W. Bowersock, *Hellenism in late antiquity* (Cambridge 1990), e.g., p. 13.
[3] R. Williams, *Arius: Heresy and tradition* (London 1987).

was to overcome the many challenges it encountered. The Church that valued its Fathers never wholly lost esteem for revelation's privileged individual interpreters, but we should not imagine that the patristic canon has been any less invidious in its effect than that of the classicists. Although capable of sanitizing by reattribution suspect writings such as the pseudo-Dionysian corpus, with its profound influence from late Platonism, the official ecclesiastical canon has marginalized much other Christian philosophy, whose reintroduction into our field of vision is fortunately now lending new range and nuance to the understanding of late antiquity. Giants like Origen and Evagrius Ponticus have long been of obvious interest to scholars; but recent work on figures such as Synesius,[4] Nemesius of Emesa,[5] John of Apamea,[6] and John Philoponus[7] reminds us how the patristic canon has deemphasized many other important individuals who remained close—sometimes too close—to the world of Greek philosophy. Because of the abundance of references to it in patristic literature, Hermetism occupies in this respect a central position. Not that Hermes was treated with high seriousness as a doctrinal authority. He was more likely to be quoted with approval by a Lactantius than an Augustine, while Cyril of Alexandria was not alone in using him mainly as a stick with which to beat "pagan" opponents like Julian. But the study of Hermetism is undeniably much more dependent on Christian sources than is that of late Platonism, and as such it offers us a privileged viewpoint from which to survey the cultural interactions of late antiquity.

The present edition corrects some minor errors that survived the corrected reprint of 1987 (the reprint of 1990 being uncorrected). Valuable criticisms may be found in the reviews by G. Geraci, *Aegyptus* 68 (1988) 275–6; J. G. Griffiths, *C.R.* 38 (1988) 293–5; and R. Lane Fox, *J.R.S.* 80 (1990) 237–40. In the light of these and other recent publications, the following points should be noted:
p. xiv n. 3:
The bibliography of Hermetism is brought up to date by J.-P. Mahé, "La voie d'immortalité à la lumière des *Hermetica* de Nag

[4] S. Vollenweider, *Neuplatonische und christliche Theologie bei Synesios von Kyrene* (Göttingen 1985); and cf. below, 179.
[5] M. Morani, ed., *Nemesii Emeseni de natura hominis* (Leipzig 1987); and cf. below, 10.
[6] R. Lavenant, ed., *Jean d'Apamée: Dialogues et traités* (Paris 1984).
[7] R. Sorabji, ed., *Philoponus and the rejection of Aristotelian science* (London 1987).

Hammadi et de découvertes plus récentes," *V. Chr.* 45 (1991) 372–5, to which add B. P. Copenhaver, *Hermetica. The Greek Corpus Hermeticum and the Latin Asclepius in a new English translation, with notes and introduction* (Cambridge 1992).

pp. 3 and 21:

More could have been made of the mid-second-century B.C. Sarapeum archive from Memphis, which indicates both the period at which the technical Hermetica must have emerged, and the mixture of Greek and Egyptian in the Memphite milieu. See now the excellent discussion by D. J. Thompson, *Memphis under the Ptolemies* (Princeton 1988) ch. 7, esp. 252–65 on the papyrus containing the *Art of Eudoxus*. This "earliest illustrated scientific work to have survived from antiquity" calls itself "oracles of Hermes"; and the whole papyrus is labelled "Within, concerns of Hermes."

p. 10:

Mahé, *V. Chr.* 45 (1991) 368 n. 35, draws attention to the ambiguity of my remark that the Greek original of the Armenian *Definitions* offers "an interesting parallel to the dismemberment of the *Perfect discourse* performed during the prehistory of *N.H.C.* VI." I meant that the *D.H.* reflect a literature in the process of becoming, and probably made up of concurrent textual versions at varying stages of development, rather than a literature that was being decomposed into florilegia (though that was happening too).

In the same article (loc. cit.), Mahé restates his view that *N.H.C.* VI.7, the prayer of thanksgiving, was not extracted from the *P.D.*, because the prayer's narrative framework differs from that in the *P.D.*, as known to us from its Latin translation, the *Asclepius* (for a new critical edition of which see C. Moreschini, ed., *Apulei Platonici Madaurensis opera quae supersunt 3: De philosophia libri* [Stuttgart, 1991] 39–86). But our dependence on the *Ascl.* imperils direct deductions from it about the lost *P.D.*'s text, and Mahé does not counter the idea that, if the compiler of the Hermetic collection contained within *N.H.C.* VI. decided to treat the prayer as the conclusion of *N.H.C.* VI.6 (*The Ogdoad reveals the Ennead*), it would have been natural for him to make some small adjustments to its narrative framework (as for example the change from second to third person). See also below, 86 n.50.

To my account of the surviving Hermetic texts should now be added the "Hermetica Oxoniensia" from Bodleian Library, Clarke gr. 11, published by J. Paramelle and J.-P. Mahé, "Extraits hermétiques inédits dans un manuscrit d'Oxford," *R.E.G.* 104 (1991) 109–39, and "Nouveaux parallèles grecs aux *Définitions* hermétiques arméniennes," *R.E.Arm.* 22 (1990–1) 115–34. I. G. Taifacos, *C. Iulius Romanus and his method of compilation in the Aphormai* (diss. London 1988) 31–5, draws attention to a previously unnoticed Hermetic fragment quoted by C. Iulius Romanus (third century) ap. Charisius (fourth century), *Ars grammatica* II.239 (p. 312.4–7 Barwick): "nam, ut Hermes ἐν τῷ κρυφίῳ λόγῳ scribit, ὑὸς ἐλέχθη σαπρὰ σπορά. τὸ γὰρ ὕσπορός ἐστιν, τὸ δέ ὗον οὐσία, καθότι τὸ γένος ἀνθρώπων ἐκ πυρὸς καὶ θανάτου στολῆς ἐγένετο."

pp. 22–4:

On the descent of Hermes Trismegistus from the all-powerful Thoth of the ancient Egyptian scribes, see the thought-provoking article by B. Couroyer, "Le 'Dieu des sages' en Egypte," *R.Bi.* 94 (1987) 574–603; 95 (1988) 70–91, 195–210.

pp. 29–31:

In connection with the two Hermeses, note also Synesius's asssertion, *De regno* 7 and *De providentia* I.11, that the Egyptians make double images of Hermes in which an old and a young man stand side by side, in order to signify that Hermes is both wise and brave.

p. 36 n.139:

The view that Hermetism was influenced by Christianity, and in particular by Christian gnosticism, has gained ground of late: J. Büchli, *Der Poimandres, ein paganisiertes Evangelium. Sprachliche und begriffliche Untersuchungen zum 1. Traktat des Corpus Hermeticum* (Tübingen 1987); M. Simonetti, "Alcune riflessioni sul rapporto tra gnosticismo e cristianesimo," *Vet. Chr.* 28 (1991): 337–74, esp. 362. But Büchli's argument for Christian influence on the Hermetica rests on an exclusively philological investigation of just one tractate, the *Poimandres*. While not wishing to exclude the possibility that some Hermetist writers were in contact with Christianity, I see as yet no reason to abandon the cautious tone of my remarks on Hermetism's relationship to Christian gnosticism (113–14).

p. 73:

Egyptian elements in the Hermetica continue to attract scholarly attention: see, e.g., H. Jackson, "Κόρη κόσμου: Isis, pupil of the eye of the world," *C.E.* 61 (1986) 116–35; J.P. Sørensen, "Ancient Egyptian religious thought and the XVIth Hermetic tractate," in G. Englund, ed., *The religion of the ancient Egyptians: Cognitive structures and popular expressions* (Uppsala 1987) 41–57.

pp. 87 and 161–2:

K. Alpers, "Untersuchungen zum griechischen Physiologus und den Kyraniden," *Vestigia Bibliae* 6 (1984) 17ff., and D. Bain, "'Treading birds': An unnoticed use of πατέω (*Cyranides* 1.10.27, 1.19.9)," in E. M. Craik, ed., *'Owls to Athens.' Essays on classical subjects presented to Sir Kenneth Dover* (Oxford 1990) 296, place Harpocration in the fourth century, ignoring or dismissing the allusion in Tertullian. Yet Tertullian's observation that "Liberum, *eundem apud Aegyptios Osirim*, Harpocration industria ederatum argumentatur," may imply that his Harpocration was, like the Harpocration of the *Cyranides*, Egyptian; and his explanation ("quod ederae natura sit cerebrum ab heluco defensare") recalls similar material in our Harpocration: *Cyr.* 46.3–8 (Kaimakis). A further argument for placing Harpocration in the fourth century is the notion that the Magnus and Marcellinus referred to in acrostics reused by Harpocration are the iatrosophist Magnus of Nisibis and either the historian Ammianus Marcellinus, or the Marcellinus to whom Libanius addressed his *ep.* 1063 (if these are not, as G. W. Bowersock, *J.R.S.* 80 (1990) 247–8, and T. D. Barnes, *C.Ph.* 88 (1993) 57–60, now argue, the same person). But there is no known direct link between these figures, nor any other reason to identify them with the Magnus and Marcellinus of the acrostics. It seems best to keep Magnus, Marcellinus, and Harpocration in the second century, and admit that Libanius's Marcellinus, if he is not the historian, may be otherwise unknown to us.

p. 101:

On my discussion of the relationship between *epistēmē* and *gnōsis*, note the critical remarks by Mahé, *V.Chr.* 45 (1991) 367 n.11a.

p. 132:

On Porphyry's "universal way," see some further comments in my *Empire to commonwealth*, 39–40.

pp. 156–61:

This historical use of the Hermetic texts is implicitly rejected by R. Valantasis, *Spiritual guides of the third century: A semiotic study of the guide-disciple relationship in Christianity, Neoplatonism, Hermetism, and Gnosticism* (Minneapolis 1991), according to whom "the guides and the relationships result from the textual strategies, not from a description of historical reality" (151). The purpose of Porphyry's *Vita Plotini* is therefore "to sell [Plotinus's] books" (154). On *Lese-*

mysterien see below, 149–50. I persist in thinking there is more to life than literature.

p. 172:

I agree with R. Lane Fox, *J.R.S.* 80 (1990) 239, that "the jury is still out" on the question whether the Nag Hammadi codices belonged to a Christian gnostic group or a monastery (Pachomian or other). But casting doubt on Epiphanius's explicit statement that such gnostic groups still existed in fourth-century Egypt (C. Scholten, "Die Nag-Hammadi-Texte als Buchbesitz der Pachomianer," *Jb.A.C.* 31 (1988) 169–70, without serious arguments, but accepted by Lane Fox) does not prove the inherent improbability of such survival, especially when one takes into account the unambiguous evidence from Syria: K. Koschorke, "Patristische Materialien zur Spätgeschichte der Valentinianische Gnosis," *N.H.S.* 17 (1981) 120–39. Although the outcome of this debate is not crucial to my attempt to locate the milieux that produced the Hermetica, since *N.H.C.* VI merely reuses Hermetic materials originally composed elsewhere, the Nag Hammadi phase in the history of these particular Hermetica is distinctive in that it is Coptic, not Greek. And just because the overwhelming majority of Coptic texts is Christian, we cannot exclude an element of bilingualism in the Hermetic milieu, especially since the Thebes cache also (below, 168–73) points in this direction.

ch. 8:

On the late antique Latin sources for Hermetism, see C. Moreschini, *Dall' Asclepius al Crater Hermetis. Studi sull' ermetismo latino tardo-antico e rinascimentale* (Pisa 1985).

Finally, I would like to thank Anthony Grafton for proposing and the editorial staff of Princeton University Press for facilitating the inclusion of *The Egyptian Hermes* in the Mythos series.

Princeton, February 1993   GARTH FOWDEN

Preface

This book was born of a certain dissatisfaction I felt after several years spent writing a historical thesis about Platonist philosophical circles in late antiquity.[1] That milieu, for all its intellectual inventiveness and diversity, had turned out to be, from the social point of view, asphyxiatingly exclusive; and at the end of my researches I was left with a sense that there was still much more to be discovered about the social milieu of late pagan thought. How, in particular, could I uncover what the literate but not especially learned pagan, in the Greek-speaking world, believed to be his actual or potential relationship with God? And if he himself did not know, how did he find out? Where could he find a teacher, and what might be their relationship?

There was ready to hand a body of philosophical texts which clearly were not produced in the elite milieu of the Platonist circles, but reflected analogous patterns of thought and experience. These were the so-called Hermetica, treatises composed in Roman Egypt and attributed to the god Hermes Trismegistus and to other members of his circle, such as Asclepius. And besides these philosophical texts there is a body of 'technical' Hermetica, works on magic, alchemy, astrology and other branches of what modern scholars are pleased to call 'pseudo-science'. Those of the philosophical texts which were transmitted in Greek or Latin were impressively edited by A. D. Nock and A.-J. Festugière (Paris 1946–54), and are well known to students of antique thought. The technical texts, for their part, though not as yet gathered into a *corpus*, are known to specialists in ancient occultism, and were also treated at length in various studies by Festugière. But historical and sociological questions

---

[1] 'Pagan philosophers in late antique society, with special reference to Iamblichus and his followers' (unpubl. diss., Oxford 1979); and cf. Fowden, *Philosophia* 7 (1977) 359–83; *J.H.S.* 102 (1982) 33–59.

about Hermetism have usually been regarded as of subordinate interest and importance.

The foundations of the historical approach to Hermetism were laid in 1614 by Isaac Casaubon, in his *De rebus sacris et ecclesiasticis exercitationes XVI. Ad Cardinalis Baronii prolegomena in Annales*.[2] Thanks in particular to Ficino's Latin translation (1471), the *Corpus Hermeticum* had become a source of fascination to Renaissance scholars, who were generally agreed that Hermes Trismegistus, a semi-divine sage or even a god, had lived in remote antiquity and personally composed, in Egyptian, the various treatises that circulated under or in association with his name in Greek, Latin and Arabic. Casaubon was not quite the first scholar to express reservations about this story; but his must certainly be the credit for the full exposure of the delusion, and the redating of the philosophical *Corpus Hermeticum* to the late first century A.D. – a thesis with which it is dispiritingly difficult to quarrel even today, and whose publication marks, as well as any other single event, the watershed between Renaissance occultism and the scientific rationalism of the new age. Hermes now fell gradually into disrepute, and languished in unaccustomed obscurity for almost three centuries. From this pathetic condition he was at length rescued by the German philologist Richard Reitzenstein, who in 1904 published his ingenious and learned book *Poimandres: Studien zur griechisch-aegyptischen und frühchristlichen Literatur*, in which it is maintained that the Hermetica were produced by a religious community whose members had a self-consciously Egyptian cast of mind. The Hermetica immediately became the focus of a lively debate about origins, influences and historical context generally, Reitzenstein himself coming to emphasize much more the Iranian element in Hermetism.[3] This phase of Hermetic scholarship culminated in the appearance, between 1944 and 1954, of Festugière's four immense volumes, *La révélation d'Hermès Trismégiste*, which highlighted the literary and intellectual Hellenism of the philosophical Hermetica, fixing their doctrine in the matrix of Greek philosophical thought and especially of the long-standing controversies about the interpretation of Plato. The magisterial and wide-ranging manner of this work stifled further discussion, and might well have suppressed Hermetic studies for several generations, had it not been for the discovery in

[2] Yates, *Giordano Bruno* 398–403; Grafton, *J.W.I.* 46 (1983) 78–93.
[3] For a survey of late nineteenth- and twentieth-century Hermetic scholarship see Mahé 2.9–32. An extensive but inaccurate bibliography of the whole of Hermetic studies has now been provided by González Blanco, *A.N.R.W.* 11.17.4 (1984) 2240–81.

1945 of the Nag Hammadi library of Coptic gnostic texts, and among them of several Hermetic treatises, one previously unknown.

Festugière was saved from immediate embarrassment by the malice and misfortune that delayed publication of the sensational Nag Hammadi documents until the 1970s. The Dominican scholar even thought he could afford a certain irony: how could the contents of 'une jarre d'Egypte'[4] possibly undermine the immense edifice of his erudition? The answer is now becoming clearer: the intellectual origins and context of Hermetism, viewed in ever closer relationship to traditional Egyptian thought and to gnosticism, are the subject of a fast-increasing number of scholarly studies, most notably those of J.-P. Mahé (a professor, significantly enough, of Armenian). But in one sense Festugière was right, in that, as he himself had observed a few years earlier, 'en ce qui touche les idées...on peut, avec quelque érudition, soutenir ce qu'on veut'.[5] This remark was intended as a warning, but there was an element of self-revelation in it too. Festugière was a philologist and a historian of ideas, his mind formed in the study of classical philosophy. In this realm he moved with assurance; and in his learning he, like the Hermetists, sought God.[6] But Festugière's work on the Hermetica does not reveal the fascination with social history that is indispensable if one is to press ideas into the humus of everyday reality – to see them as the expression of experience as well as the sediment of tradition. Truth, for the Hermetists, was not an object of scholarly enquiry that might adequately be discussed in the pages of a philosophical treatise, but a seen and catalytic force in their personal lives. Behind the text stand the master and the disciple, in everyday interaction. To enumerate their (supposed) intellectual debts, and leave it at that, is to approach the followers of Hermes in a state of mind which they would have found alien. Even at our distance in time, it is to invite rebuff.[7]

[4] Festugière I².427.

[5] *Id.*, *Etudes de religion* 142; and cf., for a cautionary tale, Momigliano, *Alien wisdom* 128–9.

[6] See the moving memoir by Saffrey, in *Mémorial Festugière* vii–xv.

[7] Dörrie too, *Platonica minora* 110–11 (echoing Bousset's 1914 review (= *Religionsgeschichtliche Studien* 97–191, esp. 100) of Kroll, *Hermes Trismegistos*), criticized Festugière's obsession with the doctrines of Hermetism to the exclusion of 'die Frage nach der Glaubwürdigkeit der darin sich äussernden Religiosität' – but provided an answer absolutely antithetical to the conclusions of the present study: 'Der Hermetismus war immer nur Literatur – und er war eine Literatur mit den geschilderten Inkonsequenzen und Abhängigkeiten und vor allem mit jener bemerkenswerten Schablonenhaftigkeit... Bei diesem Befund ist es wohl berechtigt, in Zweifel zu ziehen, ob der Hermetismus je das besass, was ich menschliche Realität nennen möchte... Ich glaube nicht, dass es ein zu hartes Urteil ist, wenn man den Hermetismus nicht zu den lebendigen Kräften der Spätantike rechnet.'

This question of the historical and social milieu of Hermetism has come to seem particularly worth investigating in the light of the Nag Hammadi texts and other evidence, much of it papyrological, that has come to light in recent decades. It is time, at long last, to take up Casaubon's cue, and ask who were the men and women who hid behind the name of Hermes Trismegistus, and how their search for God was articulated in their everyday experience. Not, it must be said from the outset, that there can be any easy or even very specific answers, when they have to be sought for the most part between the lines of philosophical texts. Even as an approach to the late pagan mind, our search will have its limitations. Hermetism was only one of a number of non-elite currents of thought which drew on Greek philosophy; and anyway it is easy to overestimate how non-elite it was. Among what seem to us the murkiest and least credible of all the pseudepigrapha which exploit Hermetic materials are the prophecies of Christ attributed in late antiquity to pagan gods and sages and deployed with enthusiasm by numerous Christian apologists. And yet, speaking of just such prophecies as these, the ecclesiastical historian Sozomen observed that, 'being for the most part in verse and expressed in words more elevated than the crowd is accustomed to, they were known [only] to the few who were distinguished for their education'.[8] Even so, my conclusions touch on broader areas of society than did those which emerged from my earlier investigation of the circles of Plotinus and his successors. And just as we shall see the doctrines of Hermetism playing a part in the emergence of the intellectual synthesis fostered, notably, by Iamblichus, my treatment of the movement's historical milieu represents, I hope, a useful step forward in the wider sociological analysis of late paganism – a subject whose neglect is now slowly being overcome.

The book is arranged in three parts. The first locates the Hermetic literature's origin in the fusion of Egyptian and Greek ways of thought that occurred in the Nile valley during the Ptolemaic and Roman periods. Part II argues that Hermetism can only be properly understood if the technical and philosophical books are seen as enshrining related aspects of Man's attempt to understand himself, the world around him, and God – in fact, as a practical spiritual 'way' (chapters 3 and 4). That at least is how they were perceived in antiquity, notably by two contemporary thinkers, Zosimus of

---

[8] Soz. 1.1.7. Photius, though, was unimpressed by either the literary or the intellectual quality of what he knew of this genre: *Bibl.* 170.117ab.

Preface

Panopolis and Iamblichus of Apamea, whose full importance for the study of Hermetism has not been appreciated; and Iamblichus made use of Hermetism in formulating his own widely influential doctrine of theurgy (chapters 5 and 6). Finally, part III addresses itself to the historical evidence for the milieu and audience of Hermetism, both within Egypt and in the rest of the Graeco-Roman world.

In writing this book I have incurred debts both institutional and personal. At Cambridge, the Master and Fellows of Peterhouse and of Darwin College, by electing me to Research Fellowships, gave me the leisure and peace of mind I needed in order to embark on my journey, though I had not guessed its length and difficulty. In Washington, D.C., I was able through the kindness of Bernard Knox to enjoy the delightful environment of the Center for Hellenic Studies, in a year in which the Fellows did not perhaps wholly eclipse that unsung breed, the spouses. My labours have also been alleviated by the staff of libraries in Britain, Greece, the Netherlands and the U.S.A., particularly the British School, the American School of Classical Studies and the Ecole Française in Athens, and the Dumbarton Oaks Center for Byzantine Studies in Washington, D.C. I am deeply indebted to the British Academy, the Faculty of Oriental Studies, University of Cambridge (Wright Studentship Fund), the Seven Pillars of Wisdom Trust, the Society for the Promotion of Roman Studies (Donald Atkinson Fund) and the Wolfson Foundation for financing visits to America, the Near East and North Africa.

Numerous individuals have responded to requests for advice and the supply of σπάνια καὶ δυσεύρετα. With ineluctable invidiousness I single out here Han Drijvers, Oliver Nicholson, Andrew Palmer, John Ray and Eve Reymond. And I owe special gratitude to David Jordan, whose enormous erudition has led me to things I would never have found, and saved me from things I ought never to have thought.

Lastly I wish to thank Peter Brown and Henry Chadwick, the two remarkable teachers to whom I owe inexhaustible inspiration and daunting example; and Polymnia Athanassiadi, for her constant and at times infuriating reminders that 'the letter killeth, but the spirit giveth life'. I have failed to take this as much to heart as I might have done; but to one who has I dedicate this book, in vivid awareness that without her it would not be.

GARTH FOWDEN

Groningen, 29 April 1985

INTRODUCTION:

The texts

A text, for us, is its author's possession. It mirrors the individuality of its creator, and is not properly understood unless we know who and what that creator was. Approaching a literary work, we are reassured if we are first told something of the person who produced it. To a certain extent this is true also of scientific writing. Anonymity and pseudonymity alike arouse suspicion.

Though this habit of mind was not unknown to the ancient world, it was less the norm than it is with us. There, anonymity and pseudonymity flourished. And even authors who were willing to reveal their own identity often regarded attribution of texts they quoted as unnecessary and, no doubt, inelegant. The historian who studies a pseudepigraphical genre finds himself, then, in a quandary. To enquire immediately after the 'author' is, to say the least, impolite, and suggests one may simply have missed the point. But nor can one wholly suppress one's historical *curiositas*. Clearly a middle way has to be found. The texts must be described, and something said of the manner in which they have reached us. Questions of a more personal sort can then be postponed until the circumstances and the inner nature of the texts have been better understood.

We may begin with the technical Hermetica, whose various genres can be enumerated briefly, since Festugière has surveyed them in the first volume of *La révélation d'Hermès Trismégiste*. A firm foundation of Hermes Trismegistus's authority in this sphere, as we shall see in chapter 1, was his position as a patron of magic. The content of magical texts was admittedly so fluid that they were frequently not ascribed to an individual author at all; and Hermes is pushed and jostled in the surviving magical papyri by numerous other figures from every corner of the earth and heavens. Even so, he exercised an authority that was not easily gainsaid, so that we possess, or know of, a number of magical texts specifically attributed to him.[1] And power over magic brought authority in other fields as well. For example, the literature that dealt with the occult properties of different substances and organisms – of obvious practical relevance to the magician – was dominated by the Hermetic *Cyranides*, which in turn draw, among other sources, on a treatise called the *Archaic Book*, also attributed to Hermes.[2] Alchemists too were at pains to claim Hermes as one of the founders and propagators of their art;[3] and his name is to be found at the head of the lists of alchemical authorities drawn up by late antique and Byzantine writers.[4] But it is in the astrological literature that we find the most frequent attributions to Hermes,[5] to the point that even the other generally acknowledged authorities in this field – the gods Asclepius and Isis, for example, the priest Petosiris and King Nechepso – were all thought of as pupils of Hermes, or at least as expositors of Hermetic doctrine.[6] To this subdivision of the technical Hermetica belong also a number of books on astrological medicine ('iatromathematics') and astrological botany, applying astrological data to the diagnosis and cure of disease.[7]

Viewed generally, the technical Hermetica combine a broad intellectual kinship and similarity of style with a heterogeneity which stems in part from their varied subject-matter, but extends also to the internal structure of individual treatises. Many of our texts have been repeatedly remodelled over many centuries by people who seem to have regarded divine pseudonymity as compensating for any degree of editorial licence.[8] Had it not been for the vogue which alchemy and astrology continued to enjoy in Byzantium (and, indeed, meta-Byzantium), the texts would have been lost completely, having no claim to preservation on literary grounds. But precisely this continuing fashionability has made reconstruction and dating of

---

[1] Gundel 23–4, to which add *P. Graec. Mag.* xxiva, and *P. Berol.* 21243 (= Brashear, *Z.P.E.* 33 (1979) 262–4).   [2] *Cyranides*: below, 87–9. *Archaic Book*: Festugière 1.211–15.

[3] For a list of the 'reliques médiocres' of the alchemical Hermetica see *ibid.* 1.241–60.

[4] *Alch. gr.* 25–6, 424–5, 447.12–14.

[5] Festugière 1.102–23 (though note that the Ἑρμοῦ τοῦ Τρισμεγίστου πρὸς Ἀσκληπιὸν λόγος καθολικός contained in National Library of Greece MS. 1180, and described *ibid.* 107 n.1 (no. 9), and by Mahé 2.5 n.13, after verification by J. Paramelle (*sic*), as an unpublished astrological Hermeticum, is in fact *C.H.* ii.4ff.); Gundel 10–16, 21–4.

[6] Festugière 1.103; Gundel 25–36.   [7] Festugière 1.137–86; Gundel 16–21.

[8] See e.g. *Cyr., passim*, esp. the prologue and book 1; and the *Lib. Herm. Tris.* (and Festugière 1.113–22 on its evolution over more than five hundred years). Also Cumont, *Die orientalischen Religionen* 156, esp. n. 33, and Kaimakis's edition of the *Cyr.*, 7, on Byzantine bowdlerization.

the original versions very difficult. In the case of the magical texts we at least have a large number of papyri, though again they represent a mature phase in the development of the tradition, being mostly of late antique date.[9] We are fortunate though that one of the earliest surviving magical papyri, firmly datable to the period of Augustus, happens also to be the oldest Hermetic text preserved in that medium[10] – which tends to confirm what one might anyway suspect on intellectual grounds, and deduce from the character of the god himself, namely that magic must have been among the first fields in which Greek texts were attributed to Hermes Trismegistus. And the Ptolemaic origins which may be assumed in the case of Hermetic magic can be asserted as regards some of the more evolved technical genres. Although most of the surviving astrological and iatromathematical Hermetica are of Roman date, at least in the form in which they have reached us, some were already in circulation in the first century B.C., and perhaps earlier.[11] Texts belonging to these genres were being widely read by the first century A.D.,[12] and soon afterwards we first find evidence for the existence of the *Cyranides*.[13] The alchemical Hermetica are perhaps somewhat later, since it was only in the Roman period that alchemy began to assume its classical form.[14]

We have no sound evidence that the technical Hermetica circulated in antiquity in any way other than as individual treatises. Some of the magical papyri, it is true, have a decidedly anthological character, but formal collections of technical Hermetica we first encounter in Byzantium, as for example in our two oldest alchemical manuscripts, *Marcianus* 299 of the tenth or eleventh century, and the thirteenth-

---

[9] The evidence is summarized by Festugière, *Idéal religieux* 281 n. 2.

[10] *P. Berol.* 21243; cf. Brashear, *Z.P.E.* 33 (1979) 261, 278.

[11] Our first unambiguous external *testimonium* is provided by Antiochus of Athens, who probably lived in the first century B.C.: see *C.C.A.G.* 8(3).111 n. 2, and Gundel 115–17, who also suggests that Antiochus spent some time in Alexandria. Antiochus refers in turn (*C.C.A.G.* 8(3).116.10) to an earlier interpreter of Hermes called Timaeus, about whom we lack any historical information: Gundel 111–12. In general Gundel 104–15 (and cf. 22 n. 28; 92) inclines to believe that Antiochus's predecessors had access to Hermetic writings; and Festugière 1.76–8, with Fraser 1.437–9, agree that some astrological Hermetica will have been of Ptolemaic origin. Much turns on the dating of Petosiris and Nechepso, generally regarded (see above, 2) as purveyors of Hermetic doctrine. Kroll's hitherto accepted view that they should be placed *c.* 150 B.C., albeit 'mit Spielraum nach unten' (*R.E.* 16.2164), has recently been argued to be much too optimistic (Schwartz, in *Livre du Centenaire* 311–21, esp. 318 n. 5, 320). The earliest firmly datable allusion to either authority is that of the Tiberian astrologer Thrasyllus, *C.C.A.G.* 8(3).100.19–20. The Neronian epigrammatist Lucillius refers to Petosiris (*Anth. gr.* xi.164) as if he was a household name. [12] See previous note, and below, 161–2.

[13] Below, 87, 162. [14] Gundel, *R.L.A.C.* 1.242–3.

century *Parisinus* 2325. But it is of considerable significance for our historical investigation of Hermetism that *philosophical* Hermetica were already being grouped into collections in antiquity. Such collections are abundantly attested both within the text themselves – as when they cross-refer, for example, to the so-called *General discourses* (γενικοὶ λόγοι)[15] – and by writers who quote from the philosophical Hermetica, and frequently mention collections of *Discourses* addressed by Hermes to Tat, Asclepius and Ammon, and by Isis to Horus.[16] A reference by Cyril of Alexandria (d. 444) to 'the man who put together at Athens the fifteen so-called Hermaic books' is of particular interest, since this may have been the source whence Cyril derived some at least of the Hermetic texts he himself quotes; though all he vouchsafes at this point is a quotation from the 'separate compositions' of the Athenian Hermetist, a passage from a dialogue in which a priest describes the civilizing achievements of the historical Thoth–Hermes.[17] And the tendency for certain passages from the Hermetica to be quoted again and again in the non-Hermetic literature points to the existence of anthologies as well, organized in more readily digestible form than the collections.[18] We have a good example of such an anthology in the work of Stobaeus (early fifth century?) – though the *Anthologium*'s forty Hermetic texts, including as they do such lengthy items as the *Korē kosmou* (*S.H.* xxiii), almost deserve to be called a collection in their own right.[19]

More concrete evidence about the philosophical collections is to be found, once again, among the papyri. Some scrappy late second- or third-century fragments in Vienna, for example, preserve parts of at least two *Discourses* (λόγοι) *of Hermes to Tat*, numbered nine and ten and devoted to philosophical discussion of such commonplace Hermetic themes as the (divine) energies and the difference between Man, endowed with reason and able to know God, and the animals.[20] Though none of these texts is preserved elsewhere, we indisputably have here early and direct evidence for the circulation of at least one collection of philosophical Hermetica. But the most spectacular papyrological addition to our knowledge, and one which has affected every aspect of the study of Hermetism, was made in 1945, with the discovery near the hamlet of Hamra Dum in Upper Egypt of a library

---

[15] Below, 98 n. 12.   [16] Below, 179–80, 197.   [17] Cyr. Al., *Jul.* 1.548bc.

[18] For the various quotations of *S.H.* 1, for example, see Pépin, *V. Chr.* 36 (1982) 251–60. *S.H.* xxviii appears to be an extract from an anthology.

[19] See further below, 197.

[20] *P. Graec. Vindob.* 29456 *recto* and 29828 *recto*, ed. Mahé, in *Mémorial Festugière* 51–64.

of mainly gnostic texts in Coptic,[21] including a number of philosophical Hermetica. Of the eight texts contained in codex VI of the Nag Hammadi library, as it is called after the nearest large town to the find-spot, those that interest us here are numbers 6–8. Other texts from the collection, including some in codices other than number VI, present doctrinal parallels with these three indisputably Hermetic tractates;[22] but none claims to be Hermetic, or makes use of the Hermetic *dramatis personae*.

What exactly the grouping together of three Hermetic texts at the end of *N.H.C.* VI signifies is for the time being controversial. In the context in which we know them their primary function is as part of a wider, essentially gnostic collection. But were they originally a specifically Hermetic collection (or at least a part of one); or did the compiler of codex VI bring the treatises together himself?

The first of the triad, no. 6, is an initiatory dialogue between Hermes and Tat.[23] The title is missing, but references in the text suggest that it was called *The Ogdoad reveals the Ennead*[24] – a reference to the eighth and ninth spheres which constitute the divine realm and lie above the seven planetary spheres.[25] There is no good reason to doubt the natural assumption that we have to do here, as in most early Coptic literature, with a translation from the Greek.[26] As we shall see, this treatise is of considerable interest from the doctrinal point of view, and not only because it was previously unknown; but its uniqueness makes it relatively unhelpful as a source for its own history, because there is no parallel tradition to compare it with. Fortunately we do not have this problem with the other two texts, which are both translations from the Hermetic *Perfect discourse*, known to us in Latin guise as the *Asclepius*. No. 7 has no title, and begins directly with the words: 'This is the prayer that they spoke:...' There then follows the prayer of thanksgiving from the end of the

---

[21] On the discovery see most recently Rudolph, *Gnosis* 40–8 (with map); Robinson, in *Textes de Nag Hammadi* 21–58, and *Facsimile edition of the Nag Hammadi codices: introduction* 3–14.

[22] *Mahé* 1.12–14; Ménard, in *Mélanges Marcel Simon* 287–92.

[23] Tat is not explicitly identified, but there is a clear analogy with *C.H.* XIII.

[24] *N.H.C.* VI.6.61.21–2; and cf. Mahé 1.88.

[25] *C.H.* 1.26 (where the powers 'above the Ogdoadic nature' are clearly in the Ennead), XIII.15; and cf. XVI.17, and Mahé 1.40–1, 120 (on the possibility that God Himself is envisaged as dwelling in a tenth sphere above the Ogdoad and the Ennead).

[26] *Pace* Keizer, *Eighth reveals the Ninth* 35–51, who produces no substantial evidence for his notion that *N.H.C.* VI.6 is an original composition in Coptic. For some evidence that the Hermetic texts in *N.H.C.* VI were not all translated by the same person, and cannot therefore all (or necessarily any) of them have been translated by the compiler of the codex, see Mahé 2.462–3.

5

Perfect discourse (Ascl. 41), and the concluding sentence of the treatise, which in the Coptic version reads: 'When they had said these things in prayer, they embraced each other and they went to eat their holy food, which has no blood in it.' The last of the three treatises, no. 8, likewise lacks a title, but corresponds to sections 21–9 of the Latin *Asclepius*, and contains Hermes's famous prophecy.

Unlike the Vienna Hermetica, which belonged to a numbered sequence, the Nag Hammadi Hermetica show no sign of having ever been conceived of as a connected series. The only clue to their origin is a scribal note inserted between items 7 and 8:

I have copied this single discourse (*logos*) of his, because many indeed have reached me, but I did not write them down, thinking that they had reached you [pl.]; and what is more I hesitate to copy these for you, because possibly they did [already] reach you, and the matter was troublesome for you; for the discourses which have reached me from that source are numerous.[27]

There has been considerable disagreement about whether this note refers to the preceding or the following text, or perhaps even to nos. 6 and 7 together;[28] but one would most naturally expect a note in this position to refer to the immediately preceding item, the prayer of thanksgiving. On this assumption, one might even translate the loan-word *logos* as 'formula' or 'prayer' – a sense it frequently bears in the Greek magical papyri.[29] The note has important implications about the compiler's attitude to the *Perfect discourse*. We know that the Greek text of the prayer of thanksgiving acquired at some point an identity of its own, separate from the *Perfect discourse*, which may indeed not have been its earliest origin.[30] But the Coptic text is indisputably derived from the *Perfect discourse*, because it includes part of the narrative framework of that treatise.[31] Since *N.H.C.* VI.8 is also an extract from the *Perfect discourse*, it is clear that the compiler of the codex excerpted from this lengthy text the two passages that he deemed most suitable for his purpose – and perhaps he also had in mind the practical consideration that there was not room in his codex for the whole treatise. Having decided that the prayer of thanksgiving suited his requirements, he no doubt realized how appropriate it would look following straight on after *The Ogdoad reveals the Ennead*, concluding it as it concluded the *Perfect discourse*.

---

[27] *N.H.C.* VI.7a (tr. J. D. Ray).   [28] Parrott, *N.H.S.* 11 (1979) 389–91; Mahé 2.464–5.
[29] *P. Graec. Mag.* 2.269, *s.v.*; cf. *C.H.* XIII.16.   [30] Below, 84–6.
[31] Since it is in the third person, like the other narrative elements in the *Ascl.*, the Coptic version of the narrative framework must be closer to the Greek than is the Latin of the *Ascl.*, which abruptly changes the narrative into the first person.

Hence the ambiguous join on p. 63 of the codex – a decorated *incipit* for the prayer, but no title or space between it and *N.H.C.* vi.6, as is the custom elsewhere .between treatises; and hence too the inversion of the original sequence of the two extracts from the *Perfect discourse*.[32] Probably the compiler/scribe knew that the prayer of thanksgiving was also in circulation as a separate unit. Certainly he will have known that there were many other Hermetic prayers similar to it. So when he finished copying it out he added a note excusing himself for having perhaps brought owls to Athens, but implying (quite rightly) that this particular prayer was worth having anyway, as an important example of Hermetic spirituality. Indeed, the *Perfect discourse* as a whole was among the most frequently quoted of all Hermetic texts. The prophecy in particular, with its moving account of God's desertion of the holy land of Egypt, and its desolation in 'the senescence of the world', exercised a perennial fascination, finding its way into Lactantius's *Divinae institutiones* and Augustine's *De civitate Dei*, just as it caught the eye of our anonymous Coptic compiler.[33] It is also easy to see why *The Ogdoad reveals the Ennead* was included in this mini-anthology – it is strikingly typical of the more initiatory type of philosophical Hermetica, and has much more Egyptian colour. In short, the Hermetic treatises in *N.H.C.* vi look very much as if they were selected partly because they were well-known, partly for their representative character, and partly for patriotic motives too. They are exactly what one would choose in order to convey a first impression of Hermetism to a Coptic audience if that audience were completely unfamiliar with it. Though they are not, nor ever were, a formal Hermetic collection, their presence as a loose group in this wide-ranging gnostic library speaks eloquently of philosophical Hermetism's appeal in late antiquity.

But the most important, if also most imponderable, of our collections of philosophical Hermetica continues to be the *Corpus Hermeticum* itself. The key to our lack of understanding of the *Corpus*'s origins is the simple fact that we cannot prove its existence, *qua*

---

[32] Note that the *P.D.* itself may well have evolved in a similar fashion: N.F. 2.290–5. Mahé 1.137–9, in effect ignores both the separation implied by the decorated *incipit*, and the narrative framework included in *N.H.C.* vi.7, and argues, from the distinctly secondary consideration of the inverted order of the two extracts from the *P.D.*, that the compiler of *N.H.C.* vi cannot have known the prayer of thanksgiving as part of the *P.D.*, and that it must therefore have been attached to *The Ogdoad reveals the Ennead* before the compilation of *N.H.C.* vi.

[33] See also Fodor, *A. Orient. Hung.* 23 (1970) 347–62, on a much later Egyptian apocalyptic narrative preserved in Arabic but apparently translated from Coptic, and not dissimilar to the *Ascl.* prophecy.

collection, before Michael Psellus's references to it in the eleventh century[34] – even though, tantalizingly, the alchemist Zosimus of Panopolis mentions *C.H.* I and IV in the same breath and context as early as the turn of the third century.[35] If these two treatises were already associated in late antiquity, can the same be said of any of the other texts – a total of seventeen[36] – that appear in the fullest manuscripts of the *Corpus*? Stobaeus included in his *Anthologium* extracts from *C.H.* II, IV and X; but since he also knew many otherwise unattested Hermetica, it seems ill-advised to draw further conclusions about the nature of his sources. In fact, the only thing we can be sure of is that, however they were put together, the contents of the *Corpus Hermeticum* did *not* all come from the same place: *C.H.* XVIII, for example, is not Hermetic at all, but a straightforward panegyric addressed to certain unnamed emperors, perhaps members of the Tetrarchy.[37] It is also noticeable that the contents of the *Corpus*, for all their variety, do not include the popular *Perfect discourse*. If we look at a writer who knew the philosophical Hermetica well, like the Christian Lactantius (d. *c.* 320), it becomes clear not only that he was acquainted with many more Hermetic writings than we are, but also that he tended to quote only from those that fitted with the particular doctrinal points that he wanted to make. From Lactantius we learn a great deal about, for example, Hermetic doctrine on the nature of God, since it corresponded closely with his own understanding of Christianity; but about Hermetic mystical teaching, which could not easily be accommodated to a Christian context, he leaves us largely in the dark. That a writer as sympathetic to Hermetism as Lactantius could convey, albeit for understandable reasons, such an unbalanced picture of its doctrine, arouses a suspicion that the composition of the *Corpus* too, though it may go back to a late antique core, reflects the taste of the Christian Byzantine readership to which we owe our manuscripts.[38] Byzantine disapproval of certain aspects of Hermetism is vividly conveyed by the abusive epithets – λῆρος, φλυαρία – that spatter the margins of one of our manuscripts.[39] Perhaps this is the explanation for the absence of *C.H.* XVI–XVIII from many of our manuscripts, XVI and XVII being

---

[34] N.F. I.XLVII–LI.
[35] Zos. Pan., *fr. gr.* 245.
[36] Numbered I–XVIII but omitting XV, for reasons explained by Scott 1.18–20.
[37] N.F. I.XLVII, 2.244.
[38] N.F. I.XI–XII, LI–LIII.
[39] Reitzenstein, *Poimandres* 323; below, 9.

too pagan, and XVIII, the last treatise in the collection and anyway not Hermetic, being naturally likely to fall out with them.[40]

Nor is it just the *Corpus qua* collection that is the product of an evolutionary process, since its individual constituent parts were also altered in the course of transmission, just as were the technical Hermetica. Here again, quotations made from Hermetic books by late antique writers provide a useful control on the *Corpus*, this time on the fidelity of the text itself. Adjustments might, for example, be made for stylistic reasons – Stobaeus's *Anthologium* in particular, where it reproduces passages also to be found in the *Corpus*, clearly rests on a much purer textual tradition.[41] More significantly, material offensive to Christian and Greek taste might also be allowed to drop out in the course of the long process of transmission from scribe to scribe – *N.H.C.* VI.6, for instance, includes references to magic, astrology and pagan cult, and a variety of Egyptian decor, of a sort conspicuously absent from the otherwise closely analogous *C.H.* XIII. And, conversely, extraneous material might be introduced into the tradition. One can see the process by which this came about in the two fourteenth-century manuscripts *Parisinus* 1220 and *Vaticanus* 951. In the former, a later hand has added a lengthy and aggressive marginal scholium on *C.H.* I.18, with the superscription τοῦ Ψελλοῦ – the author, in other words, was Michael Psellus. In the Vatican manuscript the scholium has already entered the text itself, and has lost its superscription.[42] This particular scholium could never be mistaken for an integral part of the text – but less conspicuous additions often were.

Apart from the *Corpus*, the Stobaean fragments and the Vienna and Nag Hammadi papyri, we have three other sources of information about the doctrines of philosophical Hermetism. These are the *Perfect discourse*, the *Definitions of Hermes Trismegistus to Asclepius* (*Hermeay Eṙameci aṙ Asklepios sahmank'*), preserved in an Armenian translation, and a variety of testimonia from late antique writers both pagan and Christian. The testimonia will be discussed extensively in the course of this study, particularly in part III. But the two independently-preserved treatises require some introduction at this point. The *Perfect discourse* survives intact only in a Latin translation, the so-called

---

[40] That *C.H.* XVI is attributed to Asclepius, while in *C.H.* XVII Tat, not Hermes, is assigned the role of teacher, may also have contributed to the exclusion of these treatises.

[41] N.F. I.XXXVII–XLVI; and cf. below, 10, on the relationship between the *Ascl.* and its Greek original.

[42] The scholium is printed in Scott 4.244–5; and cf. N.F. I.XLIX and XI n. 5.

Asclepius, apparently made during the fourth century,[43] and attributed in some mediaeval sources to Apuleius. Of the Greek text we have only a few fragments, mainly citations by Lactantius, while *N.H.C.* VI, as we have seen, preserves one large and one small fragment in a Coptic version. Comparison with the Greek and even the Coptic fragments reveals that the Latin version is decidedly paraphrastic[44] – though the *Perfect discourse* itself was clearly a long and composite text, whose incoherences were rather unsuccessfully camouflaged by a feeble editor.[45] Yet the *Asclepius* has its moments, notably Hermes's great prophecy of the demise of Egypt. And doctrinally it is almost encyclopaedic. So it was widely read in late antiquity; and the loss of the original is surprising, to say the least. No doubt we have here another symptom of Byzantine censorship, since the work contains several openly – even, to the Christian mind, shockingly – pagan passages. As for the Armenian *Definitions*, these are preserved in a number of manuscripts, the earliest dated 1273, but most of them copied in the sixteenth to eighteenth centuries.[46] The *Definitions* were probably translated from the Greek as part of the concerted attempt mounted by the 'Hellenizing School' (*c.* 570–730) to endow Armenia with a learned literature in its own language.[47] They were first provided with a scholarly edition only in 1956. The text consists of a collection of brief definitions (as its title suggests), arranged thematically around such common Hermetic ideas as the three spheres of being (God, the World and Man), and Man's aspiration to know God. Apart from the last section, interpolated from Nemesius of Emesa, all the definitions are more or less closely paralleled in the other Hermetica; and one of them is in fact the beginning of one of the Stobaean fragments.[48] The Greek original of the Armenian *Definitions* reflected, then, a high degree of fluidity in the textual tradition of the Hermetic literature; and in this the *Definitions* offer an interesting parallel to the dismemberment of the *Perfect discourse* performed during the prehistory of *N.H.C.* VI.

As for dating the earliest strata of the philosophical Hermetica, it is difficult to improve on what the Vienna papyri have already told us – namely that there were specimens in circulation (and even in collected form) by the end of the second century. This is also the

---

[43] Below, 198.   [44] Mahé 1.153–5; Wigtil, *A.N.R.W.* II.17.4 (1984) 2286–97.
[45] The structure of the *P.D.* has most recently been analysed by Mahé, in *Textes de Nag Hammadi* 405–34.   [46] Mahé 2.320–1.
[47] *Ibid.* 327–8; Terian, in *East of Byzantium* 175–86.
[48] *D.H.* x.7 = *S.H.* XIX.1; cf. Mahé 2.329–30.

period when we first find allusions to the philosophical writings of Hermes in other sources.[49] Two prayers known from the Hermetica have also been preserved in papyri of the late third and early fourth centuries;[50] but we have no way of knowing how long before that they had been in circulation, and it is possible that their origins were quite unconnected with Hermetism. The Nag Hammadi find likewise provides only a *terminus ante quem*: the three Hermetic texts must antedate their translation into Coptic, and the subsequent production of codex VI in the mid-fourth century.[51] The doctrine of the one previously unknown treatise (*N.H.C.* VI.6) suggests a milieu similar to that of the initiatory texts in the *Corpus Hermeticum*.

In dating the treatises of the *Corpus* itself, the *Perfect discourse* and the Stobaean fragments, our manuscripts cannot offer even the limited help one gets when dealing with the papyri. References to philosophical Hermetica in non-Hermetic writers provide only another *terminus ante quem* – and anyway the earliest known quotation from a philosophical Hermeticum that actually survives is in Ps.-Justin's *Cohortatio ad Gentiles*, which was written only in the middle or latter part of the third century.[52] So we are thrown back on the vaguest of all criteria for dating, that of doctrine. It can be said here, by anticipation, that none of the conclusions reached in this study conflict with the current scholarly consensus, which assigns the composition of the philosophical Hermetica to the period from the late first to the late third centuries A.D.[53]

---

[49] Below, 198, on Tertullian.

[50] Below, 84–5.

[51] Keizer, *Eighth reveals the Ninth* 7–21; Mahé 1.11–12. The criteria for dating are mainly palaeographic.

[52] Ps.-Just., *Coh.* 38, quoting *S.H.* 1.1; and cf. Grant, *H. Th. R.* 51 (1958) 128–34.

[53] *C.H.* I, assigned by Dodd, *Bible and the Greeks* 201–9, to the late first or early second century, is perhaps among the earliest of our texts – Mahé's arguments (2.278) for dating *D.H.* before it are flimsy. (J.-P. Mahé has kindly communicated to me an article on 'Hermes Trismegistos', forthcoming in M. Eliade (ed.), *The encyclopedia of religions* (New York), in which he suggests that the Jewish liturgical influences detectable especially in *C.H.* I (below, 36) are unlikely to have been felt after the revolt of A.D. 115–17, which resulted in the virtual disappearance of Egyptian Jewry for almost two centuries: see *C.P. Jud.* 1.86–96.) *S.H.* XXIII appears to be relatively late (Nock, *Essays* 31, esp. n. 16; and cf. Burkert, *E.A.C.* 18 (1972) 51–5, emphasizing parallels with Ecphantus, *Regn.*, and speculating on a Severan date for both works), and *C.H.* X may be too, since it purports to be an epitome of the *General discourses* of Hermes to Tat. Probably most of the treatises were in existence by the time of Ps.-Justin and Zosimus of Panopolis. It is uncommon to find direct evidence for the relative chronology of the Hermetic treatises: exceptions are the apparent cross-reference to *C.H.* I at *C.H.* XIII.15, and *C.H.* IX's claim (1) to be a sequel to the *Perfect discourse* – not necessarily the original of the *Ascl.*, whose composite character suggests a late date. (Lactantius knew *C.H.* XVI as *Sermo perfectus*: *Inst.* II.15.7, and below, 206.)

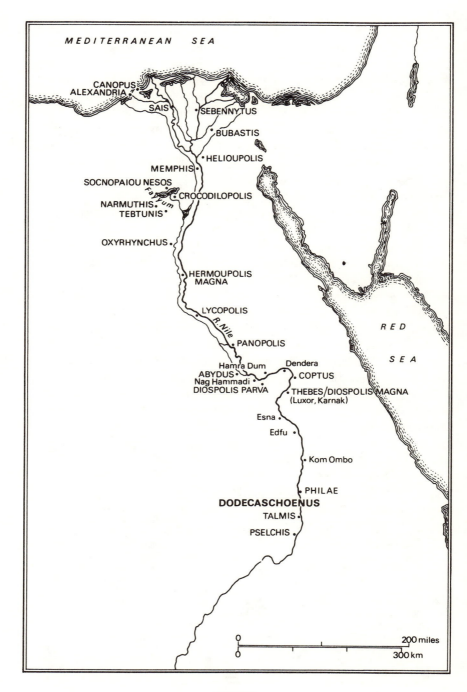

MEDITERRANEAN SEA

CANOPUS
ALEXANDRIA
• SAIS
• SEBENNYTUS
• BUBASTIS
• HELIOUPOLIS
MEMPHIS •
SOCNOPAIOU NESOS
• CROCODILOPOLIS
NARMUTHIS •
TEBTUNIS •
Fayum
OXYRHYNCHUS •
HERMOUPOLIS
MAGNA •
• LYCOPOLIS
R. Nile
• PANOPOLIS
Hamra Dum   Dendera
ABYDUS •   • COPTUS
Nag Hammadi •
DIOSPOLIS PARVA
THEBES / DIOSPOLIS MAGNA
(Luxor, Karnak)
Esna •
Edfu •
• Kom Ombo
• PHILAE
DODECASCHOENUS
TALMIS •
PSELCHIS •

RED

SEA

0 ————————————————— 200 miles
0 ————————————————— 300 km

EGYPT

12

PART I

MODES OF CULTURAL INTERACTION

[1]

The durability of Egypt

Egypt, we read in the Hermetic treatise called *Asclepius*, is 'the image of heaven...the temple of the whole world'.[1] Even today Upper Egypt, which has preserved traditional ways more faithfully than other parts of the country, is a land dominated by the immense stone temples of the old gods. The sprawling shrines of Amun at Karnak and Luxor still stand, while the walls and palaces of 'hundred-gated' Thebes have crumbled into the earth. The holy places of Hathor at Dendera, Chnum at Esna, Horus at Edfu, of Sobek and Haroeris at Kom Ombo and Isis at Philae still mark the stages of one's journey as one travels along the narrowing valley towards the confines of Egypt. And in the time of the Pharaohs this was already an ancient and holy land. It had witnessed the emergence of the primeval hill from the all-encompassing waters, and the birth and burial of the very gods themselves.[2] Egypt's whole being was wrapped up with the rhythms of the divine world; and its inhabitants believed that their land would survive only while the gods were still worshipped – a conviction not dispelled until the collapse of paganism itself.[3]

Of all the wonders past and present, natural and man-made, that Egypt had to show, it was her gods and temples that most caught

---

[1] *Ascl.* 24: 'An ignoras, o Asclepi, quod Aegyptus imago sit caeli aut, quod est verius, translatio aut descensio omnium, quae gubernantur atque exercentur in caelo? et si dicendum est verius, terra nostra mundi totius est templum.'

[2] Morenz, *Ägyptische Religion* 44–52, 167–91; Hornung, *Conceptions of God* 143–65.

[3] Iam., *Myst.* VI.7; Soz. VII.20; Derchain, *Papyrus Salt 825* 3–21; Crawford, in *Ptolemaic Memphis* 7; Thelamon, *Païens et chrétiens* 199–201, 273–5; Assmann, in *Apocalypticism*, esp. 371–3.

the imagination of the foreign visitor. But the whole of Egypt's cultural and social life, like the configuration of the land itself, was unique. So too was the Egyptian mind, with its immovable conviction that the cultural identity of Egypt and the stability of the physical universe itself were one and the same thing.[4] Egypt had shown itself time and time again a land that might be subjected, but never assimilated. And so it was that Alexander's conquest of the Nile valley marked a profound caesura in the country's political history, in that the crown of Upper and Lower Egypt was never again to be worn by a native Pharaoh, but brought no such clear-cut results in the cultural sphere. When the two alien cultural traditions of Egypt and Greece began to mix, it was on terms that bore little relation to political realities. In the centres of power, Hellenism was triumphant; but in cultural terms Egyptianism, instead of being submerged by Hellenism, exercised so strong a gravitational and assimilative pull on it that the product of their interaction was at least as much Egyptian as Greek.[5] Nowhere was this truer than in matters of religion.

The gods of Egypt

The Greek world at large, and after it the Roman, was firmly persuaded that the Egyptians had been the first people to organize formal religious cult. Men of these less ancient nations were prepared to admire quite uncritically the temples and rituals of the Egyptians,[6] and even to accept the idea that the land of Egypt was intrinsically holy.[7] The priesthood, which retained not a little of the vast social and political power it had wielded under the Pharaohs,[8] enjoyed a reputation among men of Greek and Latin culture[9] usually accorded only to the sages of nations safely and romantically remote from the

[4] Assmann, in *Apocalypticism* 345–77.
[5] Préaux, *C.E.* 35 (1943) 148–60, and *M.H.* 10 (1953) 203–21; Dunand, in *Modes de contacts* 45–87.
[6] Lucian, *Syr. D.* 2; *Exp. tot. mundi* 34, 36; Amm. Marc. xxii.16.19–20; and cf. next note.
[7] E.g. Thphr., *Piet.* fr. 2(ἱερωτάτη χώρα) (= Porph., *Abst.* ii.5.1 = Eus. Caes., *P.E.* i.9.7); Jul., *ep.* 111.433b (ἦν κοινωνία μὲν πρὸς θεοὺς Αἰγύπτῳ τῇ πάσῃ); and, under protest, Plut., *Is. Os.* 66. For Egyptian expressions of the idea see Engelmann, *Sarapis* 7, line 31 (θείας...Αἰγύπτοιο), and n. *ad loc.*; *Ascl.* 24; *N.H.C.* ii.5.122–3.
[8] Crawford, in *Ptolemaic Memphis* 1–42.
[9] Lucan x.172–92; Thess., *Virt. herb.* 1. prooem. 12, on the 'erudite priests and elders full of abstruse learning' of Diospolis Magna (Thebes); Jos., *Ap.* ii.140–1; Lucian, *Philops.* 34; Clem. Al., *Strom.* 1.15.71.3–4 (who, though a native of Alexandria, treats the Egyptian priests as 'barbarian' philosophers); Diog. Laert. i.1, 10–11; Or., *Cels.* i.12; Heliod. Em. iii.11.3.

The gods of Egypt

well-trodden highways of the Mediterranean world, such as the
Brahmins and Gymnosophists of India. Even the wisest representatives of other traditions – Moses among the Jews, Solon, Pythagoras
and Plato among the Greeks – were acknowledged to have sat at the
feet of Egyptian priests.[10] In the imperial Roman period men
continued to believe sufficiently in the wisdom of Egypt to travel there
and seek out its far-famed temple-dwellers,[11] leaving behind clouds
of awe-struck graffiti which may still be read on the monuments. In
the fourth century the Platonist philosopher Iamblichus of Apamea
thought it no anachronism to impersonate a learned Egyptian priest
in his *De mysteriis Aegyptiorum*; while the author of the *Expositio totius
mundi*, in a passage that accurately reflects the belief of the Egyptians
themselves, emphasized the crucial link between the holiness of the
land of Egypt and the wisdom of its inhabitants:

It is impossible, in whatever matter you may wish, to find such a wise man as the
Egyptian; and so of all philosophers and men versed in the wisdom of letters, the
best have been those who have always dwelt in this country.[12]

But this sort of adulation was not necessarily reciprocated. Herodotus
had already remarked on the Egyptians' hostility to foreign ways:

They keep the ancestral laws and add none other...They avoid the use of Greek
customs, and generally speaking the customs of all other men.[13]

The priesthood in particular, virtually undiluted as it was by Greek
blood,[14] remained deeply absorbed in its own tradition; and the
priests' ambivalent feelings about the alien culture that had struck
root in their country was reflected in the slightly disdainful smile[15]
and infuriating reserve[16] with which they greeted their Greek visitors.
According to Philostratus, Apollonius of Tyana was told in India that

the visitors who come here from Egypt...defame the Greeks. They maintain that
they themselves are holy men and wise, and that it was they who decreed the

---

[10] Ph. Al., *V. Mos.* 23; Plut., *Is. Os.* 10 (with Griffiths's n. *ad loc.*).
[11] E.g. Aelius Aristides: see Behr, *Aelius Aristides* 16–17.
[12] *Exp. tot. mundi* 34; and cf. next note.
[13] Hdt. II.79, 91; cf. 49. Compare *P. Insinger* XXVIII.4–7, and Chaer. fr. 10, on the moral perils
of foreign travel; and in general Morenz, *Ägyptische Religion* 44–57.
[14] Peremans, *Anc. Soc.* 4 (1973) 59–68. Priests of Greek temples might also be native
Egyptians: *P. Michigan* 4244/4a.5, dated 142 B.C. (= Lüddeckens, *Ägyptische Eheverträge*
156; cf. Quaegebeur, in *Egypt and the Hellenistic world* 306); *P. Oxy.* 3471.1–9 (A.D. 131).
[15] Plato, *Tim.* 22b; Dio Chr., *or.* XI.37, 39–43.
[16] E.g. Str. XVII.1.29 on the experiences of Plato and Eudoxus; and Thess., *Virt. herb.* 1.
prooem. 13 (perhaps also reflecting fear of Roman legislation against magic). The
Macedonian *katochoi* who lived in the Sarapeum at Memphis were occasionally beaten up
by lay temple-workers: *U.P.Z.* 7–8.

15

sacrifices and rites of initiation which are customary among the Greeks. To the Greeks they deny any good quality, declaring them to be ruffians, a rabble given up to every sort of anarchy, story-tellers, miracle-mongers, and people who, while indeed poor, make their poverty not a title of dignity, but just an excuse for stealing.[17]

Many Egyptian priests, it is true, knew Greek. They were also a major source of information about the country for Greek visitors and scholars. Some, as we shall see in the next chapter, were even sufficiently Hellenized to write books in Greek about Egyptian religion, and perhaps also to translate some of the sacred priestly books for the benefit of those who could not read the originals.[18] Yet these were probably the activities of a small minority; and most priests learnt the language of the conqueror only for practical, everyday purposes, and no doubt spoke it much better than they wrote it.[19] There was no shortage either of the sort of priests whom the Greek papyri chauvinistically call 'unlettered' (ἀγράμματοι), in other words ignorant of Greek.[20] Clearly there was ample margin for misunderstanding, which will have been compounded by the prejudice and arrogance of some of the less sensitive Greek visitors – of Dio Chrysostom for example, who regarded the whole of Egypt as a mere 'appendage' (προσθήκη) of the Greek metropolis, Alexandria.[21]

[17] Philostr., V. Apol. III.32.
[18] Below, 52–6; and Merkelbach, Z.P.E. 2 (1968) 7–30, for a second-century A.D. Oxyrhynchus papyrus containing Greek versions of Egyptian priestly writings. A hieroglyphic and a demotic text from Dendera, datable probably to the reign of Augustus, allude to 'scribes of Greek writings': B.M. 57371.16, 57372 (hieroglyphic text).9, ed. Shore, in Glimpses of ancient Egypt 138–60. Quaegebeur, Anc. Soc. 11–12 (1980–81) 227–40, argues that the clergy were involved in the production of laws in both demotic and Greek. Derchain, R. Egypt. 26 (1974) 15–19, claims to find evidence of Greek ideas in the temple inscriptions at Edfu. Porph., Abst. IV.10, quotes a translation of an Egyptian prayer, similar in content to Book of the dead §125, made by Euphantus, an Egyptian (so hardly to be identified with Euphantus of Olynthus, pace Jacoby, F. Gr. H. 74).
[19] See Schönborn, Pastophoren 42–3; and the unpublished priestly archive from Narmuthis, which, though largely demotic, contains a surprising amount of Greek material: Donadoni, Acme 8 (2–3) (1955) 73–83, esp. 75, on the Greek of the Narmuthis archive as a 'lingua parlata ma non studiata nella sua tradizione se non letteraria, almeno grammaticale ed ortografica'. On other bilingual priestly archives see Peremans, in Egypt and the Hellenistic world 278–9. On the transparently Egyptian Phthomonthes, a pterophoros and enthusiastic inscriber of Greek graffiti in the jabal at Thebes, who spelt his title differently every time, and never correctly, see Bataille, B.I.A.O. 38 (1939) 151–3 (nos. 15–16), 156–7 (no. 26). On the disinclination of Egyptian priests to adopt Greek names, see Crawford, in Ptolemaic Memphis 25.
[20] Youtie, Z.P.E. 19 (1975) 101–8; and see Lucian, Philops. 34, on the hierogrammateus Pancrates, 'speaking incorrect Greek'. Otto's conservative estimate, Priester und Tempel 2.209–38, of the degree of Hellenization of the average priest in Hellenistic and Roman Egypt still stands.
[21] Dio Chr., or. XXXII.36; and cf. below, 21 n. 46.

The gods of Egypt

No doubt such reactions were quite common among Greek intellectuals on the Grand Tour – and they might easily develop into, or reinforce, much more deep-rooted prejudices, especially against the Egyptians' idosyncratic way of imagining their gods.[22]

One naturally wonders, then, to what extent it was possible for the interaction of Egyptianism and Hellenism to lead to their fusion, in the religious or any other sphere.[23] Did the centuries that followed the conquest of Egypt by Alexander see the emergence of a new, Graeco-Egyptian consciousness? Undeniably, attempts to demonstrate a 'fusion' of Egyptianism and Hellenism run the constant risk of being undermined by a considerable body of evidence that the two cultures often contrived, especially in the Ptolemaic period, to exist in contiguous isolation.[24] Greek immigrants, and the more urban and educated among their descendants, often persevered in Greek ways of thought and behaviour. They spoke their own language, keeping it free even of loan-words, and exploiting its flexibility, consciously or not, to disguise the uniqueness of their adopted land, bequeathing us in the process 'pyramids', 'obelisks', 'sphinxes' and 'labyrinths'.[25] They read their own literature, and stuck to the company and customs of their own kith and kin. Since they made no attempt to eradicate the autochthonous culture, and since that culture might be ignored, but hardly dismissed, they could never pass for autochthonous themselves – unless perhaps in the eyes of outsiders, who called settlers and natives alike 'Egyptians'.[26] We have already seen that parts of the Egyptian elite were similarly narrow in their outlook – and we may assume that the native peasantry was too, if only out of ignorance. But some of this ignorance was bound to be dispelled with the passing of time, and through the physical fact of cohabitation in the same claustrophobically narrow river-valley between hostile expanses of desert. By the Roman period, and especially in the cities and those rural areas, such as the Fayyum,

---

[22] E.g. Cic., *Nat. D.* 1.43; Lucian, *Deor. conc.* 10; Salutius IV.3. Many Jewish and Christian writers saw Egypt as the very incarnation of irreligiosity: Tardieu, *Trois mythes gnostiques* 270–2; Mahé 2.83–8.

[23] Since the meaning of the word 'acculturation' is not generally agreed, it seems better to speak of cultural 'interaction' or 'fusion', as appropriate; and, when an unbalanced fusion is meant, to say so.

[24] Bingen, in *Sixteenth Cong. Pap.* 3–18; Samuel, *Athens to Alexandria*, esp. 75–101; and the more general remarks on Greek cultural exclusivism, even in the Hellenistic and Roman periods, by Dubuisson, *R.B.Ph.* 60 (1982) 5–32 – though his argument is more valid for the educated than the popular milieu.

[25] Bergman, in *Syncretism* 208–11.

[26] Neugebauer, *Ancient mathematical astronomy* 562.

where Greek settlement had been intensive, there had emerged a mixed race with a distinctive cast of mind, 'neither Greek...nor Egyptian, but a hybrid: a joint', as Lawrence Durrell remarked of pre-Second World War Alexandria. Polybius observed of the Alexandrians that they came from Greek stock and had not forgotten their Greek ways – even though they had clearly become a mongrel race.[27] And Livy thought the Macedonian colonists of Alexandria had 'degenerated' into Egyptians.[28] Furthermore, any Egyptian who wanted to rise socially was bound to absorb the language, culture and manners of the politically dominant Greeks; and the bilinguality of this increasingly numerous class of men and women fulfilled the *sine qua non* for a genuine cultural fusion. It is to this educated native milieu, rather than to the very small number of Greeks who took the trouble to learn Egyptian (usually out of a desire to gain access to the world of the temples[29]), that we most naturally look for the genesis of a Graeco-Egyptian consciousness.

Religious belief, though, was an element of the Egyptian identity which proved especially resistant to fusion with imported Hellenism. Not of course that the phenomenon of syncretism between Egyptian and Greek deities was unknown. It manifested itself in various forms (even if we disregard the henotheist tendency[30] that became conspicuous in the Roman period). The most elementary, of which Herodotus provides numerous examples, was the straightforward verbal identification of an Egyptian and an alien divinity whose character, attributes, rituals or even names seemed similar[31] – Thoth and Hermes, for example, because of their functional resemblance (of which more below). More elaborately, it was possible to synthesize, however partially, two gods who were thought to enjoy some such kinship,[32] and even to produce from them a conglomerate – Hermes Trismegistus from the fusion of Thoth and Hermes, Hermanubis from Hermes and Anubis, or Helioserapis from the merging of Helios and Sarapis. Or a wholly new god might be created by a more subtle

---

[27] Plb. xxxiv.14.5.

[28] Livy xxxviii.17.11. For a brilliant investigation of the modes of cultural interchange in late Ptolemaic Edfu see Yoyotte, in *Religions en Egypte* 127–41. Cf. also Bell, *M.H.* 10 (1953) 222–37.

[29] Rémondon, *C.E.* 39 (1964) 132.

[30] Perfectly illustrated by *I. mét. Eg.* 165: σέβου τὸ θεῖον, θύε πᾶσι τοῖς θεοῖς ('reverence the divine, sacrifice to all the gods'); and cf. the remarks of Dunand, in *Syncrétismes dans les religions de l'antiquité* 161–5, especially on the henotheist tendency of the Isis cult.

[31] Bergman, in *Syncretism* 214–26.

[32] On the many modalities of this sort of synthesis, see Morenz, *Religion und Geschichte* 496–509.

theological fusion, as Sarapis, although adapted from the Memphite deity Osor-Hapi (in Greek Oserapis), was freshly conceived in terms of both Egyptian and Greek theological beliefs,[33] and worshipped in ritual that drew on both Egyptian and Greek practice. Yet religious syncretism is a more ambiguous process than we usually allow for. Although it presupposes the interaction of at least two religious cultures, interest in this process may fluctuate widely among different categories of worshippers, and produce an extremely uneven effect on their conception of the gods involved, and on the way in which they worship those gods. This was certainly the case in Greek and Roman Egypt, where the independence and tenacity of the native Egyptian religion precluded a true union of the two traditions, especially in the initial stages, while the Egyptian cults were still strong. In fact, 'Graeco-Egyptian' religion turns out to be based on a profound imbalance, in favour of the autochthonous, between its two constituent elements.

If it is perhaps not surprising that the Sarapis cult evolved in the overwhelmingly Greek milieu of Alexandria, what undoubtedly is significant is that nearly all our best evidence for cultic syncretism, of whatever sort, comes from the more heavily Hellenized parts of Egypt, such as Alexandria and the Fayyum. It was, after all, the Greeks who needed to acclimatize in a foreign land; and so it was they who took the initiative in identifying their gods with native divinities. The sparsity of evidence for the worship of purely Greek or Roman gods[34] suggests that there was little satisfaction to be had merely in clinging to what was familiar – the Olympians seemed out of place on the banks of the Nile. Even in areas that had a large Greek population, the immigrants were often happy to attach themselves

[33] The formulation is that of Fraser 1.246.
[34] This is occluded by the narrow Graeco-Roman perspective adopted by much modern scholarship. Fraser 1.193–212 makes much of the exiguous evidence for Greek cults in Alexandria, and suggests (189) that our ignorance about Egyptian religion in the city 'corresponds to a lack of religious activity on the part of the Egyptian population'(!). Rübsam, *Götter und Kulte in Faijum*, fails adequately to emphasize that 'Greek' gods are often Egyptian divinities masquerading under the name of their Greek equivalent (see e.g. 40 *ad fin.*). (*P. Oxy.* 3471.8–9, a reference to priests of a 'Greek temple of Zeus and Hera', suggests that Greek divine names were likely to be taken to refer to Egyptian gods unless otherwise stated.) Kiessling, *A.P.F.* 15 (1953) 25–45, lists the Egyptian cults attested in Greek and Roman Memphis, but asserts (44) that the Greek community (οἱ Ἑλληνομεμφῖται) had nothing to do with them; whereas in fact the Greek community was highly Egyptianized (Świderek, in *Hommages à Claire Préaux* 670–5, esp. 673–4), and we know next to nothing about native Greek cults in the city (Kiessling, *A.P.F.* 15 (1953) 43–4). Crawford, *Kerkeosiris* 86–92, 136–7, is more balanced, concluding that 'there is generally more evidence... for the egyptianization of Greeks than for the adoption of Greek beliefs and practices by the native Egyptians'.

to the dominant local gods, not excluding those, such as Sobek (Souchos), the crocodile-god of the Fayyum, for whom even the most imaginative syncretist would have been hard put to it to find a Hellenic counterpart.[35] Naturally the syncretic process had some effect on the native milieu as well – one has only to look at the humble terracotta figurines that survive from the Hellenistic and Roman periods to see how the ordinary people of the *chōra*, themselves increasingly mixed racially, envisaged their gods in a form that was at once Greek and oriental.[36] Yet, behind the terracotta facade of the syncretic figurines, there lurked wholly traditional ideas about the working of the divine realm.[37] Perhaps this goes some way towards explaining the failure of the Sarapis cult to stir much interest among native Egyptians before the Roman period[38] – while as late as the third century A.D. we find the philosopher Porphyry remarking on the antipathy of Egyptians towards 'half-Greek fabrications' like Hermanubis.[39]

Even the personal participation of Greeks in native cults did not necessarily make much difference to the way those cults were conducted, or to the behaviour or beliefs of their native followers. It is instructive to examine the Sarapis cult as it was practised in the culturally antithetical cities of Alexandria and Memphis. At 'Alexandria near Egypt',[40] a Greek *polis* that happened to have been founded on the Nile delta, Sarapis was naturally enough treated as a Greek god, his statue by Bryaxis housed in a temple which, as built by Ptolemy III, was apparently a mainly Greek structure, while its Roman successor was in the Corinthian style. The priesthood and ritual were probably also largely Greek.[41] Even in Alexandria though, various Egyptian objects were to be seen adorning the Sarapeum, including a couple of statues of Psenptais, a third-century priest of Memphite Ptah, that perhaps suggest links between the

---

[35] *Chrest. Wilck.* 141–2 (though the unthinkable has now been thought: Quaegebeur, in *Egypt and the Hellenistic world* 312–16).

[36] Dunand, *Religion populaire*, esp. 5–16, 154–61.

[37] This point is argued at length, with reference to Isis, by Dunand, *Culte d'Isis* 1.78–99, esp. 99.

[38] Fraser 1.272–5; and cf. the explanation offered by Macrob., *Sat.* 1.7.13–15.

[39] Porphyry, *De imaginibus* 18*.1–2. Cf. Plutarch's rather abject plea (*Is. Os.* 66) for the Egyptians to take a more ecumenical view of their gods.

[40] 'Alexandrea ad Aegyptum' /'Αλεξάνδρεια ἡ πρὸς Αἰγύπτωι was the city's official name in the Roman period: Fraser 1.107–9. The distinction between Alexandria and Egypt was common currency: see the quotation from the *Oracle of the Potter*, below 21–2; Ph. Bybl. fr. 1 (804.28–9); MacMullen, *Aegyptus* 44 (1964) 183–4.

[41] Fraser 1.27–8, 264–70.

clergy of the two cities.[42] And Egyptian elements in both the personnel and the cult of the temple undoubtedly multiplied in the Roman period, as emerges both from the excavations and from accounts in Rufinus and other late sources.[43] But at Memphis, once the Pharaohs' capital and still strongly Egyptian in character, 'Sarapis' was but a name for Osor-Hapi, whose presentation was scarcely Hellenized at all.[44] The processional way that led to his temple may have been adorned with statues in the Greek style – there was even an exedra bearing images of Greek poets and philosophers such as Pindar and Plato;[45] but the Sarapeum itself, its priesthood and ritual, remained as Egyptian as ever, and in that the Greek community in Memphis, and (with some exceptions[46]) their compatriots who came from afar to visit the sanctuary, were content to acquiesce. Amidst the immense neighbouring complex of pyramids, temples and catacombs of animal gods – the Apis bulls, the hawks of Horus, the ibises and baboons of Thoth – the occasional papyri and inscriptions left by Greek worshippers reflect a passive, transitory presence. The decree of the priests of Memphis, preserved on the Rosetta Stone, by which statues and ceremonies were ordained in honour of Ptolemy V, emphasized that they were to be in the Egyptian manner;[47] but the most striking of all testimonies to the quintessential Egyptianism exuded by the 'arcana Memphitica'[48] is contained in a Ptolemaic prophecy called the *Oracle of the Potter*:

And the belt-wearers [the Greeks[49]] will destroy themselves, for they are followers of Typhon. Then Agathos Daimon will abandon the city that is being built [Alexandria] and will emigrate to god-bearing Memphis. And it will be deserted, the city of foreigners that will be built among us. These things will come to pass when all evils have come to an end, when the foreigners who are in Egypt disappear as leaves from a tree in autumn. And the city of the belt-wearers will be deserted...on acount of the impieties they have committed. And the Egyptian statues which were carried thither will be restored to Egypt, and the city by the sea will be transformed into a drying-place for fishermen, for Agathos Daimon and Mephis [= Knephis]

[42] Quaegebeur, in *Ptolemaic Memphis* 53–9, 77–8.
[43] Fraser, *loc. cit.*; Thelamon, *Paiens et chrétiens* 194–9, 201–5.
[44] On this and what follows see Harder, *Karpokrates von Chalkis* 40–5; Kiessling, *A.P.F.* 15 (1953) 17–19, 44–5; Fraser 1.253–4; Gallotta, *P.P.* 167 (1976) 129–42; Ray, *W.A.* 10 (1978) 149–57.   [45] Lauer and Picard, *Statues ptolémaïques*, esp. 26–7.
[46] E.g. Dio Chr., *or.* XXXII.13: the Alexandrian Sarapis is 'more perfect' than his Memphite progenitor.
[47] *O.G.I.S.* 90. On the role of Memphis in the political concessions made to Egyptianism at this period see Crawford, in *Ptolemaic Memphis* 31–6.
[48] Apul., *Met.* II.28.
[49] If such was not the original meaning, the expression was certainly understood in this sense subsequently: cf. *Oracle of the Potter* P_3.33, and Koenen's introduction, 189–91.

will have departed to Memphis; so that passers-by will say: 'This was [once] the all-nurturing [city], that was inhabited by all races of men.'[50]

Hermes Trismegistus

The evolution of Hermes Trismegistus himself, out of the syncretism of Thoth and Hermes, well illustrates the tensions which arose from the encounter of these two strong-minded cultural traditions. And to understand the genesis of the Egyptian Hermes is to take a first step into the historical milieu of the Hermetica.

Thoth was among the most diverse and popular of all the Egyptian gods.[51] Like many of his colleagues he was a composite, even an accumulation, rather than a figure cast whole and unambiguously defined; he was a powerful national god who yet had certain specialities and local associations. In particular, Thoth was regarded even in the most primitive period as the moon-god; and from this lunar association arose many of his most distinctive functions. Just as the moon is illuminated by the sun, so Thoth derived much of this authority from being secretary and counsellor to the solar divinity Re. The moon, 'ruler of the stars, distinguishes seasons, months and years';[52] and so Thoth became the lord and multiplier of Time, and the regulator of individual destinies.[53] Indeed, so important were the moon's phases in determining the rhythms of Egyptian national life, that Thoth came to be regarded as the origin both of cosmic order and of religious and civil institutions. He presided over almost every aspect of the temple cults, law and the civil year, and in particular over the sacred rituals, texts and formulae, and the magic arts that were so closely related. To him, as divine scribe, inventor of writing and lord of wisdom,[54] the priesthood attributed much of its sacred literature, including, for example, parts of the *Book of the dead*. And of the occult powers latent in all these aspects of the cult of the gods, Thoth was the acknowledged source. By extension he came to be regarded as the lord of knowledge, language and all science – even as Understanding or Reason personified. 'Without his

---

[50] *Oracle of the Potter* P₃.49–62.

[51] For what follows see Rusch, *R.E.* 6A.351–88 (with a summary of earlier bibliography); Altenmüller, *Synkretismus* 235–43; Derchain-Urtel, *Thot*.

[52] Inscription from the temple of Amun at Hibis: Brugsch, *El Khargeh* Taf. XVI. 33–4 = Davies, *Temple of Hibis* pl. 31 (tr. Boylan, *Thoth* 83).

[53] On Thoth's important role in the Egyptian doctrine of fate see Morenz, *Rolle des Schicksals* 28–9.

[54] Schott, *Z.Ä.S.* 99 (1972) 20–5.

knowledge nothing can be done among gods and men.'[55] Esoteric wisdom was his special preserve, and he was called 'the Mysterious', 'the Unknown'. His magical powers made of him a doctor too; and when the body finally succumbed to mortality, Thoth conducted the dead man to the kingdom of the gods, and participated in the judgment of his soul. But it was at Hermoupolis Magna (al-Ashmunayn), the main centre of his cult, that Thoth attained the pinnacle of his glory[56] – indeed, his distinctively Hermoupolitan character was recognized throughout Egypt.[57] Naturally enough his clergy were eager to aggrandize their patron; and the obvious way to do so was through the development of a distinctive cosmogony, Hermoupolis being widely regarded as the oldest place on earth. So it was that Thoth acquired a leading role in the drama of creation itself, as a demiurge who called things into being merely by the sound of his voice. Besides the common near Eastern idea that speech has creative power,[58] we can surely detect here the influence of Thoth the god of magic.

Perhaps, though, it was to his role as guide of souls and judge of the dead that Thoth most owed his popularity with ordinary people. And he continued to inspire strong popular devotion throughout the Ptolemaic and Roman periods.[59] His was an inescapable presence; and it is easy to see why foreign settlers in Egypt were tempted to try to establish some sort of link with him. The second-century B.C. Jewish romancer Artapanus, for instance, wrote an account of the life of Moses in which he assimilated his hero to 'Hermes' (i.e Thoth), making him responsible for introducing the Egyptians to ships, machines, weapons and philosophy; for dividing the country up into nomes, each with its own divine patron; for inventing the hieroglyphs; and for assigning lands of their own to the priests.[60] And the Greek settlers identified Thoth with their god Hermes.[61] Like Thoth, the classical Greek Hermes was associated with the moon, medicine and the realm of the dead.[62] Furthermore, both had a reputation for

---

[55] *Aeg. I. Berl.* 2.63–71 (tr. Roeder, *Urkunden* 56).

[56] Boylan, *Thoth* 149–58; Roeder, *A.S.A.E.* 52 (1952–4) 315–442; Kessler, *Lex. Äg.* 2.1137–47.

[57] Noberasco, *O.A.* 20 (1981) 268.

[58] Morenz, *Religion und Geschichte* 328–42, esp. *ad init.*

[59] Boylan, *Thoth* 165–72; Kákosy, *A. Arch. Hung.* 15 (1963) 123–8; Quaegebeur, *Enchoria* 5 (1975) 19–24; below, 26 n. 77.

[60] Artap. fr. 3; Mussies, in *Studies dedicated to Professor Jan Zandee* 89–120.

[61] Festugière 1.69–70. Heliod. Em. III.14.2, alludes to the story that Homer was an Egyptian, and a son of Hermes.

[62] Fauth, *Kl. Pauly* 2.1069–76. For comparisons of the two divinities see Kolta, *Gleichsetzung* 134–9; Derchain-Urtel, *Thot* 136–42.

inventiveness and trickery, and both functioned as messenger of the gods, which in Hermes's case prepared him as well for his characteristic function in the Hellenistic period, as the *logos* or 'word', the interpreter of the divine will to mankind.[63] This Hellenistic Hermes-*logos* was a thoroughly cosmopolitan divinity: the Lycaonians, who were sufficiently un-Hellenized to have retained their native language, had no difficulty in recognizing the apostle Paul as Hermes come down to earth, 'because he was the chief speaker' (ὁ ἡγούμενος τοῦ λόγου).[64] The Stoics assigned Hermes a still more central role in their theology, magnifying his function from the merely expressive to the creative, and regarding him as both *logos* and demiurge. It may even be that this development owed something to the Egyptian understanding of Thoth as creator.

Hermes Trismegistus, then, was the cosmopolitan, Hellenistic Hermes, Egyptianized through his assimilation to Thoth, and in fact known throughout the Roman world as 'the Egyptian' *par excellence*.[65] To some extent this intermingling of Egyptian and Greek theology and Hellenistic philosophy produced a sum that was greater than its parts, a divinity who could deservedly be placed among the *dei magni* of the pagan pantheon that presided over the Roman world.[66] Yet around and within the Egyptian Hermes there persisted serious tensions, mirroring the peculiarities of the Graeco-Egyptian milieu that had produced him.

In the beginning it no doubt seemed enough to say that the Greek god Hermes was equivalent to the Egyptian god Thoth, and leave it at that. But the temptation to provide a mythological explanation could not be resisted for ever; and that was one of the reasons why Cicero was eventually able to enumerate no less than five different individuals who claimed the name Hermes, the third being the familiar offspring of Zeus and Maia, while

the fifth, who is worshipped by the people of Pheneus [in Arcadia], is said to have killed Argus, and for this reason to have fled to Egypt, and to have given the Egyptians their laws and alphabet – he it is whom the Egyptians call Theyn [Thoth].[67]

---

[63] Leisegang, *R.E.* 13.1061-5; Orth, *Logios* 77-86.

[64] Acts XIV.11-12; cf. Iam., *Myst.* I.1.1 (Θεὸς ὁ τῶν λόγων ἡγεμών, Ἑρμῆς), and *Cyr.* 41 on Hermes Trismegistus as λόγων ἡγούμενος.

[65] Porph., *Abst.* II.47.1; Festugière, *Etudes d'histoire* 143-4.

[66] Versnel, *Mnemosyne* 27 (1974) 144-51.

[67] Cic., *Nat. D.* III.56. Pease's notes document the influence of this passage; Lactantius adds the detail that Hermes founded Hermoupolis. For further accretions to the story see Mar. Vict., *In Cic. Rhet.* I.26, p. 223 (with Hadot, *Marius Victorinus* 91-2); Puech, *En quête de la gnose* I.117-18; N.F. 4.148-9.

In other words, the story that was produced – and widely circulated – to explain the emergence of Hermes Trismegistus invoked a relatively human Hermes who was recognized to be distinct from the messenger of the gods. So it is not surprising to find that people of Greek culture did not always envisage Trismegistus in the same terms as did those of a more Egyptian background.

It is in the Greek magical papyri rather than in the Hermetica that we most clearly discern the lineaments of Hermes Trismegistus, and that the Egyptian aspects of his identity are given fullest rein.[68] In a country as renowned for its magic as was Egypt, that was only to be expected.[69] The papyri present the new syncretistic Hermes as a cosmic power, creator of heaven and earth and almighty world-ruler (παντοκράτωρ, κοσμοκράτωρ). Presiding over fate[70] and justice, he is also lord of the night, and of death and its mysterious aftermath – hence his frequent association with the moon (Selene) and Hecate. He knows 'all that is hidden under the heavenly vault, and beneath the earth',[71] and is accordingly much revered as a sender of oracles – many of the magical spells that are addressed to Hermes aim to elicit arcane information, frequently by inducing the god to appear in a dream. In this capacity, Hermes often becomes involved in the minutiae of his devotees' everyday existence – there are interesting parallels to be drawn here with the small amount of material that has survived in demotic on Thoth-oracles,[72] and with the demotic letters, both Pharaonic and Ptolemaic, in which ordinary people who consider themselves to have been wronged in some way seek redress from the god Thoth as we might from a court of law or an industrial tribunal.[73] The Hermes of the magical papyri is then a cosmic deity, but one who may also dwell within the heart of man (ἐνκάρδιος); and the magician often assumes towards him a tone of intimacy shading off into self-identification. One magical invocation

---

[68] For what follows see *P. Graec. Mag.* v.400–21; vii.551–7, 668–85; viii.1–52; xviib; Heitsch, *Philologus* 103 (1959) 223–36 (cf. *P. Graec. Mag.* 2.249); Ray, *Archive of Hor.* Hermes is actually called τρισμέγας/τρισμέγιστος at *P. Graec. Mag.* iv.886, vii.551, and explicitly identified with Θαθ = Thoth at vii.551–7. Festugière 1.287–308 collects all the *P. Graec. Mag.* texts relevant to Hermes. *Pace* Nilsson, *Opuscula* 3.130–1, there is no reason why the hymns to Hermes transmitted in the magical papyri should not have been written by the magicians themselves. Even if they were not, their use is indicative of Hermes's image in the magical milieu.

[69] See further below, 65–7.

[70] An important function from the point of view of Hermetism, and one already performed by Thoth: above, 22 n. 53.

[71] *P. Graec. Mag.* viii.14–15.

[72] Kaplony-Heckel, *F.B.S.M.* 14 (1972) 85–90; Ray, *Archive of Hor* 130–6.

[73] Quaegebeur, *Enchoria* 5 (1975) 19 n. 4.

begins: 'come to me, Lord Hermes, as foetuses into the wombs of women', and after a modest shopping-list of gifts which the god is asked to bestow ('attractiveness,[74] nourishment, success, a happy life, sex-appeal, a nice face, and the prowess of all men and women'), ends with the round assertion that: 'I know you, Hermes, and you know me. I am you and you are me.' On occasion the magician might even impersonate Thoth–Hermes (or any other god) in order to put pressure on one of his divine colleagues.[75]

This self-identification with a god, common in the magical papyri, is an authentically Egyptian trait.[76] It highlights both the variety of the magician's approach to his gods, and the persistence of Egyptian ways of thought. The traditional Greek Hermes, clad in chlamys and winged hat and sandals, is not unknown to the magical papyri, but the autochthonous Thoth is commoner;[77] and if Hermes succeeded in becoming a dynamic element in Graeco-Egyptian popular religion, it was largely thanks to his alliance with his native counterpart, which allowed him to be thought of as more Egyptian than Greek. At first Hermes Egyptianized by translating, either literally or metaphorically, the attributes of Thoth. Once can see this clearly in his titulature. From the third century B.C. onwards we find attached to the name of Hermes formulae, such as μέγιστος καὶ μέγιστος θεὸς μέγας, which clearly originated in Egyptian designations of Thoth,[78] while the familiar title 'Trismegistus' acquired canonicity only in the Roman period.[79] Similarly, the Greeks fell into the habit of celebrating their god Hermes in a festival, the Hermaea, which coincided exactly – in fact was identical – with one of the major festivals of Thoth.[80] With time, naturally enough, this carefulness bred of unfamiliarity came to seem less necessary. As far as Hermes was

---

[74] On χάρις in the magical papyri see Bell, Nock and Thompson, *P.B.A.* 17 (1931) 259–61.

[75] *P. Graec. Mag.* VIII.2–6, 49–50; V.246–51.

[76] See e.g. the address to Osiris inscribed on the statue of Setne-Khamwas in the British Museum: 'He [Setne] hath caused thee to become great of form, he liveth through thee, O god, and thou livest through him': Shorter, in *Studies presented to F. Ll. Griffith* 130.

[77] Nilsson, *Opuscula* 3.139–40; Bonner, *Magical amulets* 24; Delatte and Derchain, *Intailles magiques* 141–51 (emphasizing, in the depiction of Thoth on magical gems, 'une tradition égyptienne authentique, préservée des influences étrangères'), 175–7; Tardieu, in *Studies presented to Gilles Quispel* 412–18.

[78] Ray, *Archive of Ḥor* 159–60; Thissen, *Lex. Äg.* 2.1134 nn. 6–8; Daumas, in *Gnosticisme et monde hellénistique* 7–10. That the title τρισμέγιστος was still unknown in the second/first century B.C. is proved by an inscription erected by the priests of Thoth at Hermoupolis, who could think of no way to describe their god precisely in Greek except by transliterating his Egyptian titles: ΘΩΥΘ ΩΩΩ ΝΟΒ ΖΜΟΥΝ (Pestman, *Recueil* 1.106–7, 2.113–14).

[79] Below, Appendix.

[80] Casarico, *Aegyptus* 61 (1981) 122–4.

concerned, the popularity of his cult at Hermoupolis[81] must have contributed a great deal to the dissolving of cultural barriers and the evolution of the composite Hermes Trismegistus of late antiquity. We can see the same process at work in the centuries-long accumulation of pious inscriptions and graffiti left by pilgrims Egyptian, Greek and Roman, of all stations in life, at the temple of Thoth–Hermes Paotnouphis at Pselchis (al-Dakka) on the Nubian frontier;[82] and in a mid-third-century soldier's votive inscription at Panopolis to 'the great god Hermes Trismegistus'.[83] By the later Roman period there had emerged a *koinē* of Graeco-Egyptian religious discourse; and of this *koinē* Hermes Trismegistus was a central constituent.[84] But for all that, the native Thoth was never wholly absorbed. He was too commanding a figure. Even in the Greek literary milieu there were those prepared to take the line of least resistance and propagate a version of Trismegistus that was scarcely Hellenized at all except in name. Cyril of Alexandria quotes a good example of this approach from a Hermetic text which he says was composed at Athens.[85] The author presents 'our Hermes' as seen through the eyes of an Egyptian priest. He is an adept of the temple cults, a law-giver and an authority on astronomy, astrology, botany, mathematics, geometry, the arts and grammar. He it was who divided the country into nomes and other units, measured it, cut irrigation canals and established the exchange of contracts. In short, the anonymous Athenian Hermetist depicts Hermes in the same unmistakably Egyptian terms as those in which Artapanus had envisaged Moses.[86]

But most of those who looked at things from a Greek point of view had a rather different image of Hermes Trismegistus, which to some extent played down specifically Egyptian elements and assumed that, in origin at least, Hermes had been human. After all, Plato had

---

[81] Below, 174–6.

[82] Griffith, *Demotic graffiti* 17–32; Bresciani, *Graffiti démotiques*, pls. XLVII–XCIV; Ruppel, *Inschriften von Dakke*.

[83] *S.B.* 8917.

[84] On the absorption of Thoth–Hermes into the cult of the Egyptian Church in the guise of the archangel Michael see Wortmann, *B.J.* 166 (1966) 102. Cf. the assimilation of Hermes to Michael common in the Greek world: Lawson, *Modern Greek folklore* 45. On Hermes as archangel in the pagan tradition see Lewy, *Chaldaean Oracles* 225 n. 197.

[85] Cyr. Al., *Jul.* 1.548ac.

[86] As it happens, Cyril draws the parallel, observing that Hermes was of like mind with Moses, 'though he was not correct and above reproach in everything'. Clem. Al., *Strom.* 1. 21.134.1 (on 'Hermes the Theban' and 'Asclepius the Memphite', who 'in the opinion of men became gods'; and cf. Cyr. Al., *Jul.* VI.812d) probably refers to the deified Eighteenth Dynasty sage Amenhotep son of Hapu, not to Thoth–Hermes: Quaegebeur, *Enchoria* 5 (1975) 22; Wildung, *Imhotep und Amenhotep* 98, 236.

queried whether even Thoth was a god or just a divine man.[87] Ammianus Marcellinus mentions Trismegistus, alongside Apollonius of Tyana and Plotinus, as an example of a human endowed with a particularly strong guardian spirit;[88] and it is usually in human or at most heroic company that Hermes appears when cited as one of a string of authorities (as often happens) by late antique writers.[89] So too in the philosophical Hermetica. Hermes is a mortal who receives revelations from the divine world and eventually himself achieves immortality through self-purification, but remains among men in order to unveil to them the secrets of the divine world.[90] It is significant how many of the philosophical Hermetica are presented in epistolary or dialogue form. In this way the Hermetist, while preserving the divine and revelatory character of his doctrines, imparts to their exposition a certain air of historical reality, stirring in his audience, perhaps, echoes of Socrates and his circle as depicted in the Platonic dialogues.

Yet if once Hermes had been a mortal, that had been in remote antiquity,[91] and he had long since been assumed into the company of the gods. The technical Hermetica are studiously vague, usually envisaging Trismegistus as a sage who lived at a remote period and conversed freely with the gods,[92] though on occasion they speak of him as a divine being.[93] The *Korē kosmou*, which Stobaeus included in the selection of Hermetic philosophical texts for his *Anthologium*, but which was considerably influenced by technical Hermetism, treats Hermes straightforwardly as a god, and surrounds him with an unashamedly mythological narrative. The figure of Thoth, the divine author of the Egyptian temple literature, lurks only just below the surface of the *Korē*'s Hermes, all-knowing revealer of wisdom to

---

[87] Plato, *Phlb.* 18b.

[88] Amm. Marc. xxi.14.5.

[89] E.g. Tert., *An.* ii.3 (Silenus, Hermotimus, Orpheus, Musaeus, Pherecydes), xv.5–6 (Orpheus, Empedocles, Protagoras, Apollodorus, Chrysippus); Arn. ii.13 (Pythagoras, Plato); Marc. Anc., *Eccl.* 7, 9, 16 (Plato, Aristotle); Did. Al., *Trin.* ii.27 (Orpheus, Plato Comicus, Porphyry); Aug., *Faust.* xiii.1, 15 (Sibyls, Orpheus), *ep.* 234.1 (Orpheus, Agis); Fulg., *Mit.* iii.9 (Orpheus), *Exp. Virg.* pp. 85.20–86.2 (Pythagoras, Heraclitus, Plato, Chrysippus, Aristotle); *F. Gr. Th.* 177.19–26 (Moses, Apollonius of Tyana).

[90] E.g. *C.H.* i and xiii, esp. 3; and cf. Athenag., *Leg.* xxviii.6; N.F. 3.cxxxvi–cxliii.

[91] Lact., *Ira* xi.12: long before Plato, Pythagoras and even the Seven Sages; *Inst.* 1.6.3: 'antiquissimus'; Aug., *Civ. Dei* xviii.39.

[92] Festugière 1.102–4, 240–1; below, 151.

[93] E.g. *Cyr.* 14 (Ἑρμῆς ὁ τρισμέγιστος θεός), 42 (μάκαρ θεῶν Ἑρμῆ); Firm. Mat., *Math.* iii.1.1: 'potentissimum Mercurii numen'. *C.C.A.G.* 1.167.4–5 calls Hermes θειότατος, but humans might also be so designated. Whether the Taautos (= Thoth: below, 216) alluded to by Philo of Byblos is man or god is left ambiguous: Ebach, *Weltentstehung* 60–2.

mankind – and in general Egyptian ideas are particularly prominent in this text.[94]

The ambiguity of a figure who hovered between the divine and human worlds will have struck many as an advantage and attraction. Late paganism cultivated with enthusiasm such figures as Heracles, Dionysus, Asclepius and Orpheus. Hermes was one more of these intermediaries, who were much in demand in a world increasingly fascinated by the transcendental quality of the Divine.[95] But not everybody relished such ambiguities. Just as what seemed to some the simplistic identification of Hermes with Thoth was eventually 'explained', so too the tension in Trismegistus's character between the venerable and remote figure of Thoth and the more human Hermes of the Greeks had to be accounted for, if only to clear up the doubts of those who, like the Christian writer Lactantius, were not sure whether to treat the Hermetic books as divine revelation or human speculation.[96] So at some point the Hermetists began to propagate the idea that there had been *two* Egyptian Hermeses, grandfather and grandson. In the *Perfect discourse (Asclepius)*, Hermes Trismegistus refers to the tomb of his grandfather and namesake Hermes in Hermoupolis, 'the city where he was born (*patria*) and which is named after him'.[97] Clearly the author envisages Hermes I as identical with Thoth[98] – and the Egyptians were indeed used to the idea that gods might be born and then die, not in the euhemeristic sense, but as part of a perpetual process of regeneration.[99] The identification is made explicit in a passage from a text attributed to the early Ptolemaic priest and historian Manetho, but certainly of much later date, in which reference is made to 'stelae inscribed in the sacred language and with hieroglyphic characters by Thoth, the first Hermes'.[100] But who was his grandson, the second Hermes?

The Hermetists, while insisting that their compositions had indeed been written in Egyptian, and inscribed on stelae in hieroglyphic characters,[101] were also well aware that they could not have been

---

[94] Below, 35–6.

[95] Athanassiadi-Fowden, *Giuliano* 146–9, 150, 181–3.

[96] Lact., *Inst.* I.6.1, VII.13.4.   [97] *Ascl.* 37; and see below, 174–5.

[98] Aug., *Civ. Dei* XVIII.39, alludes to this passage, but wrongly assumes that Hermes I was the Greek god Hermes, son of Zeus and Maia. (*Pace* (e.g.) N.F. 3.CLXIII n. 3, Augustine's reference here to 'Trismegistus iste Mercurius' cannot have been derived from Varro, even if the rest of the passage was: cf. below, Appendix. This is a gloss by Augustine himself, based on *Ascl.* 37.)

[99] Hornung, *Conceptions of God* 143–65.

[100] *Ap.* Geo. Sync. 72; and cf. Laqueur, *R.E.* 14.1100.

[101] E.g. *N.H.C.* VI.6.61.18–62.15.

29

rendered into Greek without losing the authority that attached to sacred texts in the native language – 'for the very quality of the sounds and the [intonation] of the Egyptian words contains in itself the force of the things said'.[102] A translation would require, at the very least, the active assistance of the priestly guardians of the originals. Iamblichus, for example, records that an Egyptian priest named Bitys was supposed to have translated some of the hieroglyphic texts of Thoth into Greek,[103] and had made use of (Greek) philosophical vocabulary in doing so.[104] These texts Bitys had found 'in temples at Sais in Egypt', which of course is where Solon was supposed to have encountered Egyptian priests more learned in the history of Greece than any Greek, and to have translated parts of their archives.[105] Iamblichus also tells us that Pythagoras and Plato, during their visit to Egypt, 'read through' the stelae of Hermes with the help of native priests.[106] Whether or not these stories are true is fortunately not what concerns us here. What is important is firstly that the Hermetists wished it to be believed that their compositions were books of Thoth rendered from Egyptian into Greek; and secondly that the legitimacy and prestige of these books depended on the finding of a plausible explanation of how this translation had been brought about. Hence the last twist in the evolution of the myth of the Egyptian Hermes, namely the presentation of none other than Hermes the younger as the translator of the Thoth texts. At any rate, this appears to be the idea underlying the obscure and corrupt ps.-Manethonic passage already mentioned. After referring to the hieroglyphic texts inscribed by Thoth, the first Hermes, ps.-Manetho goes on to assert that 'after the Flood they were translated from the sacred language into Greek, and deposited in books in the sanctuaries of Egyptian temples by the second Hermes, the son of Agathos Daimon and father of Tat'.[107] That the Thoth-literature was believed

---

102 *C.H.* xvi.1–2; and cf. below, 37–8.
103 Iam., *Myst.* viii.5, x.7. That (μεθ)ἡρμήνευσε signifies translations into Greek rather than interpretations in Egyptian is clear from the context.
104 Iam., *Myst.* viii.4.265.
105 Plato, *Tim.* 21e ff., *Critias* 113ab. Like Iamblichus, Plato explains that a certain amount of Greek terminology inevitably creeps into these priestly sources in the course of transmission.
106 Iam., *Myst.* i.1.3 (reading ἱερογραμματέων for ἱερογραμμάτων), 2.5–6; and cf. *P. Ryl.* 63, a third-century A.D. fragment of an astrological dialogue between Plato and some Egyptian priests.
107 *Ap.* Geo. Sync. 72–3. The punctuation of the text is uncertain (cf. N.F. 3.CLXIII n. 1), and could be taken to mean that Agathos Daimon was the translator. To him too was ascribed the authorship of treatises that circulated in the Hermetic milieu: N.F. 3.CLXV.

to have been rendered into Greek at such an early date has struck modern scholars as so improbable that they have emended the passage.[108] But Plato had spoken of the translation of Greek records into Egyptian after the deluge(s);[109] and anyway this was exactly the sort of claim the Hermetists *had* to make if they were to overcome the well-known inadequacies of translations from Egyptian into Greek.

And so the two Hermeses in the *Asclepius* now stand revealed as separate embodiments of the divine Egyptian and the more human Greek dimensions of the composite deity Hermes Trismegistus.[110] The significance of this arrangement will gradually emerge in the coming chapters. It not only provided a mythological explanation and sanction for the existence of a Hermetic literature in Greek, rather than in the sacred tongue of Egypt, but also left the Greek Hermes flexible enough to play his traditional role of intermediary between God and men, as we shall see him doing to particular effect in the more initiatory of the philosophical Hermetica. But not everything in our texts is that harmonious. They too manifest the deep-seated cultural tensions that moulded their patron; and they too testify, in a surprising way, to the durability of Egypt.

The Hermetica

Here is not yet the place to describe the internal structures or the doctrines of Hermetism (part II). But the texts do have a distinctive *mise en scène*, and they do make occasional allusion, as we have already begun to see, to exoteric aspects of the various cults that were practised in the valley of the Nile. By examining these externals we can establish the Graeco-Egyptian origin of the Hermetica – which

---

[108] See Scott 3.491–2, and all other commentators. The only words that need to be excluded are γράμμασιν ἱερογλυφικοῖς, a doublet. Zos. Pan., *fr. gr.* 230.23–7, asserts that Asenas, the High Priest of Jeruselem, sent Hermes (Ἑρμῆν) to one of the Ptolemies (presumably Ptolemy II, who ordered the production of the Septuagint) in order to translate Hebrew texts into Greek and Egyptian. This is extremely odd, and anyway rather a remote parallel to ps.-Manetho. Scott's emendation πέμψαντα ἑρμηνέα is tempting, especially in view of the pun on Ἑρμῆς/ἑρμηνεύς a few lines earlier.

[109] Plato, *loc. cit.*

[110] Cf. the distinction of two Asclepii in the same passage (*Ascl.* 37), and at *S.H.* XXVI.9, where one is clearly the Greek Asclepius, the other the Egyptian Imhotep. But *pace* Gundel 26, the illiterate horoscope of A.D. 137 (Neugebauer and van Hoesen, *Greek horoscopes* 137c, p. 42) which refers to Asclepius, ὁ⟨ς⟩ ἐστιν Ἰμούθου [read Ἰμούθης] υἱὸς Ἡφήστου, plainly means that Asclepius is identical with Imouthes and the son of Hephaestus (Ptah) (cf. *P. Oxy.* 1381. 201–2, 228–9; *S.H.* XXVI.9), not that Asclepius is the son of Imouthes and Imouthes the son of Hephaestus.

should not be taken for granted – and we can create a context for the discussion of literary and doctrinal issues.

First of all, the *dramatis personae*. The Hermetica are presented as revelations of divine truth, not as the product of human reason; and in the philosophical as in the technical texts those who do the revealing are the typical deities of Graeco-Egyptian syncretism[111] – in other words even allowing for the presence of some characteristically Greek elements,[112] and of certain ambiguities already discussed, the overall atmosphere is Egyptian. Alongside Hermes Trismegistus himself and Isis, who had long been associated in the Egyptian as well as the Greek tradition,[113] we find Asclepius, identified with the Egyptian Imhotep/Imouthes;[114] Ammon, the Egyptian god Amun, euhemeristically regarded by some as one of the country's early kings;[115] Horus, the son of Isis;[116] and Agathos Daimon.[117] Rather more unusually, the *Korē kosmou* alludes to Kamephis as an intermediary between Hermes and Isis,[118] while *S.H.* xxvi.9 identifies the god of philosophy as Arnebeschenis, a Greek transcription of the Egyptian for 'Horus of Letopolis'.[119] Both of these divinities are attested elsewhere in the Greek literature of or on Egypt, but they were considerably less well-known than the other figures just mentioned, and their presence indicates a more than superficial familiarity with the native milieu. There are also figures unique to the Hermetica: Poimandres, Tat and the priest Bitys. Of Bitys there will be more to be said in a later chapter. The origin and meaning of the name Poimandres is unclear, though it may well be Egyptian.[120] As for Tat,

---

[111] See esp. *S.H.* xxvi.9, *Ascl.* 37.

[112] *C.H.* x.15 (reference to Olympus); *Ascl.* 9, 19, 27; *S.H.* xxiii.28, xxix; Mich. Psel., *Tant.* 348 (Hermes reported to have used Greek myths in instructing Tat, but only exceptionally); and cf. Kroll, *Hermes Trismegistos* 97–8.

[113] N.F. 3.cxxvi–cxxvii; Griffiths, *Plutarch's De Iside* 263–4; Hani, *Religion égyptienne* 38–9; Ray, *Archive of Ḥor* 159.

[114] Gundel 25–7; below, 50–2.

[115] Plato, *Phdr.* 274d; Manetho 105.31. Plato has Thoth reveal all the arts to Ammon (hence Ph. Bybl., *fr.* 1 (805.8–10), on texts by Thoth found in temples of Ammon: cf. Baumgarten, *Philo of Byblos* 77–80); and on this idea *C.H.* xvi (ὅροι Ἀσκληπιοῦ πρὸς Ἄμμωνα βασιλέα), *S.H.* xii–xvii (Ἑρμοῦ ἐκ τῶν πρὸς Ἄμμωνα), the Hermetic iatromathematical treatises addressed to Ammon (*Phys. med. gr.* 1.387, 430), and Iam., *Myst.* viii.5.267 (see below, 140) are simple variations. Ps.-Just., *Coh.* 38, quotes Ammon alongside Hermes on god as 'utterly hidden'; and cf. Syn., *Dion* 10 (for the form 'Amous' see Hdt. ii.42; *S.H.* xiv *tit.*).

[116] *P. Oxy.* 1381.230–1 calls Horus the son of Hermes.

[117] N.F. 3.clxv–clxviii, 1.135 n. 78; Fraser 1.209–11.

[118] *S.H.* xxiii.32; cf. N.F. 3.clxii–clxiv.

[119] Quaegebeur, *Lex. Äg.* 2.998–9.

[120] Marcus, *J.N.E.S.* 8 (1949) 40–3. Haenchen, *Gott und Mensch* 338, prefers to derive it from ποιμήν ('shepherd').

he began humbly enough as a Greek misspelling of Thoth,[121] but ended up taking on an identity of his own as Thoth–Hermes's son, both bodily and spiritual.[122] The Hermetists apparently saw nothing inconsistent in this – an indication that philosophical Hermetism is not just a haphazard accumulation of separate elements, but a self-validating structure with its own conventions.

According to the *Korē kosmou*,[123] Hermes was a god who succeeded in understanding the mysteries of the heavens, and revealed them by inscribing them in sacred books, which he then hid here on earth, intending that they should be searched for by future generations, but found only by the fully worthy. Having finished his task he returned to the celestial abode of the gods; but he left behind a successor, Tat, together with Asclepius–Imouthes and others not named. This plurality of authorities in Hermetism is not much noticed in modern accounts of the subject; but since the Hermetists themselves insisted on it, we ignore it at our peril. Rather than assigning all their treatises to the unimpeachably authoritative figure of Trismegistus, and having done with it, the authors of the Hermetica fully exploited their other *dramatis personae*, even allowing them on occasion to shine in their own right. Though most of the philosophical Hermetica are either attributed to Hermes's personal authorship or at least feature him as teacher in conversation with a more or less stage-struck pupil, *C.H.* xvi is attributed to Asclepius, while *C.H.* xvii is a dialogue in which Tat replaces Hermes in the role of teacher. *S.H.* xxiii–xxvii, though identified by their titles as Hermetic compositions, are strictly speaking dialogues between Isis and her son Horus. And similar examples could be produced from the technical genres.[124]

In this context, the mysterious Poimandres is of special interest. In *C.H.* i Poimandres, identified as divine intellect (ὁ τῆς αὐθεντίας νοῦς), instructs none other than Hermes Trismegistus himself. The only other allusion to Poimandres comes at *C.H.* xiii.15, where Hermes mentions Poimandres's teaching, speaking of him once more as ὁ τῆς αὐθεντίας νοῦς and acknowledging his superior authority; but in *C.H.* xi Hermes is again shown receiving instruction from *Nous*, and it is clear that Poimandres is intended. The alchemist Zosimus of Panopolis exhorts his pupil Theosebia, once perfected, to 'hasten towards Poimenandres [*sic*]'.[125] Even in the light of these few al-

---

[121] E.g. *P. Graec. Mag.* vii.551–7.
[123] *S.H.* xxiii.5–8.
[125] Zos. Pan., *fr. gr.* 245.

[122] *C.H.* xiv.1; *S.H.* xxiii.6.
[124] See e.g. below, 163–4.

lusions, Poimandres clearly deserves more attention than he usually gets. And we now have a suggestive new item for the dossier in the Syriac *Prophecies of the pagan philosophers in abbreviated form* recently published by S. Brock[126] and dated by him to the late sixth or early seventh century. Here we find (§21) an abbreviated and somewhat Christianized version of *C.H.* XIII.1-2, 4, under the heading: 'Poimandres, on Christ'. Unlike most of the pagan 'prophecies' of the Christian dispensation contained in this collection, which are familiar to us from Cyril of Alexandria and the various similar oracle-collections that circulated in late antiquity, this passage from *C.H.* XIII does not occur elsewhere; so we have to consider the possibility that whoever put it into circulation under the title 'Poimandres, on Christ' had access to the whole treatise. And if he did, he will have known that Hermes Trismegistus acknowledged Poimandres as his teacher. But this is hardly a sufficient explanation of the heading attached to the 'prophecy', especially since the Syriac text makes clear that the dialogue takes place between Hermes and a 'questioner' (i.e. Tat). The allusion to Poimandres will have puzzled the original readers of the *Prophecies* as much as it does us – unless Poimandres was much better known in antiquity than appears from what we have of the Hermetic literature. After all, to have been Hermes Trismegistus's teacher was no insubstantial claim to fame. And it may be recalled that, from Ficino's time up to the beginning of the twentieth century, and until our own day in certain theosophical circles, the whole of the *Corpus Hermeticum* passed under the name of 'Poemander'.[127]

It is clear then that our Hermetists were not just Hermetists. Rather, they were accustomed to think in terms of a whole milieu populated with ancient Egyptian gods and sages, some of whom seem to us distinctly *recherchés*. They are of course syncretistic figures set to act in intellectual modern dress. Agathos Daimon shamelessly plagiarizes Heraclitus,[128] and in some of the philosophical Hermetica the mere names of the interlocutors are the nearest one gets to any sign of Egyptianism at all. Even so, when the surviving fragments of the Hermetic mythology are put together, there is undeniably a hint of the Golden Age about it. To assert grandly, as does Festugière, that 'nous sommes en plein τόπος',[129] does not explain much. Are all

---

[126] Brock, *O.L.P.* 14 (1983) 203-46, esp., for the passage in question, 220 (text); 231 (translation); 206, 241-2 (commentary).
[127] Scott 1.17.   [128] N.F. 1.185 n. 21.   [129] N.F. 3.CLXIII.

these names marshalled just to dazzle us? Or do they also reflect the Hermetist's particular self-awareness?

The idea of the Golden Age is worth pursuing. But first we should glance at some other manifestations of Egyptianism in the Hermetic texts, besides the *dramatis personae*. This is controversial territory. When, for example, at the end of *The Ogdoad reveals the Ennead*, Hermes bids Tat inscribe their dialogue in hieroglyphs on turquoise stelae to be set up in 'the temple [of Thoth–Hermes] at Diospolis', in order that they may be read by those who come after, there is a predictable reaction from scholars over-familiar with this tired device of writers hard up for Nilotic colour. But even an invention need not be uninformed. In this case our author is recalling and adapting formulae from inscriptions he has seen lining the *dromoi* of Upper Egyptian temples – a good example from Karnak has recently been published.[130] The ogdoad of frog- and cat-faced divinities he deploys in the same passage is also unlikely to be a complete fabrication.[131] But if for all that the Egyptian elements in the new Coptic Hermeticum seem a bit incidental, the *Korē kosmou* (*S.H.* XXIII) shows how such materials might also play a more integral role in the evolution of a Hermetic text. The word 'evolution' is used advisedly, since the *Korē kosmou* is anything but a coherent structure. It shows the scars of maladroit editing apparently designed to recast a straightforward Hermetic treatise as a dialogue between Isis and Horus, and to insert within that framework a joint aretalogy of Isis and Osiris.[132] Though this aretalogy is not dependent on the Egyptian prototype at Memphis which inspired, as we shall see in chapter 2, so many of the Greek Isis-aretalogies, there is a general resemblance of subject-matter[133] and even of form – the *Korē kosmou* aretalogy is constructed as a series of brief statements to the effect that 'these' (οὗτοι), i.e. Isis and Osiris, bestowed such-and-such a benefit on the human race. The link between Isis and Hermes is more emphatically stated than in the Memphite text, which arouses suspicions of editorial intervention, and there is a marked element of philosophical elaboration analogous to the literary elaboration of the version of the Memphite

---

[130] Wagner, *B.I.A.O.* 70 (1971) 7: ἀναγράψαντας [εἰς στήλ]ην λιθίνην τοῖς τε ἱεροῖς καὶ ἐγχωρίοις καὶ ἑλληνικοῖς γράμμασιν τὰς γεγεν[ημένας] ὑπ' αὐτοῦ εὐεργεσίας εἰς τὸ ἱερὸν καὶ τοὺς κατοικοῦντας τὴν πόλιν ἀν[αθεῖναι] ἐν τῶι ἐπιφανεστάτωι τόπωι ἐπὶ τοῦ δρόμου τοῦ Ἄμμωνος ὅπως ὑπάρ[χωσι εἰ]ς τὸν ἅπαντα χρόνον; and cf. *O.G.I.S.* 56.74–5 (Canopus decree), 90.53–4 (Rosetta decree). On the Upper Egyptian milieu of *N.H.C.* VI.6 see below, 170–1.

[131] But cf. Mahé 1.36–7.

[132] N.F. 3.CXXXI–CLVIII. The aretalogy is *S.H.* XXIII.65–8.

[133] Festugière, *Études de religion* 165–7.

35

text found on Andros; but whatever the precise origin and history of the *Korē kosmou* aretalogy, its native Egyptian inspiration is unmistakable. And the same can be said of much else in the *Korē kosmou*, especially its cosmogonical passages.[134]

Even the non-Graeco-Egyptian elements that one can detect in the Hermetica are precisely those that one would expect in texts written in Ptolemaic or Roman Egypt – a land which, however enclosed and autonomous it had been in the past, was now not only politically a part of the cosmopolitan Hellenistic and Roman world, but also host to important and numerous foreign communities. If Iranian influences, emphasized by R. Reitzenstein in the later period of his Hermetic studies, are best regarded as remote and indirect,[135] still Egypt was certainly not innocent of them. And that Hermetic writers absorbed Jewish ideas is anything but surprising when one recalls the wide distribution and (one assumes) numerousness of Egypt's Jewish population.[136] The Hebrew creation-myth was bound to be of interest to anyone who, like the Hermetists, regarded cosmology as one of the foundations of philosophy; and the *Poimandrēs*'s debt to *Genesis* was already remarked on by Psellus.[137] Recent scholarship has elaborated this perception,[138] unearthed evidence for Jewish influence on other philosophical Hermetica too, and shown that the sources of this influence are to be looked for not just in the reading of the Septuagint, but also in personal contact with the liturgical life of Jews living in Egypt.[139] And the Jewish writer Artapanus's identification

---

[134] Kroll, *R.E.* 8.801–2; Bousset, *R.E.* 11.1389–91; above, 28–9; and cf. N.F. 3. CLXXVII–CLXXIX.

[135] Nock, *Essays* 195–9; Nilsson, *Geschichte* 2.605–9.

[136] *C.P. Jud.* 1, pp. 4–5 (pouring cold water on the figure of a million proposed by Ph. Al., *Flacc.* 43); 3, pp. 197–209.

[137] Above, 9; and cf. the allegation in *P. Graec. Mag.* XIII.14–16 that Hermes plagiarized a magical treatise by 'Moses'.

[138] Dodd, *Bible and the Greeks* 99–200 (but also the criticisms of Haenchen, *Gott und Mensch* 335–77, who considerably reduces Dodd's estimate of the Jewish, or at least LXX, material in *C.H.* 1); Philonenko, in *Syncrétismes dans les religions de l'antiquité* 204–11, and *R.H.Ph.R.* 59 (1979) 369–72; Pearson, in *Studies presented to Gilles Quispel* 336–48. The *Anthrōpos* doctrine of *C.H.* 1 seems to have been paralleled in the *pinax* of Hermes/Bitys, whose relations with Jewish teachings were remarked by Zosimus of Panopolis: see below, 151–2.

[139] *C.H.* III: Dodd, *Bible and the Greeks* 210–34. *C.H.* VII: *ibid.* 181–94. *Ascl.*: N.F. 2.289–90; Philonenko, in *Studies for Morton Smith* 2.161–3. *S.H.* XXIII: Philonenko, in *Int. Coll. Gnosticism 1973* 153–6. *N.H.C.* VI.6: Philonenko, *R.H.Ph.R.* 59 (1979) 369–72. Cf. also Dodd, *Bible and the Greeks* 235–42, esp. 242: 'while in *Corp.* I., III. and VII. there is definite evidence of dependence on biblical sources, in the rest of the Corpus there are indications that among the variety of elements contributory to the Hermetic philosophy of religion Jewish influence is to be included. It will have been in most cases indirect, but in *Corp.* V. and in the hymn appended to *Corp.* XIII., direct influence of the LXX is probable.' On the difficulty of asserting categorically that a text is influenced by the Jewish rather than

of Moses with Thoth–Hermes is one sign among many that these contacts did not just go in one direction.[140]

But not all cultural contacts and interactions are necessarily constructive. That native Egypt resisted the Ptolemies, and bore Roman rule in resentful apathy,[141] are facts of political history that need no restating here; and this hostility naturally found expression in the religious sphere too, as for example in native antipathy to syncretistic deities such as Sarapis and Hermanubis. It is, needless to say, of considerable significance for our present investigation that expressions of the ethnic Egyptian point of view are also to be found in the philosophical Hermetica.

The overwhelming prestige of Greek as a literary tongue meant that anti-Greek feeling, cultural as well as political, had often to be expressed in the language of the enemy – one thinks most readily of our Greek versions of the *Oracle of the Potter*. Inevitably the language-question became a sensitive point with educated Egyptians. Hence this extraordinary passage from the beginning of *C.H.* xvi, put into the mouth of Asclepius:

Hermes...often used to say to me...that those who read my books will think that they are very simply and clearly written, when in fact, quite on the contrary, they are unclear and hide the meaning of the words, and will become completely obscure when later on the Greeks will want to translate our language into their own, which will bring about a complete distortion and obfuscation of the text. Expressed in the original language, the discourse conveys its meaning clearly, for the very quality of the sounds and the [intonation] of the Egyptian words contains in itself the force of the things said... Preserve this discourse untranslated, in order that such mysteries may be kept from the Greeks, and that their insolent, insipid and meretricious manner of speech may not reduce to impotence the dignity and strength [of our language], and the cogent force of the words. For all the Greeks have...is empty speech, good for showing off; and the philosophy of the Greeks is just noisy talk. For our part, we use not words, but sounds full of energy.

This goes much further than would be necessary simply to assert the antiquity and oriental provenance of a text that had no claim to either. Clearly we have to do here with an Egyptian who, desiring to convey the impression that his work is but a translation from his native tongue, acts on the principle that attack is the best form of

some other milieu, see Zuntz, *Opuscula selecta* 165–9, and Mahé 2.287–8, 313 n. 175, 433–4, 445–8. Between Essenism and the Hermetica Braun, *Jean le Théologien* 2.253–76, finds nothing more than parallels. Direct influence of Christianity on Hermetism has also yet to be proved: Grese, *Corpus Hermeticum XIII* 44–7, 55–8, 198.

[140] Above, 23; and Görg, in *Das ptolemäische Ägypten* 177–85.

[141] E.g. Amm. Marc. xxii.16.23.

defence. He may himself have had no choice but to write in Greek, but he shared with many Hellenized oriental intellectuals a suspicion of the debilitating effect of translation – understood in the broadest sense – on the distinctive essence of his own tradition.[142]

Language has always of course been at the centre of efforts to define and maintain separate ethnic and even national identities; and the subordination and eventual elimination of once independent linguistic traditions is among the least attractive side-effects induced by some types of cultural interaction. But it is only one of many such consequences. Another Hermetic treatise, the *Perfect discourse* (*Asclepius*), contains a memorable and moving account of the total effect of cultural oppression on a traditional society. For that reason alone it deserves discussion in the present context. It happens also to be among the most misunderstood of all Hermetic texts.

In the form in which it has come down to us, the *Asclepius* is a compilation of materials from various sources, loosely linked together. Despite its paraphrastic manner, there is no good reason to suppose that the translator materially altered the original Greek *Perfect discourse*.[143] Paragraphs 24–7 (= *N.H.C.* vi.8.70–5)[144] contain a more or less self-sufficient narrative foretelling the demise of Egypt and its gods, which modern scholarship has analysed as a compound of apocalyptic *topoi* and allusions to the persecution of paganism by victorious fourth-century Christianity. That it is indeed related to other literary prophecies, especially Egyptian ones such as the *Oracle of the Potter*, there can be no dispute;[145] but its allusions to legal penalties for pagan worship, and even for those who devote themselves to *religio mentis*,[146] are certainly not, as has been alleged,[147] fourth-century insertions in response to the anti-pagan laws of the Christian emperors, since the eschatological prophecy in book vii of Lactantius's *Divinae institutiones*, composed during the first decade of the fourth century,[148] is not only based on the *Perfect discourse*, but actually makes

---

[142] E.g. *Ep. Arist.* 312–16; and cf. Clem. Al., *Strom.* 1.21.143.6–7; Or., *Cels.* v.45; Iam., *Myst.* vii.4.256; *C.P. Jud.* 1, p. 31.

[143] Above, 10.

[144] The author allows himself to be distracted by somewhat irrelevant theological speculations at *Ascl.* 26–7 = *N.H.C.* vi.8.74–5, but the main theme re-emerges at (N.F.) 332. 18 = *N.H.C.* vi.8.75.26.

[145] N.F.'s nn. *ad loc.*, esp. n. 201; Festugière 2.23 n. 1; Krause, *Z.D.M.G.* Supp. 1(1) (1969) 52–7; Schamp, *A.C.* 50 (1981) 727–32; Mahé 2.68–113.

[146] *Ascl.* 24 ('quasi de legibus a religione, pietate cultuque divino statuetur praescripta poena prohibitio'), 25 ('capitale periculum constituetur in eum, qui se mentis religioni dederit. nova constituentur iura, lex nova').

[147] E.g. N.F. 2.277, 288.   [148] Barnes, *Constantine* 13.

use of both the passages in question.[149] In fact, Hermes's prophecy cannot be shown to contain any necessary reference to Christianity.

This basic fact has not hitherto penetrated the scholarly mind[150] precisely because Lactantius, and later Augustine too, were already reading the prophecy as a forecast of the collapse of paganism.[151] They gleefully and very naturally added it to their catalogues of self-incriminating material from the enemy camp; and there it has remained ever since. Its real nature, though, is quite different. Since pagan Egyptians believed that their land would survive only while the old gods continued to be worshipped, eradication of the distinct identity of Egypt, if it ever came about, was bound to be accompanied by the demise of the traditional cults. And an unprejudiced reading of our text shows that it was this question of ethnic and cultural identity that was uppermost in its author's mind, as indeed it had been in the thoughts of earlier Egyptian contributors to this genre.[152]

The Hermetic prophecy begins by asserting an uncompromisingly Egyptocentric view of the world: Egypt is 'the image of heaven', the focus of all celestial energies, 'the temple of the whole world'. This is the same attitude that we have already seen expressed in more specific form in *C.H.* xvi; and it is exactly mirrored in *S.H.* xxiv, which returns repeatedly to the theme of Egypt the holiest land, set in the centre of the earth as the heart in the body, its inhabitants the most intelligent of all human-kind.[153]

And yet [our prophecy continues] a time will come when it will seem that the Egyptians have in vain honoured God (*divinitatem*) with pious heart and assiduous devotion, and all holy reverence for the gods will become ineffective and be deprived of its fruit. For God will return from earth to heaven, and Egypt will be abandoned.

---

[149]

Ascl.	*Div. Inst.*
24: esp. 'statuetur praescripta poena prohibitio'	vii.15.10: 'prima omnium Aegyptus stultarum superstitionum luet poenas'
25: esp. 'nova constituentur iura, lex nova'	vii. 16.4 'nova consilia in pectore suo volutabit, ut proprium sibi constituat imperium, leges commutet et suas sanciat' (= *Epit.* lxvi. 3: 'novas leges statuet, veteres abrogabit...')

These parallels (the first of which invalidates Schwartz's hypothesis, *R.H.Ph.R.* 62 (1982) 165–9, that *Ascl.* 24–5 *ad init.* (N.F. 2.326.15–328.15) is in its entirety a fourth-century (post-Lactantian) insertion) are all the more striking when we recall that Lactantius is not quoting from our *Ascl.*, but is making his own translation from the original Greek of the *P.D.*

[150] Mahé 2.58–60, is an exception, but ignores the evidence of Lactantius.
[151] Lact., *Inst.* vii.15.10; Aug., *Civ. Dei* viii.23.
[152] Assmann, in *Apocalypticism* 345–77, esp. 351, 357, 373. [153] *S.H.* xxiv.11, 13, 15.

The durability of Egypt

This passage and others similar to it have much impressed modern commentators, who have concluded that we have to do here with a prophecy of a final and definitive *Götterdämmerung*. In fact it is Egypt whose doom is foretold, while the gods merely withdraw to heaven, whence they return to earth after its purification by flood, fire or plague. And even then, when all things will be new, Egypt will still be the true home of the gods.

> Those [gods] who rule the earth will be restored,[154] and they will be installed in a city at the furthest threshold of Egypt (*in summo initio Aegypti*), which will be founded towards the setting sun and to which all human kind will hasten by land and by sea.

This no doubt is a city of the imagination;[155] but in answer to Asclepius's enquiry where these gods are at the moment, Trismegistus replies (at *Ascl.* 27): 'In a very great city, in the mountain of Libya (*in monte Libyco*)', by which is meant the edge of the desert plateau to the west of the Nile valley.[156] A subsequent reference (*Ascl.* 37) to the temple and tomb of Asclepius (Imhotep) *in monte Libyae* establishes that the allusion at *Ascl.* 27 is to the ancient and holy Memphite necropolis, which lay on the desert *jabal* to the west of Memphis itself. In this later passage the Hermetist shows his awareness that the temple of the god Asclepius enshrined the tomb of a deified man, Imhotep;[157] and it may be that both passages also consciously preserve the native Egyptian habit of referring to the area in which the sanctuary of Asclepius lay, as the 'mountain' or 'peak'.[158] As an

---

[154] *restituentur* conj. Ferguson, for *distribuentur* (codd.) (which arose simply by repetition of the last word in the previous sentence – so the original verb is likely to have been homophonous). Mahé's *dis* ⟨*cedent*⟩ (by analogy with the Coptic version) contradicts the theme of the return of the gods, emphasized by Mahé himself, 2.78.

[155] Not Alexandria, *pace* Mahé 2.77, 252, who ignores the context and draws an over-literal parallel with the *Oracle of the Potter*'s 'city by the sea' (quoted above, 21–2).

[156] Kees, *R.E.* 13.146–8, *s.vv.* 'Libyae', 'Libyci montes'; Calderini, *Dizionario* 3.200; and cf. *I. Memn.* 62, on the Memnonia Αἰγύπτου Λιβυκῆισιν ὑπ᾽ ὀφρύσιν. In Egypt, ὄρος/*mons* meant both 'mountain' and 'desert', the abrupt edge of the desert plateau to either side of the Nile being the only 'mountain' visible to the Egyptian eye: L.S.J. *s.v.*, and cf. *jabal* in Egyptian Arabic. (There is therefore no reason to read καταβάσεως against the manuscripts' μεταβάσεως at *C.H.* XIII.1 (ἐπὶ τῆς τοῦ ὄρους μεταβάσεως), as N.F. do, following Reitzenstein. Hermes and Tat are to be understood to have been conversing in the desert.) Van Rinsveld's assertion, in *Textes et études* 239, that the *Ascl.* passage may have been taken as an allusion to Alexandria, ignores both usages of ὄρος/*mons*.

[157] Sethe, *Imhotep* 7–8. *Ascl.* 37 also states that the Asclepeum was situated 'circa litus crocodillorum', which may well refer to the lake (now drained) of Abusir, to the north of the necropolis: see Emery, *J.E.A.* 51 (1965) 8 and plate II.1; Ray, *Archive of Ḥor* 150.

[158] Ray, *Archive of Ḥor* 149–51; and cf. *U.P.Z.* 114(1).11–12, 117.7–9, associating the Asclepeum with 'the western mountain/desert' (λιβὸς ὄρος). On the precision of the information about Egyptian religion in this passage see also N.F. 2.395 n. 324.

ancient stronghold of the native Egyptian gods, and a flourishing centre of paganism as late as the fourth century,[159] Memphis was a potent symbol in Egyptian eyes, an antitype, as has already been pointed out, of the Greek metropolis of Alexandria; and the author of the *Perfect discourse* well knew how to invoke these associations in support of his cause.

The tragedy of Egypt, then, is a parenthesis within eternity, a temporary departure of the gods from earth before the return of the Golden Age. But in human terms the catastrophe is ineluctable. What precisely is to be its nature? In the first place foreigners, barbarians, will entirely fill the country, and the ancient temple cults and rituals will not only be neglected, but actually forbidden. Egypt will be filled with the tombs of the dead, the Nile will be swollen with blood and overflow, and the whole country will be left a desert. 'As for anyone who survives, only by his language will he be recognized as an Egyptian – in his way of behaviour he will seem an alien.' Men will be reduced to total despair; and of this state of mind Hermes provides a most remarkable description:

In that day men will be weary of life, and they will cease to think the World worthy of reverent wonder and of worship. This whole good thing, than which nothing was or is or will be deemed better, will be threatened with destruction; men will think it a burden, and will come to scorn it. They will no longer love this world around us, this incomparable work of God, this glorious structure, this sum of good made up of things of many diverse forms...Darkness will be preferred to light, and death will be thought more profitable than life; no one will raise his eyes to heaven; the pious will be deemed insane, and the impious wise; the madman will be thought brave, and the wickedest will be regarded as good...Only the evil angels will remain, who will mingle with men, and drive the poor wretches by main force into all manner of reckless crime, into wars and robberies and frauds, and all things hostile to the nature of the soul. Then will the earth no longer stand unshaken, and the sea will no more be navigable; heaven will not support the stars in their orbits, nor will the stars pursue their constant course in heaven; the voice of the gods will of necessity be silenced and dumb; the fruits of the earth will rot; the soil will turn barren, and the very air will sicken in sullen stagnation.

These last lines recall the imprecations heaped by funerary inscriptions on the heads of those guilty of the ultimate violation, that of the grave.[160] Perhaps they also consciously reverse the praises of Isis and other cosmic divinities that we find in the Graeco-Egyptian aretalogies.[161] What the gods gave they will also take, in the time of the world's senescence (*senectus mundi*).

---

[159] Kees, *R.E.* 15.666–7.   [160] Robert, *C.R.A.I.* (1978) 270.
[161] Below, 46–7.

The durability of Egypt

But the background and implications of this striking prophecy are best grasped if we compare what has happened in more recent history to traditional societies as they first came in contact with Western colonizers. Faced with such unexpected and incomprehensible intrusion, it is not unknown for these societies to disintegrate culturally and eventually to commit, in varying degrees, communal suicide.[162] Faced with the impossible demand of finding a *modus vivendi* between the old values and structures of life on the one hand and Western intrusion and pressure on the other, a relatively primitive traditional society may lose all faith in its own symbolic universe and, thus disorientated, slide gradually into complete despair. Social life at first atrophies, and may eventually be actually perverted, as for example by role-reversal of the sexes, neglect of friendship and other social bonds, dissolution of the family, abandonment of the weak and sick, avoidance of procreation, exposure of children and, ultimately, self-starvation. As in the *Perfect discourse*, so in these doomed societies of the contemporary world, the demise of belief in and worship of the gods is a function of social despair. From a growing other-worldliness and lack of contact with the here-and-now, religion degenerates into a parody of itself. A particularly striking illustration is provided by the Unambal, a tribe of Australian aborigines, whose cults involve the use of pidgin-English and are directed, not towards the traditional gods, but towards malevolent daemons who look like white men and infect their worshippers with disease. The old gods are believed to have abandoned the country and passed beyond the horizon; and the objects sacred to them have been sold to white ethnologists. There is no alternative except a bitter, despairing capitulation to the all-powerful alien.

Traditional societies of a more sophisticated type, as for example those of the Far East, have tended to experience a lesser trauma. But there too contact with the West has bred Messianic movements and resulted in the assimilation of Christian elements into non-Christian religious systems.[163] And the pre-Columbian civilizations of central and southern America, while anything but primitive, were even so quite unprepared for the irruption of the Spanish into their continent.[164] Indian tradition maintains that the coming of the conqueror was foretold by omens affecting the whole of the natural realm; and the collapse of the Inca *ancien régime*, for example,

---

[162] On what follows see Versnel, in *Studi Angelo Brelich* 541–618, esp. 595–601.
[163] Lanternari, *Movimenti religiosi*.   [164] Wachtel, *Vision des vaincus* (mainly on Inca Peru).

identified as it had been with cosmic order through the Sun-cult, was certainly perceived as a universal rupture. The Aztecs and the Mayas likewise saw their defeat as the dethronement and death of their previously all-powerful national gods. The conquest was followed by demographic catastrophe – not just the death of countless natives from war, oppression and diseases from which they had no immunity, but a decline in the birth-rate too. Many committed suicide; despairing women killed their new-born children. The Indians lost their lands and had imposed on them a wholly alien market economy. Worse still, their gods were outlawed and even their burial-customs forbidden. In short, along with the *ancien régime* there disintegrated too a whole world of the mind. Nothing illustrates this better than the Mayas' abandonment of the calendar which they had so long and meticulously maintained. No more were the traditional stelae erected in public to mark the beginning of each twenty-year cycle. Time itself had lost its meaning. No wonder that the past now seemed like a Golden Age.

The Egyptians too were heirs to a highly developed civilization; but that did not stop some of them feeling despised and threatened by their foreign rulers, as witness the *Oracle of the Potter* (Ptolemaic in origin, but preserved only in copies of the second and third centures A.D.), *C.H.* xvi's violent attack on the Greek language, and the crystallization under the Ptolemies of traditional Egyptian anxieties about the stability of the universe represented for instance by the ritual for the conservation of life in *P. Salt* 825.[165] The author or compiler of the *Perfect discourse* was more reticent, and the function of the prophecy within his composition is not easily defined. The forecast of the demise of Egypt can hardly be said to relate integrally to what precedes and follows it; yet it is sufficiently permeated by Hermetic concepts[166] to exclude the possibility that it is a pure intrusion. Perhaps it is a Hermetized recension of an earlier text, like the aretalogy of Isis and Osiris in the *Korē kosmou*. But be that as it may, the presence of this passage within the *Perfect discourse* indicates a strain of passionate Egyptianism in the milieu which produced and preserved it. It was a milieu that had been long and, so it seemed, irreversibly Hellenized in its language and thought-patterns;[167] *but*

---

[165] Derchain, *Papyrus Salt 825* 28, 111. See further Dunand, in *L'apocalyptique* 65–7.

[166] E.g. *Ascl.* 25 (N.F. 329.5–11); and Mahé, in *Textes de Nag Hammadi* 405–34.

[167] See Mahé 2.68–113, esp. 112–13, on the 'origines égyptiennes et remodelage hellénistique' of Hermes's prophecy; and note as well the distinctly detached, anthropological tone of the explanation of Egyptian animal-cults at *Ascl.* 37.

that had not made it a Greek milieu.[168] That our prophecy should have been translated into Coptic and included in the strikingly Egyptian selection of Hermetic texts in Nag Hammadi codex vɪ will not now surprise us. Its author would have been consoled had he known that, in Syriac and Arabic guise, Hermes Trismegistus was to outlive by many centuries the dominance of Hellenism in the lands of the eastern Mediterranean.

[168] Compare the similar conclusions of Lewy, *Chaldaean Oracles* 399–400, on the background of the *Orac. Chald.*

[2]

Translation and interpretation

It was not of course always, or even very often, that the durability of Egypt was expressed as hostility or defiance. We may be sure that much less of the autochthonous tradition would have endured had it not been for a preparedness to make compromises and to co-exist with Hellenism within the cultural compound discussed in the previous chapter. This process is often called 'interpretatio graeca', a doubly suspect phrase. In the first place it conveys the impression that the authors of the 'interpretatio graeca' were Greeks, when in fact they were not infrequently Egyptians. And secondly, 'interpretatio' means 'translation' as well as 'interpretation'. Since one can have neither without the other, that is fair enough. But the modern understanding of 'interpretation' covers methods of approach to a situation or text too far removed from 'translation' to be confused with it. And the following pages are designed to show, precisely, how Egyptian ideas, once articulated in Greek, inevitably acquired new dimensions and lost old ones. Translation evolved rapidly into interpretation; and a proper understanding of this distinction, obscured by the expression 'interpretatio graeca', can help us understand better the nature and extent of the relationship between the various Hermetic genres and the native intellectual tradition.

Aretalogies of Isis and Asclepius

Fortunately we are able to follow both the initial stage of translation[1] from Egyptian into Greek, and several subsequent phases of inter-

---

[1] I employ the word 'translation' to denote, not only the rendering of a text from one language into another, but also the production of texts in the spirit of a language or thought-world other than that in which they are actually written down. Cf. below, on the possibility that the Cyme aretalogy was originally composed in Greek.

pretation, within just one very specific genre, that of the Isiac aretalogies. These texts were designed to present a goddess of universal appeal to a mass audience ignorant of Egyptian and likely to be impatient of undue theological sophistication. The Graeco-Egyptian Isis was the product of a fusion between the native Egyptian Isis and a variety of Greek goddesses such as Demeter and Aphrodite. She inspired an enormous devotional literature in virtually all parts of the Greek-speaking world and over a wide chronological span; and fundamental to any understanding of this literature is an inscription discovered in 1925 at Cyme in the Aeolid.[2] It begins, after a dedication, with the statement that 'these things were copied (τάδε ἐγράφηι) from the stele in Memphis that stood near the temple of Hephaestus'. The remainder of the inscription is an Isiac aretalogy cast in a ringingly declaratory first person:

I am Isis, the ruler of all land...I separated earth from heaven. I showed the stars their path. I ordered the course of the sun and the moon...

and so on. Other versions or fragments of the same text exist in inscriptions from Thessalonica and Ios, and in Diodorus of Sicily's description of Egypt.[3] Despite the fact that Diodorus was a foreigner, and that none of the inscriptions was found in Egypt, there is no reason to doubt the Memphite origin of the aretalogy. It is true that Diodorus refers to a tradition that it was originally inscribed on the tomb of Isis at Nysa in Arabia; but he himself appears to believe the more popular tradition that Isis was buried in the *temenos* of Hephaestus (Ptah) at Memphis[4] – which corresponds with what the Cyme inscription tells us. Whether the original version of the text was composed in Egyptian or Greek, and how one should characterize its doctrinal content, is much more controversial;[5] but one can be reasonably certain that the aretalogy was composed either in or on behalf of Memphite priestly circles, and contains important Egyptian doctrinal and stylistic elements, presented in a manner comprehensible, though not perhaps very appealing, to a Greek public. In other words it is a straightforward product of what one might call the

[2] For editions and bibliography of the Isiac texts discussed in the following paragraphs see Grandjean, *Nouvelle arétalogie* 8–11. The Cyme inscription is now *I. Cyme* 41.
[3] The relationship of the four texts is most clearly visible in Harder's version, *Karpokrates von Chalkis* 20–1.
[4] Diod. Sic. 1.22.2.
[5] The history of the debate is outlined by Grandjean, *Nouvelle arétalogie* 12–15. Strong support has since been lent to the Egyptianizers by Ray, *Archive of Ḥor* 155–8, 174.

translator's approach to the expression of Egyptian religious material in Greek.

The first Isiac aretalogy to be discovered in modern times was that of Andros (1838). Scholarly fixation with the Memphis version has hitherto ensured that the Andros inscription is usually regarded as important, not for its many distinctive characteristics, but because it too ultimately derives from, and therefore provides evidence for the dissemination of, the Memphite text. Although it is earlier (first century B.C.) than any of the three inscriptions that depend directly on the Memphite text – the Ios version dates only from the third century A.D.[6] – the Andros aretalogy represents a much more advanced stage in the presentation of the text. It is still cast in the first person, Isis addressing her adepts; and it shares a good deal of thematic material with its model. But its external manner is markedly Hellenistic. Out of an austere catalogue of virtues has burst a flood of baroque bombast, replete with mythological allusions; out of Cyme's

> I am the mistress of sea-faring; I make the navigable [seas] unnavigable, when I wish,[7]

has grown this in the Andros inscription:

> When the weather was clear it was possible for vessels to sail across Amphitrite, their prows blackened with the drought of winter, after I had opened wide the grey arms of Tethys with a smile and a blush on my gay cheeks. Over the navigable depths I drove my pathless way when my heart moved me. Speeding in every direction with dark roar the ocean gave deep bellow from its inmost shrine, amid its profound caverns. I was the first to guide the keel of the swift ship, its sails billowing, as I rode on its planked deck above the swell. The beautiful family of Doris started their winding dance as the sea was brought under control by swift vessels of pine. Their minds trembled with amazement as they gazed and gazed on the crew their eyes had never known.[8]

A further stage in this evolution away from translation towards a more interpretative approach – and this time affecting content as well as style – may be seen in the Isiac aretalogy discovered in 1969 at Maroneia on the coast of Thrace.[9] This new text derives, like the Andros inscription, from the Memphite aretalogy; but it is cast in

---

[6] The evidence for the dating of the Isiac aretalogies is summarized by Grandjean, *Nouvelle arétalogie* 8–11.

[7] *I. Cyme* 41.49–50.

[8] Peek, *Isishymnus* 21, lines 145–57 (tr. Witt); and cf. *ibid.* 83–98. With the Andros version compare also the Isis aretalogy from Cyrene (*ibid.* 128–31).

[9] Grandjean, *Nouvelle arétalogie* 17–18 and *passim*.

the second person, as an address to Isis, and its author is in consequence projected into the foreground. We learn that the aretalogy is offered in return for the healing of the dedicant's eyes; and the personal relationship between the goddess and her worshipper is made prominent in the inscription's opening lines. Indeed, the hymn is presented as nothing less than a co-operative effort: 'these praises are written by the mind of divinity, but by human hands'. Moreover, the tone of the Maroneia text, for all its schematic debt to Memphis, is resolutely Greek. Not only does it contain none of the references to Bubastis and Memphis that occur in the other aretalogies, but it includes a passage about the religious significance of Athens and Eleusis that is unique in the genre:

It pleased you to dwell in Egypt; in Greece you honoured above all Athens... That is why in Greece we hasten to gaze upon Athens, and in Athens, Eleusis, for we deem the city the ornament of Europe, and the sanctuary the ornament of the city.

One's impression is that the Greek author of this text is trying as best he may, while remaining broadly within the framework of a consecrated model, to detach Isis from her native habitat, and make of her a Greek divinity. Isis dwelt in Egypt – one could hardly avoid acknowledging that much; but her heart, it is implied, was in the land of the Olympian gods to whom – and especially to Eleusinian Demeter – she was so often assimilated in the Hellenistic period. Here we see the interpretative approach to the Memphite aretalogy pushed further than in any other text discovered hitherto.[10]

In view of the enthusiasm with which the Hellenistic world outside Egypt took her to its heart, it was predictable and natural that Isis's character should evolve in its new environment. But the Isiac aretalogies from outside Egypt merely illustrate in exaggerated and more readily comprehensible form what was happening at the same time in Egypt itself, where the authority of the native tradition restrained somewhat the wilder flights of the Isiac imagination, but did not seriously compromise its natural evolution from translation to interpretation. Among the few Greek 'Isiaca' that the land of the Nile has so far yielded[11] is an aretalogy of Isis written on a papyrus from Oxyrhynchus (*P. Oxy.* 1380) dating from the first half of the second century A.D. The fragmentary second-person invocation of

[10] But cf. the aretalogy of Harpocrates from Chalcis in Euboea, which claims the god as a native of that city: Harder, *Karpokrates von Chalkis* 8, line 12.

[11] There is no need to discuss here the Isiac texts contained in the papyri discussed by Merkelbach, *Z.P.E.* 1 (1967) 55–73, which all stand very close to the Memphite prototype.

Isis breathes the atmosphere of cosmopolitan Hellenism – the list of Isiac cult-sites with which the surviving part of the papyrus begins ranges from Rome as far eastwards as India. Yet the centre of gravity is Egypt. Not only is the list of Egyptian Isea extremely detailed, but the latter, aretalogical part of the text emphasizes Isis's Egyptian origin and associations, while its dry, staccato and repetitive style is more Egyptian than Greek – indeed, it seems likely that much of the invocation was translated directly from the Egyptian.[12] This dual character – the factual and conceptual essence, and to some extent even the form, Egyptian, and the linguistic medium Greek – tends to support the aretalogy's first editors' suggestion that its author was a priest of Isis at Oxyrhynchus or Memphis. His extensive knowledge of the cult of Isis overseas perhaps favours Memphis, especially if we accept that the wide dissemination of the Memphite aretalogy was not accidental, but owed something to deliberate and informed propagation.

Earlier in date, but much more Hellenized in expression, are the four hymns written in the first(?) century B.C. by one Isidore, and carved on the walls of the temple of Isis in the village of Narmuthis on the southern edge of the Fayyum.[13] Three of Isidore's hymns (I–III) praise Isis as the omnipotent, all-embracing goddess whom the whole world adores, under a myriad of different names. She is the teacher, protectress and consoler of mankind, bringer of gifts and fount of life and prosperity. The fourth hymn relates the story of the temple's foundation by Porramanres (Amenemhet III). Although the hymns are addressed to the goddess (in the second person), rather than spoken by her, and for all that Isidore appends his name to each of the inscriptions, we learn nothing about the author himself. He contents himself with remarking, in the final lines of hymn IV, that

reliably informed by men who enquire into these things, and having publicly inscribed all the facts in person, I have explained to the Greeks the power of the god and the prince, showing that no other mortal had power such as this.

Earlier in the same hymn he refers to his source as 'those who have read the sacred writings'. If he could not read them himself (and was

---

[12] Cf. the introduction and commentary to *P. Oxy.* 1380; and van Groningen, *De papyro Oxyrhynchita 1380* 77–82. The presumed Egyptian source would have resembled the recently-published *P. Tebt. Tait* 14, a second-century A.D. demotic invocation of Isis; cf. also *ibid.* 36.

[13] *I. mét. Eg.* 175. Vanderlip, *Isidorus*, is inaccurate and largely superfluous. Bollók, *Stud. Aeg.* 1 (1974) 27–37, has argued for a date in the late third century B.C.

prepared to admit it), he was probably not an Egyptian priest; while his style, with its numerous allusions to Homer and others, suggests that he was of a Greek cultural background.[14] Certainly his audience was Greek, as he himself unambiguously states. Yet his compositions could not have been inscribed in so conspicuous a position without the sanction of the temple authorities. Although Isidore's hymns are not modelled on the Memphite aretalogy, from which so much of the non-Egyptian Isiac literature derived, they must have originated close to the same (Egyptian priestly) circles, and served the same end – the propagation of Isis in the Hellenophone world. Evidently the priests of Narmuthis were concerned that the 'men of mixed races'[15] who dwelt around their sanctuary should not remain in ignorance either of the universal power of Isis, or of the religious traditions of the immediate locality.

Isidore's hymns are carefully attuned to the task he sets himself. His basic materials are Egyptian, but he emphasizes the universal authority of Isis,[16] and his style is unashamedly Greek.[17] A text of similar intention is to be found on the verso of the Oxyrhynchus aretalogy already discussed. *P. Oxy.* 1381 dates from the later second century A.D., and contains the extended prologue and first few lines of an aretalogy of Imouthes–Asclepius, which in its original form was probably not much earlier than our papyrus. From the prologue it transpires that the writer had for some time been starting, and then putting off, the translation into Greek of a book describing the god's 'miraculous manifestations', 'immense power', gifts, benefits and 'undying virtue'.[18]

While I was in the full tide of composition my ardour was restrained by the greatness of the story, because I was about to make it public; for to gods alone, not to mortals, is it permitted to describe the mighty deeds of the gods.

After some years passed by, our author fell gravely ill. Convulsed with pain, and lying half asleep one night (when 'divinity shows itself more effectively'), he saw Asclepius appear to him in a dream – 'someone whose height was more than human, clothed in shining raiment and carrying in his left hand a book, who after merely regarding me two

[14] Though on his metrical shortcomings see Keydell, *Kleine Schriften* 313–14.

[15] Isid. Narm. III.30–1.

[16] See especially *id.* 1.14–24. On the Egyptian elements in Isidore's hymns, see Drijvers, *Vox theologica* 32 (1962) 139–50.

[17] One might compare, in the field of the plastic arts, the bronze statuettes of priests of Isis discussed by Charbonneaux in *Mélanges Piganiol* 1.407–20.

[18] *P. Oxy.* 1381.46–7, 218–22. (Translations are the editors', slightly amended.)

or three times from head to foot disappeared'. The illness passed immediately; but in return Asclepius demanded, 'through the priest who serves him in the ceremonies', the fulfilment of his patient's long-standing undertaking. The narrative continues:

Since thou hadst once noticed, Master, that I was neglecting the divine book, invoking thy providence and filled with thy divinity I hastened to the inspired task of the history. And I hope to extend by my proclamation the fame of thy inventiveness; for I unfolded truly by a physical treatise in another book (ἐν ἑτέρᾳ β[ί]βλῳ φυσικῷ...λόγῳ) the story of the creation of the world, in terms calculated to persuade ([τὸ]ν τῆς κοσμοποιίας πιθ[α]νολ[ο]γηθέντα μῦθον). Throughout the composition I have filled up defects and struck out superfluities, and in telling a rather long tale I have spoken briefly and narrated once for all a complicated story. Hence, Master, I conjecture that the book has been completed in accordance with thy favour, not with my aim; for such a record in writing suits thy divinity... Every Greek tongue will tell thy story, and every Greek man will worship the son of Ptah, Imouthes.

We have to do here, then, with a man who knows both Egyptian and Greek; so even if his Greek were not as poor as it is, it would still be more likely that his first language was Egyptian. Apparently the content of his book was largely 'historical' and aretalogical – what we would call hagiographical. It was regarded as holy; and should clearly be assigned to the same broad genre as the Isis-literature. The writer's concern, unambiguously, is the propagation of Imouthes–Asclepius among the Hellenophone population of Egypt. To this end he sets out to produce, not a straightforward translation of the Egyptian text he has in front of him, but an adaptation or interpretation that allows him not only to introduce new material, but also to soften and 'render plausible' (πιθανολογεῖν) anything that might alienate a Greek audience – especially, no doubt, the abundant and confusing mythological narratives to which so many Egyptian religious texts were devoted.[19] And, in a manner that is unmistakably Greek rather than Egyptian, and recalls the Maroneia aretalogy, our author faces his work as a co-operative enterprise, in which the god's inspiration and direction is indispensable, while his own part is to formulate the narrative.[20]

The reference to a cosmogonical treatise, the close association in Graeco-Egyptian literature between Asclepius and Hermes, the revelatory atmosphere, the text's date and certain stylistic

---

[19] Compare the Greek translation by one Hermapion, *ap.* Amm. Marc. xvii.4.18–23, of the inscriptions on a Heliopolitan obelisk, drastically simplifying distinctively Egyptian elements, especially titles: Erman, *S.P.A.* (1914) 245–73.

[20] Cf. Leipoldt, in *Festschrift Wilhelm Schubart* 56–63.

51

considerations[21] all show that this interesting aretalogy emanated from a milieu similar to that of Hermetism, and warn us against trying too hard to isolate the aretalogical texts from the theological and philosophical speculations of the more educated. Likewise, the formulaic construction and didactic manner of many of the Isiac aretalogies may perhaps imply a popular audience; but the actual translator or author of the aretalogy was likely to be of a higher educational level than his intended audience, while the more complex compositions presuppose both an author and an audience of considerable literary accomplishment.[22] Indeed, the same variation between translation and interpretation is detectable in the learned as in the popular religious literature of Graeco-Roman Egypt; and in the one sphere as in the other the exponents of the interpretative approach were as likely to be native Egyptians as Greeks – further proof of the leading role played by Hellenized native Egyptians in the moulding of the Graeco-Egyptian consciousness.

Manetho and Chaeremon

Not long after the Macedonian conquest of Egypt there began to emerge an ethnological literature, mostly written by Greeks who were resident in Egypt or at least had visited the country, and designed to satisfy the appetite of the more educated part of the Greek public for information about Egyptian theology and cultic traditions.[23] Among the earliest and most influential commentators, after Herodotus, was Hecataeus of Abdera (late fourth century), who drew on both priestly records and his own experience to produce a personal and interpretative account of Egypt that strongly influenced later writers.[24] Unfortunately, neither Hecataeus's book nor much of what his successors wrote has survived intact,[25] probably because it was inferior in quality both to Herodotus and to the accounts of Egyptian religion that were now being written, for the same audience, by

[21] See below, 159, esp. n. 13. Note also the close parallels between *P. Oxy.* 1381 and Thess., *Virt. herb.* (below, 162–4).

[22] Henrichs, in *VII Cong. Class. Studies* 1.339–53, argues for Prodicean influence on the aretalogies, mediated by Hecataeus. Compare also the Isiac aretalogy incorporated in the Hermetic *Korē kosmou*: above, 35–6.

[23] See Diod. Sic. 1.46.8 on the 'many Greeks who made their way to Thebes...and compiled their "Egyptian histories"'.

[24] *F. Gr. H.* 264; cf. Fraser 1.496–505.

[25] Otto, *Priester und Tempel* 2.217–18, lists the main authors; cf. Fraser 3, *s.vv.*

certain Egyptian priests of Greek culture. Here was an inside view, and its success is impressive testimony to the Greeks' desire to see things as they actually were.

As far as we know, the first priest to write about Egypt in Greek was Manetho,[26] who flourished in the first half of the third century B.C., and did more than any Egyptian before him to instruct foreigners in the history and culture of his country. His *Aegyptiaca* contained records of all the Egyptian dynasties down to the thirtieth, was mined by later Jewish and Christian historians and chronographers, and exerted through them a considerable influence on later antiquity's view of its past. Other of Manetho's writings, judging from citations, were even more popular. His *Sacred Book* dealt in particular with Egyptian religion; and he is known to have composed treatises *On festivals, On ancient ritual and religion*, and *On the making of kyphi* (which the Egyptians used as both incense and medicine) – unless these were subdivisions of the *Sacred Book*. A book on physical doctrines (τῶν φυσικῶν ἐπιτομή) is also recorded.

One can catch something of what Manetho's table-talk must have been like through Heliodorus's portrait of the fictional Egyptian priest Calasiris, in the *Aethiopica*. Telling of his visit to Delphi, Calasiris observes how the Greeks

plied me with questions on various matters. One would ask how we Egyptians worship our country's gods, while another wished to know how it came about that different animals were adored by different sections of our people, and what was the reason of each cult. Some wished to know about the construction of the pyramids, others about the subterranean mazes. In brief, they omitted not a single point of interest in their enquiries concerning Egypt; for listening to any account of Egypt is what appeals most strongly to Greek ears.

Somebody else, continues Calasiris, asked him about the sources and behaviour of the Nile; and

I told him what I knew of these matters, giving him all the information which is recorded in sacred books about this river, and which prophets alone may read and learn.[27]

Like Calasiris, Manetho was well aware of his special qualifications for his task, as a native priest with access to the archives; and this no doubt was the motive for the attack he made, according to Josephus, on the 'ignorance' of Herodotus[28] – for even though

[26] *F. Gr. H.* 609; cf. Laqueur, *R.E.* 14.1060–1101, and Fraser 1.505–10.
[27] Heliod. Em. 11.27.3–28.2.
[28] Jos., *Ap.* 1.73.

Herodotus too claimed priestly authority for much of his narrative, he was after all a Greek and spoke no Egyptian. In fact, it was really Manetho's linguistic medium that was innovative, far more so than his message. His interests did not stray far beyond those customary for members of his caste, and he clearly intended his material to speak for itself once rendered into Greek. His was clearly the mentality of the translator rather than the interpreter or commentator. Indeed Ptolemy II Philadelphus, who was thought to have been responsible for the translation of the Jewish scriptures (the Septuagint), is also said to have ordered the translation of Chaldaean, Egyptian and Roman(!) books into Greek.[29] If there is any truth in this, perhaps Manetho was one of the scholars so employed.

Three centuries later we find a comparable figure in Chaeremon, who flourished in the middle of the first century A.D. Chaeremon held the grade of *hierogrammateus* in the Egyptian priestly hierarchy, and was presumably of Egyptian birth, though he was also a man of genuinely Hellenic culture.[30] Various Greek writers accord him the epithet 'philosopher' – indeed, Origen and Porphyry are more specific, and classify him as a Stoic. Like Manetho, Chaeremon concerned himself with subjects such as the hieroglyphic script (we possess fragments of his *Hieroglyphica*), the history of Egypt, and astrology – Origen refers to a treatise *On comets*. But in the present context his famous account of the Egyptian priesthood, preserved by Porphyry, and perhaps originally part of the *Egyptian history*, is of much greater interest. It is a unique attempt by an insider to convey an impression of temple life in terms comprehensible to non-Egyptians. Chaeremon idealizes unashamedly, and we read him, of course, at one remove, mediated by Porphyry;[31] but nothing impunes the essential authenticity of what survives.

In his account of the Egyptian priests, who, he says, were regarded in Egypt as being also philosophers, Chaeremon the Stoic tells how they chose the temples for places wherein to pursue wisdom (ἐμφιλοσοφῆσαι). In view of their desire for contemplation, it was natural for them to pass their time in the temples, for there they found security on account of the reverence that men have for the divine – everyone honoured the philosophers, as if they were sacred animals. Besides, their living in the temples brought them peace, for they only mixed with other people during festivals and feasts. At other times, access to the temples was for practical purposes forbidden to ordinary people, since they could visit the temples only when in a state of purity,

[29] Geo. Sync. 516; and cf. Fraser 1.330.
[30] See the introduction to van der Horst's edition.
[31] Porphyry tended to adjust his quotations, but not seriously to distort them: Schwyzer, *Chairemon* 100–6; Pötscher, *Theophrastos* 5–13.

and after considerable fasting – that is as it were a general rule in all Egyptian temples.

Renouncing all other work and human ways of earning a living, the priests dedicated their entire lives to the thought and contemplation of God. The practice of contemplation endowed them with dignity, piety and a feeling of security. The fruit of their contemplation of God was knowledge; and through contemplation and knowledge they attained to a way of life at once esoteric and old-fashioned. For constant contact with divine knowledge and inspiration makes one a stranger to greed, calms the passions, and encourages a life of wisdom. The priests cultivated frugality and moderation, continence and steadfastness, and they made justice and hatred of greed the ruling principles of their lives. The augustness of their bearing was intensified by the fact that they kept away from other people – during the so-called purifications they did not even mix with their own kith and kin. Indeed, they were not seen by anyone who was not observing the necessary purifications.

At other times they mixed more easily with men of their own order, but kept away from the profane who had nothing to do with the cult of the gods. One always saw them near to the gods or to the divine statues, either carrying them or going before them or arranging them in an orderly and dignified procession – actions not the product of pride, but rather indicating the underlying principles of the natural world.[32] Their gravity was apparent also in their general demeanour. They walked in an orderly way, their gaze fixed, so that they did not blink even when they wanted to. They laughed but rarely, and when they did it was no more than a smile. Their hands they kept always inside their habit; and each of them wore a symbol that indicated his rank in the hierarchy, for they were divided into many grades.

As for their diet, it was frugal and simple. [There follow details of dietary regulations and other forms of asceticism.]

Proof of the priests' self-control was the fact that, though they practised neither walking nor swinging exercises, they spent their lives in good health, and were energetic enough for all normal activities. For the duties they incurred in maintaining the cult of the gods were very onerous, and their labours surpassed the capacity of a man of average strength. They divided the night for the observation of the heavens, sometimes also for the divine ritual; and the daytime for the adoration of the gods, to whom they addressed hymns three or four times a day, at dawn and evening and when the sun was in the middle of its course and when it was about to set. The rest of their time they spent in the study of arithmetic and geometry, and they were constantly searching for and discovering something new – in short, their whole lives were devoted to scholarly investigation. These researches they also pursued through the winter nights, burning the candle at both ends for the love of letters, and caring nothing for reward, for they had freed themselves from that bad master, luxury. Their hard and unceasing labour attests their endurance, and their absence of desire attests their self-control.

To sail away from Egypt they thought among the greatest impieties, for they were wary of the wantonness of foreign habits, and regarded travel as permissible only for those who were obliged by necessity of state. They had indeed good reason to adhere to the ancestral traditions; for if they were found to have trespassed even in a minor matter, they were driven out.[33]

---

[32] Ἔνδειξις φυσικοῦ λόγου. This reflects the symbolic character of Egyptian theology, much emphasized in Greek writings on the subject: below, 74 n. 117.

[33] Chaer., *fr.* 10 (= Porph., *Abst.* iv.6, 8).

Translation and interpretation

It is the tone of this account, more than its factual content, that marks Chaeremon off so clearly from Manetho. Three hundred years of exposure to Greek and then Roman rule have had their effect. Not only is the objective manner of the narrative Greek – so too is the vocabulary and the whole framework of ideas within which the description is constructed. The priests of the Egyptian gods have become, not just 'philosophers', but covert Pythagoreans;[34] and while Manetho, though writing in Greek, presented his material as he had found it in his sources – as more or less a translation – Chaeremon is more self-conscious, careful to represent in terms that will not seem shocking or incomprehensible a remote and apparently self-sufficient culture that, as he well knew, by turns fascinated and alienated the Greek world. Chaeremon is an Egyptian who consciously adopts the interpretative approach – one cannot mistake his deliberate self-distancing. Perhaps in his comment on the priests' xenophobia we should even detect an implied criticism of such provincial attitudes. After all, he himself went to Rome to tutor the young Nero.[35]

In the course of this discussion of how Egyptian *Gedankengut* put off its old garments and gradually assumed Greek dress, the Asclepius aretalogy has already once brought us very close to the Hermetic milieu; and Chaeremon, the Egyptian Stoic, is open to similar suspicions – later we shall find Porphyry and Iamblichus speaking of him in a distinctly Hermetic context.[36] One naturally asks: did the Hermetica in fact have Egyptian literary antecedents or models? Two areas of native literature promise, *prima facie* at least, profitable

---

[34] Cf. Porph., *Abst.* 1.36.1–2, and van der Horst's commentary on Chaeremon. Plut., *Is. Os.* 10, says that Pythagoras went to Egypt, admired and was admired by the priests, and 'imitated their symbolism and mysterious manner, interspersing his teaching with riddles; for many of the Pythagorean sayings are not at all lacking in the lore of the writing which is called hieroglyphic' (tr. Griffiths). But even if it was not Chaeremon's fault that his priests sounded like Pythagoreans, he can hardly have been unaware of the usefulness of the resemblance.

[35] *Suda* A 1128. Manetho and Chaeremon were not unique. There was, e.g., Apollonides, the 'Archprophet-Orapis' of Memphis, who lived in the later first century A.D. and wrote in Greek on Egyptian religion: Parsons, *C.E.* 49 (1974) 153–6, and cf. 143–5 (ignored by Sijpesteijn, *Mnemosyne* 33 (1980) 364–6). Whether or not the priest and astrologer Petosiris actually existed (see above, 2), his image in later times had much of Manetho and Chaeremon in it – see Suda Π 1399: 'Petosiris, an Egyptian and philosopher, selected passages about the gods from the sacred books, according to the views of the Greeks and the Egyptians; [he also wrote] *Astrologumena*, and a treatise *On the mysteries of the Egyptians*.'

[36] Below, 139–40.

comparison: the sacred literature of the priests, which was mostly attributed to Thoth; and the so-called 'wisdom' or 'instruction' texts.

Books of Thoth and technical Hermetica

The sacred books of the ancient Egyptian priests were copied out in the 'Houses of Life', which served, subordinately to their primary cultic purposes, as temple *scriptoria* or libraries,[37] and were manned by scribe-priests known to the Greeks variously and somewhat indiscriminately as *pterophoroi* or *hierogrammateis*.[38] A fine example of a room in which sacred books were stored survives intact in the temple of Horus at Edfu.[39] This temple was built between 237 and 57 B.C., and the library dates from 140 to 124 B.C. Inscribed on its inner walls is to be found a document of immense interest: a catalogue, divided into two parts, of the books that were kept in the room. Both lists occur in the context of an address to Horus himself. The first contains titles mainly of mythological and liturgical interest; and the second runs as follows:

I bring to you [Horus and his Ennead] caskets containing excellent mysteries, to wit the choicest of the Emanations of Re [i.e. holy books]:[40]
Book of the temple-inventory.
Book of the threatening [of Seth?].
Book containing all the writings about the struggle [of Horus against Seth?].
Book of the plan of the temple.
Book of the guardians of the temple.
Specification for the painting of a wall.
Book of the protection of the body.
Book of the protection of the king in his house.
Spells for the averting of the evil eye.
Knowledge of the recurrence of the two stars [sun and moon].
Control over the recurrence of the stars.

[37] Gardiner, *J.E.A.* 24 (1938), esp. 170, 175–8; Volten, *Demotische Traumdeutung* 17–44; Derchain, *Papyrus Salt 825* 47–111; all conveniently summarized by Weber, *Lex. Äg.* 3.954–7.

[38] Posener, *R. Ph.* 25 (1951) 167–8; Zauzich, *Lex. Äg.* 2.1199–1201.

[39] For a general account of the temple, see Sauneron and Stierlin, *Derniers temples* 11–97 (esp. 34–42), 115–36. The library inscriptions are published by Chassinat, *Temple d'Edfou* 3.339–51 (tr. Weber, *Schrift = und Buchwesen* 131–4). Derchain, *Papyrus Salt 825* 57–61, argues that the room was used to store books required for certain specific rituals, and was too small to be the principal library.

[40] On the 'Emanations of Re' see Blackman and Fairman, *J.E.A.* 29 (1943) 22–3.

Translation and interpretation

Enumeration of all places, and knowledge of what is to be found in them.
All the protective formulae for the departure of Your Majesty from your
temple for your feasts.

No mention here of Thoth – but we may assume that most of these
texts were attributed to him as 'lord of the Emanations of Re',[41]
especially in view of the striking parallel to the Edfu inscription
supplied by Clement of Alexandria in the sixth book of his *Stromata*.[42]
The passage in question is inserted abruptly into Clement's argument,
and looks like a borrowing from somewhere else.[43] It describes a
procession of Egyptian priests, each carrying the symbols and books
associated with his particular position in the hierarchy. Altogether,
forty-two fundamental treatises (αἱ πάνυ ἀναγκαῖαι...βίβλοι) are
mentioned; and Clement attributes them all unequivocally to
Hermes.[44] Their subject matter is as follows (in the order in which
Clement mentions them):

(1) Hymns to the gods (1 book).
(2) Account of the king's life (1).
(3) The astrological books (4):
   (a) on the ordering of the fixed stars;
   (b) on the position of the sun, the moon and the five planets;
   (c) on the conjunctions and phases of the sun and the moon;
   (d) on the times when the stars rise.
(4) The hieroglyphic books (10),[45] on cosmography and geography,
    Egypt and the Nile, the construction of temples, the lands
    dedicated to the temples, and provisions and utensils for the
    temples.
(5) Books on education and the art of sacrifice (10), dealing in
    particular with sacrifices, first-fruits, hymns, prayers, processions
    and feasts.

---

[41] See *ibid.*

[42] Clem. Al., *Strom.* VI.4.35–7 (written *c.* 200–10).

[43] *Ibid.* VI.4.35.2–3: 'The Egyptians follow a philosophy of their own, as is indeed apparent
from their sacred religion. For first of all advances the singer (ᾠδός), carrying with him
one of the symbols of music...' etc. Cf. Chaer., *fr.* 10 (= Porph., *Abst.* IV.6), on the
deportment of Egyptian priests: 'Their hands they kept always inside their habit; and
each of them wore a symbol that indicated his rank in the hierarchy.' Perhaps Clement
has preserved a portion of Chaeremon's account omitted from Porphyry's summary? – cf.
Vergote, *C.E.* 31 (1941) 37–8.

[44] See also Str. XVII.1.46, on Thebes: 'The priests there are said to be noted astronomers and
philosophers...They attribute to Hermes all wisdom of this particular kind'; Diog. Laert.'s
observation, I.11, that the Egyptian priests 'formulated laws on the subject of justice, which
they ascribed to Hermes'; and Iam., *Myst.* I.1.1–2 (quoted below, 136).

[45] The number, not given by Clement, is easily worked out.

(6) The hieratic books (10), on laws, the gods and the whole of priestly training.
(7) The medical books (6):
    (a) on the construction of the body;
    (b) on diseases;
    (c) on organs;
    (d) on drugs;
    (e) on diseases of the eyes;
    (f) on the diseases of women.

If these were just the 'fundamental books', Clement must have known of others; but in the thirty-six non-medical volumes it was none the less possible, so he assures us, to find 'the whole philosophy of the Egyptians', as expressed in their religion.[46]

The mysterious power of these compositions, which Thoth was believed to have written with his own hand, and the fascination that they exercised over the pious Egyptian, is illustrated by a story about Setne-Khamwas, High Priest of Ptah at Memphis and son of Ramses II, preserved in a demotic papyrus of the Ptolemaic period.[47] Setne, an adept of divine writings, hears of a book by Thoth deposited in the tomb at Memphis of one Naneferkaptah. He breaks into the tomb, and hears from the ghost of Naneferkaptah's wife, Ahwere, how one of the Memphite priests of Ptah told her husband that he would find, hidden in the midst of the 'water of Coptus', a book

> that Thoth wrote with his own hand, when he came down following the other gods. Two spells (*ḥp*) are written in it. When you [recite the first spell you will] charm the sky, the earth, the nether-world, the mountains and the waters. You will discover what all the birds of the sky and all the reptiles are saying. You will see the fish of the deep [though there are twenty-one divine cubits of water] over [them]. When you recite the second spell, it will happen that, whether you are in the nether-world or in your form on earth, you will see Pre appearing in the sky with his Ennead, and the Moon in its form of rising.

Setting forth in the boat of his father the Pharaoh, Naneferkaptah found the spot described, three days' voyage beyond Coptus. He slew the endless serpent that guarded the intricate casket in which the book was deposited; he took out the book itself; and he recited the formulae, experiencing all that the priest had predicted. Returning to Coptus, Naneferkaptah,

---

[46] Clem. Al., *Strom.* vi.4.35.2 (quoted above, 58 n. 43); 37.3.
[47] See Lichtheim, *Ancient Egyptian literature* 3.125–38, whose translation is used below.

Translation and interpretation

a good scribe and very wise man, had a sheet of new papyrus brought to him. He wrote on it every word that was in the book before him. He soaked it in beer, he dissolved it in water. When he knew it had dissolved, he drank it[48] and knew what had been in it.

But the anger of Thoth quickly overtook Naneferkaptah. As he sailed from Coptus towards Memphis, first his son, then his wife, then Naneferkaptah himself fell overboard and were drowned.

Nothing abashed at this warning, Setne demands to be given the book that has been buried along with Naneferkaptah. After a dramatic magical duel involving a game of draughts, Setne seizes the book and makes off with it. This time it is Naneferkaptah himself who brings retribution upon the thief. He induces in Setne a hallucination. As the priest takes a stroll in the forecourt of the temple of Ptah at Memphis, he sees the beautiful Tabubu and longs to make love to her. He offers her ten pieces of gold (to the horror of his retinue), and she invites him to her house, receiving him in a fragrant and elegant upper room. Setne presses the provocatively dressed Tabubu to lie with him immediately, but Tabubu demands first a marriage-contract, then the consent of his children. Not satisfied even with this, Tabubu has Setne's children killed and their bodies thrown to the dogs and the cats. 'They ate their flesh, and he [Setne] heard them as he drank with Tabubu.' Then Tabubu takes Setne to her bed. He reaches out to caress her...and suddenly awakes to find himself lying naked on the ground, in an embarrassingly aroused state. As ill luck would have it, the Pharaoh passes by at that moment, and seeing Setne assumes he has been drinking. The hapless High Priest is now easily persuaded to return the book of Thoth to Naneferkaptah's grave.

If it be objected that sources of the Ptolemaic and Roman periods are unreliable guides to the priestly literature of Pharaonic Egypt, one can point to examples that survive from the Pharaonic era of several of the literary genres enumerated by the Edfu catalogue and Clement.[49] Fashions in priestly reading did not change much. The

---

48 A perennial and widespread magical practice: see e.g. Dornseiff, *Alphabet* 20, 50; Kákosy, *Lex. Äg.* 3.61; Borghouts, *Lex. Äg.* 3.1145; Speyer, *Jb. A.C.* 8–9 (1965–6) 92; Thompson, *Semitic magic* lv, lxi–lxii; van Lennep, *Travels in Asia Minor* 1.285 (on a British Consul at Samsun who satisfied Turks who importuned him for medicine by making them swallow a piece of paper stamped with the consular seal and soaked in water); Makal, *Village in Anatolia* 148. The practice gave special point to the gnostic *topos* of 'drinking down knowledge': Festugière, *Hermétisme* 105.

49 See nn. *ad loc.* in the Stählin-Früchtel edition of Clement; Neugebauer and Parker, *Egyptian astronomical texts*; Brunner et al., *Ägyptologie* ii.

Pharaonic temple-texts continued to be carefully, though not slavishly, transmitted,[50] in their traditional language and format. The first-century B.C. Greek writer Diodorus of Sicily speaks of priests teaching their sons the 'sacred' (i.e. hieroglyphic or hieratic) and demotic scripts, along with geometry and arithmetic;[51] and ability to read the hieroglyphic or hieratic script was still a *sine qua non* of priestly status in the second century A.D.[52] An important cosmological papyrus now in Copenhagen, and dating from about this period, contains a hieratic text also known from the cenotaph of Seti I at Abydus and the tomb of Ramses IV at Thebes, together with an interlinear translation and commentary in demotic, possibly for teaching purposes.[53]

This Copenhagen papyrus is just one of a whole series of documents emanating apparently from temple circles in the Fayyum town of Tebtunis and covering every imaginable area of priestly concern: ritual, hymns to the gods, cosmology, astrology, magic, wisdom-literature (i.e. moral instruction, usually in the form of brief maxims), the interpretation of dreams, medicine, temple-administration and so on.[54] They are written in hieroglyphic, hieratic, demotic and Greek, and the greater part of them belong to the Roman period, most commonly to the second century. But the Tebtunis material is widely scattered, and has not been studied as a whole; so particular interest attaches to a recently published group of late Ptolemaic and Roman demotic papyri, also from the Fayyum region, which may have belonged to the temple-libraries of the crocodile-god Sobek (Souchos) at Crocodilopolis and Socnopaiou Nesos.[55]

Among these texts, which are evidently considerably older than the copies in which they are preserved, are two which their editor has entitled respectively *On the history of the building of temples* (*P. Vindob.* D.6319) and *On the management of temples* (*P. Vindob.* D.6330); while

[50] Žabkar, *J.E.A.* 66 (1980) 127–36.
[51] Diod. Sic. 1.81.1–6. On the hereditary character of the priesthood (and therefore of priestly learning) see Otto, *Priester und Tempel* 1.203–30; Engelmann, *Sarapis* 7, lines 2–12, and nn. *ad loc.*
[52] *P. Tebt.* 291.40–48 (A.D. 162) = *Chrest. Wilck.* 137. The phrase ἱερατικὰ γράμματα might refer to either the hieroglyphic or the more cursive hieratic script: Vergote, *C.E.* 31 (1941) 23. This Greek testimonium is confirmed by a text from the temple at Dendera: Sauneron, *B.I.A.O.* 61 (1962) 55–7.
[53] Lange and Neugebauer, *Papyrus Carlsberg No. 1*, esp. 8–9.
[54] To Donadoni's useful list, *Acme* 8 (2–3) (1955) 74–5, add *P. Tebt. Tait passim.*
[55] Edited by Reymond, *Hermetic writings*. (The title is not justified by anything in the texts.) On the origin of the papyri see esp. 19–21. In view of the character of these texts, it is interesting to note the extremely Egyptian and priest-dominated character of Socnopaiou Nesos in the Greek and Roman period: Samuel, in *Sixteenth Cong. Pap.* 389–404.

a third (*P. Vindob.* D.6321) contains a fragment from the 'mysterious writings of Ptah', and provides instructions for protecting sacred places by magical rites. These titles present notable parallels with some of the inscriptions on the walls of the Edfu temple, and belong at least to the same genre as the Edfu library catalogue's 'Book of the plan of the temple', Clement's treatise 'On the construction of temples' and the various apotropaic writings referred to by both sources.[56] The other three papyri in the group[57] provide unique examples of Egyptian speculative literature. They show a strong interest in cosmogony and the understanding of the powers latent in the material world, and make several references to the god Thoth and his writings[58] – the situation they envisage is one in which a teacher, perhaps Thoth himself, instructs a pupil in divine wisdom, apparently in the setting of a temple.[59] In text c_1 we find a reference to the *ḥp n nṯr*, the 'law of the god'.[60] The god with whom the concept *ḥp* was most commonly associated was Thoth; and it will be recalled that the book, written by Thoth's own hand, that Setne sought in the sea of Coptus contained two 'formulae' – *ḥp* – with which Setne was able to enchant the whole of creation, and see the gods. The assumption behind all these texts is that knowledge comes from the gods, and in particular from Thoth, and that its possession endows one with power which (by implication) is analogous to that of the gods themselves. Once in c, and twice in c_1, we find written in red ink the words *mre rḫw*, 'pursuing wisdom',[61] which thus repeated can hardly be, as Reymond has suggested, the title of a treatise, but more likely constitute a sort of refrain or *Leitmotiv*, defining the underlying purpose of these compositions.[62]

It was, then, this quintessentially Egyptian tradition of magico-theological erudition, a tradition that even in its latest phase contained little if anything necessarily Greek, that Clement had in

---

[56] Reymond, *Hermetic writings* 25–34, 45–116.

[57] *P. Vindob.* D.6336, 6343, 6614, hereafter (as in Reymond's edition) c, c_1, D respectively.

[58] c. 1.3, 6, 9; c_1, II.13, 19–20; c_1, III.11, 14–15 ('He is the wisdom. He is Thoth [   ] who provides for nourishments for them [   ] made (by) his hand. This is the feather of the scribe of records, ⟨of⟩ his boo[ks   the] books, saying...'); D, a. 1, 8; and Reymond's commentary *ad loc.*

[59] c_1, III.6 ('Thy teaching in the god's law'), 8 ('thy teaching [is?] in the temple about thy likeness of men...'), 11 ('Do [not] fail to draw nourishment from sayings [?of Thoth]...').

[60] c_1, III.6. Cf. Reymond's n. *ad loc.*, 137, and another reference to *ḥp* at D, a. 2.

[61] c, I.4; c_1, I.17, III.16. Cf. Reymond's commentary *ad loc.*; and *Setne* I.3 *ad init.* (= Lichtheim, *Ancient Egyptian literature* 3.128), on Naneferkaptah's zeal for 'writings' = learning.

[62] Cf. the refrain which concludes many sections of *P. Insinger*: 'The fate and the fortune that come, it is the god who sends them'; and Mueller, *O.L.Z.* 67 (1972) 122–3.

mind when he spoke of 'the philosophy of the Egyptians'. It was in the Roman period a thought-world whose prestige and stability could not wholly mask its inner decay or its obsession with the refining of its own processes. The decline was apparent even to outsiders. Strabo lamented the evaporation of the learned tradition from the temples of Heliopolis;[63] and Dio Chrysostom remarked on the 'ignorance' and 'negligence' of contemporary custodians of the Egyptian temple-records.[64] It is true that the more sophisticated among the hiero-glyphic texts in the temple at Esna, inscribed during the period between Domitian and Antoninus, give the impression that Egyptian theology was still evolving even at that late date; but the evolution resulted not so much from new insights as from a desire to impart order and lucidity to the bewildering multiplicity of doctrines already in circulation.[65] Likewise at Kom Ombo, the temple texts show a certain tendency towards elaboration, but strictly within the con-ventions of the variation on a theme.[66] The theological fundamentals remain immutable; only the details are adjusted. This airless immo-bility of the priestly mind is reflected in every detail of the temple regime. The ancient rituals are performed in temples whose archi-tecture, even under the Ptolemies and the Romans, remains austerely Pharaonic; and from their walls the gods stare out in poses first struck in furthest antiquity. At Kom Ombo the last royal portraits, depicting Roman emperors of the third century, are iconographically indistinguishable from the early Ptolemaic images, except in their debased execution; while at Esna adjacent panels depict Ptolemy VI and the emperor Decius in the act of sacrificing to the gods, both in exactly the same manner as thirty dynasties of Pharaohs before them.[67]

But the most telling sign of what was happening to the native Egyptian mind was the condition of the hieroglyphic script. The ancient Egyptians believed, not only that an object's or being's whole nature was implicit in its name, so that knowledge of the name

---

[63] Str. XVII.1.29.

[64] Dio Chr., *or.* XI.38.

[65] Sauneron, *Quatre campagnes* 43–4; *B.S.F.E.* 32 (1961) 43–8; *Fêtes religieuses* 268–9. (The symmetries pointed out by Sauneron between a late creation-account at Esna and that to be found in the Leiden *kosmopoiia* (*P. Leid.* I 395 = *P. Graec. Mag.* XIII) tell us more about the eclecticism of the *kosmopoiia*'s author than about the intellectual milieu of the Esna priesthood.)

[66] Gutbub, *Kom Ombo* 502–5.

[67] Porter and Moss, *Topographical bibliography* 6.179–203, esp. 197 (nos. 230–1); 114 (no. 23) and 116 (nos. 32–3).

conveyed power over what it designated,[68] but also, as we have already seen in the story of Setne, that a supernatural force was inherent in the actual written or engraved letters that made up the name.[69] Without, then, falling into the error of imagining that the hieroglyphs were above conveying anything as vulgar as words and sentences, but were symbols of arcane and divine truths,[70] it is possible to recognize how essential knowledge of the priestly script was to the survival of traditional Egyptian ways of thought. Yet Clement of Alexandria asserts that familiarity with the sacred characters had in his day become the preserve of a minute elite;[71] and the Esna texts, which go into abrupt decline in the later second century, confirm that Clement was well-informed. The latest known dated hieroglyphic text (A.D. 394) is to be seen on the Gate of Hadrian in the island sanctuary of Isis at Philae, which from A.D. 298 marked the southern frontier of Roman Egypt.[72] It is so corrupt that parts of it would be incomprehensible were it not for a related demotic inscription nearby;[73] and one easily understands why it was that the fifth-century Alexandrian writer Horapollo's treatise on hieroglyphs (*Hieroglyphica*) already belonged, at least in part, to the realm of fantasy.[74] To the alchemist Olympiodorus (perhaps identical with the sixth-century Alexandrian Platonist of that name), the hieroglyphic inscriptions that he searched out in the abandoned temples beside the Nile, and in the quarries along the edge of the western desert, were plainly full of power and wisdom – but by his day impenetrably mysterious.[75]

Remote Philae, though, where the use of demotic as well as the hieroglyphs is attested later than anywhere else, does stand as a

---

[68] Hence *Instr. Merik.* 47 (= 138): 'God knows every name' (the culmination of a catalogue of His powers).

[69] Schott, *Studium generale* 6 (1953) 278–88; Fischer, *Lex. Äg.* 2.1195–6; above, 60 n. 48.

[70] E.g. Plut., *Is. Os.* 10; Plot. v.8.6.

[71] Clem. Al., *Strom.* v.4.20.3.

[72] Barnes, *Constantine* 17–18; Pestmann, *Chronologie égyptienne* 118–27.

[73] *Philae* 436; cf. 353, 361 for similarly garbled, but undated, hieroglyphic inscriptions.

[74] Below, 185. Jul., *ep.* 59, takes for granted that the Alexandrians will be more than pleased to swap an obelisk 'with Egyptian inscriptions' for a colossal bronze statue of himself.

[75] *Alch. gr.* 87–8. If the hieroglyphs still exercised some fascination even in Islamic Egypt (see Blochet, *R.S.O.* 6 (1914–15) 49–63, but also Mayer, *Saracenic heraldry* 12–13), that was thanks to appreciation of their artistic form rather than to comprehension of their meaning: Drioton, in *Studi Calderini* 2.471–7. But for a suggestion that at least one hieroglyphic symbol may have retained something of its original significance (in this case in popular beliefs concerning pregnancy and birth) down to the twentieth century, see Blackman, *A.I.Ph.O.* 3 (1935) 91–5.

symbol for the durability as well as the conservatism of Egyptian paganism. It was as autochthonous a sanctuary as one could hope to find, thanks especially to its close links with the tribes to the south – the Nubians and the Blemmyes.[76] Fifth-century demotic graffiti from the island[77] reveal priests of either Egyptian or more southerly origin, with not a single Greek name among them, busily employed about a cult which continued to attract pilgrims, and whose fame was such that Marinus of Neapolis, writing towards the end of the century in far-away Athens, could speak of 'Isis who is still honoured at Philae'.[78] And she continued to be, until the cult was suppressed in the reign of Justinian.[79] But if Esmet senior, a priest of Isis, states in one graffito that he 'acted as lord[?] of writing divine words[?]',[80] neither the script nor the language encourages one to believe that Esmet represented a still living tradition of priestly learning.[81]

It is as well to have in mind this long-drawn-out senescence of the native tradition of sacred learning when one turns to consider the possibility that the Hermetica may have been modelled on it. It was a tradition already suffering from sclerosis when the books of Hermes were composed; but access to it was not yet impossible, and it enshrined certain types of knowledge and skill which were no less in demand among Greek Egyptians than among the natives. Magic, medicine and the movements of the stars were major preoccupations both of the Thoth-literature – as a glance at the Edfu catalogue and Clement's list confirms – and of the technical Hermetica. So how deep did the Hermetic sciences push their roots into the cultural subsoil of native and even Pharaonic Egypt? Can the books of Hermes be regarded as in any sense translations or interpretations of the books of Thoth?

The question can be answered least equivocally with regard to magic – and we are helped by an abundance of surviving texts in both Egyptian and Greek. The native tradition regarded Thoth as

---

[76] *I.G.L.P.* 2, pp. 29–31; Procop., *Bell.* 1.19.34.
[77] E.g. *Philae* 96, 240, 258, 332, 343, 355, 365, 366, 375, 376, 450, a group dated between 408–9 and 452 (the latest known demotic text), and all related to a single family, most recently discussed by Burkhardt, in *Graeco-Coptica* 77–83.
[78] Marin., *Proc.* 19.
[79] Nautin, *C. Arch.* 17 (1967) 3–8.
[80] *Philae* 366a; cf. 259, 450. The demotic expression alludes to those whom the Greeks called *pterophoroi/hierogrammateis*: *Philae* p. 304.
[81] Zauzich, in *Das römisch-byzantinische Ägypten* 77.

Translation and interpretation

the patron of both magic and the priestly books; and naturally the most authoritative magicians were the priests themselves,[82] men like Setne-Khamwas, who had the training and leisure to study and experiment with the traditional magical formulae. And indeed the influence of Egypt, 'mother of magicians, who discovered and passed on to others every kind of witchcraft',[83] was felt wherever magic was practised in the Graeco-Roman world. In the land of the Nile itself it was inevitable that magical books would before long be translated for the benefit of the Greek settlers. The tendency of magicians to claim indiscriminately that any spell they composed had been found in such-and-such a temple, graven in hieroglyphs on a stele by Hermes himself,[84] has induced in modern scholars the comfortable illusion that all such assertions are *topoi*, to be disregarded save as a symptom of Egyptomania. But it is hardly a secret that a good deal of Egyptian magic really was transliterated, translated or adapted into Greek;[85] and there is much in the Greek magical formulae that can only be explained in terms of Egyptian antecedents.[86] That is not to deny that there is a difference in style between Pharaonic and Graeco-Egyptian magic – with the demotic texts coming somewhere in the middle, and in many respects closer to the contemporary Greek idiom than to the Pharaonic material. A particularly notable feature of Pharaonic magic is its rich mythological content, which was drastically simplified before it passed into Greek. But this is perfectly explicable when one considers the difficulty that the Greeks would have experienced in understanding the significance and function of the plethora of arcane divinities one encounters in the Pharaonic texts. What we are seeing here is not a cultural break, but precisely

[82] Hopfner, *Offenbarungszauber* 2.§§7–17; te Velde, *J.V.E.G.* 21 (1969–70) 181; and Gardiner, *J.E.A.* 24 (1938) 176, on the association of magical texts with the 'House of Life'.

[83] Ioh. Chr., *Hom. in Mt.* VIII.4.

[84] See most notably *P. Berol.* 21243.i.1–5 = Brashear, *Z.P.E.* 33 (1979) 262: 'Extract from the spells in the holy book found in the sanctuary in Heliopolis, called (the book) of Hermes, written in the Egyptian language and translated into Greek'; also Brashear's n. *ad loc.* for further examples.

[85] Lexa, *Magie* 1.155–66; Preisendanz, in *VIII Kong. Pap.* 120. The well-known demotic magical papyrus preserved partly in London and partly in Leiden contains material in Greek as well. At XV.24–31 is a spell transmitted in both Greek and demotic. Griffith and Thompson, *Demotic magical papyrus* 1.10–13, argue that the demotic is probably translated from the Greek, rather than vice versa, but that the Greek looks, from its mythological content, as if it may itself have been translated from the Egyptian. (Cf. also Johnson, *Enchoria* 7 (1977) 95–7.)

[86] See Nock's commentary on *P. Brit. Mus.* 10588 (Bell, Nock and Thompson, *P.B.A.* 17 (1931) 256–86); Riesenfeld, *Eranos* 44 (1946) 153–60, on the marked Egyptian elements in Greek magical hymns; Wortmann, *B.J.* 166 (1966) 62–112, on magical gems; and Bergman, in *Studies dedicated to Professor Jan Zandee* 28–37, and *Mélanges Adolphe Gutbub* 1–11.

that 'rendering plausible' (πιθανολογία) of Egyptian material for the benefit of a Greek audience of which the translator of the Imouthes–Asclepius aretalogy (*P. Oxy.* 1381) speaks in his prologue – and which no doubt there too consisted mainly in the paring down of the mythological elements.

If Graeco-Egyptian magic provides a relatively clear-cut illustration of cultural continuity, the intellectual roots of the other technical Hermetica are more diverse, not least because of the important contribution made by Babylonia in these areas.[87] In the case of alchemy, the ancient Egyptians are known to have been interested in the origin and nature of precious stones and metals, while the Greek alchemical texts of late antiquity contain various allusions to Egypt and its traditions; but there is no sign of anything approaching the continuous evolution that links Pharaonic to Graeco-Egyptian magic.[88] Similarly with astrology.[89] We have no records that the ancient Egyptians made astronomical observations; but some form of time-keeping was essential to the smooth functioning of the temples. Coffin lids and the ceilings of Ramesside tombs reveal crude efforts to divide the night into 'hours' on the basis of observations which will presumably have supplied the material of the astronomical Thoth-literature attested by the Edfu catalogue and Clement of Alexandria. Especially characteristic was the system whereby (in its fully-developed Hellenistic form) the zodiacal belt was divided into thirty-six 10° segments, or 'decans'. And the use of this decanal system, together with a penchant for alluding to the temples and priests of old Egypt and to specific events in the country's history,[90] does impart an air of Egyptianism to the astrological texts of the Hellenistic and Roman periods. Indeed, later Pharaonic Egypt had been by no means unfamiliar with the idea that the stars might directly influence the course of human affairs;[91] nor should we exclude the possibility that some of the texts which expounded Egyptian star-lore were translated into Greek[92] – after all, a parallel

---

[87] Astrology: Gundel 9–75, 89–90; Neugebauer, *Ancient mathematical astronomy* 2–5, 559–68, 589–614; Rochberg-Halton, *J.N.E.S.* 43 (1984) 115–40. Alchemy: Forbes, *Ancient technology* 1.125–48.

[88] Daumas, in *Die römisch-byzantinische Ägypten* 109–18, takes a rather optimistic view of the evidence.

[89] On what follows, see Parker, in *Place of astronomy* 51–65; Neugebauer, *Ancient mathematical astronomy* 559–68.

[90] Cumont, *Egypte* (but also Robert's criticisms, *Etudes epigraphiques* 76–88).

[91] Kákosy, *Oikumene* 3 (1982) 163–91.

[92] As suggested by Gundel 11, 12–14, 92, who probably over-estimates the importance of such translations (if they existed) to the evolution of Hermetic astrology.

process is well attested in Hellenistic Babylonia.[93] But Babylonia of course had more to offer. Graeco-Roman astrology was essentially an amalgam of Babylonian and Greek currents of thought and practice, and there is no real need to invoke ancient Egypt in order to explain it. The native priesthood continued to produce astronomical books in the name of Thoth,[94] and to carve zodiacs and other heavenly representations on the walls of their temples, as in the roof-chapels at Dendera. But all that must have seemed archaic to the adepts of 'Petosiris' and 'Nechepso', who made Egypt into the astrologers' cynosure, but only by decking her out in foreign garb.

In short, the evidence for substantial continuities between the Egyptian priestly literature and the technical Hermetica is patchy, not surprisingly in view of Egypt's successive exposure to Babylonian influences at the time of the Persian supremacy, then to the Greek world as a result of Alexander's conquest. But Graeco-Egyptian magic, which was to a large extent conceived of as Hermetic, can certainly be seen in terms of translation and interpretation of native materials; and if the same cannot be said of Hermetic alchemy and astrology, it is nevertheless clear that Hermes's patronage of such disciplines was modelled on Thoth's patronage of ancient Egyptian science. It is significant too that, as we shall see in a later chapter,[95] Hermetic astrologers and alchemists were keen to convey the impression that their learning did in fact emanate from the temples of old Egypt. While one does not have to believe them, it is likely that native clergy who knew Greek will have found much to interest them in the technical books of Hermes.

Instructions *and philosophical Hermetica*

The other area of Egyptian literature that seems to bear investigation in the light of Hermetic hindsight is the so-called 'wisdom' or (more appropriately) 'instruction' genre.[96] The earliest examples date from the Old Kingdom, the latest from the Roman period; and the texts

---

[93] Cumont, *Astrology and religion* 56–65.
[94] Str. XVII.1.46 (quoted above, 58 n. 44), who must have in mind texts such as are occasionally encountered in the papyri discussed above, 61, and by Gundel 36–8, 348.
[95] Below, 166–8.
[96] See most recently Williams, *J.A.O.S.* 101 (1981–2) 1–19, and Lichtheim, *Late Egyptian wisdom literature*, which includes new translations of the demotic *Instructions*. The earlier texts are translated in the same author's *Ancient Egyptian literature* 1–2.

were widely disseminated on both papyrus and ostraca. They were not unknown in the temple milieu,[97] and indeed a number of them reveal a particular reverence for Thoth. But their content is quite different from that of the priestly Thoth literature. In sequences of brief exhortations usually delivered by father to son, they set out the profane, everyday wisdom of the ancient Egyptians, aspiring neither to the status of divine emanations, nor even to secrecy. The genre attained its highest degree of integration and coherence in the New Kingdom, each text concentrating on a few themes arranged into numbered chapters. Here is a specimen from the *Instruction of Amenemope*:

> Do not lie down in fear of tomorrow:
> 'Comes day, how will tomorrow be?'
> Man does not know how tomorrow will be;
> God is ever in His perfection,
> Man is ever in his failure.
> The words men say are one thing,
> The deeds of the god are another.
> Do not say: 'I have done no wrong',
> And then strain to seek a quarrel;
> The wrong belongs to the god,
> He seals [the verdict] with his finger.
> There is no perfection before the god.
> But there is failure before him;
> If one strains to seek perfection,
> In a moment he has marred it.
> ...[98]

The latest, demotic texts are much more aphoristic and staccato in style, though sayings on related themes continue to be grouped together. A more personal relationship with God becomes apparent, but the tone is for the most part severely practical. The *Instruction of Ankhsheshonq*, for example, apprises us that 'The owner of the cow is he who is able to run', and that 'He who sends spittle to the sky, upon his face it falls'. He reminds us that 'Man is even better at copulating than a donkey; his purse is what restrains him', and that 'Instructing a woman is [having] a sack of sand whose side is split open'; and he bids us not laugh at cats.[99]

On the grounds that this aphoristic manner is shared by *S.H.* XI and the Armenian *Definitions of Hermes Trismegistus to Asclepius*,

---

[97] Above, 61.
[98] *Instr. Amen.* 18.
[99] *Instr. Ankh.* IX.23, XI.10, XIII.20, XVI.15, XXIV.10.

J.-P. Mahé has recently compared the doctrine of the *Instructions* with that of the philosophical Hermetica.[100] He interprets, for example, the *Instructions*' indifferent allusions to 'the god' and 'the gods' as an anticipation of the complex Hermetic God, who is both the One and the All; but the meaning of these expressions in the *Instructions* is much disputed, and in any case the *Instructions* nowhere show the sustained interest in the nature of the divine world that is so characteristic of the Hermetica. To the anthropocentrism of the Egyptian texts, on the other hand, it is easy to find parallels in the Hermetica's high view of Man, formed by God with loving care. The understanding of the wise man as one who allows his heart to be opened to divine or paternal guidance, who follows the 'way' that will be shown him and prefers silence to empty talk is also common to the two genres. But the assumptions underlying these ideas in the *Instructions* are far more anthropocentric than in the Hermetica, where the essence of Man is the God within, and silence is offered as a sacrifice of praise during the divine vision, not practised as a means to secure one's own wants. As an exceptionally explicit example of interior, reflective discourse, Mahé offers the following from the *Instruction of Any*:

> Do not raise your voice in the house of God,
> He abhors shouting;
> Pray by yourself with a loving heart,
> Whose every word is hidden.
> He will grant your needs,
> He will hear your words,
> He will accept your offerings.
> Libate for your father and mother,
> Who are resting in the valley;
> When the gods witness your action,
> They will say: 'Accepted'.
> Do not forget the one outside,
> Your son will act for you likewise.[101]

Whereas the Hermetic ideal of silence is clearly conveyed in Hermes's description of the divine vision in *The Ogdoad reveals the Ennead*:

I have seen! Language is not able to reveal this. For the entire Ogdoad, O my son, and the souls that are in it, and the angels, sing a hymn in silence.[102]

In short, the outlook of the *Instructions*, though pious, is this-worldly, ethical, social, that of the philosophical Hermetica – as we

---

[100] Mahé 2.278–308; and cf. 308–12 for other examples of Hermetic aphorisms.
[101] *Instr. Any* 4.   [102] *N.H.C.* vi.6.58.16–21.

shall see more clearly in chapter 4 – gnostic, contemplative, individualist.[103] Mahé's diligent and at times ingenious accumulation of parallels between the two genres reflects a shared geographical and, in the case of the latest *Instructions*, chronological ambience, but no more. It is particularly improbable that the philosophical Hermetica enjoyed the wide circulation that the *Instructions* must have done, to judge from the numerous surviving copies. What then of the claim that the aphoristic manner of certain of the Hermetica is modelled on that of the *Instructions*? An aphorism is strictly speaking a definition, more loosely speaking an axiom or pithy saying; but while the Armenian *Definitions* are precisely what they claim to be,[104] so too are the *Instructions*, albeit pithily expressed. So to link the two genres on the basis of their 'aphoristic' structure is once again to neglect the essence for the letter,[105] especially in view of the fact that the *Instructions* were, by the time the Hermetica came to be written, just one manifestation among many of an international, cross-cultural gnomic literature, as abundant in Greek as in any other language.[106] Why then lay such particular emphasis on rather fragile resemblances with the Egyptian *Instructions*? A similar objection could be made to the assertion that the *Instructions* and the Hermetica are related because of their suitability for use in a school context. This could be said of many otherwise dissimilar literary genres.

Mahé's valuable perception that the philosophical Hermetica and the Egyptian instructional literature have certain things in common (whether or not as a result of direct influence) is spoilt by the attempt to make too much of it. But to abandon Mahé at this point would do scant justice to his grand Darwinian design; for from the 'sentences' (γνῶμαι) of the Armenian *Definitions* and *S.H.* xi he goes on to derive all the other varieties of philosophical Hermetic text, even those apparently least reducible to a string of maxims, as for instance *C.H.* I, the *Poimandrēs*.[107] The process begins with the simple, unadorned gnomology, an unclassified sequence of statements which

---

[103] As partially acknowledged by Mahé himself, 2.305–7.

[104] The same title would suit *S.H.* xi.

[105] Mahé's demonstration, 2.410–13, that the term γνώμη ('sentence') eventually became a catch-all expression covering definitions, aphorisms and all other brief declarative statements can obviously not justify failure to distinguish between those genres when it is clear that the ancients themselves continued to distinguish them.

[106] Lichtheim, *Late Egyptian wisdom literature*.

[107] Mahé 2.407–36 (with detailed illustrations of the argument).

may later be grouped into chapters according to theme. The third stage is to conjoin the sentences into the semblance, at least, of connected prose. Such texts are handy teaching-aids, because they lend themselves both to reduction to lists of points for memorization, and to expansion into commentaries – they become the chapter-headings of the teacher's exposition. This then is the next phase of the evolutionary process, as the remnants of the original maxims are reduced to the role of thematic markers in a continuous explanatory text. Finally comes the introduction of myth, expressed in past-tense narrative – as for example the various Hermetic accounts of creation, amidst which, despite the amplitude and autonomy of the mythic element, the original gnomic declarations may still at various points be distinguished. The same can be said of the prayers, though these are even further removed from the original gnomologies because of the marked alien, particularly Jewish, influences to which they were subject.

As an exercise in speculative philology this is neat enough, but it lacks historical realism. Mahé plays down even the Jewish influences,[108] which at least he admits. But the Hermetists can hardly have been so absorbed in the stitching together of their maxims that they forgot about the Platonic dialogues. Diotima's speech in the *Symposium*, and the *Timaeus* generally, strike a didactic and almost revelatory note highly congenial to the adepts of Hermes.[109] Then there was the type of popular sermon called the diatribe, particularly associated with the Cynics. The diatribe widely influenced the philosophical literature of the Roman east, and is plainly echoed by *C.H.* vii and the similar sermon at the end of *C.H.* i.[110] And the Hermetic device of having Hermes instruct a pupil in a temple may find a better analogy in the Egyptian priestly literature[111] than in the *Instructions*, which never deploy either Thoth or temples on active service. Mahé's scheme does not formally exclude any of these influences; but they should not be passed by in silence.

More germane to the question from which we started, though, is the fact that Mahé's thesis is intended to bolster his proposition that the philosophical Hermetica are lineal descendants of the Egyptian *Instructions*; and the purpose of that proposition, in turn, is to refute

---

[108] Above, 36.
[109] Festugière 2.30–1; Dörrie, *Platonica minora* 107–10.
[110] Nock, *Essays* 26–32.
[111] Above, 62.

the view, argued most notably by Festugière, that Hermetism is wholly comprehensible in terms of the Greek philosophical tradition, particularly of Platonism and Stoicism.[112] For Mahé, as once for Reitzenstein, Hermetism is mythical Egyptian thought translated into Greek 'dans un vocabulaire qu'il faut bien qualifier de philosophique parce qu'il a, en effet, une longue histoire littéraire extérieure à l'Egypte'.[113] That the Egyptian element in the philosophical Hermetica must indeed be greater than was allowed by Festugière has increasingly been suspected in recent decades.[114] Mahé has now posed the problem in an acute form. But what we have already seen of the Egypt in which Hermetism emerged makes clear that neither of the extreme positions occupied by Festugière and Mahé are likely to be justifiable, since we are dealing with a syncretistic culture whose elements, especially by the Roman period, were not easily separable. The (relatively) unhellenized Egyptian expressed himself in the language and thought-patterns of the indigenous tradition, but what he wrote, as in the *Instructions*, might well draw on and be drawn on by what was being written at the same time in Hebrew, Aramaic and Greek. By the same token the Hellenized Egyptian wrote the Greek language, to whose expressiveness he was sensitive, and thought in Greek categories, whose subtlety he exploited. But once he had been moulded by that culture, he became first its bearer, then its arbiter. Indeed by late antiquity most of the leading exponents of Hellenism were orientals. Inheriting a tradition which once had professed respect for the wisdom of the Orient from a safe distance, they tipped its whole centre of gravity eastwards. Plato was now an 'Atticizing Moses';[115] and if in certain matters he seemed to say the same as Hermes, that was obviously because he had copied Hermes.[116] Hellenism, then, was held captive by those it had conquered; nor could it expect of its captors that they would ignore the possibilities offered by the unique monotheist theology of the Jews, the star-lore of the Babylonians (on which they built the whole new discipline of

---

[112] See esp. Festugière's minimization of the Egyptian element at 1.85.

[113] Mahé 2.291, without acknowledgement to Iam., *Myst.* viii.4. 265 (quoted below, 137); and cf. Stricker, *Brief van Aristeas* (summarized by Préaux, *C.E.* 33 (1958) 153–6), arguing that the Hermetica were all produced in the early Ptolemaic period as part of a Greek initiative to codify Egyptian religion.

[114] E.g. Derchain, *R.H.R.* 161 (1962) 175–98 (but on the basis of a restricted range of texts, including the non-Hermetic *C.H.* xviii); Mahé, *N.H.S.* 7 (1975) 143–4; Ponsing, *R.H.Ph.R.* 60 (1980) 29–34; Iversen, *Egyptian and Hermetic doctrine*. Mahé 2.278–308 draws on much other Egyptian material besides the *Instructions*.

[115] Num., *fr.* 8, and cf. *fr.* 1a.   [116] Proc., *In Tim.* 117d.

astrology) or, most beguiling of all in the case of the Egyptians, the resources of mythic and symbolic expression available in their own native tradition.[117] These influences, translated and interpreted, fertilized the investigations of the divine realm into which thinkers of the Roman period threw themselves with such enthusiasm. So it should not surprise us to find that the Hermetists combined openness to the international civilization of Hellenism with a deep, sometimes even aggressive awareness of their roots in Egypt. Indeed, our best evidence for this comes in the writings of the philosophical Hermetists, whose thought had far fewer direct links with the Egyptian past than did that of the technical Hermetists. To a remarkable extent, though, Hermetic scholarship, overwhelmingly philological and philosophical in its emphases, has remained blind to these modes of cultural interaction – for all that the tensions of local and international cultures have never played themselves out on a stage broader or more open than that provided by our own times.

[117] This aspect of the Egyptian tradition is often mentioned by Hellenophone writers, e.g. Chaer., *fr.* 2 (and van der Horst's n. 8); Ph. Al., *V. Mos.* 23; Plut., *Is. Os.* 9–10; Iam., *Myst.* vii.1; Dam., *V. Isid.* 1–2 (*E. Ph.*); and cf. Schott, *Studium generale* 6 (1953) 278–88.

PART II

THE WAY OF HERMES

[3]

Magister omnium physicorum

The time has come to look more closely at what it was that the cultural interactions described in part I actually produced. But just as we have reached this point by following a path of historical investigation, so here in part II the questions to be asked will be determined by historical considerations. Our concern will be neither the origin nor the development of doctrines, but their interrelationships and their role in the overall Hermetic world-view. The objective is to paint a portrait of the Hermetic mind as the texts reveal it – a canvas which will then be provided with a historical frame in part III. Such a scheme demands selection, and results naturally in an interpretation rather than a comprehensive description (if that is possible) of Hermetism. But the account in this chapter of the technical Hermetica, and in the next of the philosophical texts, will be followed by a demonstration in chapters 5 and 6 that the interpretation offered is not only implicit in the books of Hermes themselves, but also well-attested in other ancient sources.

Sympatheia

Of the omniscience of Hermes Trismegistus something has already been said. In the magical papyri he appears as the god who knows 'all that is hidden under the heavenly vault, and beneath the earth';[1] while in the *Korē kosmou* we read that it was he who instructed Isis

[1] *P. Graec. Mag.* VIII.14–15.

and Osiris in 'the secret ordinances of God' and conveyed to mankind knowledge of 'the arts, the sciences and all the professions'.[2] In other words the Graeco-Egyptian Hermes was still very much the old Thoth; and it comes as no surprise to find him regarded in Egypt as the inventor and leading exponent of all the sciences, particularly of those which fell outside the purview of the Alexandrian Museum and its rationalist Greek scholars.

The intellectual distinctiveness of the technical Hermetica is best appreciated, not so much by comparing them with other pseudonymous orientalizing literatures (the books of Zoroaster, Ostanes and others), to which they are very similar, as in relation to conventional Greek and Roman science. The technical Hermetica build on the disinterested investigation and classification of phenomena that had been the hallmark of Aristotelian science[3] – indeed, Marius Victorinus reports that Trismegistus's division of the day into twelve hours was inspired by his observation in Egypt of the regular urinatory habits of what other authorities variously identify as the baboon or the cat.[4] But to this practical streak the technical Hermetica add a belief in universal forces that are empirically uninvestigable, yet capable of being turned to Man's advantage once access has been gained to the necessary occult knowledge. Among the basic intellectual common denominators of the technical Hermetica – and an important element also in the philosophical texts – is the notion that all phenomena, in the divine and material realms alike are linked together by 'sympathetic' powers or energies into one pleroma. This is an idea that anyone who reflects on what he sees around him – for example, the connection between the sun and the growth of plants – may quite easily arrive at; and it can be found in theological and philosophical systems both primitive and sophisticated. In ancient Egyptian religion it manifests itself in the magical power, *heka*, that pervades the universe, and in the divine, especially solar, energies that enliven the whole world, and that were depicted in the time of Akhenaton as rays of the sun each ending in an outstretched hand, clustering especially round the person of the Pharaoh himself.[5]

---

[2] *S.H.* xxiii.5, 68; and cf. Tert., *Val.* xv.1('Mercurius ille Trismegistus, magister omnium physicorum'); Cyr. Al., *Jul.* 1.548bc; and Cumont, *Égypte* 153–4. Tertullian's phrase is adopted for the title of this chapter in conscious disregard of the likelihood that 'physici' are here natural philosophers, not occultists: see Fredouille's n. *ad loc.*

[3] On the ease of mistaking a scientist for a magician, see Apul., *Apol.* 36–41.

[4] Mar. Vict., *In Cic. Rhet.* 1.26, p. 223; and cf. Reitzenstein, *Poimandres* 265.

[5] Hornung, *Conceptions of God* 199–200 and 247 (and cf. *C.H.* xviii.11), 207–13; te Velde, *J.V.E.G.* 21 (1969–70) 175–86. On the later notion of 'divine power' (*nḫt* [*n ntr*]) see

Sympatheia

Among Greek philosophers the idea of nature as a universal principle, founded on the observable regularities of natural phenomena, was common currency from the Presocratics onwards;[6] and from this the Stoic doctrine of universal sympathy (συμπάθεια) was a relatively late and sophisticated development.[7] The importance of the idea in the technical Hermetica is therefore no surprise; but it is difficult to find in these texts any explanatory rather than merely formulaic statement about what sympathy is.[8] In the circumstances, it seems wise to make some use at this point of what is said about sympathy in the philosophical Hermetica, in the hope that an acquaintance with the doctrine in its fully developed form will provide a context for the sympathy-related ideas contained in the technical writings.

The fullest accounts of cosmic sympathy in the philosophical Hermetica can be found in *C.H.* XVI and the *Asclepius*,[9] and may be summarized as follows. God is one, and the creator of all things, which continue to depend on God as elements in a hierarchy of beings. Second in this hierarchy after God himself comes the intelligible world, and then the sensible world. The creative and beneficent powers of God flow through the intelligible and sensible realms to the sun, which is the demiurge around which revolve the eight spheres of the fixed stars, the planets and the earth. From these spheres depend the daemons, and from the daemons Man, who is a microcosm of creation.[10] Thus everything is part of God, and God is in everything, his creative activity continuing unceasingly. All things are one[11] and the pleroma of being is indestructible.

The divine powers that bind this closely-knit structure together are sometimes called 'energies',· and may also be spoken of in terms of light.[12] These energies derive from the sun, the planets and the stars;[13] and they operate on all bodies, whether immortal or mortal, animate or inanimate. They are what causes growth, decay and sensation;

Sauneron, *S. Or.* 7 (1966) 58 n. 6; and for sympathetic ideas applied to medicine and the parts of the human body see *ibid.* 59 n. 27.

[6] Lloyd, *Magic, reason and experience* 49–58.

[7] Festugière 1.90 n. 1; Vogel, *Greek philosophy* 3, index 3, *s.v.* συμπάθεια.

[8] On the well-known formula that 'Nature rejoices in Nature, and Nature masters Nature, and Nature conquers Nature' see Fraser 1.442–3.

[9] *C.H.* XVI *passim*; *Ascl.* 3, 19. Note also *Ascl.* 24 *ad init.* (quoted above, 13 n. 1), on Egypt as the focus of sympathetic forces.

[10] On the idea of the microcosm–macrocosm see Festugière 1.92–4, 125–31.

[11] *C.H.* XII.8; XIII.17, 18; XVI.3.

[12] E.g. *C.H.* XVI.5; *Ascl.* 19 (N.F. 2.318.21); cf. Festugière, *Hermétisme* 121 n. 3.

[13] This is graphically illustrated by *P. Graec. Mag.* 1.154–5, LVII; and see below, 78.

and they are also the origin of the arts and sciences and every other human activity.[14] By establishing sets of sympathetic correspondences, or 'chains', they maintain affinities between the most disparate areas of the natural realm, so that each animal, plant, mineral or even part of the human or animal body corresponds to a particular planet or god whom (or which) they can be used to influence, providing the right procedures and formulae are known.[15] And just as the elements of one chain are mutually sympathetic, so those of different chains may be antipathetic – a principle with obvious applications in the sphere of medicine, as the iatromathematical literature attests.

As for the daemons, they are simply personifications of these sympathetic energies – they may be either good or bad, but they are emanations, possessing neither body nor soul.[16] Needless to say, their effect on human beings is all the more insidious for that. They penetrate to the very core of the body, and attempt to subject the whole man to their will. This, expressed figuratively, is the crucial doctrine of fate (εἱμαρμένη, *fatum*), that played so large a part in the late antique consciousness. There will be more to say about this in both the present and later chapters. Here it suffices to draw attention to the close link between fate and the stars; for it was the opinion of the Hermetists that all the forces and energies just spoken of, and to which the whole of sublunary creation was subject, derived directly from the heavenly bodies. 'The overthrow of kings, the insurrection of cities, famines, plagues, the sudden fluctuations of the sea, and earthquakes, none of these things occurs...without the action of the decans.'[17] In short, the Hermetists' understanding of cosmic sympathy was intimately linked with their daemonology and their astrology; and it underlies too the philosophical spirituality of later Hermetism, with its insistence on the soul's need to transcend the realm of fate before it can be united with God. The technical Hermetica, developing stage by stage the doctrine of sympathy in its application to Man both body and spirit, thus provide a *propaideia* to the philosophical Hermetica, whose peculiar preoccupations and style they occasionally approach. Clearly, the spiritual dimension of technical Hermetism is of considerable interest for the historian who wishes to locate the roots of the late pagan mentality.

[14] *S.H.* iv.6–17; and cf. N.F. 1.140–2.
[15] Hopfner, *Offenbarungszauber* 1.§§378–425.
[16] *C.H.* xii.21, xvi.10–16; *S.H.* vi.10; cf. *P. Graec. Mag.* xii.254–5, and Gundel, *R.E.* 7.2635.
[17] *S.H.* vi.8; cf. *C.H.* xvi.17–18; *Ascl.* 3; and Gundel, *R.E.* 7.2633.

Magic

We may begin with the Graeco-Egyptian magical literature. Hellenistic and Roman magic was designed to harness the unpredictable divine powers that filled the universe, making nonsense out of generally accepted theories of causation, and breeding all manner of fears, anxieties and insecurities in the human mind. These powers were not normally regarded as a legitimate sphere for mortal interference; but magicians claimed to be able to manipulate them, in particular by exploiting the sympathetic links between material substances and the corresponding 'energies', whether daemons, planets or gods.[18] Although most magical procedures aimed at immediate, practical objectives – success in love, perhaps, or an enemy's ruin – it was essential that the magician acquire and demonstrate, even flaunt, *knowledge* of the divine realm, for knowledge bestowed the power (δύναμις) that the operative had to possess in order to compel the higher beings' acquiescence in his schemes. Hence the preoccupation displayed by many magical papyri with the extraction of oracles from the gods[19] – a process that required intimate contact with and understanding of the divine world. Not surprisingly, magicians frequently used the vocabulary of the mystery religions in formulating their incantations; and they might even claim to effect some sort of personal union with the gods they invoked.[20]

The magicians' concentration on knowledge and power rather than personal virtue, and their tendency to flatter, exploit and even threaten the gods in order to get their way, caused some of the more refined minds to condemn them as unspiritual. Plotinus, for example, in his attack on the gnostics, asks:

When they address the magic chants they have composed to these powers, not only to the soul but to those above it as well, what are they doing if not saying spells to conjure and persuade them? They say that these powers obey and are led by a mere word, by whoever among us is better skilled in the art of saying just the right things in the right way, songs and cries and aspirated and hissing sounds and everything else which their treatises say has magic power in the higher world. But even if they do not want to say this, how are the incorporeal beings affected by

[18] Above, 78 n. 15; Festugière, *Idéal religieux* 294–303; Annequin, *Recherches* 20–79.
[19] E.g. *P. Graec. Mag.* I.1–2, 327–31; IV.717–32, 870–916, 930–1033, 3172–208; VI; VII.319–34, 348–58; XIII.708–14. Cf. Apul., *Apol.* 26, on the 'popular' view of magic as 'union through speech with the immortal gods'; and Thess., *Virt. herb.* I. prooem. 11, 17, 22, on Thessalus's attempt 'to speak to a god / the gods' by magical means.
[20] Festugière, *Idéal religieux* 284–93, 303–10, 317–25; Nock, *Essays* 34–45.

sounds? So those who think that they are using especially exalted words to address the gods end up, without realizing it, by depriving their incantations of their sacred quality.[21]

But there is little profit, from the historian's point of view, in condemning magic just because it failed to measure up to the sublime conceptions of a Plotinus, or, even more irrelevantly, because it conflicts with the Christian or 'scientific' prejudices of modern scholars.[22] Traditional religion in most societies is based on the principle of reciprocity between men and gods, on the assumption that the performance of specific cultic actions can induce a favourable disposition in the divine beings they are addressed to;[23] and neither in principle nor, often enough, in practice, is there any difference between this sort of religion and what later, more sophisticated generations call magic. So much was clear even to the elder Pliny, who otherwise yielded to none in his detestation of 'magicae vanitates':

The most fraudulent of arts [magic] has held complete sway throughout the world for many ages. Nobody should be surprised at the greatness of its influence, since alone of the arts it has embraced three others that hold supreme dominion over the human mind, and made them subject to itself alone. Nobody will doubt that it first arose from medicine, and that professing to promote health it insidiously advanced under the disguise of a higher and holier system; that to the most seductive and welcome promises it added the powers of religion, about which even today the human race is quite in the dark; that again meeting with success it made a further addition of astrology, because there is nobody who is not eager to learn his destiny, or who does not believe that the truest account of it is that gained by watching the skies. Accordingly, holding men's emotions in a threefold bond, magic rose to such a height that even today it has sway over a great part of mankind, and in the East commands the Kings of Kings.[24]

Ancient (and indeed modern) Egyptian religion provides a precise illustration of this point – in fact, it was so deeply coloured by magic that the verbal distinction is almost redundant.[25] And it is to ancient

---

[21] Plot. II.9.14.2–11.

[22] See e.g. Festugière, *Idéal religieux* 324, 327 (on magic as 'exactement à l'opposé du sentiment religieux'); Nilsson, *Opuscula* 3.129–66. The extent to which even ancient commentators could fail to understand the rationale behind magic is illustrated by Synesius's assertion, *Calv.* 68b, that knowledge and power are, in magical terms, antithetical rather than interdependent categories.

[23] See Plato, *Euthphr.* 14e: 'Then piety, Euthyphro, is an art which gods and men have of trafficking with one another?'; and cf. the wrath of Cain at God's rejection of his sacrifice, Genesis IV.5.   [24] Pliny the Elder XXX.1.1–2 (tr. Jones).

[25] Gardiner, *E.R.E.* 8.262–3; Borghouts, *Lex. Äg.* 3.1138–9; and cf. Viaud, *Magie et coutumes populaires*, on modern Coptic magic; and Ḥusayn, *Al-ayām* ch. 16, on village Sufism and magic.

Egyptian magic that we should look for the origin of the idea that the magician could constrain the gods to do his will by abuse and threats.[26] It is perhaps difficult for us to see how feelings of reverence and awe could be generated by divinities who were to such an extent the victims of their worshippers, unless the Egyptians' view of the relationship that should prevail between Man and his gods was quite different from that which has been propagated by the higher forms of (say) Judaeo-Christianity. And it is essential to recognize that this was indeed the case. In the first place, the magician's potential power was considered to be unlimited, certainly equivalent to that of the gods, once he had learned the formulae by which the divine powers that pervaded the universe could be bound and loosed – such was the logical corollary of the Egyptians' belief in the dynamism of words and spells.[27] Ritual purity was essential to the magician's success, but personal, ethical purity was deemed irrelevant. In the second place, the display of piety was normally a *quid pro quo*. Gods were worshipped while effective, and discarded when not,[28] just as the longevity of the dead Pharaoh's divine honours and funerary cult was a function of his achievements as a ruler rather than of theological dictate or even ecclesiastical custom. Malevolent divinities were honoured just as much as their more favourably disposed colleagues, on the perfectly logical grounds that evil must be averted at all costs. That certain ancient Egyptians entertained what we might choose to regard as more elevated theological conceptions cannot be denied – but their influence never transformed the essential character of Egyptian religion.[29]

In classical Greece, by contrast, the magico-religious world-view was exposed to systematic criticism by the natural philosophers; but one of the more important advances of recent research[30] has been the recognition that these arguments had to await the advent of 'critical' scholarship in the nineteenth century to find their most receptive audience. In antiquity their success was at best patchy. Most would have sympathized with Lucian's Deinomachus when he declared that disbelief in magic was tantamount to atheism.[31] One may of course

---

[26] Sauneron, *S. Or.* 7 (1966) 36–42.

[27] See above, 23, 59, 64; and Zandee, in *Verbum* 33–66, but also the qualification insisted on by Hornung, *Conceptions of God* 210–11.

[28] On 'the limits of divine power and efficacy' see *ibid.* 166–9.

[29] Morenz, *Religion und Geschichte* 77–119, esp. 115–17.

[30] Dodds, *Greeks and the irrational*; Lloyd, *Magic, reason and experience* 10–58, 263–4.

[31] Lucian, *Philops.* 10.

agree with Plotinus's attack on the *naïveté* of the magicians, especially in the general terms in which he expresses it; but that is no excuse for glossing over the full range of the Greek magical papyri. The beauty of magic had always lain in the infinite different possibilities of learning and action that it offered its practitioners. Once a god's favour had been secured, it was up to the individual magician to pursue a limited, easily-definable objective, or to ask, as Solomon had, for some less tangible benefit. And a reading of the Greek magical texts leaves the impression that a few of those who wrote and used them were indeed evolving towards the idea that intimate contact with the gods could be an end in itself. This is to some extent a subjective judgement, and may well not be very widely applicable, especially if, as will be suggested in chapter 7, the principal texts in question derive from a single collection put together in fourth-century Thebes. Nor even in these texts do we have a true 'spiritualization' of magic, since the acquisition of knowledge and power remained the primary goal. But we can at least speak of a revitalization of the old forms, by applying them to less mechanistic, more intimately personal aspirations.[32]

The injection of these more spiritual elements into magic is best exemplified by an important early fourth-century papyrus now in the Paris Bibliothèque Nationale (*P. Graec. Mag.* IV).[33] The papyrus is a miscellany, and offers a rare synoptic view of the potentialities of late antique magic. Beginning (and ending) with the customary accumulation of vulgar spells, it turns at line 475 into something unusual in the magical papyri, a rite for obtaining a divine revelation or oracle by means of a spiritual initiation, a mystery.[34] Like any

---

[32] Cf. (J. Z.) Smith, *Map is not territory* 188–9. (M.) Smith, *Secret gospel* 221–2, errs exemplarily in treating *P. Graec. Mag.* IV.154–222 as betraying 'considerable religious feeling' (by the writer's own standards, of course) because, e.g., the magician claims to have acquired a 'godlike nature'. This is merely another example of the Egyptians' traditional bragging before their gods: above, 26 n. 76.

[33] The section that mainly concerns us here (475–750) is what Dieterich misleadingly dubbed 'eine Mithrasliturgie' in his book of that name. It was perhaps composed at some time in the second century: Dieterich 43–6. Dieterich's commentary usefully discusses the pronounced magical and Egyptian elements in the text, the presence of which is largely taken for granted in what follows.

[34] *P. Graec. Mag.* IV.476, 723, 746 (μυστήριον/-α); 477, 744 (μύστης/-αι); 732–3 (συνμύστης). Cf. Arn. II.62, on 'magi' who claim to have 'commendatory prayers whereby they mollify certain powers and incline them to make easy the way of those who are struggling to fly up to heaven'. Dieterich's attempt (see esp. *Mithrasliturgie* 82–5) to deny the rite's origin in the magical milieu by positing two stages in its textual history (first, a spiritual initiation; and secondly, additions made by a magician who wanted to use the rite for oracular purposes) is founded on the traditional assumption that magic cannot use spiritual vocabulary, and can only anyway be maintained by special pleading. Dieterich found

magical text, this ritual is aimed at anyone who desires the particular end, namely an oracle containing an answer to some specified question, that it is designed to achieve – even to the point of leaving the user to insert his own name, and the subject of his enquiry, at the appropriate points in the rite.[35] At one level, then, we have to do with an impersonal formula conceived in the mechanistic spirit typical of magical procedures.[36] It is, though, a notably ambitious formula: the prologue (475–85), for example, speaks of the rite as having been 'communicated' (μεταδοθῆναι) by the archangel of the great god Helios Mithras 'so that I alone...may ascend into heaven and behold all things'. And although, like most magical texts, the rite in the Paris papyrus is designed to be followed by a lone operative, it also envisages the possible presence of a 'co-initiate', whose worthiness is to be judged by the first operative.[37] Here we have in effect the relationship, well-known from many other late antique religious and philosophical texts, and especially from the Hermetica, of spiritual father with spiritual son. What is more, there are particularly personal and spiritual dimensions to this text which parallel the initiatory elements in the philosophical Hermetica,[38] to be discussed in the next chapter.

The rite, which naturally presupposes a period of asceticism and abstinence,[39] may be summarized as one of ascent, rebirth, vision and communication. After a first *logos* or prayer (485–537), intended to invoke the assistance of God's power in the completion of the rest of the rite, the initiate sees himself being lifted up and ascending into the heights (537–57). Already at this point his vision is beginning, though as yet he sees no more than the heavens, the planets and the rising and setting stars (which are of course gods of a sort). Once the hostile heavenly powers have been neutralized, by making hissing and popping sounds and uttering certain magical incantations

---

it particularly difficult to account for the last section of the initiation, which combines the actual giving of the oracle with mystery-language and references to an ἀπαθανατισμός ('immortalization'), which is a strikingly appropriate name for this part of the text (see below, 84).

[35] *P. Graec. Mag.* IV.717–18.

[36] *Ibid.* 746–8: 'this immortalization can be performed three times a year'.

[37] *Ibid.* 732–46.

[38] The comments of Cumont, *R.I.P.B.* 47 (1904) 6–10, and Festugière 3. 169–74, do not aim to exhaust the subject. Compare e.g. our ritual's assertion that the initiate's soul becomes a star during its progress towards immortalization with *C.H.* x.7: 'Human souls acquire immortality by changing into daemons and then [passing] in this way into the choir of the gods. There are two choirs of gods, that of the wandering [stars] and that of the fixed.'

[39] *P. Graec. Mag.* IV.734–6.

(557–68), the second and third prayers are offered as the vision intensifies (569–620). Just as in Egypt magicians liked to pass themselves off as the gods they were invoking, so here the initiate pronounces himself to be already a star, wandering about with the other heavenly bodies. When he has completed the third prayer, and as he concentrates all his faculties on the unfolding vision of the divine world, he beholds the youthful and beautiful god Helios, whose duty it is to announce the vision of the supreme god Aion (620–57).[40] It seems to be at this point that the crucial process of rebirth begins. It is a noetic experience,[41] rendering the initiate 'immortal'[42] – indeed the whole rite is on this account called an 'immortalization' (ἀπαθανατισμός).[43] In the wake of a sequence of animal-faced divinities of a decidedly Egyptian character, there now occurs the epiphany of the supreme god himself (657–704). This is the moment for the initiate to demand his oracle, even as he hovers on the point of death, so overwhelming is the divine power in whose presence he now stands (704–32). This *apathanatismos* is designed, it is true, only for the temporary purpose of receiving an oracle, ordinary human organs being unable to behold the divine.[44] Yet the notion of immortalization, and the allusion to the initiate's finding himself on the edge of bodily extinction, remind one perforce of the rituals of death and rebirth in which certain of the mystery religions culminated.[45] There too they were part of an evolution towards more spiritual conceptions.

Another Parisian papyrus, *P. Louvre* 2391 (= *P. Graec. Mag.* III), presents a more precise, though still far from unambiguous, link with the philosophical Hermetica. Like most of the larger magical papyri, this is a late antique miscellany. The part that concerns us here is lines 494–611, a formula designed to persuade Helios to do whatever the magician bids. The operative begins by addressing the god in the usual hectoring manner, impressing him with his knowledge of names and attributes. But his tirade ends by merging (583[46]) into a prayer quite different in tone and of markedly

---

[40] *Pace* N.F. 1. 165 n. 58, the initiate sees but does not become Aion: *P. Graec. Mag.* IV.516–21, 594.

[41] *Ibid.* 508–9: ἵνα νοήματι μεταγεν⟨ν⟩ηθῶ.

[42] *Ibid.* 477 (ἀθανασία), 501 (ἀθάνατος γένεσις), 647–8 (με⟨τα⟩γεννηθείς…ἀπαθανατισθείς).

[43] *Ibid.* 741, 747; and cf. previous note.

[44] *Ibid.* 523 (πρὸς ὀλίγον), 746–50; 529–32; and cf. Nilsson, *Geschichte* 2.687: 'Es ist eine zauberische Vergöttlichung, nicht ein Unsterblichkeitsmysterium.'

[45] See esp. Apul., *Met.* XI.23 (the Isiac initiation): 'I approached the border of death'; and Meslin, *R.H.* 252 (1974) 305–7.　　　[46] I follow Reitzenstein, *Poimandres* 156.

liturgical construction, praising God and thanking Him for the gift of divine *gnōsis* vouchsafed to the pious worshipper. This prayer looks as if it has been borrowed from elsewhere and incorporated into its present context regardless of stylistic considerations. That need cause no surprise – magicians were adept with scissors and paste. What is unique about this particular text is that it recurs in one of the philosophical *Hermetica*, as the conclusion of the *Asclepius*. Indeed, we have its Hermetic version both in the expanded Latin of the *Asclepius* and in a much more faithful Coptic translation among the Hermetic texts in Nag Hammadi codex vi (*N.H.C.* vi.7).[47] Since the Coptic version also includes parts of the narrative framework from the *Asclepius*, it must have been extracted (and translated) direct from the *Asclepius*'s Greek original, the *Perfect discourse*. But it cannot be taken for granted that the same is true of the Greek version of the prayer in *P. Louvre* 2391, which lacks the narrative framework. Admittedly our sketchy information about dating poses no obstacle to such a hypothesis. The *Perfect discourse* will have been composed in the second or third century;[48] while all we can say of the relevant section of *P. Louvre* 2391 is that it evolved before the particular miscellany we possess was committed to papyrus in the fourth century. Much more germane, though, to our understanding of the prayer of thanksgiving's history is the fact that the *Perfect discourse*'s central section is translated into Coptic at the end of the same Nag Hammadi codex in which our prayer appears, and separated from it by a scribal note. Although the compiler of *N.H.C.* vi knew that the prayer belonged to the *Perfect discourse*, he decided on his own initiative to append it to *N.H.C.* vi.6. This was but the first step in a process well known in the magical and analogous literature, where prayers and hymns circulated freely and might be re-used many times, losing in the process most of their original associations.[49] It is impossible, then, to be certain that the Greek text of the prayer of thanksgiving preserved in *P. Louvre* 2391 was extracted directly from the *Perfect discourse*. Our magician may have come upon it in some quite different source. In fact, the prayer may not even have

[47] See Mahé 1.160–7 for a parallel edition of all three texts.
[48] Above, 11.
[49] Heitsch, *Philologus* 103 (1959) 216–20, 223–4; Mahé 1.139–41. Compare also a British Museum amulet, of ambiguous character but probably more pagan than Christian, containing part of the hymn at *C.H.* 1.31 (Bonner, *Magical amulets* 181–2), which also reappears in a Christian, perhaps gnostic and semi-liturgical context in the late third-century *P. Berol.* 9794: McNeil, *Numen* 23 (1976) 239–40. The prayer that concludes this hymn (31–2) is strikingly similar to *Ascl.* 41 etc.

been an original composition by the author of the *Perfect discourse,* but a borrowing from elsewhere.[50]

In the end, it is precisely this elusiveness and ambiguity of the magical material that emerges as its most instructive characteristic. Granted that magic exercised a strong influence over the educated levels of Hellenistic and Roman society as well as over the less instructed, it is perverse to assume that any text that does not display a wholly mechanistic view of the relationship between Man and God, but is known to us in a magical context, must have been borrowed by the magician from a more 'respectable' source. *Some* magicians were capable of writing grammatical Greek, quoting Homer[51] and, we must suppose, thinking abstractly; and there is no reason to treat the Paris 'immortalization', for example, as anything other than the speculation of an educationally above-average magician. But the ordinary magician, knowing his limitations, adopted a more empirical approach to his craft. He had to cover all the options, because he could never be certain which precise form of words would compel the gods to do his will. His ignorance made him a natural opportunist, who on the circuitous road to the particular objective he had in mind might pick up some pearl of whose price he had only the faintest intuition. (Indeed, one philosophical Hermetist issued an explicit warning against such marauders.[52]) In the form in which they have come down to us, the magical texts are very late; and they were compiled in an age when what we think of as the distinctive insights of late paganism were already being vulgarized.[53] If in the midst of a magical spell we suddenly come on echoes of the philosophical Hermetica, it is realistic to allow as much credit to chance as to

[50] There is nothing *a priori* falsifiable in Mahé's suggestion, 1.141–6, that the history of the prayer of thanksgiving should be thought of in terms of a common archetype giving rise to various recensions, of which the most influential was that incorporated in the *P.D.* – though we cannot exclude the possibility that the version in the *P.D.* was itself the archetype. But Mahé's arrangement of the lower part of the stemma (146) is highly questionable. While there is nothing to prove that the Greek version in *P. Louvre* 2391 derived from the *P.D.*, the Coptic of *N.H.C.* VI.7, as well as the Latin of the *Ascl.*, definitely did, and directly too (see above, 85). None of the minor linguistic divergences emphasized by Mahé (esp. 1.145) in order to show that the Latin and Greek versions derive from the *P. D.* while the Coptic does not, can seriously undermine this sibling relationship between the Latin and Coptic texts. On possible Hermetic elements in *P. Leid.* I 395 (= *P. Graec. Mag.* XIII) see below, 171–2.

[51] *P. Graec. Mag.* VII *ad init.* ('Ομηρομαντεῖον); *op. cit.* 3.287–8 (index of Homeric citations). Cf. Preisendanz, in *VIII Kong. Pap.* 117 n. 50.

[52] *N.H.C.* VI.6.62.22–7.

[53] Festugière, *Idéal religieux* 281 n. 2, concludes that it is from the third century A.D. onwards that the magical papyri begin to reveal an interest in the spiritual relationship between the operative and the god he invokes.

informed choice. It is a question of the seed having fallen, not perhaps by the wayside, but on stony ground and among thorns.[54]

Occult properties and alchemy

Despite the eclecticism of the magical papyri, though, it is true of *all* Graeco-Roman magic that it concerns itself with the spell, the magical *action*, rather than with the principles that lie behind it. We have already remarked that the technical Hermetica yield no theoretical account of the workings of cosmic sympathy; but we do possess – characteristically of this frontier-land between Aristotelian observational science and popular and magical lore – various treatises that describe and catalogue the occult properties of different substances and organisms, and the uses they can be put to, especially in the medical sphere. This is systematization, not yet theory; but still it represents an advance on the *ad hoc* character of the magical papyri. Bolus of Mendes, writing under the pseudonym 'Democritus', was an early and influential representative of this trend;[55] but our present concern is with those parts of the occult literature that were ascribed to Hermes Trismegistus.

By the Hermetic occult literature we effectively mean the *Cyranides*, which deal in exhaustive detail with the sympathies, antipathies and other occult properties of birds, fishes, plants and stones. In the form in which we have it, the *Cyranides* is a compilation from several earlier treatises, mostly Hermetic.[56] But one of them goes under the name of Harpocration of Alexandria, who must have flourished about the middle of the second century A.D.,[57] and is quoted in the prologue

[54] Betz's proposition, *H.R.* 21 (1981–2) 156–71, that formulae in the magical papyri for compelling one's personal daemon (ἴδιος δαίμων) (or by extension some other divine being) to give oracles were an *interpretatio magica* of the philosophical maxim 'Know yourself' is excessively ingenious. Magicians had no need of philosophers to tell them that it was possible to identify oneself with and constrain the gods – least of all in Egypt. And anyway the maxim was exactly that – one did not need to be a philosopher to have heard it.

[55] Festugière 1.197–200.

[56] Festugière 1.201–16.

[57] The *terminus ante quem* is provided by Tert., *Cor.* VII.5, who quotes Harpocration. (*Pace* Boudreaux, *C.C.A.G.* 8 (3).133, Harpocration's visit to Seleucia on the Tigris (*Cyr.* 15–16) may conceivably have taken place after its capture by Lucius Verus in 165, since the city was not totally destroyed: McDowell, *Seleucia* 234–6.) And a *terminus post quem* can be deduced from *Cyr.* 1, which is a conflation of Harpocration's treatise with the Hermetic *Cyranis*, and contains various verse passages (*Cyr.* 28–9, 42–3, 50–2, 58–9, 96–7) with acrostics reading ΜΑΓΝΟΥ or ΜΑΓΝΟΣ ΜΑΡΚΕΛΛΙΝΩ. These acrostics were first pointed out to me by D. R. Jordan, and have since been published by West, *C.Q.* 32 (1982) 480–1, and Führer, *Z.P.E.* 58 (1985) 270. That the verse passages were derived, by the compiler

of the *Cyranides* as describing an inscription, 'carved in Syrian characters', which he saw and had translated for him at Alexandria in Babylon.[58] The inscription contains the following address to the soul:

O immortal soul, clothed in a mortal body, you are borne from on high by the evil bonds of Necessity, for God Himself declared that you would rule over mortal bodies and bear with the sinful, being the yarn spun by the Fates and Necessity. For like a man who is imprisoned and in bondage, so you too are held by the harsh bonds of Necessity. But when you escape from the mortal and oppressive body, you will truly behold God ruling in the air and the clouds, He who eternally brings upon the earth thunder and earthquakes, lightning and thunder-bolts, and moves the foundations of the earth and the waves of the sea. Such will be the eternal works of God the mother of all things. God has made known to mortals all things, and their opposites.[59]

Here is announced the grand theme of late Greek philosophy: the ensnarement of the soul in the bonds of fate, its liberation, and its return to its creator. Similar preoccupations can also be traced in those parts of the first book of the *Cyranides* which are derived from Harpocration. Here is the most explicit example:

A question to the master: 'Tell me first of all: is the soul immortal or mortal?' And he said: 'My child, listen. Many of the inexperienced have false opinions as to the intellectual aspect of the immortal soul. But the soul is its own master; for when the body is at rest on its bed, the soul is reposing in its own place (in the air, that is to say), whence we received it; and it contemplates what is happening in other regions. And often, feeling affection for the body in which it dwells, it foretells good or ill years before it comes to pass – in what we call a dream. Then it returns to

of the *Cyr.* as we know it, from the treatise of Harpocration is clearly stated (28.127–9; 54.86–7 (proving that the whole of 49–54.85 is by Harpocration); 98.93); but their original author was one Magnus, whose work Harpocration later incorporated into his own mainly prose composition. Since our *terminus ante quem* for Harpocration excludes West's suggestion that Magnus and Marcellinus be assigned to the fourth century, it is worth considering the claim of the two doctors whose portraits twice occur together in Bologna University Library MS. 3632 (saec. xv), fol. 17–26 (where they are entitled μάγνος – μαρκελῆνος), 213 (ὁ μάγνος σωφηστῆς – ὁ μαρκελῆνος): Olivieri and Festa, *S.I.F.C.* 3 (1895) 454. These must be Magnus of Ephesus (Kroll, *R.E.* 14.494, no. 28; Kudlien, *R.E.* Supp. 11.1098) and the Marcellinus who shared with him an interest in the pulse (Kroll, *R.E.* 14.1488–9, no. 51). Both were members of the Pneumatist school, and seem to have lived *c.* A.D. 100.

[58] *Cyr.* 14, 16–18. Quotations are from the Greek text, though there is a Latin translation dated 1169, a century earlier than the oldest Greek manuscript (see the introduction to Delatte's edition).

[59] *Cyr.* 18. The manuscripts' prose is a mangled version of what were originally verses; but there is no acrostic, so we may have to do with a composition by Harpocration himself, not Magnus. With θεὸς παμμήτωρ compare e.g. *C.H.* 1.9 (ὁ δὲ Νοῦς ὁ θεός, ἀρρενόθηλυς ὤν...); *P. Graec. Mag.* III.603 (= *Ascl.* 41) on God as μήτρα πάσης γνώσεως (Mahé 1.165 emends ⟨φυ⟩σεως); and the references collected by Mahé, *N.H.S.* 7 (1975) 131–3. The coyer Western mind consistently expurgates: the Latin version of the *Cyr.* has 'haec sunt opera Dei Patris aeterni' (18.8), and the *Ascl.* substitutes 'fecunda praegnatio' for the over-concrete μήτρα.

its own habitation and, waking it [the body] up, explains the dream. From this let it be clear to you that the soul is immortal and indestructible. This then is what Harpocration said...[60]

Such passages are less irrelevant to the mundane subject-matter of Harpocration's treatise than appears at first sight, since an interest in the return of the soul to its divine source was the ultimate extension of the study of natural sympathies. And anyway both the *Cyranides* and Harpocration's treatise are composites,[61] whose many facets reflect a long evolution of thought and practice. For all that the literature on occult powers is more systematic than the magical texts, its original intention, in common with most of the technical Hermetica, was to describe techniques rather than to reflect on their theoretical implications; but with the passing of time alterations and additions were made *ad libitum* in accordance with changing fashions and preoccupations. Hence the impossibility, already alluded to, of assigning a single date to many of these texts – and the clumsiness of such categories as 'technical', 'philosophical' and 'spiritual', which reflect a schematic way of thinking quite alien to that of the Hermetists. This particular problem is encapsulated, in an acute form, in the alchemical literature that circulated under the name of Hermes.

Alchemy was the art by which base metals were supposed to be transmuted into silver and gold.[62] But while the alchemist's practical techniques were rooted in the banausic skills of the jeweller, the glass-maker and such like, his theoretical pretensions touched ultimately on the human soul in its relationship to God. An interest in imitating the appearance and colour of precious metals evolved gradually into a habit of thinking of metals as composed of a lifeless physical base, or 'body', and an invigorating principle, or 'soul', which imparted character and distinctiveness to the physical base. The physical base was the same for all metals; but the 'soul' was present in varying degrees of purity – hence the different characteristics of each metal, and the belief that it was possible to transmute base metals into gold by manipulating the 'soul'. But the same distinction between the body and soul of metals stimulated in some alchemists another, more analogical line of thought, which used alchemical imagery in order to describe the purification of the human

---

[60] *Cyr.* 54 (reading θεωρεῖ in line 81). Compare also 50.   [61] Above, 87, esp. n. 57.
[62] On the following see Gundel, *R.L.A.C.* 1.239–60; Forbes, *Ancient technology* 1.125–48; Festugière, *Hermétisme* 233–40.

soul and its ascent to its divine source, so that a physical process became a generative symbol of a spiritual experience. The alchemists themselves were 'philosophers',[63] and the aim of their 'philosophy' or 'divine art' was 'the dissolution of the body and the separation of the soul from the body'.[64]

Some, it is true, were over-literal in this alchemization of the spiritual life. In the Pseudo-Democritean *Physica et mystica* we find an attack on 'those who, on an unconsidered and irrational impulse, want to prepare a remedy for the soul and a release from all suffering, and do not think of the harm they will come to';[65] and earlier in the same text we read that the Persian sage Ostanes 'died intestate, according to some, having used poison to release the soul from the body'.[66] But though the idea of using poison to purify the soul may seem comical, the conclusion that some alchemists seriously thought of spiritual experience in these terms seems inescapable. Plotinus's attack on the idea that suicide is a short cut to spiritual perfection suggests that it had been broached among his pupils;[67] and we have to accept that 'Ostanes' and those who thought like him may well have been pursuing genuine spiritual goals in good faith. It would be foolish, then, to dismiss as meaningless the vocabulary of mystery and revelation deployed in such alchemical treatises as the *Dialogue of the philosophers and Cleopatra*,[68] the *True book of Sophe the Egyptian*,[69] or the Hermetic dialogue *Isis the prophetess to her son Horus*.[70] But one may be forgiven some caution as regards the profundity of the religious experience that lies behind the bare words. It is noticeable too that, although alchemy was a creation of the Hellenistic and Roman mind, and most of the surviving alchemical literature is late,[71] none the less neither the Hermetic nor any of the other treatises show much sign of the personal religious feeling that is so characteristic of the period. It is only with Zosimus of Panopolis, at the turn of the

---

[63] Note also the tendency to attribute the origins of alchemy, and the authorship of alchemical treatises, to well-known philosophers: e.g. *Alch. gr.* 25–6, 425; and cf. below, 178.

[64] *Alch. gr.* 136.10–11 (Stephanus: seventh century).

[65] *Ibid.* 47.12–14.

[66] *Ibid.* 43.5–6 = Bidez and Cumont, *Mages* 2.317. There is a reminiscence here of Plato, *Phd.* 64c, a discussion about the definition of death; but the alchemical context suggests that Ostanes did not simply commit suicide, but was attempting to separate soul from body for a specifically spiritual purpose. (Cf. also below, 121–2, on Zosimus of Panopolis.)

[67] Plot. 1.9, esp. 14–15; and cf. Olymp., *In Phd.* 1.1–9, 111.11, arguing that suicide may be justifiable if beneficial to the soul.

[68] Ed. Reitzenstein, *N.G.G.* (1919) 14–20; cf. Festugière, *Hermétisme* 241–6.

[69] *Alch. gr.* 213–14; cf. Festugière 1.261–2.

[70] *Alch. gr.* 28–35; cf. Festugière 1.253–6.   [71] Above, 3.

fourth century, that alchemy comes fully of age in this sense; and Zosimus's spirituality is so clearly the product of his contact with the philosophical Hermetica that we must postpone our discussion of him until a later point in this study.

Astrology

It will be recalled that the elder Pliny, in the passage quoted a little earlier, spoke of magic embracing in its universal dominion not just religion, but medicine and astrology too; and it is to astrology (with which, as already mentioned,[72] various therapeutic techniques were closely associated) that we must now turn. Astrology, as befitted its prominent place in the Hellenistic and Roman world-view, generated an extensive Hermetic literature; and its doctrines, relevant as they were to all aspects of human experience, exercised a pervasive influence on the philosophical as well as the technical Hermetica.[73]

Something was said at the beginning of the present chapter about the crucial role played by the stars in the dissemination of divine 'energies' through the universe, and in the related workings of cosmic sympathy and fate. This complex of beliefs – and, by extension, their religious dimension to be discussed here – was a characteristic product of the Hellenistic and Roman periods; for while such general notions as cosmic sympathy, fate, and even the influence of stars on human affairs can be traced in ancient Egypt and classical Greece,[74] the fundamental presupposition of astrology – namely belief in a direct and calculable connection between planetary movements and human actions – first emerged in the aftermath of Alexander's conquests, through a fusion of Greek with Egyptian and Babylonian ideas effected principally by the Stoics.[75] The mechanistic character of this doctrine, with its vision of Man as the helpless victim of ineluctable forces, seems inimical to the religious spirit, at least in the individualistic sense in which the modern Western mind understands

---

[72] Above, 2.

[73] On astrology and the philosophical Hermetica see below, 100, 119. On the astrological element in the magical Hermetica see Gundel 23–4; and in magic generally, id., *Weltbild*. On astrology and alchemy (including the Hermetic texts), see id., *R.L.A.C.* 1.256–7.

[74] Sympathy: above, 76–7. Fate: Gundel, *R.E.* 7.2626–7. Astral influences: Kákosy, *Oikumene* 3 (1982) 163–91.

[75] For a recent relatively cautious view of the Stoics' involvement with astrology see Long, in *Science and speculation* 165–92.

such things. By their very nature, astrological prognostications tended to induce gloom, or at least a sense of impotence; and there was often a temptation to dismiss the whole subject with a strong dose of Lucianic irony.[76] Yet the astrologers saw themselves as men of religion, and clothed their teachings in the language of sacred cult. It is important to gain some understanding of the reasons for the wide appeal of astral religion in late antiquity.

There is a sense in which even the simple, untutored contemplation of the heavens can be a religious act. The glittering, star-strewn Mediterranean skies confront and bewitch those who dwell beneath them, and often enough provoke in the sensitive soul the first stirrings of a truly spiritual religion. The emperor Julian, addressing a hymn to the Sun, recalled how

from my childhood I was consumed by a passionate longing for the rays of the god, and my mind was utterly absorbed from my tenderest years in his ethereal light. Not only did I desire to gaze intently upon it, but if I ever happened to find myself out of doors during a cloudless clear night, I would leave everything else aside and devote all my attention to the beauties of the heavens, oblivious both of what anyone might say to me and of what I myself was doing. I gave the impression of being seized by excessive curiosity for these things, and I was already taken for an astrologer when the down was still scarcely on my chin ... And that the celestial light utterly dazzled me, exciting me and stimulating me to contemplate it – to the point that, having as yet read no special treatise on the subject, I had by myself discovered that the motion of the moon is the opposite of that of the universe – let what I have already said attest.[77]

Likewise the Hermetist describes the heavens before our world came into being:

The ordering of the heavenly bodies is superior to that of our world below. It is immovable for all time, and transcends human understanding. And so the lower world was seized with fear and sighed before the extraordinary beauty and eternal stability of the things above. For it was truly a worthy object of contemplation and of mental struggle, to see the beauty of the heavens presenting a reflection of the God as yet unknown, and the sumptuous majesty of the night, adorned with a clear light, though one less than that of the sun; while the other mysteries moved severally amidst the heavens according to fixed movements and periods of time, ordering and nourishing the lower realm through certain secret effluences.[78]

It was natural, then, for men to persuade themselves that the luminous beings hovering in the night sky were powerful beyond their

---

[76] See e.g. Apul., *Met.* xi.15, on *Fortuna* as *caeca* and *nefaria*; and Lucian, *J. Conf.*

[77] Jul., *or.* xi.130c–131b; and cf. Plot. ii.9.16.48–56.

[78] *S.H.* xxiii.2–3. (The sudden change of tense after the first sentence is important evidence for the obscure textual history of the *Korē kosmou*.) Cf. *ibid.* 5, 68; *C.H.* v.3–4, x.25.

apparent sphere, and that they were the source of the 'energies' that were thought to operate constantly on all bodies, whether immortal or mortal, animate or inanimate. Some astrologers were consequently predisposed towards the belief that Man's highest aspiration in this life, if he happens to be endowed with a kingly soul, is to contemplate the stars and commune with them, separated for a time from his bodily envelope:

> I know that I was mortal born, creature of but a day.
> But when the revolving spirals of the stars in mind I trace,
> My feet touch earth no more – I feast with Zeus,
> Filled with ambrosia, nourished as the gods themselves.[79]

Those who thought in this way were little inclined to reflect on what lay beyond death, for which the dominion of fate absolved them of all responsibility;[80] and they rejected prayer and sacrifice to the gods, since the notion that by these means one might improve one's lot in the after-life was to them a vanity.[81] The astrologer might foretell the future, but he could in no way influence it.

We may doubt, though, whether the number of those who adhered to this sort of strict determinism was very large. It was a highly controversial doctrine even in the narrow circle of philosophers who occupied themselves professionally with such matters;[82] and in practice its exponents tended to allow some margin for free will,[83] and even for religious cult, or at least its vocabulary.[84] As for the average man, even if he paid lip-service to the doctrine of fate, and believed in the astrologer's ability to foretell future events, he felt it unwise to neglect the more conventional cult of the gods.[85] The magical papyri largely ignore fate, even though their few references to it show that their compilers were well aware of its inexorable force. By contrast, magicians made frequent use of the concept of necessity (ἀνάγκη), which they often conveniently envisaged, not as a hostile power at all, but as an ally in their attempts to compel the gods to do their will.[86]

---

[79] For this epigram, attributed to Ptolemy, see Boll, *Sternkunde* 143–55; and cf. in general Cumont, *Egypte* 26–7, and *Die orientalischen Religionen* 162–3. These ideas were said to have been present already in the supposedly Hermetist writings of Petosiris and Nechepso (Reitzenstein, *Poimandres* 4–7; Gundel 29–34), and are particularly conspicuous in Vettius Valens, on whom see Festugière, *Idéal religieux* 120–7.

[80] Gundel, *R.E.* 7.2632–3, to which add *Lib. Herm. Tris.* 28.1–6.

[81] Cumont, *Egypte* 205 n. 2.   [82] Schröder, *R.L.A.C.* 7.546–62.

[83] *Ibid.* 532–46, esp. 540–1.   [84] E.g. Firm. Mat., *Math.* 1.6.1–2.

[85] Cumont, *Die orientalischen Religionen* 165–6, esp. n. 69.

[86] Gundel, *Weltbild* 70–4. Even the Paris 'immortalization' makes no reference to fate, but only to necessity (*P. Graec. Mag.* IV.606).

But it would be wrong to suggest that those who did believe firmly in the universal power of fate (whether diluted or not by an admixture of free will) never aspired to be freed from it. The austerity of the doctrine of fate, calmly accepted and thus in a sense overcome by the Stoics,[87] gave rise in others to a strong religious impulse, and to the belief that the more powerful gods – Sarapis and Isis for example – might abrogate the decrees of destiny[88] – perhaps one of the main reasons for the appeal of the Egyptian gods in the Graeco-Roman world.[89] This was certainly thought to be true of Hermes;[90] and it need not surprise us to find that the priest Petosiris, whose doctrine was considered to be authentically Hermetic, was believed to have been able himself to exercise some control over the workings of necessity.[91] Such ideas, though, are the exception rather than the rule in the astrological literature, implying as they do the evolution of the astrologer, whose primary interest is in the working of the stars, into the adept of some divinely revealed 'way' by which the soul can be purified, and freed from the bonds of matter. This sort of religious 'mystery' might be primarily cultic, such as the mysteries of Isis, or it might be more philosophical in manner. A number of the philosophical Hermetica fall into this latter category; and it is to the corpus of philosophical Hermetica in general that we must now turn.

[87] This idea is well expressed by Heliod. Em. II.24.6–7.
[88] See e.g. *P. Graec. Mag.* XIII.613–14, 633–5, 708–14; Apul., *Met.* XI.15 (and cf. Griffiths, *Isis-Book* 241–4); Zos. Pan., *fr. gr.* 229–30 (quoting Zoroaster); and Müller, *Isis-Aretalogien* 79–85, on the Egyptian as well as Greek background of this idea.
[89] Cf. Morenz, *Ägyptische Religion* 78.
[90] Above, 25.
[91] Proc., *In Remp.* 2.344–5; and see above, 2. Firm. Mat., *Math.* 1.6.2, asserts that we should worship the gods so that, 'reassured of the divinity of our own minds', we may resist the power of the stars.

[4]

Religio mentis[1]

The spiritual and religious dimension of Hermetism, which is no more than incidental to the majority of the technical treatises, becomes prominent (though not monopolistic) in the philosophical writings. Some scholars have gone so far as to speak of 'theological' rather than 'philosophical' Hermetica, and not unjustifiably, since many ancient sources too call Hermes a theologian.[2] But these texts, like their technical cousins, cover an extensive range of themes and approaches, which is better described as philosophical, in the wider sense of the word employed by the ancients, than as theological – especially since there apparently was a Hermetic genre devoted specifically to the description of the traditional gods.[3] Indeed, the variety of the philosophical Hermetica is so great as to impose on the student a basic methodological decision. Does one start from their differences or from what they have in common? Reacting against J. Kroll's attempt in his book *Die Lehren des Hermes Trismegistos* (1914) to construct a single Hermetic synthesis, most scholars this century have preferred to isolate groups of conceptually similar treatises and make out of them divergent streams united little more than nominally under the label 'Hermetism'.[4] This approach, which goes hand-in-hand with a tendency to regard Hermetism as a 'Sammelbecken' for heterogeneous older doctrines, without an independent identity of its own, is understandable granted the philosophical preoccupations of most

---

[1] *Ascl.* 25.

[2] Porph., *Abst.* II.47.1, associating 'the theologians' with 'the Egyptian' (= Hermes Trismegistus: Festugière, *Etudes d'histoire* 143–4); Greg. Naz., *or.* XXVIII.4 (and cf. Pépin, *V. Chr.* 36 (1982) 251–60); Amm. Marc. XVI.5.5, associating the 'teaching of the theologians' with Mercury; Ioh. Lyd., *Mens.* IV.53, 64, recording various teachings of the 'theologian' Hermes concerning the gods (cf. N.F. 4.145); and various later Byzantine writers enumerated by Pépin, *art. cit.* Also *C.H.* XVII *ad fin.*: τῇ δὲ ἐπιούσῃ περὶ τῶν ἑξῆς θεολογήσομεν.

[3] See below, 138–9.

[4] The literature is succinctly surveyed by Tröger, *Mysterienglaube* 4–6. Bousset's important review of Kroll is reprinted, in expanded form, in his *Religionsgeschichtliche Studien* 97–191.

95

Hermetic scholars, and can even be made to seem historical by reference to the evident fact that not all the texts were written at the same time or place or by the same person. One might compare the remarks of a recent student of the Orphic poems, writing, he tells us, under the 'clear old sceptical gaze' of Wilamowitz:

It is a fallacy to suppose that all 'Orphic' poems and rituals are related to each other or that they are to be interpreted as different manifestations of a single religious movement. Of course, in some cases there are connections between different poems, between separate rituals, or between certain poems and certain rituals. But the essential principle to remember is that a poem becomes Orphic simply by being ascribed to Orpheus. By the same token, Orphics are simply people who in their religious beliefs or practices, whatever these may be, accord a place of honour to texts ascribed to Orpheus. There was no doctrinal criterion for ascription to Orpheus, and no copyright restriction. It was a device for conferring antiquity and authority upon a text that stood in need of them.[5]

It is, admittedly, easier to believe a little than a lot; but one need not stray outside the bounds of Anglo-Saxon common sense to see that repeated ascription of texts to such figures as Orpheus or Hermes had a cumulative effect. As M. Foucault put it:

Hermes Trismegistus did not exist, nor did Hippocrates – in the sense that Balzac existed – but the fact that several texts have been placed under the same name indicates that there has been established among them a relationship of homogeneity, filiation, authentification of some texts by the use of others, reciprocal explication, or concomitant utilization. The author's name serves to characterize a certain mode of being of discourse: the fact that the discourse has an author's name, that one can say 'this was written by so-and-so' or 'so-and-so is its author', shows that this discourse is not ordinary everyday speech that merely comes and goes, not something that is immediately consumable. On the contrary, it is a speech that must be received in a certain mode and that, in a given culture, must receive a certain status.[6]

Not that the discovery that Hermetism is an autonomous mode of discourse had to await the twentieth century. One has only to recall that the philosophical texts were gathered together into collections from an early date; and that Iamblichus spoke with admirable concision of the 'way of Hermes'.[7] Our most interesting evidence, though, is internal to the treatises themselves. It has not hitherto been taken seriously by scholars in this field, perhaps because it compels a view of the Hermetic tradition strikingly different from their own.

[5] West, *Orphic poems* 3, and cf. 262–3, but also the implicity less reductive observations at 39.

[6] Foucault, in *Textual strategies* 147.

[7] Iam., *Myst.* VIII.4–5.

The *philosophical* paideia

The philosophical Hermetica, for all the vicissitudes of their transmission to us, are not just so many disembodied statements of doctrine. They reveal quite a lot both about their relationship to each other and to Hermetica now lost, and about the way in which the Hermetists understood the *raison d'être* and function of their writings and of the spiritual and intellectual values that those writings enshrine. Their dialogue form emphasizes their primarily didactic intention; and even a superficial reading quickly reveals that different texts are aimed at readers or auditors at differing levels of enlightenment. As one might expect, statements about the general direction and form of the 'way of Hermes' are more explicit in those texts aimed at a relatively experienced and sophisticated audience; and it is in particular from initiatory texts such as *C.H.* i (*Poimandrēs*), *C.H.* xiii and *N.H.C.* vi.6 (*The Ogdoad reveals the Ennead*)[8] that we can construct a general picture of the different 'steps' (βαθμοί)[9] of the Hermetic *paideia*, before we go on to look at its constituent parts.

Towards the end of *The Ogdoad reveals the Ennead* Hermes bids Tat write the whole dialogue down 'in hieroglyphic characters on stelae of turquoise for the temple at Diospolis'; and he continues in these words:

Write an oath in the book, lest those who read the book bring the language into abuse, or oppose the acts of fate. Rather, they should submit to the law of God, without having transgressed at all, but in purity asking God for wisdom and knowledge. And he who will not be begotten at the start by God – that happens in the general and *exōdiakoi* discourses – will not be able to read [or: proclaim] the things written in this book, although his conscience is pure within him, since he does not do anything shameful [and] which is not in agreement with it [sc. the book]. Rather, by stages he advances and enters into the way of immortality. And thus he enters into the understanding of the Ogdoad that reveals the Ennead.[10]

Here we have a sketch-map for the aspiring traveller along the way of Hermes. Its obscurities are lessened if we compare it with the opening passage of *C.H.* xiii, the dialogue *On rebirth*:

In the *General* (*discourses*), O father, you spoke about the divine nature enigmatically and without shedding much light. You did not give a revelation, saying that nobody

---

[8] For comparisons of these treatises see Keizer, *Eighth reveals the Ninth* 135–41, 169–79; Mahé, *R.S.R.* 48 (1974) 54–65; Mahé 1.38–47. In the following discussion of Hermetic concepts of knowledge I am much indebted to the lucid exposition by Dodd, *Fourth gospel* 10–30; cf. also Keizer, *Eighth reveals the Ninth* 180–96.

[9] *C.H.* xiii.9; *N.H.C.* vi.6.52.12–13, 54.27–8, 63.9; and cf. *S.H.* xxiii.7: Hermes did not teach the whole of his doctrine to Tat because of the latter's youth.

[10] *N.H.C.* vi.6.62.22–63.14 (tr. Dirkse, Brashler, Parrott, with adjustments); cf. Bellet, *Enchoria* 9 (1979) 1–3.

can be saved before rebirth. And when, as we were coming out of the desert,[11] after you had spoken with me, I became your suppliant and asked you about the doctrine of rebirth so that I might learn – since it is the only part of all [the teaching] that I do not know –, you said that you intend to convey it to me 'when you are ready to become a stranger to the world'. And now I am prepared. I have fortified my spirit against the deceit of the world. So, for your part, make up for my shortcomings in the way you said when you proposed to convey to me the process of rebirth, either by word of mouth or in some secret way. O Trismegistus, I do not know from what womb Man was born, and of what seed.

Central to both passages is the proposition that the divine vision is granted only to those who are reborn – and rebirth can be brought about only by divine action, as *C.H.* xiii goes on to explain at length. But before the initiate can be reborn he must acquire wisdom and virtue; and these preparatory stages of the Hermetic *paideia* are set out, according to the Coptic treatise, 'in the general and *exōdiakoi* discourses'. The importance of the *General discourses* is illustrated by the frequency of allusions to them in the surviving philosophical Hermetica.[12] And presumably it is they that Hermes has in mind when he remarks to Tat, at the beginning of *The Ogdoad reveals the Ennead*: 'It is right [for you] to remember the progress that came to you as wisdom in the books.'[13] Apparently, then, this stage in the Hermetic *paideia* might take the form of private study; but the scenario of *C.H.* xiii, in which the *General discourses* are treated as courses of instruction recently delivered in person by Hermes to Tat, perhaps better reflects usual practice. Certainly the journey could be completed only under the guidance of a spiritual master.

The preparatory character of the *General discourses* is apparent from their name and put beyond doubt by Tat's remark in *C.H.* xiii that they treat of the divine realm 'enigmatically and without shedding much light'. We know that some of them dealt with astronomical and astrological doctrine;[14] and it may be that they should be identified with the 'physica exoticaque' addressed by Hermes to Tat and attested in the *Asclepius*.[15] Their purpose was to provide a general grounding in the Hermetic world-view; and since they were presumably the most numerous and commonly read of the philosophical Hermetica, it seems improbable that they can all have perished. In fact *C.H.* x, suggestively entitled *The key*, states that it

---

[11] See above, 40 n. 156.

[12] *C.H.* x.1, 7; xiii.1; *S.H.* iii.1, vi.1; and Vienna fr. B.6 (ed. Mahé, in *Mémorial Festugière* 54).

[13] *N.H.C.* vi.6.54.6–9, 14–16. Mahé 1.42–3, 95–6, points out that there is perhaps a deliberate ambiguity here, as the Coptic might equally well signify either 'book' or 'generation'.

[14] *S.H.* vi.1. [15] *Ascl.* 1.

is an epitome of them; and certainly it provides a wide-ranging conspectus of Hermetic doctrine on the three spheres of being, God, the World and Man, and on the fall of the soul and its longing to return to its source. Indeed, most of the surviving philosophical Hermetica, other than the specifically initiatory treatises, would fit quite happily under the heading *General discourses*. As for the *exōdiakoi* discourses, their contents remain obscure. Perhaps they were the same as the *diexodikoi logoi* of Hermes to Tat referred to by Cyril of Alexandria[16] – *Detailed discourses* complementing the *General discourses*. What is certain is that they were preliminary to the initiation itself.

But even the initiatory discourses, while dwelling on the culminating 'steps' of the Hermetic way, do not lose sight of the fact that they will serve as guides or manuals for other aspirants to the divine vision. That is why in *The Ogdoad reveals the Ennead* Hermes bids Tat inscribe their discourse on stelae of turquoise; and the same idea is present in *C.H.* I and XIII.[17] *C.H.* I, the *Poimandrēs*, illustrates particularly well the higher levels of Hermetic instruction. To a Hermes cast exceptionally as pupil the secrets of the origin of the World and of Man, and of the soul's destiny, are revealed by Poimandres, who is no less than divine intellect (νοῦς) itself. The whole dialogue is pitched at an unusually exalted level, and the instruction is conveyed with the aid of visions. *C.H.* I is also unusual in that it treats the vision of God as something of which one may have knowledge before but experience only after the soul has been finally separated from the body by death, whereas the Hermetica more commonly maintain that contemplation of the divine realm is possible even for those who are still attached to the body's mortal envelope.[18] But, for all that, the Hermetist who picked the *Poimandrēs* up and read it will have had no difficulty understanding it, not just as a mythical statement, but simultaneously as a paradigm for his own spiritual quest.[19]

That aspiring Hermetic initiates were expected to proceed systematically from elementary to more sophisticated texts, just as the Platonist philosophers of the age graded Plato's dialogues, for teaching purposes, according to their greater or lesser explicitness about the things of the spirit,[20] is confirmed precisely by those

---

[16] Cyr. Al., *Jul.* 1.553a, II.588b; cf. L.S.J. *s.v.* ἐξοδικός.
[17] *C.H.* 1.30, XIII.13.   [18] Below, 109–10.
[19] Festugière 4.204–5 makes a similar point with regard to *C.H.* XIII.
[20] E.g. *Prol. phil. Plat.* 26. Plato himself had insisted on the purificatory as well as practical function of the study of mathematics, geometry etc.: *Resp.* 524d–527b; and cf. Plot. 1.3.

variations of manner and doctrine between the texts themselves that are so often adduced as evidence of the incoherence of Hermetism. *S.H.* vi is a good example of the sort of text that a neophyte would have been given to read at a relatively early stage. Tat asks Hermes to keep his promise, made 'in the preceding *General discourses*', to explain the doctrine of the thirty-six decans. This Hermes then does, in some technical detail, though he can hardly be said to live up to his promise that this will be 'the chiefest and most eminent discourse of all'. He is more realistic at the end, when he speaks of knowledge of the stars as an essential *preliminary* to knowledge of God, and part of the 'preparatory exercise' (προγύμνασμα) that the soul must perform in this world, so that when it reaches the point where it may contemplate the divine realm it will not lose its way.[21] To end on a note of piety and praise of God is a characteristic Hermetic trait, a significant and economic device for indicating the wider religious context of the necessarily limited information conveyed by an elementary text such as *S.H.* vi. *All* knowledge leads to God – and this particular treatise illustrates the special significance of astrological beliefs in the overall 'way of Hermes'.

C.H. ix, superficially similar in structure and manner to *S.H.* vi, in fact prepares the transition to a subtler level of instruction. Like *S.H.* vi, this treatise specifically presents itself as part of a didactic sequence:

Yesterday, O Asclepius [Hermes begins], I expounded the *Perfect discourse*.[22] Now I think it necessary, in succession to that discourse, to discuss the doctrine of sensation.

What follows is a decidedly technical philosophical discussion emphasizing the indissociability of sensation (αἴσθησις) from intellection (νόησις), as touching in turn Man, the World and God. But the treatise concludes by indicating, somewhat gnomically, what the next stage of instruction will reveal. Neither reason in general, nor specifically the Hermetic discourse – the word *logos* may of course mean either – can of itself bring one to the truth. The *logos* guides the intellect 'as far as a certain point'; but thenceforth the intellect must proceed on its own, with nothing but reminiscence of the teachings it has received in the sphere of reason to compare its

---

[21] Compare also *C.H.* ii (a treatise on movement, place and the nature of God), which describes itself (17) as 'preliminary knowledge of the nature of all things'; and *C.H.* xi, esp. 22.   [22] See above, 11 n. 53.

experiences with. In this manner the intellect may eventually attain to faith (πίστις) – 'for to have understood is to have believed (τὸ γὰρ νοῆσαί ἐστι τὸ πιστεῦσαι), and not to have understood is not to have believed'. One could hardly wish for a more concise statement of the ancients' conviction that human and divine knowledge, reason and intuition, are interdependent – a view which continued to prevail in Islam, particularly in Shiite and Sufi circles, but which the Western intellectual tradition has often rejected, decomposing knowledge into independent categories, separating philosophy from theology, and in so doing setting up serious obstacles to the understanding of more unified world-views.

More will be said shortly of the higher levels of understanding (νόησις) according to the doctrines of the Hermetists. But here is the place to mention a useful distinction made elsewhere in these texts between two types of knowledge, *epistēmē* ('science') and *gnōsis*, which are the products respectively of reason (λόγος) and of understanding[23] with faith, as stated at the end of *C.H.* ix. As *C.H.* x.9 puts it: '*gnōsis* is the goal of *epistēmē*'—a particularly neat formulation of the cognitive transition that the 'way of Hermes' was designed to bring about. The meaning of this statement – namely that knowledge of God's creation is an essential preliminary to knowledge of God himself – emerges best from one of the Stobaean fragments:

Without philosophy it is impossible to be perfectly pious. He who learns of what nature things are, and how they are ordered, and by whom, and to what end, will be thankful for all things to the Creator, as to a good father, a kindly fosterer and a faithful guardian. He who is thankful will be a pious man, and the pious man will know where and what truth is and, through this knowledge, will become still more pious.[24]

Here the emphasis is mainly on philosophy as *epistēmē*; while the *Perfect discourse* (*Asclepius*) makes the same point, but from the perspective of philososphy as *gnōsis*:

Pure philosophy, that which depends only on piety towards God, should pay no more attention to the other [sciences] than is required in order to admire how the return of the stars to their first position, their predetermined stations and the course of their revolutions obey mathematical laws; and in order, by knowledge of the dimensions, qualities and quantities of the earth, the depths of the sea, the power of fire, and the effect and nature of all these things, to admire, adore and praise the art and

---

[23] Cf. *C.H.* I.3: μαθεῖν θέλω τὰ ὄντα καὶ νοῆσαι τὴν τούτων φύσιν καὶ γνῶναι τὸν θεόν; and *C.H.* IV.4: ὅσοι μὲν οὖν...ἐβαπτίσαντο τοῦ νοός, οὗτοι μετέσχον τῆς γνώσεως καὶ τέλειοι ἐγένοντο ἄνθρωποι, τὸν νοῦν δεξάμενοι. But note that at *N.H.C.* VI.8.66.5–13, *epistēmē* is said both to issue from, and to be identical with, *gnōsis*. [24] *S.H.* IIB.2–3.

mind of God. And to be instructed in music is precisely to know how all this system of things is ordered, and what divine plan has distributed it. For this order, having brought all individual things into unity by creative reason, will produce as it were a most sweet and true harmony, and a divine melody.[25]

In the light of these distinctions between different types of knowledge, it is worth returning briefly to the problem raised earlier about the significance of doctrinal divergences within Hermetism. It hardly needs spelling out that anyone who accepted the basic Hermetic teachings about the three spheres of being, God, the World and Man,[26] and their unity through sympathetic interlinking,[27] was committed to a more or less immanentist or monist position. To have denied that God is present in all His works, and that His genius may be glimpsed through their beauties,[28] would have been at least inconsistent. Yet some conception of the transcendence of God (as for example the creator of the All rather than Himself the All) can often be found even in the most immanentist treatises;[29] and as he rose in due course from *epistēmē* towards *gnōsis*, the Hermetist was increasingly likely to face the World and Man as of lesser intrinsic interest than God, and to long for knowledge *of* God rather than merely knowledge *about* Him. And in this way there might easily arise a tendency to devalue the World and Man and to undermine their integral relationship with God – in other words to cultivate a philosophy of dualist tendency and to emphasize the transcendent nature of the Divinity.[30] The authors of *C.H.* vi and *S.H.* IIA–IIB, for instance, speak of a world in which there is no absolute truth or goodness, and in which knowledge of these things is granted only to a select few. Any good there is on earth is a mere appearance, an absence of excessive evil. 'The World is the *plēroma* of evil, and God the *plēroma* of goodness.' We, of course, dwellers in the Platonic cavern, call some things good and beautiful, and struggle to increase our store of them; yet we are tragic-comic figures, for we never even dream what the divine goodness and beauty really are.[31]

[25] *Ascl.* 13.
[26] E.g. *C.H.* v. and IX *passim*; x.14; *Ascl.* 10; *D.H.* 1.
[27] E.g. *C.H.* x.22–3; *Ascl.* 3, 19; and above, 77–8.
[28] *C.H.* v.1–8 (and cf. N.F. 1.46 n. 9; Festugière 1.92–4); *Ascl.* 25 = *N.H.C.* vi.8.72; *D.H.* 1.4.
[29] Festugière 2.51–71.
[30] With reference to Philo, Festugière speaks, 2.583, of 'la nécessité enfin de dépasser le spectacle du Kosmos, et même, en un sens, de fuir ce spectacle, pour approcher l'essence divine par la voie tout intérieure de recueillement'.
[31] *C.H.* vi.3–6; *S.H.* IIA. 6–10. The extreme position that the World (κόσμος), rather than just the earth (γῆ), is evil is specifically rebutted at *C.H.* IX.4.

The philosophical *paideia*

It is possible, then, to point to both monist and dualist elements in our texts. The Hermetists themselves were not unaware of such apparent or even real inconsistencies, as we can see from the very first sentence of *C.H.* xvi, a discourse of Asclepius to Ammon:

> I am sending you, O king, an important discourse, the culmination, as it were, of all the others, and an explanation of them, not composed according to the opinion of the many, but rather in many respects refuting them – indeed, you will find that it contradicts even some of my own discourses.

There is even an instance in which one treatise appears to dismiss another as apocryphal;[32] and one can find elsewhere less explicit but equally unmistakable signs of internal Hermetist polemics.[33] But it is a fatal mistake to imagine, with most scholars this century, that treatises of monist and dualist tendency should be consigned to independent, *parallel* categories. Such doctrinal variations, as should now be clear, in fact reflect an intention that different *successive* levels (or 'steps') of spiritual enlightenment should provide access to different *successive* levels of truth about Man, the World and God, so that for example knowledge of the World, which the Hermetists regarded as desirable at the earlier stages of spiritual instruction, is subsequently rejected as 'curiosity' (περιεργία, *curiositas*), the pursuit of knowledge for its own sake, and branded as sin.[34] And so we find monist treatises that convey *epistēmē* and say little or nothing about the spiritual life;[35] and dualist texts that impart *gnōsis* and describe the actual experience of contemplation – in fact the word *gnōsis* and its correlates tend not to occur except in such texts.[36] Others, such as *C.H.* v, a contemplative text that none the less adopts a very positive attitude to the material world, steer a middle course and represent the gradual transition that the initiate effected from *epistēmē* to *gnōsis*. And, as one would expect, the transition was not without its pitfalls – even within individual treatises it is possible to find blatant self-contradictions,[37] not always such as can be explained away in terms of later adjustment and corruption. Most resistant of

---

[32] Compare *C.H.* xii.8 and xiii.15, in which Hermes respectively asserts and denies that his teacher had conveyed to him doctrines that had not been written down. Zieliński, *Iresione* 2.179–82, exaggerates the significance of this passage when he attempts to use it in support of his belief in two fundamentally different doctrinal strands within Hermetism.

[33] Compare e.g. *C.H.* ix.4 with vi.4, and ix.9 with ii.5.

[34] *Ascl.* 13–14 (with N.F. 2.369 n. 115); *S.H.* xxiii.24, 44–6; and cf. Labhardt, *M.H.* 17 (1960) 206–24.

[35] E.g. *C.H.* ii. *C.H.* iii.4, exceptionally, envisages Man's whole development and fulfilment in terms of his earthly life.

[36] Cf. Delatte, Govaerts and Denooz, *Index s.vv.*; and *N.H.C.* vi.6.62.33.

[37] Compare e.g. *C.H.* ix.3–4 and 8.

all to classification in terms of parallel rather than successive doctrinal developments are those treatises that were designed as compendia – notably *C.H.* x (*The key*) and the *Perfect* (i.e. 'complete', 'encyclopaedic') *discourse*, which is anyway a composite whose elements have not been very well co-ordinated. If we are to take Hermetism seriously, we must give an account of it that assigns due weight to all these different levels of approach to the truth, rather than obscuring them so that they can be accommodated to some predetermined doctrinal scheme.[38] And we should bear in mind too the possibility that the Hermetists deliberately formulated mutually contradictory statements about God, in order to convey something of His transcendence and the comprehensiveness of His power, indescribable in the language of human reason.[39] It is to the mysteries of such *gnōsis* that we must now turn.

Gnōsis

So far, Hermetic *gnōsis* has simply been defined as the knowledge of God that the initiate longs for. In order to understand better what this *gnōsis* is, two further points should be borne in mind.

In the first place, Man's contemplation of God is in some sense a two-way process. Not only does Man wish to know God, but God too desires to be known by the most glorious of His creations, Man;[40] and to this end He freely bestows on the initiate some of His own power, mediated through a spiritual instructor.[41] Indeed, Hermes goes so far as to assert, in *C.H.* xiii, that the mysteries of the spirit 'are not taught, but we are reminded of them by God, when he wishes'.[42] It is interesting in this connection to note what some of the more straightforwardly didactic treatises, like *C.H.* x and the *Perfect discourse*, have to say about *nous*, the divine intellect[43] – or, as another

---

[38] It is unfortunate that Festugière, while recognizing that the monist and dualist approaches are inextricably entwined in virtually all the Hermetic texts (e.g. 3.36 n. 3; 4.54–5), nevertheless constructed *Révélation* around this distinction, imposing his own preoccupations on material that is decidedly recalcitrant to them.

[39] Cf. *C.H.* xiii.1: Tat complains to Hermes that he has spoken 'enigmatically' about God; Mahé 2.436–40.

[40] *C.H.* 1.31; x.4, 15; *Ascl.* 41 = *N.H.C.* vi.7; and cf. *C.H.* vii.2.

[41] *C.H.* 1.27, xiii.8 (note also the reference to God's 'mercy'); *N.H.C.* vi.6.55–7, esp. 55.15 (contemplation a 'gift'); and cf. N.F. 3.9 n. 7, and Mahé 1.94–5, 100–1. Also *S.H.* iia.6, on the 'power to see God' accorded by God to certain individuals.

[42] *C.H.* xiii.2; cf. 3, 16, and *S.H.* iia.2.

[43] See esp. *C.H.* x.21–4; *Ascl.* 10, 18, 41. On the soul as the vehicle of *nous* see *C.H.* x.16–17.

of the Hermetic books succinctly puts it, 'the soul of God'.[44] The basic function of *nous*, according to these texts, is to link together the hierarchy of God, the World, Man and the animals, and especially to enable the soul, its vehicle, to free itself from the snares of the flesh and be illuminated by 'the light of *gnōsis*'. The Hermetist's most fervent prayer must therefore be for 'a good *nous*', strong enough to repel the assaults of the world and the flesh; and it is fully consistent with this attitude that the more initiatory tracts make the spiritual teacher into something like a personification of divine intellect. Poimandres announces himself in *C.H.* I as 'the *nous* of the Highest Power' (ὁ τῆς αὐθεντίας νοῦς), to whose guidance Hermes is to entrust himself;[45] while in *The Ogdoad reveals the Ennead* Hermes, in his more accustomed role of master, becomes one with *nous* in the course of his initiation of Tat.[46] The Hermetic initiation, then, is not merely an encounter, but an interaction, between Man and God; and it is only by grasping the genuine reciprocity of this experience that we can appreciate the deeply gnostic core of Hermetism.

The second point arises from this first. Why should a transcendent God wish to be known by mere mortals? The Hermetists' answer is that the most glorious of God's creations is animated by a divine spark, and therefore himself divine.[47] Man is of double nature, and so the difference between the divine and human spheres is less substantial than it seems. The idea is deceptively simple. In fact, very few men have any inkling of their own divinity;[48] and it was for this reason that the Hermetists regarded an understanding of the origin and nature of the World and Man as an essential preliminary to spiritual illumination. 'To know the stages of the creative process is also to know the stages of one's own return to the root of all existence.'[49] Man's crippling disability is his ignorance;[50] and the Hermetist's highest aspiration was to overcome that ignorance and, by helping Man to understand his true nature, bring him at last to know God and assert his own divinity.[51] The necessity of this double

---

[44] *C.H.* xii.9.   [45] *C.H.* 1.2 22; and cf. 1.30, xiii.15.

[46] See below, 110. Compare also *C.H.* vii.2 ('Ask for a guide who will lead you to the portals of knowledge, where [burns] the bright light') with *C.H.* x.21 ('When the intellect has entered into the pious soul, it guides it towards the light of knowledge').

[47] See e.g. *C.H.* 1.15, ix.5; and Dodd, *Fourth gospel* 25–7, 41–2, 45.

[48] See e.g. *C.H.* ix.4; *S.H.* iiA.6, and N.F.'s n. *ad loc.*

[49] Scholem, *Jewish mysticism* 20.   [50] *C.H.* vii; and cf. 1.27, x.8 and xiii.7, 8.

[51] *C.H.* x.9: 'The virtue of the soul is knowledge (γνῶσις); for he who has knowledge is good and pious and already divine.' The main passages on self-knowledge leading to knowledge of God are collected by N.F. 1.23 n. 47. Cf. also Betz, *H. Th. R.* 63 (1970) 465–84; Puech, *En quête de la gnose* 1.117–18.

gnōsis emerges most clearly in *C.H.* XIII, where the initiation falls into two phases, the former emphasizing self-knowledge, the latter knowledge of God.[52] It is to this central Hermetic experience of initiation, particularly as it is described in *C.H.* XIII and *The Ogdoad reveals the Ennead*, that we must now turn our attention.

The first thing that needs to be emphasized about the Hermetic initiation is that it is not envisaged as a form or a symbol, or something that one just reads about, but as a real experience, stretching all the capacities of those who embark upon it: 'for it is an extremely tortuous way, to abandon what one is used to and possesses now, and to retrace one's steps towards the old primordial things'.[53] As to the goal of the journey – 'to apprehend God', the Hermetist exclaims, echoing Plato, 'is difficult, but to tell of Him is impossible, even for the man who can apprehend Him'.[54] The earlier stages of Hermetic instruction might perhaps be embarked on alone, and bear the aspect of private study and self-discipline;[55] but for the initiation itself the guidance of a spiritual teacher was indispensable – hence the dialogue form of many of our texts, and their preoccupation with the subtle relationship that develops between the teacher and his pupil or 'son'. In fact there is a sense in which the initiation is just as much an adventure for both of them.[56] The teacher has been there before, and he can explain, as much as words allow, what the initiate may hope to experience; but unless he himself can actually attain the vision again, and describe what he sees, the pupil has no hope of following, still less of developing further, as he was expected to do,[57] the understanding granted him through the mediation of his teacher.

About the Hermetists' conviction of the need for instruction and study in the early stages of initiation something has already been said. But the way of Hermes, as Hermes himself points out at the end of the *Asclepius*,[58] was not for the mind alone; nor did the attainment of *epistēmē* or even *gnōsis* provide any automatic access to salvation. 'The pious fight consists in knowing the divine and doing ill to no

---

[52] *C.H.* XIII.7–14, 15–21, noting especially ἐπιπεφώτισται (21).

[53] *C.H.* IV.9; and cf. *S.H.* IIB.5–8, *Ascl.* 32.

[54] *S.H.* I.1; cf. Plato, *Tim.* 28c. See also *C.H.* VII.2, *S.H.* IIA.1.

[55] See e.g. *C.H.* I.1, XIII.1 (referring to the *General discourses*).

[56] Cf. *Ascl.* 3.

[57] *C.H.* IX.10, XI.22, XIII.15.

[58] *Ascl.* 40: 'It remains only for us to bless God in our prayers and to return to the care of the body. For, if I may so put it, our souls have had their full ration of matters divine in this discussion of ours.'

man':[59] the ethical virtues also had their part to play. The intending initiate must lead a life of piety, obedience and purity – that is, abstinence from the pleasures of this world.[60] The Hermetists do not seem to have been austere ascetics, though the demands they made on themselves undoubtedly increased as they advanced towards spiritual perfection. Generally they held that, just as God formed Man and his environment, so Man in turn is obliged to perpetuate his own race. No-one is unhappier, according to *C.H.* ii, than the man who dies childless;[61] while the *Perfect discourse* goes so far as to praise sexual intercourse as not merely a necessity but a pleasure, and an image of God's own creative act.[62] But the tone changes in the more spiritual treatises, where the body may be described as a prison, and sex rejected as a curse.[63] The virtues are here taken much more for granted, and at this stage it can even be pointed out, as in the key-passage quoted earlier from *The Ogdoad reveals the Ennead*,[64] that pure morals and a clear conscience are not in themselves a sufficient preparation for *gnōsis*. The relative neglect of the ethical virtues in the more spiritual treatises derives from their authors' assumption that their audience will already have made the crucial choice on which all else depends – the choice, that is, between the 'material' and the 'essential' Man, the corporeal and the incorporeal, the mortal and the divine realms. For one cannot love both simultaneously.[65]

The attainment of self-knowledge – the exposure of the 'essential' Man beneath the encrustations of materiality – is best described in *C.H.* xiii,[66] a dialogue constructed around Hermes's attempts first to explain to and then to induce in his pupil Tat the experience of 'rebirth' (παλιγγενεσία). The didacticism and awkwardness of the treatise's first stages, in which we see Tat thrown into confusion and despair by his inability to grasp the reality behind the images of Hermes's exposition, contrasts sharply with the illuminative climax, and dramatizes with particular effectiveness the whole of the gnostic

[59] *C.H.* x.19.
[60] *C.H.* i.22; *Ascl.* 11, 29; *N.H.C.* vi.6.56–7, 62.28–33. Piety as the natural function of Man, and especially of the philosopher who aspires to *gnōsis*, is a recurrent theme (e.g. *C.H.* vi.5, ix.4, x.9, xvi.11; *S.H.* iib.2–3), implicit in the phrase which provides the title of this chapter.
[61] *C.H.* ii.17; and cf. *C.H.* iii.3.
[62] *Ascl.* 20–1 = *N.H.C.* vi.8.65; and cf. Mahé, *N.H.S.* 7 (1975) 130–3.
[63] *C.H.* xiii.7; i.18–19, 24; vii.2; and cf. Mahé, *N.H.S.* 7 (1975) 137–42.
[64] Above, 97.   [65] *C.H.* iv.6.
[66] *N.H.C.* vi.6 has much less to say about self-knowledge, though there is a hint at 58.8.

experience. What is more, the drama, far from being merely a literary form, as in some of the more exclusively didactic treatises examined earlier, is an essential part of the initiation itself, which could not be completed except through the interaction of master and pupil. Thus it is that Hermes's account of the 'irrational punishments of matter', the vices inherent in all mortals, though it begins straightforwardly enough, gradually assumes an almost incantatory manner, culminating in the actual purging of Tat's mortal weaknesses 'by the powers of God'.[67] This is that same invasion of the initiate by divine *nous* of which something has already been said; and the direct result of this purification is the 'construction of the Logos',[68] in other words the reconstruction within Tat of the original, essential Man.[69] In this way Tat is brought into a state of perfect repose, balance and clarity of vision.[70] He perceives for the first time, by means of the powers with which he is now filled, his inalienable kinship with the divine world – he acquires, in other words, the true self-knowledge of the human who is able to distance himself from his natural condition.[71] It is this experience that the author of *C.H.* xiii has in mind when he speaks of 'rebirth'.

Although the actual word *palingenesia* is employed only in *C.H.* xiii, the concept is implicit in all the more initiatory texts – even the *General discourses* are said to have referred to it.[72] Rebirth is emphatically not a repetition of physical birth, but a bursting into a new plane of existence previously unattained, even unsuspected, albeit available potentially. It is, in fact, a negation of physical birth, in that our first birth imprisons the soul in the body, while our rebirth

[67] *C.H.* xiii.7–10.

[68] *C.H.* xiii.8: συνάρθρωσις τοῦ Λόγου; and cf. 3 ('I was born in *nous*'), 10 and 12 (the ten powers of God bring about spiritual birth), and *N.H.C.* vi.6.54.25–8. The philosophical Hermetica speak with many voices on the relationship between *nous* and *logos*; see e.g. *C.H.* i.6, 30; iv.3; ix.1; xii.14; Tröger, *Mysterienglaube* 121, 133–4; and compare *C.H.* i.2 and 30 on Poimandres as 'the *nous/logos* of the highest Power'.

[69] *Pace* Mahé 1.53–4, and Grese, *Corpus Hermeticum XIII* 122, 130–1, there is no substantial doctrinal divergence, only a difference of emphasis, between *C.H.* xiii (8: construction of the *Logos* in Tat *ab initio*; 3: radical change wrought in the initiate by his experience) and *C.H.* i (initiate has only to recognize his intrinsic divinity: 18, 19, 21). The Hermetists acknowledged the divergence of approach, but saw no contradiction: *Ascl.* 25 (N.F. 2.329.5–9), and cf. Dodd, *Fourth gospel* 45, 48–9. Indeed, the idea of 'purification' employed at *C.H.* xiii.7 clearly presupposes a divine nature only temporarily obscured, and, as it happens, explicitly referred to *ibid.* as the 'interior man' (ἐνδιάθετος ἄνθρωπος, feebly explained away by Grese, *Corpus Hermeticum XIII* 114–15).

[70] *C.H.* xiii.11, 13.

[71] This change of perspective is well described at *C.H.* iv.4–5.

[72] Dodd, *loc. cit.*, to which add *N.H.C.* vi.6.62.33–63.3 (quoted above, 97). On the *General discourses* see *ibid.* and *C.H.* xiii.1.

liberates it. The 'tent' of the earthly body, as Hermes tells Tat in *C.H.* XIII, was formed by the circle of the zodiac,[73] and so lay subject to the power of fate. Most astrologers maintained that the hold of fate over the body is unbreakable; and the Hermetists agreed that it was presumptuous in the extreme to oppose fate directly – that was the business of magicians, who believed in the efficacy of purely mechanical formulae.[74] Fate was instead to be overcome, so the Hermetists maintained, 'without making use of anything material, or employing any other aid, save only the observation of the appropriate moment (καιρός)' at which the originally independent divine element in Man, the soul, might be freed from its bodily prison and thus removed from the control of fate—if God so willed.[75] It is this liberation from fate and materiality that the Hermetists thought of as 'rebirth'.[76]

In envisaging such a radical re-ordering of the initiate's constitution and perceptions, the Hermetists were naturally of somewhat varying opinions as regards the temporal and spatial aspects of the process. 'This thing cannot be taught, nor can it be seen by that material element, which is all the vision we have.'[77] In the *Poimandrēs* the soul progresses – in fact 'ascends'[78] – through the planetary spheres, casting off different vices at each stage of its journey; and in *C.H.* IV Hermes points out to Tat 'how many [heavenly] bodies we must pass through, how many choirs of daemons, what continuity of substance (συνέχεια) and what courses of stars, so that we hasten towards the One and Alone'.[79] By contrast, the initiation described in *C.H.* XIII purges Tat of his vices at a stroke, and brings him at the same time to perceive his true, divine self, and to know god.[80] Again, while *C.H.* IV and XIII agree in envisaging the experience of rebirth (and the divine vision that follows it) as taking

---

[73] *C.H.* XIII.12; and cf. *Ascl.* 35 and above, 77–8.

[74] The disagreement is well summarized by Zos. Pan., *fr. gr.* 229–30 (quoted below, 124), opposing Zoroaster the magician to Hermes the philosopher. On not resisting fate see especially *N.H.C.* VI.6.62.22–30 (quoted above, 97), also apparently alluding to the abusive behaviour of the magicians.

[75] *C.H.* XII.9; *Ascl.* 29 (with N.F. 2.386 n. 242); Zos. Pan., *loc. cit.*; Iam., *Myst.* VIII.4.267 (whence the quotation), x.5–6; and cf. N.F. 1.195.

[76] Hermes offers a brief definition at *C.H.* XIII.13 (and cf. 3): 'rebirth means no longer perceiving things as bodies in three dimensions'.

[77] *C.H.* XIII.3 (and cf. the rest of the section).

[78] On the vocabulary of ascent in the Hermetica, see Tröger, *Mysterienglaube* 140–1.

[79] *C.H.* IV.8, and cf. also 9, quoted above, 106. On συνέχεια see N.F. 1.55 n. 21.

[80] *C.H.* XIII.8.

place within the span of mortal life,[81] the *Poimandrēs* holds that it may occur only after death.[82]

But in describing the actual encounter with God, the Hermetists speak with greater unanimity. According to the *Poimandrēs* the soul, 'denuded of what the planetary spheres had wrought in it, enters with its own strength into the Ogdoadic nature, and with the Beings sings hymns to the Father...[and] hears certain powers above the Ogdoadic nature hymning God with a sweet voice'. In *The Ogdoad reveals the Ennead* we find a similar but more extended account of the soul's vision as it enters the divine spheres of the Ogdoad and Ennead alluded to in the title. Divine power manifests itself in the form of light, at first to Hermes alone, who in short, ecstatic phrases describes for his pupil the noetic vision that the power brings.[83] Becoming himself *nous*, Hermes beholds the origin of the divine powers, and sees the primordial spring of life.

These indescribable depths...language is not able to reveal. The entire Ogdoad, O my son, and the souls that are in it, and the angels, sing a hymn in silence.[84] And I, Mind, understand (*noein*).

Tat, overwhelmed by Hermes's exaltation, is gradually caught up in the vision, at first empathetically, then directly. Hermes now is God, and Tat calls him 'father, aeon of the aeons, great divine spirit', pleading with him that his soul should not be deprived of the vision. Then the power comes to him too, and the vision of the eighth sphere hymning the ninth, and of God who holds sway over all.[85]

It should be clear by now that the knowledge of God that the Hermetic initiation is supposed to bring is not an external knowledge, of one being by another, but an actual assumption by the initiate of the attributes of God: in short, divinization. The way of Hermes is

---

[81] See esp. *C.H.* xiii.1, 22; also *N.H.C.* vi.6 (esp. 60.4–5); *Ascl.* 41: 'We rejoice because, while we are still in the body, you have been pleased to consecrate us to eternity.' Note that the new divine body constituted in the initiate by rebirth, according to *C.H.* xiii, is conceived of as contained (temporarily) within the old mortal body, not as superseding it.

[82] *C.H.* 1.24–6. *S.H.* vi.18 seems to say the same; but at *S.H.* iib.8 ('Before you reach the goal, you must first abandon the body, and overcome in the struggle of life, and, having overcome, begin the ascent') what is intended is detachment from care for the body rather than death: cf. Porph., *V. Plot.* 1–2. *C.H.* x.5–6 appears to concede the vision but not divinization to the embodied soul (cf. N.F. 1.125 n. 27; 3.15 n. 5). The debate had a long history in Greek thought: see Smith, *Porphyry's place*, esp. 27–39, 80.

[83] *N.H.C.* vi.6.57.28–58.22. On the experience of illumination see esp. *C.H.* x.4–6; also Filoramo, *Luce e gnosi* 19–28.

[84] This hymn, which is addressed to the Ennead (*N.H.C.* vi.6.59.29–32), is recounted *in extenso* at *C.H.* xiii.17–20, and referred to at *C.H.* xiii.3 and 1.26.

[85] *N.H.C.* vi.6.58.22–60.1; *C.H.* xiii.21.

the 'way of immortality';[86] and its end is reached when the purified soul is absorbed into God, so that the reborn man, although still a composite of body and soul, can himself fairly be called a god.[87] One gains some impression of the Hermetists' high estimate of Man's potential from the concluding passage of *C.H.* x:

> Man is a divine being (ζῷον θεῖον), to be compared not with the other earthly beings, but with those who are called gods, up in the heavens. Rather, if one must dare to speak the truth, the true Man is above even the gods, or at least fully their equal. After all, none of the celestial gods will leave the heavenly frontiers and descend to earth; yet Man ascends even into the heavens, and measures them, and knows their heights and depths, and everything else about them he learns with exactitude. What is even more remarkable, he establishes himself on high without even leaving the earth, so far does his power extend. We must presume then to say that earthly Man is a mortal god, and that the celestial God is an immortal man. And so it is through these two, the world and Man, that all things exist; but they were all created by the One.[88]

This 'way of Hermes' is to be distinguished from the routes by which other contemporaries reached the divine realm.[89] The Hermetist's was a divinization neither public and official as that of the emperor, nor accorded in consequence of death as was increasingly the custom at this time regardless of social status. It was, rather, deeply private, and the reward of conscious effort – no mere rite of passage. And while the emperor and the dead were placed among, indeed regarded as of a status somewhat inferior to, the plurality of traditional gods, the Hermetist was assimilated to the One God. He is most nearly to be compared with the 'divine man' (θεῖος ἀνήρ) of late Platonism. As Plotinus pointed out in a famous passage, the divine man had to reconcile himself to a term, albeit finite, of imprisonment in the body.

> Many times it has happened: raised up out of the body into myself, apart from all other things but self-encentred, I have seen a marvellous and immense beauty. Then I realised that truly I am a part of all that is most sublime, and I actively sought to partake in this best of lives, and I attained the condition of the divine. Yet though one settles at the core of divinity, and acquires its very attributes and transcends the noetic sphere, still after one's sojourn in the divine realm there comes the moment when one must descend from intellect to reasoning. And at that moment I ponder

---

[86] *N.H.C.* vi.6.63.11; and cf. e.g. *C.H.* x.7, xiii.3. Its opposite is the 'way of death': *C.H.* i.29.

[87] *C.H.* xiii.3, 10, 14; and cf. i.26 ('...becoming powers (δυνάμεις) they enter into God. This is the happy end for those who have knowledge: to become God'; though in this case only, as noticed above, after death), and Dodds, *Pagan and Christian* 76–9.

[88] Cf. also *C.H.* xi.20, xii.1; *Ascl.* 6, 22.

[89] On the following see Waelkens, in *Mélanges Naster* 259–307.

how it can be that I am descending, and how my soul ever entered into my body, since it is of the quality that it showed itself to be, even though contained in the body.[90]

But Plotinus himself was in no doubt about his more than merely potential superiority to everything below the One itself – even the gods. That is the meaning of his remark, when Amelius invited him to visit the gods' temples and feasts, that 'they ought to come to me, not I to them'.[91] As men of learning the Hermetists are scarcely to be compared to Plotinus, nor does their power of expression rival his; but we have no reason to assume that the spiritual experiences in which the way of Hermes culminated were any less intense than those to which Ammonius Saccas led Plotinus, or Plotinus Porphyry.

This comparison with the late antique Platonists raises a final question: How may we characterize the way of Hermes in general doctrinal terms? Since antiquity by and large believed in the historicity of Hermes and the genuineness of the books attributed to him, questions of this sort were naturally not asked. Hermetism was what Hermes had taught, just as Platonism was what Plato had taught. The historical doubt, and hence the need for a firmer doctrinal context, is an affliction reserved for the heirs of Isaac Casaubon.

The answer must lie in the central aspiration of the Hermetist to attain knowledge of God. The idea that one may 'know God' (γιγνώσκειν θεόν / γνῶσις θεοῦ, *cognoscere deum / cognitio dei*) is extremely rare in the literature of classical and Hellenistic paganism, but common in Jewish and Christian usage;[92] and its prominence in Hermetism is symptomatic of that preoccupation with the divine at the expense of the human sphere which was increasingly marked in late paganism. For the Hermetist, true philosophy was piety towards God and contemplation of His works; and although the Hermetic *paideia* embraced, in theory, all forms of knowledge of God's creation, the author of the *Perfect discourse* could reject as the sin of curiosity the high estimation in which traditional philosophers held the natural sciences, mathematics, astronomy, music and so forth, and emphasize their merely auxiliary role in the pursuit of the 'pura sanctaque philosophia'.[93] In fact, for the Hermetist no product of

---

[90] Plot. IV.8.1.1–11; and cf. the remarks of Porph., *V. Plot.* 23.23–40.
[91] *Ibid.* 10.33–8.   [92] Norden, *Agnostos theos* 87–99.
[93] *Ascl.* 13–14; and cf. *S.H.* XXIII.24, 44–6.

human intellectual investigation, not even knowledge of God, was an end in itself; for underlying all human thought and action is the desire for release from this world of flux and materiality, for the salvation of the soul. Accordingly, the only 'truly useful knowledge is that of the way of immortality; and such knowledge was treated, naturally enough, as a treasure whose existence ought not to be casually revealed to all and sundry. It is this dualist, soteriological and esoteric philosophy that lies at the heart of the gnostic systems that were so widely diffused in the Roman empire; and of the pagan aspect of this movement Hermetism is by far the best-documented example.[94]

Gnosticism as we know it, though, was primarily a Christian phenomenon; so the question naturally arises whether there was any link between pagan gnosticism, with its strongly intellectualist, philosophical tinge, and the much more radically dualist and mythologized doctrines of classical second-century Christian gnostics like Basilides and Valentinus.[95] Thanks to its esotericism and consequent lack of formal restraints, all gnosticism tended to be anarchically speculative; and Christian gnosticism was worst of all, a many-headed hydra, as the heresiologists put it, likely to devour and regurgitate, often in virtually unrecognizable form, any idea that came into view.[96] It is possible, then, to find parallels in Christian gnosticism for much of what we read in the Hermetica. There are indeed passages in the philosophical Hermetica that suggest a real intellectual kinship, such as for example *C.H.* IV's account of how God offered the souls of men the chance to be baptized in a huge bowl (κρατήρ), so that those who deserved it might receive the gift of *nous* as well as *logos*.[97] But more often the parallels are suggested by ideas that are undeniably current in Christian gnosticism, but not exclusive to it;[98] and by preoccupations, as for example with

[94] On *gnōsis* and philosophy see Armstrong, *Plotinian and Christian studies* XXI.87–124, esp. 99; Rudolph, *Gnosis* 63–4.

[95] On the distinction see Wilson, in *Mélanges Henri-Charles Puech* 423–9.

[96] Rudolph, *Gnosis* 59–63.

[97] *C.H.* IV.3–4; and cf. Festugière, *Hermétisme* 100–12.

[98] Tröger, *Mysterienglaube* 82–166, admits that many of the parallels he adduces between *C.H.*, esp. XIII, and classical gnosticism fall into this category: cf. the criticisms by Grese, *Corpus Hermeticum XIII* 50–5. Even what appears to be anti-gnostic polemic can often be interpreted as disagreement within the Hermetic tradition: compare e.g. *C.H.* IX.4 ('Evil must dwell here [below], for here is its proper place. Its place is the earth – not the World, as is blasphemously asserted by some') with *C.H.* VI.4 ('the World is the fulness of evil'); and *C.H.* IX. 9 ('God is not without sensation or understanding (ἀνόητος), as some imagine, led by excessive reverence into blasphemy') with *C.H.* II.5 ('God is not an object of thought (νοητός) to Himself': for Christian gnostic parallels see Quispel, *V. Chr.* 2 (1948) 115–16).

cosmology or asceticism,[99] which were bound to be shared by all systems of thought that started from the idea of a divine spark, the soul, imprisoned in matter, and went on to ask how its liberation could be brought about. In the restraint and (relative) philosophicality of its approach Hermetism is more Hellenic and chronologically earlier, at least in its origins, than Christian gnosticism, in which much smaller elements of Greek philosophical thought than are to be found in the books of Hermes have become heavily overlaid by exotic oriental, especially Jewish, imagery.[100] It would be a mistake, then, to imagine that Christian gnosticism either substantially influenced Hermetism, or can be used to illuminate it, except by way of general analogy. What can be asserted is that Hermetism represents the sort of pagan intellectual milieu with which Christian gnostics could feel that they had something in common. We have some evidence that Christian gnostics read the books of Hermes, both technical and philosophical;[101] and the Nag Hammadi library shows that they might even on occasion include them among their sacred books. Future research is likely to reveal more and more doctrinal common ground between the Hermetica and the Nag Hammadi literature.[102] There could after all be no purer expression of Hermetic gnosticism than the concluding prayer of the *Perfect discourse*; and in choosing to transcribe this particular text the compiler of *N.H.C.* vi makes a clear acknowledgement of the profit that mature fourth-century Christian gnosticism could still expect to derive from the literary legacy of Hermes.

Thanks be to Thee, Most High, Most Excellent, for by Thy grace we have received the great light of Thy knowledge. [Thy] name is holy and to be honoured, a unique name by which God alone is to be blessed according to the religion of our fathers. For Thou thinkest it good to display to all things paternal kindness, care, love, and whatever virtue may be more sweet, granting to us mind, reason and knowledge: mind, in order that we may understand Thee; reason, in order that by means of hints we may investigate Thee; knowledge, in order that knowing Thee we may rejoice. And, redeemed by Thy power, we do rejoice that Thou hast shown Thyself to us completely. We rejoice that Thou hast thought it good to deify us for eternity while we are yet in our bodies. For this is the only [way in which we may show our] human gratitude: by knowing Thy majesty. We know Thee and this immense light

---

[99] See (with special reference to *N.H.C.* vi.8) Mahé, *N.H.S.* 7 (1975) 130–45; and Mahé 2.120–44.
[100] Dodd, *Bible and the Greeks* 204–9.
[101] Below, 172–3.
[102] I am obliged to J.-P. Mahé for sending me an article on 'Παλιγγενεσία et structure du monde supérieur dans les Hermetica et le traité d'Eugnoste de Nag Hammadi', now published in *Deuxième journée d'études coptes, Strasbourg 25 mai 1984* (Louvain 1987) 137–49.

perceptible to the intellect alone. We understand Thee, O true life of life. O pregnancy fertile with all natures, we know Thee, eternal continuation of all nature most full of Thy procreating activity. For worshipping the good of Thy goodness in this whole prayer, we pray for this alone: that Thou willest to keep us persevering in the love of Thy knowledge, and that we may never be separated from this way of life.[103]

[103] *Ascl.* 41 (tr. Dirkse and Brashler, with adjustments).

⌈5⌉

Towards a *via universalis*

The way is now almost open for a consideration of Hermetism's place within the wider context of late pagan thought and religion. As will appear, though, certain late antique pagans did not regard as absolute the distinction that has been adopted for tactical reasons in the previous two chapters between technical and philosophical Hermetica; and it is important to establish, before advancing any further, to what extent this distinction was employed by the Hermetists themselves.[1]

Technique and philosophy: interactions

In the first place, it is clear that many of the technical texts associated with or attributed to Hermes were written and used by people who did not pretend to be anything other than working magicians, casters of horoscopes and so on – in short, straightforward technicians. They were practical men, close to the rhythms of everyday life and to the native culture of the Nile valley – hence the resemblance of much that they wrote to the products of the Egyptian tradition, whether as straight translation or, in varying degrees, interpretation. At the same time, though, there were strong influences at work from the broader Hellenistic world, especially for example in the field of astrology; and there were also, as was suggested in chapter 3, a few practitioners of these arts who took a wider view of their vocation,

---

[1] Festugière's investigation of technical Hermetism pays lip-service to the idea that it might have some connection with philosophical Hermetism (e.g. 1.87–8, 118, 355–62); but *Révélation* as a whole leaves the impression that the two branches of the Hermetic literature were easily separable. See e.g. 1.362: 'Il n'est pas impossible que les mêmes âmes païennes aient suivi tour à tour ces deux voies, qu'après s'être plongées dans les opérations de *la magie la plus grossière* elles se soient perdues ensuite dans des *élans d'amour pour le Dieu hypercosmique*. On rencontre, dans l'Empereur Julien, *de telles disparates*.' (My italics.) The success of this approach depends, of course, on the selection of extremes for comparison.

Technique and philosophy: interactions

having become aware of the ways in which their skills might be used to relieve, not just the everyday tensions of their customers, but their deeper spiritual longings too. There was then no absolute intellectual discontinuity between those who saw Hermes primarily as a technician and those who thought of him as a philosopher, though the common ground will have been more easily visible to the authors of the philosophical Hermetica than to the humble magician or fortune-teller. It is then to the philosophical Hermetica that we should turn in the first instance for a clearer understanding of the interaction between the technical and philosophical literature.

It has to be borne in mind that many of the elements in the philosophical Hermetica that might at first look like conscious borrowings from the technical milieu are really just part of the common coin of late pagan thought – one thinks of notions such as universal sympathy and belief in the influence of the stars over human character and experience.[2] Even so explicitly astrological a passage as that in *The Ogdoad reveals the Ennead*, where Hermes gives Tat detailed instructions about the astral conjuncture at which he is to commit the account of his initiation to writing,[3] clearly reflects convention rather than deliberate syncretism. It is also likely that much of the sort of material in which we are here interested was expunged from the philosophical Hermetica by Byzantine bowdlerizers, because of its overtly pagan character. Even so, some of these texts can still be seen to draw on the arcane arts in a way and to an extent that would have been recognizable in antiquity. In the first place, as was pointed out in chapter 4, the Hermetica conventionally regarded as philosophical included some treatises of extensive technical content, deemed necessary especially in the initial stages of the Hermetic *paideia* – *S.H.* VI and XXIV–XXVI are good examples. But of more interest in the present context is the subtler fusion to be found in the *Korē kosmou*, which indeed not only illustrates the practice but states the principle too, in the aretalogy of Isis and Osiris with which it concludes:

It was they [Isis and Osiris] who, recognizing the corruptibility of bodies, cleverly created the prophets' excellence in all things, so that the prophet who is to raise up his hands to the gods should never be in ignorance of any being, and so that philosophy and magic should nourish the soul, and medicine should preserve the body when it is in any way afflicted.[4]

---

[2] See e.g. *C.H.* I.24–5.
[3] *N.H.C.* VI.6.62.16–20.
[4] *S.H.* XXIII.68; cf. Festugière, *Études de religion* 167–9, and N.F. *ad loc.*

There could be nothing more characteristically late antique than this idea of philosophy and magic as nourishers of the soul; and there will be much to be said of it shortly. The same idea underlies the *Korē kosmou*'s earlier assertion that virtuous souls will become 'just kings, genuine philosophers, founders and legislators, true diviners, authentic herbalists, distinguished prophets of the gods, experienced musicians, sharp-minded astronomers...' and so on.[5] And in his account of God's creation of the spirit-realm our author provides a more practical illustration of the fusion of technical and philosophical Hermetism, for the mingling through 'secret incantations' of divine breath, fire and certain other 'unknown substances' and the production therefrom of a subtle, pure and transparent matter, from which eventually the souls themselves – and subsequently the zodiacal signs too – are formed, is in essence an alchemical operation, with plentiful parallels in the technical literature.[6] A little later we find an astrological excursus too.[7]

The initiatory texts, despite their austere noeticism, likewise show traces of impurer modes of approach to the divine world, and among them of magical practices. In particular, the new Coptic treatise preserves a feature which is probably absent from other similar Hermetica only because of the attentions of later Christian copyists – namely, the extended sequences of vowels and cryptic divine names which break abruptly into the petitions and doxologies of the initiatory prayers.[8] The most obvious Graeco-Roman parallels are to be found in certain gnostic writings[9] and in the magical papyri, where sequences of vowels and *nomina sacra* – attributed on one occasion to Hermes Trismegistus himself – are used to invoke gods and concentrate divine powers.[10] Perhaps this was originally an Egyptian cultic practice, since in the late Hellenistic or early imperial Roman treatise *De elocutione*, ascribed to 'Demetrius', we read that 'in Egypt the priests, when singing hymns in praise of the gods, employ the seven vowels, which they utter in due succession; and the sound of these letters is so euphonious that men listen to it in place

---

[5] *S.H.* XXIII.42.
[6] *S.H.* XXIII.14–21; Festugière, *Hermétisme* 230–48 (and cf. N.F. 3.CLXVIII). Note also Festugière, *Hermétisme* 230 n. 3, on the alchemical element in *S.H.* XXVI.
[7] *S.H.* XXIII.28–9; cf. N.F. 3.CXCIV–CXCVIII.
[8] *N.H.C.* VI.6.56.16–22, 61.10–15; and cf. *C.H.* XVI.2: 'We use not just words, but sounds full of efficacy.'
[9] E.g. *Book of Jeu* II.50 (p. 124), 52 (p. 135).
[10] *P. Graec. Mag.* IV.883–97; Dornseiff, *Alphabet* 35–60; Mahé 1.106–7, 124, 130–1.

of flute and lyre'.[11] In certain Buddhist texts we encounter analogous vowel-sequences with a simultaneously magical and mystical function, having their origin clearly in a belief in the supernatural powers of certain names and even letters of the alphabet, but functioning also, when constantly repeated, as aids to dissociation from the material realm and calm concentration on the divine. They might also be used in conjunction with yoga breathing-exercises.[12]

This last example alerts us, though, to the danger of taking for granted that technical material had the same function and significance before and after transference to its new philosophical context. Usually, what had previously been an end in itself would be relegated to a subordinate function. Ritual actions and magic, as will be argued at length in this and the following chapter, might be made use of provided the ultimate noetic goal was not forgotten. There was no theoretical difficulty about that, because neither temple rituals nor magical techniques necessarily implied a comprehensive doctrine of the nature of Man's place in the universe. But in the case of astrology the process of adjustment was less easy, for belief in the influence of the stars could easily turn into a fatalism that left little or no room for the liberation of the soul from matter. One might, then, reconcile belief in astral energies with a spiritual philosophy, but only if one denied the absolutism of fate and envisaged the stars, not as the axis on which all revolves, but at the most as milestones on the way of Hermes.[13] Reality is now placed without the mortal sphere, and foreknowledge of the phases of our bodily travail is deprived of the fascination it once exercised. The philosopher offers a pure, noetic cult not, *pace* the astrologer, because conventional cult is powerless to affect the decrees of fate, but because it is addressed to inferior divinities rather than to the One God he has now laboriously learned to know. The account of the soul's progress through the material and spiritual worlds that we find in the philosophical Hermetica stands in essential contradiction to the doctrines of Hermetic astrology, many of whose devotees would have found it impossible to allow that Man might transgress the planetary spheres and lose himself for ever in contemplation of the divine realm.

In rare but important cases, though, the initiative was taken by

---

[11] Demetr., *Eloc.* 71 (tr. Roberts); and cf. *Ascl.* 38, on the honouring of the statues of the gods 'with hymns and praise and sweetest sounds which recall the celestial harmony'.

[12] Hauer, *Dhāraṇī.*

[13] E.g. *C.H.* 1.25–6.

the technician rather than the philosopher, and the result was the elevation and expansion of the technique in question, rather than its demotion. In the best example of this process, the alchemist Zosimus of Panopolis, we have also one of the most striking instances of the extent to which technical and philosophical Hermetism could be brought to a genuine synthesis.

Zosimus of Panopolis

Zosimus of Panopolis is chiefly known as one of the earliest historical figures in the development of alchemy.[14] Almost no information has survived about the external incidents of his life.[15] Probably he was born at Panopolis (Akhmim) and resided later at Alexandria; and we know that he once had occasion to visit Memphis and inspect an ancient furnace that was kept in a temple there. He is commonly thought to have flourished at the end of the third century and the beginning of the fourth. But about Zosimus's thought-world his surviving writings, for all their fragmentary state, are extremely revealing. He was a man of strong spiritual urges and little conventional scholarship, who moved in an eclectic milieu compounded of Platonism[16] and gnosticism[17] together with Judaism[18] and, as we shall shortly see, the 'oriental' wisdom of Hermes and Zoroaster. Like many men of his period, Zosimus reflected on how his soul might be freed from the world of flux and illusion; and his preoccupation occasionally invaded his sleeping hours, and gave rise to dreams and visions. Of some of these he left a description which has been much discussed by Jung and his followers, but largely ignored by historians of late antiquity.[19]

[14] Plessner, *D.S.B.* 14.631–2.

[15] The evidence is discussed by Jackson, *Zosimos* 3–5. Jackson has not realized, though, that the description of a journey to Rome, which forms part of the so-called 'Book of Zosimus' contained in an unpublished manuscript in Cambridge (Zos. Pan., *fr. syr.* 299–302), is a translation of Galen 12.168–74 (*De simplicium medicamentorum temperamentis et facultatibus*) – as was noted by Berthelot, *J.S.* (1895) 382–7, but missed by Degen, in *Galen: problems and prospects* 146–7. The same applies to most of the rest of this text: compare e.g. *fr. syr.* 297–9, 302–4 with Galen 12.210–44, 178–90 respectively.

[16] *Suda* Z 168 reports Zosimus to have composed a *Life* of Plato.

[17] Zosimus refers several times to Nicotheus, mentioned together with Zoroaster by Porph., *V. Plot.* 16, and apparently of Jewish-gnostic background: Jackson, *Zosimos* 40 n. 4; Stroumsa, *Another seed* 139–43. [18] Below, 151–2.

[19] Zos. Pan., *fr. gr.* 107–13, 115–18 (and cf. 118–19); mostly re-edited by Karle, *Alchemistentraum* 26–32, with commentary 33–61. For Jung's interpretation see his *Alchemical studies* 57–108; and Franz, *Symbolon* 1 (1960) 27–38.

Zosimus of Panopolis

Falling asleep, Zosimus saw fifteen (elsewhere he says seven) steps leading up to a bowl-shaped altar where stood a priest, who said to him:

I have accomplished the descent of these fifteen steps of darkness and the ascent of the steps of light, and he who sacrifices is himself the sacrificial victim. Casting away the coarseness of the body, and consecrated priest by necessity, I am made perfect as a spirit...I am Aion, the priest of the sanctuaries, and I have submitted myself to an unendurable torment. For there came one in haste at early morning, who overpowered me and pierced me through with the sword, and dismembered me in accordance with the rule of harmony. And he drew off the skin of my head with the sword which he was holding, and mingled the bones with the pieces of flesh, and caused them to be burned with the fire that he held in his hand[?], till I perceived by the transformation of the body that I had become spirit. And that is my unendurable torment.

Later on, Zosimus saw this same priest, in the guise of 'a man of copper', presiding over the altar-bowl, which was filled with bubbling water; and in the water he saw many people, 'burnt but living'. A bystander explained to him that

'It is the place where is carried out that which is called preserving [embalming]. For those men who wish to obtain spiritual perfection (ἀρετή)[20] come hither and become spirits, fleeing the body.' Therefore I said to him: 'Are you a spirit?' And he answered and said: 'A spirit and a guardian of spirits.'

As for the priest, Zosimus explains that

the man of copper...you will not find as a man of copper; for he has changed the colour of his nature and become a man of silver. If you wish, after a little time you will have him as a man of gold.

Subsequently, Zosimus tried several times to ascend to the 'place of punishments', but kept on losing his way. Encountering on one occasion the priest and on another a venerable white-haired Agathos Daimon, Zosimus slowly mounted step by step, only to see his guide hurled into the cauldron. The last dream concerns the dismembering and sacrifice of another figure, difficult to identify, and concludes with a voice telling Zosimus that 'the work is completed'.

The significance of the individual incidents and *dramatis personae* in these texts is partly to be found in the technical alchemical processes they symbolize;[21] but although Zosimus disclaimed, like most late antique intellectuals, any intention to innovate,[22] he was

---

[20] On the meaning of *aretē* in Zosimus see Karle, *Alchemistentraum* 33–6.
[21] See Festugière 1.212 n. 4; and above, 89, on the habit of envisaging metals in terms of bodies and souls.
[22] Zos. Pan., *fr. gr.* 234.7–10.

concerned to free himself from the material emphasis of traditional alchemy. He was committed to the idea that all things, material and spiritual, are linked by universal sympathetic powers; and the corollary of this doctrine was, in the first place, that spiritual experiences may be explained by material metaphor, and, secondly, that a correct alchemical understanding of the properties of matter is indispensable if the soul is to be liberated from its bondage in the body.[23] It is, then, scarcely surprising that Zosimus was well disposed to the aims of the Hermetic philosophers. If one were to consider which of the Hermetic writings offer the nearest parallels to Zosimus's visions, one would choose the *Poimandrēs*, with its dream-like setting and doctrine of the soul's ascent and purification from accrete passion, and *The mixing-bowl* (*C.H.* IV), with its account of the baptism of the souls in the font of intellect. And it is precisely these two texts that Zosimus mentions, by name, in the treatise entitled *The final quittance* (ἡ τελευταία ἀποχή).[24] Most of the surviving part of this work is devoted to remarks about the history of alchemical techniques in Egypt, with much emphasis on the part played by Hermes in their formulation. But Zosimus is also concerned to warn the treatise's addressee, a woman called Theosebia, against the wiles of daemons hostile to mankind's happiness, who hunger 'not just after sacrifices, but for your soul too'.

So do not allow yourself [Zosimus exhorts Theosebia] to be pulled back and forth like a woman, as I have already told you in my books *According to energy*. Do not roam about searching[25] for God; but sit calmly at home, and God, who is everywhere, and not confined in the smallest place like the daemons, will come to you. And, being calm in body, calm also your passions, desire and pleasure and anger and grief and the twelve portions of death. In this way, taking control of yourself, you will summon the divine [to come] to you, and truly it will come, that which is everywhere and nowhere. And, without being told, offer sacrifices to the daemons, but not offerings, nor [the sacrifices] that nourish and entice them, but rather the sacrifices that repel and destroy them, those of which Membres spoke to Solomon the king of Jerusalem, and especially those that Solomon himself wrote as the product of his own wisdom. So doing, you will attain the true and natural [tinctures] that are appropriate to certain times. Perform these things until your soul is perfected. When you realize that you have been perfected, and have found the natural

---

[23] Cf. *ibid.* 107.2–7: 'The composition of waters, the movement, growth, removal and restitution of corporeal nature, the separation of the spirit from the body, and the joining of the spirit with the body, are not due to foreign or alien natures, but to one single nature reacting on itself, a single species, such as the hard bodies of metals and the moist juices of plants.' Also Festugière 1.260–3; Franz, *Symbolon* 1 (1960) 27–38.

[24] Zos. Pan., *fr. gr.* 239–46; §§1–9 re-edited by Festugière 1.363–8.

[25] μὴ περιρρέμβου: for parallels, see Festugière, *Hermétisme* 251–5.

[tinctures], spit on matter and, hastening towards Poimenandres [*sic*] and receiving baptism in the mixing-bowl (κρατήρ), hasten up (ἀνάδραμε) towards your own race.[26]

In other words, the procedures of conventional alchemy are strictly preparatory to the purification and perfection of the soul; and the technical alchemical Hermetica offer a *propaideia* to the spiritual doctrines of the *Poimandrēs* and *The mixing-bowl*.[27] Zosimus faces the Hermetic literature as a conceptual unity, as he makes clear in the concluding passage of *The final quittance*'s surviving fragment, when he remarks that: 'Experience will show, along with all the virtuous actions of the soul.'[28]

Zosimus's most systematic exposition of the spiritual dimension of alchemy is contained in a text entitled *On apparatus and furnaces: authentic commentaries on the letter omega*,[29] part of a treatise in twenty-eight books, addressed, like *The final quittance*, to Theosebia, and entitled *Alchemical matters* (χημευτικά).[30] Here Zosimus confronts his major spiritual problem – how should a man relate to the forces of fate that suffuse the universe? He inveighs against those who

are always following fate, now to this opinion and then to its opposite. They have no conception of anything other than the material; all they know is fate. In his book *On natural dispositions* (περὶ φύσεων) Hermes calls such people mindless, only marchers swept along in the procession of fate, with no conception of anything incorporeal, and with no understanding of fate itself, which conducts them justly. Instead they insult the instruction it gives through corporeal experience, and imagine nothing beyond the good fortune it grants.

The striking image of the marchers, 'swept along in the procession of fate', recalls, once again, *The mixing-bowl*, where Hermes speaks of those souls who have not been baptized in intellect as 'like irrational animals'; for

just as processions pass into the crowd, unable to achieve anything themselves, but getting in the way of other people, so these men make their procession in the world, led astray as they are by the pleasures of the body.[31]

[26] That is, the race of perfected souls. Cf. *C.H.* IV.4, an address to the hearts of men: 'Plunge yourself (βάπτισον σεαυτήν), you who are able, into this mixing-bowl, you who believe that you will ascend (ἀνελεύσῃ) towards Him who sent the mixing-bowl down [to earth], you who know for what purpose you came into being.' On the alchemical tinctures referred to, see Festugière 1.264 n. 10; and for commentary on other points in this passage, *ibid.* 1.280–1; 2.28.

[27] *Ibid.* 1.280 n. 4, points also to a parallel between the 'twelve portions of death' and *C.H.* XIII.7, though the idea was widespread (see N.F. 2.212 n. 37). For Zosimus's numerous allusions to Hermes, Agathos Daimon etc. in a purely alchemical context, see the index to Berthelot's edition, *s.vv.*

[28] On the practical and spiritual aspects of alchemy see also Zos. Pan., *fr. syr.* 216, 259, 308.

[29] *Id., fr. gr.* 228–35; §§1–10 reprinted with emendations and translation (used here, with adjustments) by Jackson, *Zosimos* 16–37.

[30] *Suda* Z 168. *On apparatus and furnaces* refers to Theosebia at 228.15.   [31] *C.H.* IV.4–5, 7.

Admittedly, the idea of Man as a blinded wanderer at the mercy of daemons occurs enough in the Hermetica[32] to deserve to be called characteristic, even in a genre where so many of the ideas are commonplace; but Zosimus's reference is almost certainly a specific reminiscence of *The mixing-bowl*, for which we therefore possess an alternative title: *On natural dispositions*. This is an appropriate title for a text whose theme is the division of mankind into those who seek God and those who ignore Him.

Zosimus continues by quoting Hermes and Zoroaster to the effect that 'philosophers'[33] are superior to fate because they are never mastered either by grief or by joy. Yet the Egyptian and the Persian sage differed about whether the philosopher could actually *overcome* fate:

> Zoroaster boastfully affirms that by the knowledge of all things supernal and by the magical virtue of corporeal speech all the evils of fate, both partial and universal, may be averted. Hermes, however, in his book *On the inner life*,[34] condemns even magic, saying that the spiritual man, one who has come to know himself, need not rectify anything through the use of magic, not even if it is considered a good thing, nor must he use force upon necessity; but rather he should allow necessity to work in accordance with her own nature and judgement,

for it is certain that eventually he will see God, and be received into the realm of light. In other words, the philosopher should be sensitive to the personal significance of what happens to him by unavoidable necessity, rather than seeking to subvert or transcend by magic the divine powers inherent in the universe. But fate controls only the body, not the divine part in Man; and so the philosopher may legitimately aspire, by extracting himself from his subjection to the body and its passions, to imitate God himself, and rise above the sphere that is subject to fate. This, as also the insistence on the philosopher's need for self-knowledge, is the doctrine of the philosophical Hermetica; and it is clear that Zosimus has read at least the *Poimandrēs*, *The mixing-bowl* and the lost(?) treatise *On the inner life*, and has fully absorbed what they say into his understanding of the alchemical art.

Of the remaining Hermetic material in *On apparatus and furnaces*, more mythological or at least symbolic in tone than the discussion

---

[32] *C.H.* xvi.16; *Ascl.* 7.

[33] Since Hermes's *On the inner life*, which is apparently being quoted here (see below), appears from the context of Zosimus's remarks to have been a philosophical rather than a technical Hermeticum, τὸ φιλοσόφων γένος will not originally have referred to alchemists, but to philosophers in the more conventional sense.

[34] Reading Περὶ ἐναυλίας: see Festugière, *Hermétisme* 300 n. 78, and Jackson, *Zosimos* 44 n. 24.

of fate, something will be said in the next chapter *à propos* of the Hermetist Bitys, who is one of Zosimus's main sources at this point.[35] But we have not yet exhausted what Zosimus can tell us about the role of alchemy in the process of spiritual purification. In addition to the Greek fragments drawn on hitherto, we also have some unpublished Syriac fragments,[36] some of them really by Galen,[37] but others closely related to the surviving Greek texts by Zosimus, and undoubtedly authentic.[38] The Syriac texts confirm, if it was necessary, Zosimus's debt to Hermetic and other similar alchemical writings;[39] but of more interest in the present context is what they tell us about their author's view of alchemy's role in the broader life of the intellect and the spirit.

It is only from the Syriac fragments that we begin to grasp the part played in Zosimus's life by Theosebia, whom we encounter in the Greek texts as addressee of *The final quittance* and recipient of some spiritual advice that includes allusions to the *Poimandrēs* and *The mixing-bowl*. Though she appears to have been among the most influential exponents of alchemy in her day, Zosimus openly criticizes Theosebia in the Syriac fragments on the grounds that she has kept her alchemical wisdom secret.[40] She has, he claims, founded small circles 'apart from the multitude', and insisted on the swearing of oaths by their members. She teaches that the wisdom contained in the alchemical books is mysterious, and can only be transmitted in secret. 'But if the mysteries are necessary, it is all the more important', Zosimus asserts, 'that everybody should possess a book of chemistry, which should not be hidden away.' Elsewhere Zosimus inveighs against the jealousy, vanity and mean-spiritedness of those who conceal their wisdom; and he vows that henceforth he will have nothing to do with such people.[41] In yet another fragment he exhorts

---

[35] See also Festugière 1.263–73, and Jackson's nn. Note particularly the parallels with the *Poimandrēs*.

[36] Cambridge University Library MS Mm 6.19, partly translated (not very accurately, and at times, e.g. in the alchemical formulae, merely summarily) by Duval – see Bibliography.

[37] Above, 120 n. 15.

[38] Note particularly that the Greek version of Zos. Pan., *fr. syr.* 238, is preserved by Geo. Sync. 23–4, as from book IX of Zosimus's *Imouth*. Both Syncellus and the Syriac version describe the work as addressed to Theosebia.

[39] Zos. Pan., *fr. syr.* 212 (treatise addressed by Agathos Daimon to Osiris); 214, 235, 238 (books with titles such as *Imouth*, *The key* etc.); 238 = Geo. Sync., *loc. cit.* (Hermes's *Physica*). The title *Imouth* seems to have been applied to several alchemical books, including one by Zosimus himself (see previous n.).

[40] Zos. Pan., *fr. syr.* 239 (from a work addressed to Theosebia: see above, n. 38). For other references to Theosebia see *ibid.* 216, 308.

[41] *Ibid.* 224.

Theosebia not to imitate Aristotle, the philosopher of the visible and mortal sphere *par excellence*, but to aspire to the noetic realm, and to communicate what she sees there to those worthy of it. In this way she will acquire a great and desirable possession here on earth, namely 'the souls you will save and direct towards the incorporeal and incorruptible nature'[42] – this is reminiscent of the *Poimandrēs*'s evangelistic conclusion.

Despite the signs of controversy, then, Zosimus and his 'sister'[43] Theosebia clearly agreed that the true end of the alchemist's operations is spiritual purification and contemplation; and in both the technical and the philosophical dimensions of his art Zosimus found ample inspiration in the literature attributed to Hermes Trismegistus. Zosimus was to exercise a considerable influence on the development of alchemy in the following centuries; but it was his contemporary, the Platonist philosopher Iamblichus of Apamea (d. *c.* 320–5), who, thinking along similar lines, was to make the deeper mark on the late pagan mind, by propagating the potent combination of cult, magic and philosophy known as theurgy. Since the latter part of this and the whole of the following chapter will be concerned with the relations between Hermetism and theurgy, some explanation of the background and development of the sacred science is required at this point.

Pre-Iamblichan theurgy

Since theurgy in its heyday was acutely controversial, and is again so now among scholars, it will be as well to make clear from the outset what are the suppositions from which the present discussion proceeds. Late pagans, not unlike other religious people, regarded all aspects of their lives, from the most trivial and material to the most exalted and spiritual, as being subject, or potentially subject, to divine power. This assumption was made instinctively and naturally by anybody who shared the general theistic outlook of the age. It was not the product of special theories about determinism or anything else of that sort. In consequence, religion was expected to be able to accommodate and express all the infinitely diverse aspirations of its devotees, as well as certain things – the nature of divinity or the depths of human religious emotion – that are inherently inexpressible, through an

---

[42] *Ibid.* 264.   [43] *Suda* Z 168.

inevitably finite range of visual and verbal formulae. It follows that any attempt to describe religious experience by classifying its external manifestations will be simplistic. More particularly, enough has been said in earlier parts of this study – about for example the diversity of motive behind late antique magic, and the wide range of the *paideia* on which philosophical Hermetists insisted as the preliminary to contemplation – to make clear that, in the Hermetica at least, distinctions between 'religious' and 'philosophical' mentalities, even between 'superstition' and 'rationality', are likely to prove fluid.[44] There are no easy, predictable correlations between motive and means. Similar religious actions may, on closer inspection, turn out to have been provoked by widely differing intentions and motivations.

One could illustrate this point by showing how physical purity, in particular abstention from sexual intercourse or contact with the dead, was regarded as a precondition of all the different types of communication with the gods, from the mere visiting of a temple[45] at one end of the scale, by way of the pursuit of different types of oracle,[46] to the preparation for the noetic contemplation of God described in the Hermetica.[47] But of more interest here are the prayers that pagans offered daily, or oftener, to the sun. This was a popular form of devotion at all social levels,[48] and naturally a variety of interpretations was put on it by different people. It is instructive, though, to find one and the same person, the Platonist Proclus, addressing a thrice-daily act of worship to the sun like the most ordinary of his co-religionists,[49] and at the same time choosing that act of worship as a simile for the philosopher's encounter with the One. For in the *Theologia Platonica* Proclus speaks of the experience of beholding 'the sun of the light of the intelligible gods' as of a prostration before the rising sun, when one shuts one's eyes because of its unbearable glory. 'And let us celebrate Him [God] as with a hymn', Proclus continues, as he enumerates the manifold works of the creator, both in heaven and on earth.[50] We shall see in the next

[44] Cf. the remarks of Momigliano, *Quinto contributo* 73–92.
[45] E.g. Sokolowski, *Lois sacrées des cités grecques* 238–9 (Lindus, second century A.D.); Chaer., *fr.* 10 (on the Egyptian priesthood).
[46] E.g. Paus. IX.39.5–14 (oracle of Trophonius at Lebadea); *P. Graec. Mag.* IV.734–6; *I. mét. Eg.* 166.1–9 (record of a theological oracle from Talmis (Kalabsha) in Nubia).
[47] Above, 106–7.
[48] See the note of Saffrey and Westerink (2.121 n. 12) to the passage of Proclus quoted below.
[49] Marin., *Proc.* 22.
[50] Proc., *Theol. Plat.* II.11.

chapter that the Hermetists yielded nothing to Proclus in their appreciation of these intricately interlinked strands in the pagan heritage.

The general principle that underlies all this is clearly stated by Proclus's master Iamblichus in book v of the *De mysteriis*. Here the great Syrian philosopher addresses himself in a few direct and lucid pages to the central theme of the effect of his double nature, at once spiritual and corporeal, on Man's relationship with his gods.[51] The antithesis is first stated in its baldest form: the man who has become wholly soul and consorts with the gods renders them an absolutely incorporeal cult; while he who is still tied to the body renders them a material cult subject to becoming and change. But even the man of the spirit may, Iamblichus continues, experience bodily needs; and to meet them he must address himself to those gods or good daemons who have charge of corporeal matters – and are *ipso facto* of inferior rank. So not even the sage can confine himself to the company of the heavenly upper crust, which is wholly detached from materiality and powerless to affect it, at least directly. Then Iamblichus restates and refines somewhat his argument. Most men, he says, are subject to nature and fate, ceaselessly applying their 'practical reason' to natural phenomena and nothing else. Only a few, of exceptional intellect, cut themselves off from nature and lead a purely intellectual life. These are also those who exist between these two extremes of naturalism and intellectualism, at varying levels of spiritual purity. And each group adopts the manner of cult appropriate to it, the first preferring material rites and offerings, the second (which is very small) leading the incorporeal, intellectual life of the theurgists (as Iamblichus calls them), while those who are neither the one nor the other

either participate in both ways of worship, or disengage themselves from the one, or treat the [inferior] one as a starting-point for reaching the things that are of greater value (because otherwise what is superior would never be attained), or else they treat these things in some other way, as they see fit.

Like creation itself, then, whose multiformity is made one by the bond of universal sympathy, religious experience is a continuum, no part or phase of it comprehensible in isolation from the rest.[52] In his dealings with the gods the individual human must take account of the needs of the body as well as those of the soul; but to do so he

[51] Iam., *Myst.* v.15–20.
[52] Proc., *De arte hieratica* 148–9.

disposes only of a finite religious vocabulary, so that the same actions and expressions must often be deployed and interpreted at different levels. Recognizing these complexities, even the most intellectually and spiritually sophisticated of the late antique Platonists were prepared, if they thought it necessary for the instruction of their followers or the refutation of their critics, to manifest their spiritual powers through magic and cult as well as philosophy. This is particularly worth emphasizing in the case of Plotinus, who is generally regarded as the most intellectual, the least conventionally religious, of all the late antique Platonists. For our understanding of the relationship between magic and philosophy in Plotinus's circle, we depend chiefly on the controversial tenth chapter of Porphyry's biography.

The chapter begins with an attempt by an Alexandrian named Olympius to harm Plotinus by a magical invocation of malign astral energies. Porphyry dismisses the aggressor as 'one of those who affect to be philosophers', but neither this phrase, nor Olympius's knowledge of magic, alter the fact that, on Porphyry's own testimony, he belonged to the very narrow and select circle of people known to have been taught by Ammonius Saccas – a circle that included, among others, not only Plotinus but Longinus and the great Christian philosopher Origen.[53] We need not necessarily imagine Plotinus being assaulted by a vulgar sorcerer. In any event, the power of Plotinus's soul proved to be so great that Olympius found his spells rebounding upon himself, and so was forced to give up. But in a second anecdote, that follows on immediately from this first, we see Plotinus participating willingly and premeditatedly in a magical act. An Egyptian priest came to Rome, where Plotinus had established himself after leaving Alexandria, and persuaded the philosopher to co-operate in the invocation of his own personal daemon. The experiment took place in the temple of Isis, which the priest maintained was the only sufficiently pure place in the whole city. What actually appeared was a god, not a daemon, to the astonishment of those present. The end of this section of the *Vita Plotini* shows Porphyry eager to dispel any impression that Plotinus himself was a magician. His pupil Amelius, we are told, once invited the master to attend one of the sacred feasts in his company; and Plotinus refused, remarking that 'they [the gods] ought to come to me, not I to them'. This seems to mean that Plotinus himself, through

[53] Fowden, *Philosophia* 7 (1977) 365–6.

self-purification and contemplation, has become a more powerful divinity than any of the gods to whom the traditional cults addressed themselves.[54] But it is an ambiguous remark. The perfected philosopher, who has beheld the One, may be superior to the lesser gods, but at the same time he does not disdain to describe himself in terms of, or at least in relation to, the traditional divine hierarchy and the cults devoted to it.[55] In fact, Plotinus would have agreed wholeheartedly with the views of Iamblichus mentioned above. For all his criticism of magic, he conceded that the sage, since he has a body, must be subject to occult forces just like anyone or anything else. Only in his soul, his reasoning part, is he immune from bewitchment.[56] Though Porphyry and his friends were zealous in the worship of the gods, they had grown accustomed to thinking of their teacher as a philosopher *sui generis*, and were thrown off guard, as Porphyry himself admits, when he chose to describe himself in terms of traditional religion – albeit with a provocative hint of impiety. In attempting to reassure us, as he felt bound to do, of Plotinus's austere and uncompromising intellectuality, Porphyry unwittingly reveals that Plotinus himself took a more generous view of the underlying relationship between the cult of the gods and philosophy.[57]

But the generous view is the prerogative of those who can transcend conventional categories and see the inner connections of things. Porphyry was too analytical a thinker to do that, and spent his life trying to reconcile conventional religion and philosophy without sacrificing the assumption, natural to one who had experienced a traditional philosophical education, that their levels of application are completely different. He made his attempt through the medium of theurgy; and his principal source for theurgic doctrine was a collection of texts that emerged during the second century and was known as the *Oracula Chaldaica*. Only fragments of these oracles are now preserved. They deal, for the most part obscurely, with theological matters such as the structure of the divine hierarchy, and reveal disappointingly little about the most characteristic doctrine of classical fourth- and fifth-century theurgy, namely the soul's purification from the pollution of matter and return to its source through

---

[54] Compare Zosimus's exhortation to Theosebia, quoted above, 122–3.

[55] See Plotinus's comparison at VI.9.11.17–19 of the philosopher to one 'who has penetrated the inner sanctuary, leaving behind him the images in the temple'.

[56] Plot. IV.4.43.

[57] Cf. also Plot. II.9.16.

a combination of magical ceremonies with sacred formulae.[58] But it is with the later evolution of theurgy in the Platonist milieu that we are mainly concerned, and here we find some compensation for the lacunosity of the *Oracula*.

Porphyry, so far as we know, was the first major philosopher to take the *Oracula Chaldaica* seriously, yet he never espoused them whole-heartedly.[59] There is nothing strange, especially in a pupil of Plotinus, in the sharp distinction Porphyry makes in his *De abstinentia* between the unclean magician (γόης) and the divine man (θεῖος ἀνήρ), pure both without and within.[60] It is striking, though, to find Porphyry attacking theurgy in his *Epistola ad Anebonem* (to which Iamblichus's *De mysteriis* was a reply) on the grounds of its irreconcilability with the fundamentally intellectual character of Greek philosophy, but conceding, in the *De regressu animae*, that it was a possible means of purifying the spiritual soul ('spiritalis anima') and preparing it 'to receive spirits and angels and to see gods (ad videndos deos)'. But Porphyry remains ambivalent, even in the *De regressu*, for he denies that theurgy has any effect on the higher, or intellectual soul ('intellectualis anima'), and hence that it is able to lead the soul 'to behold its God (ad videndum Deum) and to perceive the things that truly exist'. Indeed, Porphyry asserts that the intellectual soul is capable of attaining this vision of the unity that lies beyond plurality even without the prior operation of theurgy on the spiritual soul.[61] Theurgy is, in other words, no more than a possible first step in the soul's return to its source, a partial, inadequate alternative to virtue and philosophy, a technique almost as independent of the moral qualities of its practitioner as the spells of the vulgar magician.

Iamblichus of Apamea

It was left then to Iamblichus to find a way out of Porphyry's *impasse*. The nature of the problem he faced was well stated by Porphyry

---

[58] *Orac. Chald.* 110 ('joining action to sacred word'). For a summary of the doctrine of the *Orac.* see the introduction to des Places's edition, 11–18; and on theurgy and magic see below, 133.

[59] Cf. Lewy, *Chaldaean Oracles* 449–56.

[60] Porph., *Abst.* II.45.

[61] Porph., *Regr.* 2, and cf. 4: 'those who have been purified in their spiritual soul by theurgic art cannot return to the Father'. See also Augustine's comments, *Civ. Dei* X.27.

himself in the *De regressu* (which we know only from quotations by Augustine):

> Now Porphyry says...that no doctrine has yet been established to form the teaching of a philosophical sect, which offers a universal way (*universalem viam*) for the liberation of the soul; that no such way has been produced by any philosophy (in the truest sense of the word), or by the moral disciplines and teachings of the Indians, or by the 'elevation' (*inductione*) of the Chaldaeans, or in any other way; and that this universal way had never been brought to his knowledge in his study of history. He admits without any doubt that such a way exists, but confesses that it had never come to his notice. Thus he was not satisfied with all that he had taken such pains to learn on the subject of the liberation of the soul, the knowledge and the beliefs which he convinced himself – or rather convinced others – that he possessed. For he felt that he had failed to obtain any supreme authority which he was bound to follow on such an important subject.[62]

Iamblichus by contrast was convinced that he had found such a supreme authority and universal way in a synthesis of Chaldaean, Egyptian and 'philosophical' – that is, Greek – doctrines; and this synthesis – a distinctively Iamblichan form of theurgy – is expounded in the *De mysteriis*.[63] The most notable respect in which the theurgist differed from conventional philosophers was in his dependence on what Iamblichus calls

> the perfective operation of the unspeakable acts (ἔργα) correctly performed, acts which are beyond all understanding (ὑπὲρ πᾶσαν νόησιν); and on the power of the unutterable symbols which are intelligible only to the gods.[64]

The purpose of these acts and symbols was to invoke the assistance of the gods, in order to liberate the soul from the body and the bonds of sympathy, and bring about its 'theurgical union' with the divine.[65] For Iamblichus, in other words, the theurgist's field of action, confined by Porphyry to the lower soul, had come to embrace the very highest levels of mystical union. The philosopher, for Plotinus an autonomous agent in the pursuit of perfection, was made by Iamblichus into an operative dependent on the help of superhuman forces.[66]

By introducing such marked cultic elements into his exposition of philosophy's highest objective, the purifying of the soul and its unification with God, Iamblichus exposed himself to accusations that

---

[62] Aug., *Civ. Dei* x.32 (tr. Bettenson, with adjustments).
[63] Iam., *Myst.* 1.1.4–2.7.
[64] *Ibid.* 11.11.96–7 (tr. Dodds).
[65] *Ibid.*, and 1.12, 11.6.81, v1.6, x.4, etc.
[66] Cf. *ibid.* 111.1.100, on the divinatory element in theurgy as 'a work not human, but divine, supernatural, sent down from heaven above'.

his teaching was nothing but magic or sorcery, designed to do little more than evoke apparitions of the gods.[67] Nor have we any reason to doubt Eunapius's assertion that Iamblichus did indeed perform miracles on occasion, albeit under pressure from his disciples and against his better judgement.[68] After all, theurgy and magic depended for their success on the manipulation of the same network of universal sympathy;[69] and many theurgical techniques are closely paralleled in the magical papyri.[70] But to identify the two would be to contradict flatly the *De mysteriis*, in which Iamblichus makes abundantly clear that

> it is not true that this sort of [theurgical invocation] draws the impassible and pure [gods] down towards what is subject to passions and impure; on the contrary it makes us, who through generation are born subject to passions, pure and unchangeable.[71]

Iamblichus conceded both that the descent of the gods might form a part of the theurgic process, and that from the operative's point of view the theurgical act might be performed more or less spiritually, depending partly at least on experience;[72] but the ultimate object remained the purification and salvation of the soul. Iamblichan theurgy was more a development, less a contradiction of third-century Platonism than was appreciated until very recently.[73] When in the *De mysteriis* Iamblichus identifies philosophy with mere logic, and pointedly distinguishes it from theurgy, he does so in order to emphasize his rejection of the type of philosophy, based on thought (ἔννοια) alone, whose primacy Porphyry had asserted in his *Epistola ad Anebonem*.[74] In the same way Iamblichus deprecates Porphyry's reliance on reason in order to arrive at the conviction that the gods exist, for this is an intuition that was planted within us before we ever learned to judge and choose.[75] But despite this rejection of any account of mystical union that emphasizes the role of human reason,

---

[67] Cf. Aug., *Civ. Dei* x.9–11, with reference to Porphyry, who himself conceded that theurgy might be put to unworthy uses: Iam., *Myst.* x.7.293; Aug., *Civ. Dei* x.11 *ad fin.*

[68] Eun., *V. Phil.* v.2.1–7, VI.11.11.

[69] E.g. Iam., *Myst.* I.12.42, v.20.227–8.

[70] Eitrem, *S.O.* 22 (1942) 49–79.

[71] Iam., *Myst.* I.12.42.

[72] *Ibid.* v.20–1.

[73] For helpful recent discussions see Smith, *Porphyry's place* 100–10, and Zintzen, in *Festschrift Dörrie* 312–28.

[74] Iam., *Myst.* I.2.5–7, II.11.96; and cf. the distinction drawn by Dam., *In Phd.* I.172, between the φιλόσοφοι Plotinus and Porphyry and the ἱερατικοί Iamblichus, Syrianus and Proclus. The contrast drawn at *Myst.* III.25.161 between philosophy and 'wrangling' (τὸ ἐριστικόν) confirms Iamblichus's essentially positive attitude to philosophy.

[75] *Ibid.* I.3.

Iamblichus himself often uses noetic vocabulary in connection with theurgical experience;[76] and it is noticeable that he says much less about the part played by ritual acts in describing the culmination of the soul's ascent than when discussing the earlier stages.[77] Divination and sacrifice are discussed at length in the *De mysteriis* (books III and V) in order to explain the basic, indispensable skills required of the theurgist; but it is made clear that at the higher levels of ascent such techniques become wholly spiritualized.[78] The ritual element in theurgy was real enough; but it had more to do with the route than with the goal of Iamblichus's 'via universalis', and it was only in the route he took that the philosopher of Apamea differed from his predecessors. By ritualizing the initial stages of the soul's ascent, he was able to make them more accessible than the stern and lonely way of the contemplative philosopher. But the ultimate mystical union remained, as it had been for Plotinus, an intuitive leap that only a few would dare to make, and an experience to the description of which the vocabulary of the philosopher was less inadequate than that of the theurgist.

It should by now be clear that between Iamblichan theurgy and the spiritual Hermetism described in chapter 4 there is less of a gap than has often been assumed. Indeed, Iamblichus asserts that the sources of theurgical doctrine are in part Egyptian as well as Chaldaean and Greek.[79] Posing as an Egyptian *prophētēs* called Abammon, he devotes large parts of the *De mysteriis Aegyptiorum* (a title invented by Ficino) to the exposition of general Egyptian beliefs concerning the gods.[80] And, most significant of all, Iamblichus specifically claims to have found the theurgical liberation of the soul from the bonds of fate described in Hermetic books. This declaration forces us to look at our Hermetic texts in a new light. But Iamblichus drew on other Hermetica too, and it will be well to consider these first, in order to build up a full picture of his indebtedness to the Hermetic literature.

[76] E.g. *ibid.* 1.12.41 (with the Platonic, Plotinian and Porphyrian parallels adduced by Lewy, *Chaldaean Oracles* 188); V.18.225 (on the theurgists 'leading their life according to intellect alone, and the life of the intellect'); X.4, 8. The most strikingly 'Plotinian' passage is perhaps V.15.219: 'We become wholly soul, and we are outside the body, raised up into intellect'. See also n. 73 above.

[77] See *Myst.*, *loc. cit.*, discussed above, 128. On the possibility that the *Orac. Chald.* themselves taught two levels of theurgy, see Smith, *Porphyry's place* 130–2; Hadot, in Lewy, *Chaldaean Oracles* 718–19.

[78] Iam., *Myst.* III.31.178–9, V.15.219, VIII.4.267, X.6.292.

[79] *Ibid.* 1.1.4–2.7. Dam., *V. Isid. fr.* 3, treats theurgy as of wholly Egyptian origin.

[80] E.g. *Myst.* VI.5–VII.5, as well as book VIII with its more specifically Hermetic doctrine.

Iamblichus of Apamea

In pointing to the Egyptian origins of Hermetism, Iamblichus does not seem to have been making any very striking innovation. Since Porphyry had addressed his attack on theurgy to another (fictitious?) Egyptian priest, Anebo,[81] the Egyptian connection was clearly common knowledge – in fact, it looks as if Egyptian priests were regarded as the authorities *par excellence* on theurgy. Nor is there anything surprising in that, granted the magical character of Egyptian cult, its practitioner's reputation for all manner of divine wisdom, and the numerous parallels that can be adduced between the magical papyri from Egypt and what is known of theurgical practice.[82] There is admittedly little if any sign of Egyptian influence in the *Oracula Chaldaica* themselves. They can best be accounted for in terms of the Platonist ideas, mixed with Stoicism and Pythagoreanism, that were common coin in the second century – what we call Middle Platonism –, together perhaps with elements of Iranian, Babylonian and Syrian origin.[83] It was a desire to emphasize these oriental connections that gave the oracles their epithet 'Chaldaean', for the Chaldaeans, in Graeco-Roman usage, were the astronomer priests of Babylonia who, discovered by the Greeks in the aftermath of Alexander's conquests, came to enjoy so high a reputation for learning and wisdom throughout the Greek and Roman world.[84] But to the Greek and Roman mind Babylon and Egypt stood *jointly* for the wisdom of the East, so naturally they were compared, and questions of priority or possible mutual influence much discussed, especially in the fields of astronomy and astrology.[85] And the Hellenization of the Near East in the centuries after Alexander's conquests will itself have been a potent factor in encouraging more such interaction. A late but not incredible source asserts that Ptolemy II Philadelphus ordered the translation of Chaldaean as well as

---

[81] *Ibid.* 1.1.2–3.

[82] I dissent here from Dagron, *T. & M. Byz.* 3 (1968) 155 n. 39: 'Dans cette querelle, Anébon et Abammon sont "égyptiens" comme dans Thémistios les chrétiens sont "syriens"; Porphyre soulignait ainsi le caractère étranger d'innovations religieuses qu'il estimait incohérentes et dangereuses.'

[83] See Lewy, *Chaldaean Oracles* 311–441; and Dodds, in Lewy, *op. cit.* 700–1; but also the following note.

[84] Bidez, *A.I.Ph.O.* 3 (1935) 41–89; Lewy, *op. cit.* 425–8 (following Bidez and Cumont, *Mages* 1.33–8). Koster, *R.L.A.C.* 2.1018–19, and Drijvers, in *Etudes Mithriaques* 151–86, criticize the theories about Irano-Mesopotamian syncretism that underlie these older discussions of the *Chaldaioi*.

[85] See e.g. Diod. Sic. 1.81.6 and Ps.-Eupol., *fr.* 1, maintaining the priority of the Egyptians and the Chaldaeans respectively; also Clem. Al., *Strom.* 1.74.2; Chaer., *fr.* 2, and Philippus (Bardaisan), *Book of the laws of countries* 38–40, on the 'Babylonian' and 'Egyptian' traditions as indistinguishable constituents of 'the Chaldaean doctrine', i.e. astrology.

Egyptian books into Greek;[86] while a horoscope dated A.D. 137 perhaps refers to the consultations of Chaldaeans with Hermes and Asclepius.[87] So one can see how the belief may have arisen that theurgy had roots in Egypt, long before Iamblichus set about the construction of his synthesis.

The reader of the *De mysteriis* is given to understand that the immediate source for its exposition of Egyptian theology is the sacred Thoth literature. The treatise begins with these words:

Hermes, the god who presides over learning, has for long been rightly regarded as common to all priests: he who presides over true knowledge about the gods is one and the same, whatever the circumstances. It was to him that our ancestors too dedicated the fruits of their wisdom, by placing all their own writings under his name.[88]

A little further on, 'Abammon' announces that he will draw both on the 'innumerable writings of antiquity', and on 'the [writings] that the ancients later gathered into a compact book'.[89] In book VIII these allusions are expanded a little. The 'innumerable writings' of 'Hermes' (the reference is obviously to the Thoth literature) number 20,000 according to one Seleucus, or 36,525 according to Manetho; and among these are a hundred volumes each on the empyrean and ethereal gods, and a thousand on their heavenly cousins.[90] From which we deduce (with little surprise) that Iamblichus did not lose much time poring over the temple-texts, but extracted his information about the doctrines of the Egyptian priesthood from the obvious secondary sources in Greek – Manetho's *Sacred Book*, no doubt; Chaeremon and Porphyry (as we shall shortly see); and Seleucus, who is probably the same as 'Seleucus the theologian', a near-contemporary of Manetho and mentioned along with him by Porphyry in the *De abstinentia*, in the course of a discussion of human sacrifice.[91] And to this list we should add, it seems, certain Greek Hermetica. For later in book VIII Iambli-

---

[86] Geo. Sync. 516.

[87] Neugebauer and van Hoesen, *Greek horoscopes* 137c, p. 42.

[88] Iam., *Myst.* 1.1.1–2.

[89] *Ibid* 1.2.5.

[90] *Ibid.* VIII.1.260–1, 2.262 – presumably the latter passage also derives from either Seleucus or Manetho.

[91] Porph., *Abst.* II.55.1–2; cf. Bouffartigue-Patillon's n. *ad loc.*, and Jacoby, *F. Gr. H.* 3 (b). 93, suggesting that he wrote the περὶ θεῶν attributed by the *Suda* to the much later Seleucus of Alexandria. Marc. Anc., *Eccl.* 6, includes 'the followers of Hermes and Seleucus' in a list of heretical sects. On the sources of Iamblichus's Egyptian material see also below, 138–9.

chus recalls that Porphyry had encountered difficulties while perusing certain 'writings', and offers the following 'solution':

> The [books] that circulate under the name of Hermes contain Hermetic opinions, even though they often make use of the language of the philosophers; for they have been translated from the Egyptian language by men who were not ignorant of philosophy.[92]

Evidently Porphyry had been reading some Hermetic books of philosophical hue,[93] in Greek of course, and had felt that he detected elements in them that were inconsistent with what he understood, presumably on the authority of such as Manetho and Chaeremon, to be the tenets of Egyptian theology. But if Porphyry had been reading Hermetic books, so too had Iamblichus, under the impression that they had originally been written in Egyptian, by Egyptian priests,[94] and then rendered into Greek. And so it was that Iamblichus decided to pose as a *prophētēs* in order to write the *De mysteriis*, for he knew that certain of his secondary authorities were priests, and thought he knew that his primary sources originated in the temples of ancient Egypt. But what were these Hermetic books that Iamblichus relied on?

The account of Egyptian theology in *De mysteriis* VIII.2–3 begins by explaining the supreme divine power as a triad – the One, the Monad that proceeds from the One, and Essence (or the First Intelligible) deriving in turn from the Monad. 'These then are the most ancient origins of all things, which Hermes places before the ethereal and the empyrean and the heavenly gods.' And the 'indivisible One,...who is worshipped only in silence' (a characteristic Hermetic notion), is called, according to Hermes, 'Eikton'; and after him comes Kneph (MSS: Emeph), 'the leader of the heavenly gods'. Below these two come other divine beings who have charge of the work of creation, Specifically,

> the demiurgic *nous*, master of truth and wisdom, when it comes into the sphere of generation, and leads into the light the invisible power of the hidden words, is called Amun in the language of the Egyptians; but when it executes everything unerringly and artfully and truly, then it is called Ptah – which the Greeks translate as Hephaestus, applying it only to [the god's] quality as artisan; while as giver of blessings it is called Osiris. And it has other names corresponding to its other powers and activities.

---

[92] Iam., *Myst.* VIII.4.265.
[93] Cf. also *ibid.* I.1.4.
[94] Compare the passage quoted above, 136.

Iamblichus immediately continues:

And the Egyptians posit another authority over all the elements of the created world and over the powers – four masculine and four feminine – that are in them; and they assign this authority to the sun. Another sovereignty, over the whole of mortal nature, they give to the moon. Then, marking off the heavens into two or four or twelve or thirty-six portions, or twice those numbers, or effecting some other sort of division, they assign to these portions authorities either more or fewer in number, and again they place at their head the One who is over them all. And thus the teaching of the Egyptians about the principles embraces everything from on high right down to the very lowest [degrees].

Scholars have not found it easy to make sense of all this. There is some traditional Egyptian material (though not such as was unavailable in the Greek literature on the subject),[95] jumbled together with relatively late Greek philosophical speculation,[96] and little clue to how it all fits together. Iamblichus recognizes this, emphasizing the Hermetic – by which he means Egyptian – character of the doctrines he has set forth, and ascribing whatever is obviously Greek to interpretation or interpolation by the translators.[97] Fortunately Plutarch gives us a slightly clearer picture of what Iamblichus had been reading when he alludes, in his *De Iside et Oside*, to 'so-called Books of Hermes' which deal, among other matters, with the names of the gods. From these texts we learn, for example, that 'the power placed in charge of the sun's course is Horus, and the Greeks call it Apollo; while the power in charge of the wind is called by some Osiris, by others Sarapis'.[98] In other words there existed what we may best call theological Hermetica, which described the gods in the Stoic manner, in terms of the powers inherent in physical creation,[99] and discussed the names variously assigned them by the Egyptians and the Greeks.[100] There are obvious

---

[95] Thausing, *Kairos* 4 (1962) 95–8; Derchain, *C.E.* 76 (1963) 220–6; Festugière 1.115–17; Griffiths, *Plutarch's De Iside* 374. That there is Egyptian material in *Myst.*, though, no more validates Derchain's conclusion that 'Abammon' really existed than the assumption that Iamblichus had direct access to original Egyptian sources.

[96] Festugière 4.23–4, 38–40.

[97] The passage quoted above, 137, follows on immediately after the account of the divine hierarchy.

[98] Plut., *Is. Os.* 61 (tr. Griffiths).   [99] Cf. *ibid.* 40, 41, 66.

[100] As pointed out by Adler, in *Charisteria Rzach* 9, there is an important parallel to this Plutarch passage in *P. Vat. gr.* 8, an encomium of the goddess Athena (cf. Canart, in *Miscellanea papyrologica* 386). If one accepts Adler's supplements, in particular the name of Hermes at 1.6 (approved by Nock, *Essays* 517 n. 7), the papyrus provides important evidence for the contents of the theological Hermetica. But it is surprising to hear of Hermes that 'though he had apprehended all things, he came to no precise conclusion about the birth of the gods'. More probably derived from the theological Hermetica, and sharing

parallels with the passages just quoted from the *De mysteriis*; and we may assume that it was at least in part from these theological Hermetica that Iamblichus compiled his account of Egyptian doctrine concerning the gods.[101]

The authority of the Hermetica in Iamblichus's eyes can be judged from the fact that, when they seem to contradict his argument, he neither dismisses nor tries to refute them, but simply suggests that they convey a partial picture, or that Porphyry has misunderstood them. For example, in his attack on the ritual aspect of theurgy in the *Epistola ad Anebonem* Porphyry made much of the materialist view of the divine world taken by some of Iamblichus's sources.[102] Iamblichus needed to show that this was only a partial view of Egyptian theology; and he did so exclusively on the basis of other Hermetic writings – which, we should remember, he regarded as genuine translations from the Egyptian.

Immediately after his account of the divine hierarchy, then, Iamblichus turns to the question of astrology, crucial to the dispute about the materialism or otherwise of Egyptian theology. First he paraphrases a section of the *Epistola ad Anebonem*, the original of which has been preserved by Eusebius:

Chaeremon and the others consider that there was nothing prior to the visible worlds, and give pride of place to the [gods] of the Egyptians, recognizing no other gods save the so-called 'planets' and the [stars] that fill up the zodiac, and as many as rise near them; also the divisions into the decans, and the stars under which one is born and the so-called 'mighty ones' and 'sovereigns', the names of which are contained in the *Salmeschiniaka* along with the diseases that they can heal, and their risings and settings, and the indications they give of future events.[103]

Consistently with his thesis, Porphyry here emphasizes the materialist basis of the theological doctrines contained in Chaeremon and the *Salmeschiniaka*. But Iamblichus remoulds the passage for his own ends, emphasizing the partial yet complementary nature of the explanations of the divine realm given by these authorities. The astronomers

their somewhat Stoic tone, is the material preserved by Ph. Bybl., *fr.* 4 (814.23–816.12) (also by Iam. *ap.* Ioh. Lyd., *Mens.* iv.6), from a treatise by Taautos = Thoth–Hermes on the divinity of snakes: see Baumgarten, *Philo of Byblos* 254.

101 Des Places, *Études platoniciennes* 336–7, suggests some parallels with the philosophical Hermetica as well.

102 A common observation (and complaint) as regards the Egyptians: Pépin, in *Sagesse et religion* 54–6.

103 Porph., *Aneb.* II.12b; cf Iam., *Myst.* VIII.4.265–6. (On ἐν ἀρχῆς λόγῳ τιθέμενοι see van der Horst's translation of and notes to Chaer., *fr.* 5, 7. I read κραταιοὺς καὶ ἡγεμόνας, following Iamblichus's version; cf. Schwyzer, *Chairemon* 67. Τὸ ἀλμενιχιακά I have preferred the reading offered by the best MSS of Iamblichus; and cf. Heph. Theb. II.18.74: Σαλμεσχοινιακά).

(or astrologers) may deal only with 'the particular distribution of the principles', but Chaeremon and the theologians treat of 'the ultimate principles'. And we should not (Iamblichus implies) overemphasize the importance of the *Salmeschiniaka*, which are Hermetic texts, and fully congruent with the rest of the Hermetica, but contain 'only the smallest part of the Hermetic system'. It is admittedly conceivable that neither Iamblichus nor Porphyry had read the *Salmeschiniaka*, and depended for what they knew of them on Chaeremon, who could have drawn on Egyptian as well as Greek sources – the title *Salmeschiniaka* may well derive from an Egyptian word.[104] But we do have a Greek astrological papyrus from Oxyrhynchus (*P. Oxy.* 465) which strongly resembles the *Salmeschiniaka* as described by Porphyry; and Iamblichus does give the impression that he is personally familiar with them, and understands their relationship to the rest of the Hermetic literature. This important point he makes unambiguously – that the astrological Hermetica are concerned with an integral but, ultimately, subordinate part of the Hermetic world-view. And this, as one might expect, is the cue for the introduction of the philosophical Hermetica.

'The Egyptians', Iamblichus asserts,[105] 'do not say that all things are natural' – in other words, they acknowledge a spiritual as well as a material realm.

They distinguish both the life of the soul (ψυχή) and that of the intellect (νοῦς) from the life of nature, and not just in the cosmic sphere, but as regards us [men] as well.

The world is ruled by intellect and reason (λόγος), and

they [the Egyptians] do not regard these [doctrines] as merely theoretical, but encourage one to ascend by hieratic theurgy to the higher and more universal regions that are placed above fate, to God the creator, without making use of anything material, or employing any other aid, save only the observation of the appropriate moment (καιρός). Hermes showed this way too,[106] and the *prophētēs* Bitys translated it to King Ammon, finding it inscribed in hieroglyphic characters in a sanctuary at Sais in Egypt. He handed on the name of God that extends through all the world. And there exist many other [compositions] concerning the same matters, so that you [Porphyry] are, it seems to me, wrong to posit a physical cause for all the [gods] of the Egyptians. [For] they [the Egyptians] accept many principles connected with many essences, and supramundane powers which they worship by hieratic ritual.

---

[104] Gundel 15–16. Sodano's arguments in favour of Porphyry's use of philosophical Hermetica, *Porfirio* 65–71, are based on nothing but general similarities of doctrine.

[105] Iam., *Myst.* VIII.4.266–6.268.

[106] I.e. there is more to Hermetism than astrology, which is 'but the smallest part of the Hermetic system' – see above.

This then is the crucial allusion to theurgical Hermetica. Its context, together with such specific elements as the 'way' of Hermes,[107] and even the astrological *kairos*[108] and the self-consciously Egyptian scenery, established that these texts were not dissimilar to the philosophical Hermetica known to us.[109] We may also recall Iamblichus's reference sightly earlier to books translated from Egyptian into Greek by men 'not ignorant of philosophy'. But after the account of the way of Hermes given in the previous chapter, the passage just quoted inevitably causes some surprise. Indeed, in the present state of our knowledge it is only in the light of the *De mysteriis* that we can interpret the evidence that the surviving philosophical Hermetica themselves provide for a theurgical approach to the salvation of the soul clothed in matter. That is why we must now go back to look at certain more or less ritualistic features of our philosophical texts which might ideally have been considered in chapter 4.

[107] Cf. N.F. 3.xxi (adding now *N.H.C.* vi.6.63.11); Mahé 1.132–3. For the 'path of Thoth' in the Egyptian tradition see Ray, *Archive of Ḥor* 161; and cf. (on the more general background) Couroyer, *R. Bi.* 56 (1949) 412–28.

[108] Cf. *N.H.C.* vi.6.62.16–20.

[109] On other parallels between *Myst.* viii and *N.H.C.* vi.6, see Mahé 1.50–2. On the doctrine of the two souls expounded at *Myst.* viii.6.269 see below, 152–3. Much of viii.7–8 must also be Hermetic, judging from viii.6.268–9: 'You [Porphyry] say that most Egyptians regard our free will as dependent on the movement of the stars. How things really are needs to be explained to you at greater length, making use of Hermetic concepts.' But it is difficult to locate precise debts.

[6]

Hermetism and theurgy

The role and understanding of ritual

The problem of the extent to which the Hermetists employed ritual in their spiritual quest has caused much scholarly ink to flow. No consensus has yet emerged because of a tendency to over-emphasize either the (supposedly) self-proclaimed purity and spirituality of the way of Hermes or the undeniable interest of certain philosophical Hermetica in traditional religious cult. To accept the one is assumed to require the rejection of the other – with predictably unconvincing results. A new approach is required, and a useful model is already at hand in the previous chapter's discussion of the relationship between philosophy and theurgy, and in the examination in chapter 4 of 'monist' and 'dualist' strands in the philosophical Hermetica. Once one recognizes the tendency of the scholarly mind to classify and compartmentalize, and so to occlude connections between different approaches to a given goal, one is free to ask whether such variations of method may in fact be determined either by different levels of accomplishment in those who adopt them, or by the complex nature of the goal itself. These two determining factors may also themselves be related. In terms of the present investigation, he who embarks on the spiritual journey sees many gods and no clear objective; while he who has been made perfect is absorbed in contemplation of the One. As the road ascends, both the scenery and one's response to it change.

The model here proposed has, it so happens, the explicit authority of the Hermetic *Asclepius*. Dividing the crowd of divinities below God himself, 'the Lord and Father', into the celestial and the terrestrial, the *Asclepius* discusses in two separate passages[1] the relationship between Man and the terrestrial gods. Just as God created the

---

[1] *Ascl.* 23–4, 37–8.

celestial divinities, so Man creates their terrestrial cousins, those images which, infused with the presence of the god they represent, dwell in the temples in close proximity to human kind.

In this way Mankind, always mindful of its nature and origin, persists in imitating the Divine to the point that, just as the Father and Lord endows the gods with immortality, in order that they may resemble Him, so Mankind fashions its gods in its own image.

These terrestrial gods, faithful to their human prototype, may be moved by anger and even do harm, as well of course as providing such benefits as oracles and the healing of illness. So they must be kept propitious, and none may be neglected – hence the plethora of gods, including many animals, worshipped by the Egyptians, and the need to know the precise manner of their composition, in order that a correct cult may be rendered to them. For they are made, so Hermes tells Asclepius,

of herbs, stones and spices containing occult divine power. And if you would know why they are diverted with frequent sacrifices, hymns, songs of praise and concord of sweet sounds that imitate heaven's harmony, it is so that that celestial element which has been enticed into the image by repeated celestial rites may in happiness endure its long sojourn among human kind. That then is how Man makes gods.

Immediately after this passage there follows a section (39–40) on fate, which holds together the whole divine order, including the celestial and terrestrial gods; and then comes the conclusion of the whole treatise, and the prayer of thanksgiving already reproduced at the end of chapter 4. The passage which introduces the prayer may be quoted here:

Having emerged from the sanctuary they began to pray to God, facing towards the south (for, when one wishes to pray to God at sunset, one must face in that direction, just as at sunrise one must face eastwards). When they had already begun their prayer, Asclepius said in a low voice: 'Tat, shall we suggest to your father that he should have us pray to God with incense and perfumes?' Trismegistus heard him and, much disturbed, said: 'Silence, silence Asclepius. For it is a sort of sacrilege to burn incense and other such things when one prays to God. For He who is all things, or in Whom all things are, lacks nothing. So let us adore Him rather with thanksgiving; for that is the finest incense that can be offered God, when mortal men give thanks.'

Here then we find different sorts of worship offered to the terrestrial divinities on the one hand and God the Lord and Father on the other.[2] Yet, consistent with the doctrinally compendious

---

[2] Cf. Iam., *Myst.* v.14.218: 'to offer material sacrifices to immaterial gods is inappropriate, but very suitable to all material gods'.

character of the *Asclepius*, the two approaches are distinguished rather than brought into antithesis. Despite the purely spiritual emphasis of the act of thanksgiving, it takes place in a temple, and certain positions and times are marked out as specially appropriate to it. The prayer itself has a clear structure, and its use, especially (as here) by several worshippers in unison, is in a loose sense a liturgical action. There is in short nothing intrinsically shocking about Asclepius's suggestion that a prayer should be accompanied with an offering of incense. It is the destination of the prayer – God, not the gods – that makes the incense inappropriate.

The question now arises, whether this graded rather than absolute differentiation between the ways in which we communicate with God and the many gods provides a framework adequate to accommodate the other 'cultic' or 'non/anti-cultic' elements in the philosophical Hermetica. The following pages, while providing a commentary on the passages from the *Asclepius* just now presented, will also attempt to indicate the extent of the evidence for the external aspects of the way of Hermes, and so to supplement what was said in chapter 4 about the Hermetic *religio mentis*.

Without lingering over the obvious but ambiguous[3] point that the *dramatis personae* of the Hermetica are conventional deities, and that much allusion is made to the external phenomena of religion, it should first be recalled that Thoth, and by extension Hermes Trismegistus, was conceived of as the founder and patron of all sacred rites, including magic. Even in the philosophical Hermetica there are, as noticed in the previous chapter, elements of magic; while the *Asclepius*'s positive view of the temple cults is reinforced by *C.H.* xvii, a fragment of a dialogue in which Tat speaks of universal sympathy, explains how the incorporeal world is reflected in the realm of matter, and concludes by observing: 'For this reason worship the statues, O king, for they too contain forms (ἰδέας) from the intelligible world.' We also find the pagan priest Longinianus invoking the 'Orphic, Etruscan and Hermetic precepts' in a letter to Augustine about the manner in which one should worship God,[4] thus associating Hermes with the ancient divinatory techniques of the Etruscan priests. It seems safe to assert that not even the most philosophical of Hermetists will have been unaware of this element in the tradition to which they

---

[3] Note the controversy aroused by Cumont's attempt to draw concrete conclusions from Plotinus's occasional references to cult: cf. Nilsson, *Geschichte* 2.434 n. 3.

[4] Aug., *ep.* 234.1 (reading 'Tageticis' for 'Ageticis').

adhered; and indeed it is Zosimus of Panopolis and Iamblichus, of all people, who preserve almost our only evidence that the philosophical Hermetica condemned magic.[5] It is clear that this prohibition of the resort to magic occurred only with reference to the sage's attempt to pass beyond the realm of fate, in the very last stages of the way of Hermes.

One can at least then say that the author of the *Asclepius* sets his discourse not inappropriately in a temple, ending it with a prayer which is followed by an embrace and a 'pure meal without animal-flesh'.[6] That the prayer is addressed to the setting sun, and allusion made to prayers to the rising sun, reminds us of Proclus's devotion to this daily ritual and the way he used its imagery to describe the soul's encounter with the One.[7] *C.H.* XIII contrives to combine the two approaches. Just before he reveals the 'secret' and highly philosophical hymn of rebirth that he has heard sung in the Ogdoad, Hermes gives Tat the following ritual instructions, virtually identical with those in the concluding passage of the *Asclepius*: 'Stand in an open-air place, looking towards the south wind at the moment when the setting sun sinks, and make an act of adoration; and likewise at the rising of the sun, facing towards the east wind.'[8] The example of Proclus makes one wonder whether the philosophical devotees of Hermes did not also take part in such cultic practices. And if we are right to deduce from its heading in our manuscripts (ΥΜΝΩΔΙΑ ΚΡΥΠΤΗ, ΛΟΓΟΣ Δ′) that the hymn itself was extracted from an earlier collection of such texts,[9] then we may assume that it once played a more actively ritual role than is possible in its present context. Not that the Hermetists were averse to the use of hymns in their gatherings.[10] In the *Poimandrēs*, when the day's instruction is over and the sun is setting, the teacher bids his disciples give thanks to God;[11] while the treatise itself ends with a hymn or litany of markedly liturgical character,[12] and a prayer which closely resembles the conclusion of the *Asclepius*.

Most interesting of all is what happens at the actual moment of

---

[5] Above, 109.
[6] *Ascl.* 41 = *N.H.C* VI.7.65 (which alone mentions the embrace).
[7] Above, 127.
[8] *C.H.* XIII.16. On the might and divinity of the sun see also *C.H.* V.3, XVI.5–13; *S.H.* IIA.14.
[9] For further arguments to this effect see Zuntz, *Opuscula selecta* 164–5; and cf. 152–3.
[10] On the importance of hymnody see *Ascl.* 9, 26; *S.H.* XXIII.69–70.
[11] *C.H.* I.29.
[12] On the reappearance of this hymn in a Christian (?gnostic) and perhaps semi-liturgical context in a Berlin papyrus see above, 85 n. 49.

spiritual illumination, which is precisely identified in both *C.H.* XIII (§8) and *The Ogdoad reveals the Ennead*. In the Coptic treatise the access of divine power in the form of light is immediately preceded by an embrace between master and pupil.[13] Granted Hermes's crucial role in Tat's experience, and his earlier insistence that he himself is pregnant with the power, and therefore, at least in the immediate sense, its source,[14] one suspects that the embrace is no mere outward symbol of inner illumination, but a generative action. In either case, the physical presence of the master is indispensable if the pupil is to arrive at his goal.

To describe the soul's perfection through knowledge of God, *C.H.* IV uses the image of 'baptism in intellect'.[15] Here we reach even more controversial ground. Though an over-specific interpretation of what could be just a figure of speech[16] may mislead,[17] on the other hand even a figure or symbol begins as something concrete – and that there are at least informal ritual elements in the Hermetica need no longer be doubted. But have we any reason to envisage Hermetic philosophers participating in religious ceremonies in the conventional cultic sense?

Although this question has often been answered in a firm negative,[18] supposedly on the authority of the Hermetica themselves, the texts are almost innocent of unambiguous anti-ritualism. The last paragraph of the *Asclepius* has already been discussed in its full context; and other passages commonly adduced can only by special pleading be argued to entail more than the platitude that a good life is preferable to mere devotion to ritual.[19] On the other hand, the Hermetica we have cannot, with the exception of the *Asclepius*, be said to display even an average interest in matters of cult. In

---

[13] *N.H.C.* VI.6.57.26–30.

[14] *N.H.C.* VI.6.52.

[15] *C.H.* IV.3–4.

[16] Cf. *C.H.* I.29: 'I sowed in them words of wisdom, and they were nourished with ambrosial water.'

[17] See Festugière, *Hermétisme* 100–12; and, more firmly, Nilsson, *Geschichte* 609.

[18] Nock, *Essays* 28–30; Festugière I.82–3; and van Moorsel, *Mysteries*, an attempt to Calvinize the Hermetica which predictably degenerates into farce when it attempts to deal (72–6) with *C.H.* XVII and *Ascl.* 23–4, 37–8. Robuster Renaissance scholars, including Sir Walter Raleigh, cut the Gordian knot and denied the authenticity of the *Ascl.* passages: Yates, *Giordano Bruno* 11, 172–3, 403 n. 1.

[19] E.g. *C.H.* IV.7 (the procession simile), XII.23 ('There is only one way to worship God: to refrain from evil'). *D.H.* VIII.3 ('Ceux qui [adorent] les idoles, adorent [de simples] images...') appears to advocate correct worship rather than non-worship. Van Moorsel, *Mysteries* 39–40, emphasizes the doctrine that God is self-sufficient, though this is explicitly turned into an argument against sacrifice only at *Ascl.* 41 (quoted above).

explaining this climate of neither hot nor cold, the notion of the 'way' of Hermes proves once more illuminating. Common sense alone suggests that, since the Hermetic *paideia* proposed progress from a lower to a higher state, it could no more than any other religion deny provisional tolerance to states of mind and practices it deemed ultimately undesirable. Often, indeed, the lower state is best super-seded by being gradually transformed; and that this was the method commonly adopted by the Hermetic spiritual guide is confirmed by precisely those concepts which are adduced by many scholars as proof of Hermetism's uncompromising spirituality, namely mental sacrifice and silent worship.

By the concept of 'mental' (or 'spiritual') sacrifice (λογικὴ θυσία)[20] the Hermetists intended the offering of hymns of praise and thanksgiving,[21] which functioned also as evidence of the initiate's encounter with and inspiration by the divine,[22] and as a meditation on that experience. Undoubtedly the same is true of the Hermetic texts themselves. But if the use of the term 'mental' is intended to invoke in our minds some opposite such as 'material', both are none the less adjectives qualifying the notion of 'sacrifice'. There may, in other words, be different types of sacrifice, but they all have some fundamental quality or purpose in common. There are parallels which make this clearer. In the ancient world it was customary for gods to demand that accounts of their wonders be composed by their devotees;[23] and in the aretalogy of Imouthes–Asclepius (*P. Oxy.* 1381), one of the best examples of this genre and closely related also to the Hermetica, we find the clear assertion that 'every gift of a votive offering or sacrifice lasts only for the immediate moment, and presently perishes, while a written record is an undying meed of gratitude, from time to time renewing its youth in the memory'. In other words, although the aretalogy is proclaimed to be more effective than conventional ritual, it fulfils a comparable function – it is a superior form of sacrifice. The same point is made by Porphyry in his *De abstinentia*, though in a more austerely philosophical context. For him the highest form of worship is the silent, pure reflection of the sage directed towards the One. This is the philosopher's 'holy

---

[20] *C.H.* 1.31; xiii.18, 19, 21; *Ascl.* 41 (quoted above, 143); *N.H.C.* vi.6.57.18–25. On the nuances of the expression λογικὴ θυσία see N.F. 1.27 n. 83.

[21] *C.H.* xiii.21.

[22] *C.H.* xiii.18 ('Your *Logos* hymns you through me'), 21.

[23] See the instances collected by Weinreich, *Antike Heilungswunder* 4–8; 112–13; 129, esp. n. 4.

sacrifice', his hymn and his salvation. Then to the intelligible gods, the offspring of the supreme God, one offers hymns in words; and at a much lower level there are offerings of first-fruits, burnt sacrifices and so on.[24] Conventional cult is not pointless – it is simply inferior to the sacrifice of the mind and the soul. It is a question of emphasis – the many gods or the One, the traditional cults or philosophical *gnōsis*. And increasingly, in the Roman world, there was an acceptance that these two aspects of religious culture were interdependent. Man, as the Hermetists among others taught, cannot be made perfect without divine mercy and assistance; and the one way of invoking the gods with which everyone was familiar was through sacrifices. If such thoughts were not present in the Hermetic mind, it is difficult to see why the concept of sacrifice was used at all.

Parallel to the idea of mental sacrifice is the notion, associated particularly with Pythagoras and employed, as we have just seen, by Porphyry, that God is best known and worshipped in the absolute purity of silence, for speech and hearing are sensations, while knowledge of the divine is an experience of a completely different order. But for all the Hermetists' insistence on this point,[25] it is once more plain that they are talking about an ideal, a prescription for the perfected initiate's solitary intercourse with God. In practice, as we have already seen, when two or three sages are gathered together they find nothing more natural than to offer up a prayer or hymn in praise and thanksgiving. No doubt vocal and silent praise were in practice regarded as complementary; for how else could one approach the Being 'who has all names, because all things issue from this one father; and...no name, for He is the father of all'?[26]

The much-debated relationship between Hermetism and the mystery religions provides further illustration of how the ritual and the noetic were integrated within the way of Hermes. The Hermetica occasionally proclaim themselves as mysteries not to be divulged to the profane;[27] and, very rarely, they even use the more specific

[24] Porph., *Abst.* II.34; and cf. above, 129–30, on Plotinus and conventional cult; Iam., *Myst.* v, esp. the passage quoted above, 143 n. 2; and Jul., *or.* XI.158ab, applying Hesiod's Κὰδ' δύναμιν δ' ἔρδειν ἱέρ' ἀθανάτοισι θεοῖσιν not just to sacrifices, but also to prayer and praise offered to the gods.

[25] *C.H.* I.30, 31; x.5, 9; XIII, title, 2, 8; *N.H.C.* VI.6.56.10–12, 58.17–21; Iam., *Myst.* VIII.3.263.

[26] *C.H.* V.10.

[27] E.g. *C.H.* I.16, V.I, XVI.2; *Ascl.* 19, 32; *S.H.* XXV.1, 4, 11; *Cyr. H.* 23; also *Ascl.* 1,32, and *C.H.* XIII.13, 22, on secrecy.

vocabulary of the mystery religions.[28] More significantly, there is some common ground between what philosophical Hermetism and the mystery religions offered their initiates. Hermetism was, and the mysteries may with some selection of evidence be represented as, a secret discipline leading to purification, a vision of the divine realm, and spiritual illumination or rebirth.[29] Can one then say that the Hermetic initiation was a religious mystery? In answering this question one should not forget the fundamentally different backgrounds of the mysteries and the Hermetica. The mysteries had their roots in traditional cultic practice, and their main appeal was to those who simply wanted something more profound than what was available to all in the public temples. The Hermetica, by contrast, emanate from the world of philosophical reflection. Within this world there were of course variations of emphasis; and just as the mysteries aimed at something more spiritual than the public cults, so too the Hermetists aspired to pass beyond mere ratiocination. The parallel was an obvious one, and the Hermetists used it; but it was little more than a parallel. Admittedly our philosophical texts imply an actual historical milieu that was dedicated to the spiritual life. Instruction and initiation were group experiences, even when, at the highest levels, they involved only the spiritual guide and a solitary pupil; and those who participated in these encounters instinctively expressed their solidarity and joy through prayer and hymnody, and in such comradely gestures as embraces and the sharing of food. But they knew nothing of the special priesthoods, cult-places and ceremonies that were essential to the conduct of the mystery religions. The subtlety of this balance between inner spiritual experience and the human milieu in which it is attained and expressed has not often been grasped by students of Hermetism, among whom such insensitive theories as that of the so-called *Lesemysterien* have proved depressingly popular. According to Reitzenstein, followed more recently by, for example, K.-W. Tröger,[30] the Hermetica were 'reading mysteries' or 'spiritualized mysteries', which conveyed spiritual illumination and union with God simply by being read. It hardly needs saying that this sort of desk-bound religion has little connection with the way of Hermes, which certainly requires study of the Hermetica, but whose culmination comes in the personal relationship between spiritual

[28] See *C.H.* iv.4, esp. the reference to the herald; and the admittedly rather banal allusion (if such it is) at *S.H.* xxiii.2 to the Greater and Lesser Mysteries of Eleusis.
[29] Sfameni Gasparro, *S.M.S.R.* 36 (1965) 43–61.
[30] Reitzenstein, *Mysterienreligionen* 51–2, 64; and below, n. 32.

master and pupil, and the oral instruction which the one passes to the other and which may or may not be written down.[31] As for the associated theory that the books of Hermes had their origin in actual mysteries, which were then purified of their grosser elements,[32] this is to shut one's eyes to the full spiritual scope of Hermetism, which recognizes that not just the mysteries but all forms of cult may play a part in the lower stages of spiritual progress. They are not defunct, but they are intended to be superseded. And it happens to be with the post-cultic phase of the soul's experience that the Hermetica are concerned.

Bitys

In the light of the foregoing it would be tendentious to quarrel with Iamblichus's view that Hermetism and theurgy are compatible. There is no need to resort to the argument that Iamblichus knew more than us about the teachings of Hermes. None the less, he did; and one of the writings that has been lost since his day is the book which 'the *prophētēs* Bitys translated to King Ammon, finding it inscribed in hieroglyphic characters in a sanctuary at Sais in Egypt'.[33] Bitys expounding Hermetic inscriptions to Ammon reminds us of Isis expounding Hermetic inscriptions to Horus in the *Korē kosmou*, and Ammon is of course a familiar figure in the Hermetica. So the milieu is reassuring, for all that the identity of Bitys is likely to remain for ever mysterious.[34] Of this text Iamblichus says that it concerned 'ascent by hieratic theurgy to the higher and more universal regions that are placed above fate, to God the creator, without making use of anything material, or employing any other aid, save only the observation of the appropriate moment (καιρός)'. And at the end of the *De mysteriis* Iamblichus describes in more detail the 'hieratic ascent according to the Egyptians',[35] and makes a further allusion to Bitys's 'translations' from the Hermetic books,[36]

---

[31] On this last point see *C.H.* xii.8.

[32] See e.g. Tröger, *Mysterienglaube* vi, 52–3, 167; and in general the index, *s.v.* 'Lesemysterien'.

[33] Iam., *Myst.* viii.5.267–8 (quoted *in extenso* above, 140).

[34] There is no reason to identify him with the Bithys with Egyptian and priestly connections (and perhaps himself a priest) attested in a series of second-century b.c. inscriptions from Cyprus (*O.G.I.S.* 150–2), or with Bithus, a doctor with magical interests mentioned by Pliny; though the appearance of one Pitys several times in *P. Graec. Mag.* iv may be a tribute to our Hermetist: on these last two see Preisendanz, *R.E.* 20.1882–3.

[35] Iam., *Myst.* x.5–6.   [36] *Ibid.* x.7.

which are probably his main source at this point. At least in this book, then, Hermes described the ascent of the soul in explicitly theurgical terms, with reference to the undesirability of ritual aids in the final stages, and by implication to their admissibility at earlier stages. No doubt it was this treatise, which will have had more points of contact with the *Oracula Chaldaica* than do the surviving Hermetica,[37] that mainly influenced Iamblichus to use the books of Hermes in his exposition of theurgical doctrine.

Bitys's reputation as a theurgical authority is reinforced by the fact that the only other ancient writer who alludes to him is Zosimus of Panopolis. In *On apparatus and furnaces*[38] Zosimus speaks of 'the tablet (πίναξ) that Bitys [MSS: Bitos] wrote, and Plato the thrice-great (τρισμέγας) and Hermes the infinitely great (μυριόμεγας)'. Like Iamblichus, then, he was using a book that claimed to have originated as an inscription and to have been associated with Hermes (and Plato – but this is neither surprising nor, as will shortly appear, without confirmation elsewhere). Clearly our two sources are talking about the same composition.

Zosimus recalls that, according to the *pinax*, 'in the original hieratic language the first man, the interpreter of all that exists and the giver of names to all corporeal beings, is called Thouthos'. Or such, at least, is the tradition 'among us', the Egyptians; while the Chaldaeans, Parthians, Medes and Hebrews call the first man Adam. But both Thouthos and Adam are names applied only to 'the visible outer mould'. The inner man, the man of spirit, has according to Zosimus another name, which is mysterious – but he is commonly called Phos (meaning 'light' or 'man' depending how it is accented). In his age of innocence Phos (or Prometheus) was imprisoned by fate in the body, or 'fetter', called Adam (or Epimetheus), who is a product of fate and the four elements; and he will be rescued thence by the Son of God, who comes 'both now and until the end of the world' to exhort the Photes to cut off the blind and hostile Adam and to resist the blandishments of the 'Mimic Daemon', an Anti-Christ figure. A rather desperate exhibition of syncretism, one might think, even thus baldly summarized; but Zosimus ends by assuring us that

only the Hebrews and the sacred books of Hermes say these things, about the man of light and his guide, the Son of God, and about the Adam made of earth and his

[37] See Nock, *Essays* 446, esp. n. 7.
[38] Zos. Pan., *fr. gr.* 230–5, using Jackson's text (see above, 123 n. 29). See also the commentary by Jung, *Psychology and alchemy* 346–57.

guide, the Mimic, who blasphemously claims to be the Son of God in order to deceive.

Exactly what Zosimus derived from his Hermetic sources and what from elsewhere is not clear; but it seems that Bitys, beyond his conventional material on Thoth–Hermes the culture-hero, also had something to say about the 'man of light', the *Anthrōpos* or 'essential Man' of the *Poimandrēs*, who was formed by Intellect in its own image to have sway over all men and animals, but then himself fell victim to the blandishments of the material realm. Both Bitys and the *Poimandrēs* are concerned to show through this myth how 'Man, alone among all the creatures that dwell on the earth, is double, mortal with regard to his body, immortal with regard to the essential Man.'[39] But Bitys went still further along the road of dualism according to our third and last *testimonium* to his treatise, preserved in an unpublished text possibly compiled by Michael Psellus or someone in his vicinity. According to this source, Plato followed the teachings of Hermes and Bitys in maintaining that Man has two distinct souls, rational and irrational, the one emanating from the Demiurge and associated with Providence, the other from the heavenly sphere and subject to fate.[40] The surviving Hermetica know only the more usual idea of the double soul;[41] but as it happens Iamblichus has the following passage in book VIII of the *De mysteriis*, just after his reference to Bitys:

According to these writings [the books of Hermes], Man has two souls, the one issued from the First Intelligible, participating also in the power of the demiurge, the other introduced [into him] from the revolution of the heavenly bodies – and it is into this one that the soul which sees God [i.e. the higher of the two souls] enters.[42]

Whether or not our Byzantine source depends on Iamblichus, Iamblichus certainly here depends on Bitys; and he concludes the passage by reiterating, as no doubt Bitys too had done, that it is through the higher soul that we are freed from fate and given to

[39] *C.H.* 1.15, and cf. *Ascl.* 7. On the *Anthrōpos* doctrine see Rudolph, *Gnosis* 101–11; and for a comparison of the versions in Zosimus and *C.H.* 1 see Schenke, *Der Gott "Mensch"* 44–8, 52–6.

[40] MS *Parisinus gr.* 1918 fol. 146ᵛ–147ʳ, quoted by Whittacker, *Scriptorium* 33 (1979) 60 n. 15 (and cf. 62): Ἕλληνες δὲ οὐχ οὕτω φασίν, ἀλλ᾽ ὅμως ἀκριβέστατος παρ᾽ αὐτοῖς Πλάτων τοῖς Ἑρμοῦ καὶ Βίτυος παρηκολουθηκὼς δόγμασιν δύο ποιεῖ τὰς ψυχάς, τὴν μὲν λογικήν, τὴν δὲ ἄλογον. καὶ τὴν μὲν ἐκ τοῦ δημιουργοῦ ὑφιστάνει, τὴν δὲ ἐκ τῆς οὐρανοῦ φύσεως· καὶ τὴν μὲν πρώτην προνοίας πλήρη ποιεῖ τὴν δὲ δευτέραν τῶν εἱμαρμένων.

[41] See e.g. *C.H.* XVI.15, *S.H.* IIB.5–7. On the background of the two souls doctrine see Ferwerda, *V. Chr.* 37 (1983) 360–78.

[42] Iam., *Myst.* VIII.6.268–9.

see the intelligible gods. 'As for theurgy, which rises up to the Un-procreated, this is the sort of life according to which it is accomplished.'

To sum up, the *pinax* of Bitys, purportedly a translation of texts composed by Thoth–Hermes, and associated in some way with Plato too, discussed the theurgical ascent of the soul, and in doing so invoked two doctrines highly germane to theurgy, namely that of the *Anthrōpos*, which explains *why* Man can aspire to become – indeed already is – divine, and the theory of the two souls, which explains *how* the theurgist is purified from the taint of matter. The *pinax* was, in other words, a distillation of that current within later paganism which saw the true nature of Man as so divine that it was no impiety to place it above even the gods, and so alien to this world that salvation could be gained only by bending every bodily and mental effort to attaining union with the One. The θεῖος ἀνήρ, the divine man, was the highest aspiration of late paganism and its most characteristic product. And the Hermetica, remote as they may at first seem from the thaumaturgical circles lovingly recorded by Eunapius and his like, are none the less all about the theory and practice of the sort of holiness that could be manifested – though it did not have to be – in that way. One does not have to read very far between the lines of the philosophical Hermetica to see this, but it naturally becomes clearer when one adds the testimony of those who, like Zosimus and Iamblichus, could draw on Bitys and other Hermetica lost to us, and plainly regarded the teachings they found in these books as highly germane to the way which they were pursuing – a way for the soul's purification and ascent that led through technique towards intellectual contemplation. Just as Zosimus confirmed and elaborated our picture of the interdependence of technical and philosophical Hermetism, so Bitys and Iamblichus provide a vital link between Hermetism and late Platonism. Perhaps in future all three will be allowed a more prominent place in our overall picture of Hermetism than they have received hitherto.[43]

[43] There is no room or need here for a direct comparison between Zosimus and Iamblichus. But the visions of Zosimus (above, 120–1) could be described as an allegory of theurgic experience; and there are passages in Iamblichus (e.g. *Myst.* v.11–12, on the purification of matter by fire) which are very close to alchemical thought. And compare the passages in which Zosimus and Iamblichus describe the Hermetic doctrine on how to supersede fate, quoted above, 124, 140.

PART III

THE MILIEU OF HERMETISM

[7]

Hermetism in Egypt

A difficult but beguiling task remains. It was established in chapter 4 that the term 'Hermetism', though not itself used in antiquity, stands for a doctrine with some internal coherence, not just for a chance assemblage of disparate texts for which the attribution to Hermes Trismegistus was a mere flag of convenience. But does 'Hermetism' describe a historical and sociological reality as well? Or were the teachings of Hermes so feebly distinguishable from other doctrines that in practice nobody thought of calling himself or herself a 'Hermetist' rather than, say, a 'Platonist'? In other words, though there clearly were milieux *receptive to* Hermetism, is it also possible to locate milieux or individuals prepared to proclaim themselves Hermetist with some sense of exclusivity? To answer this question it will be necessary to examine systematically the evidence of the texts themselves, of the numerous Hermetic testimonia, and of other related historical sources. With good reason, such an analysis has not been undertaken before. The Hermetica, being pseudepigraphical, make no direct allusion to their own origin; while the external testimonia are overwhelmingly concerned with the teachings of Hermes, not with the character or behaviour of his adepts. We may know a lot of people who read or at least had heard of the Hermetica, and alluded to them in their writings, but there were no doubt others who read them without recording the fact for posterity, and anyway there need be no very precise correspondence between those who read a book and those for whom its author intended it. In short, most of our evidence raises more questions than it answers. The structure of this chapter is designed to accommodate such discussion as is unavoidable, and to emphasize that no cohesive account of the subject can yet (or perhaps ever) be written. Five loosely connected sections concentrate each one on a portion of such evidence as we have, and suggest by their position in relation to other sections, if in no other way, something of what else we might have known, if the Hermetists themselves, perhaps, had been less secretive. A final section draws some conclusions and parallels. We begin, as always, from the internal evidence of the Hermetic texts.

The evidence of the Hermetica

One instinctively turns first to the philosophical books, with their relatively catholic view of the nature of Hermetism and their tendency, as for the most part dialogues, to convey more of the atmosphere of instruction than do the technical texts. The philosophical texts were intended both as 'mental sacrifices', an expression, that is, of their authors' spiritual experiences or aspirations, and as protreptic, an exhortation to set out on the way of Hermes.[1] And we know that, whatever the role of private study in the earlier stages of this way, the initiation and illumination of the adept was the work of his spiritual teacher. This emerges with complete clarity from the Hermetica themselves; and once that much has been recognized, one is bound to go on to ask whether the texts can tell us anything more, behind their ideal, mythological scenery, about what being a Hermetist meant in practical social terms. We should not of course fall into the trap of imagining that the Hermetica are descriptive historical and sociological documents; but neither are they a merely literary phenomenon. It is one of the great merits of Festugière's work on Hermetism that he recognized this,[2] despite his general emphasis on doctrinal background and the need he (understandably) felt to distance himself from the formal Hermetic Church dreamed up by Reitzenstein in his *Poimandres*.[3] Festugière showed well that most of

---

[1] *S.H.* IIB.I: 'My child, I am composing this treatise in the first place because of my love for mankind and out of piety towards God'; and cf. *P. Oxy.* 1381.195–202.

[2] Festugière 2.31–4.

[3] *Ibid.* 1.81–4, though parts of the argument are suspect, and the conclusion grossly overstated, e.g. 84: 'tous ces faits obligent à tenir les écrits hermétiques pour un phénomène purement littéraire, et non pour les "liturgies" d'une confrérie de mystes' (so too Dörrie, *Platonica minora* 109–10). Mahé's judgement is more balanced: 'Ce qui est invraisemblable dans les explications de R. Reitzenstein c'est la précision des détails qu'il prétend tirer des

the Hermetica reflect a situation in which a teacher converses confidentially with a single pupil or, less usually, several. Allusion is often made to other encounters and lessons, and the individual session is regarded as part of a sequence. It is thought well to commit parts at least of this oral instruction to writing, often with the object of spreading the resulting compositions outside the immediate circle of master and pupils. But they retain the characteristic repetitions, self-contradictions and other peculiarities of the text that originates in an oral tradition. Festugière produces abundant material from the Hermetica themselves to support this general analysis,[4] which anyway is wholly consistent with our own. But it is now possible, thanks not least to the new Nag Hammadi text, to expand and refine several of these points.

In the first place the Hermetists saw the relationship between master and pupil as just one link in a long chain – the idea of the *diadochē*, or succession, so familiar from the history of the Greek philosophical Schools. Behind *The Ogdoad reveals the Ennead* lies, as we are made aware in its very first lines, a whole tradition of spiritual teaching,[5] in whose long history the initiation we witness is but one incident. Hermes's command that the dialogue be committed to writing, his possible exhortation to Tat to teach others, and Tat's (rather reluctant) acceptance of being but one of many spiritual sons fathered by Hermes – all these are pointers in the same direction.[6] Indeed, the notion of the Hermetic succession is more pervasive than has been recognized, possibly because it tends to be more mythologically expressed than in *The Ogdoad reveals the Ennead*.[7] And what cannot be transmitted in person to the next link in the succession must at all costs be preserved by being written down. This point, implicit in the new Coptic treatise's insistence on the inscription and preservation of the record, is made explicit in the *Korē kosmou*

textes, mais non pas l'existence en elle-même d'une communauté gnostique qui se serait réclamée d'une révélation de Poimandrès à Hermès' (2.12 n. 57). Reitzenstein's theory was formulated principally with regard to *C.H.* I, and contrasts with the notion of the *Lesemysterium*, which he propagated in *Mysterienreligionen* mainly as an explanation of *C.H.* XIII.

4 Festugière 2.34–47.
5 See esp. *N.H.C.* VI.6.52.6–7: *paradosis*; and the use of the words παραδίδωμι and -λαμβάνω at *C.H.* 1.26, 32; XIII.1; with the comments of Festugière, *Hermétisme* 155 n. 54.
6 See respectively *N.H.C.* VI.6.62.1–4; 54.29–30 and 63.4 (with the discussions by Mahé 1.98 and Bellet, *Enchoria* 9 (1979) 3); 53.22–3.
7 See e.g. *C.H.* x.5; *S.H.* IIB.5; XXIII.5–7, 32, 66–8; XXVI.1; also Jul., *Gal.* 176b, an allusion (though intended only in the most general sense) to Egyptian sages 'from the succession of Hermes'.

(*S.H.* xxiii).[8] *The Ogdoad reveals the Ennead* also emphasizes the importance of studying the books of Hermes in general, and in particular of not divulging its own contents, on pain of terrible penalties.[9] In short, although the ultimate revelation of divine knowledge can occur only in the personal intercourse of master and pupil, there is a parallel and supplementary literary tradition which, since it records what passes between Hermes and his adepts, has a sanctity of its own. That is why Hermetic texts, technical as well as philosophical, are frequently referred to as ἱεροὶ λόγοι, 'sacred discourses', emphasizing their scriptural status;[10] and one can imagine that access to them, and the obligation not to reveal their mysteries, will have acted as a powerful bond between Hermetic adepts. That the requirement of secrecy was controversial we have already seen,[11] and its neglect in practice is attested by the impressively wide circulation the Hermetica attained; but that does not render unreasonable the assumption that, at least to begin with, the aura which attached to the books of Hermes reinforced the group-cohesiveness of those who wrote and read them.

In fact one does not have to read far in the surviving texts to find abundant symptoms of a sense of apartness from the uninitiated majority of human kind.[12] The pious are few, the wicked many; and this is a state of affairs divinely ordained, for God gave reason (λόγος) to all, but intellect (νοῦς) only to some, and those who lack it are like the animals. To thirst after knowledge of God is to become alien to this world and to the opinion of the many, who will react in the best case by turning one to scorn, in the worst by bloody persecution. So to keep the doctrine secret is a matter of self-protection as well as of piety: the circle of adepts must be small, and its members will certainly all be well-known to one another.

As it happens, though, the most vivid glimpse that the books of Hermes themselves give us of their ideal Hermetic milieu has a memorably evangelistic streak in it. The dialogue between Poimandres and Hermes in *C.H.* i is presented in the form of a vision, a device which emphasizes from the outset the religious intention that underlies Poimandres's heavily didactic manner; while the sub-

---

[8] *Locc. citt.*
[9] *N.H.C.* vi.6.54, 63.
[10] E.g. *C.H.* iii.*tit.*; *Ascl. tit.* (and N.F. 2.263, esp. nn. 3–4), 23; *S.H.* iv.10; xxiii.1, 8; *P. Oxy.* 886.2–3; Zos. Pan., *fr. gr.* 232.19; *Lib. sanc. Herm.* (on the decans); and Dörrie, *Platonica minora* 107–8.   [11] Above, 125.
[12] For the following see *C.H.* 1.21–3; iv.3–5; ix.4, 10; xiii.1; xvi.1; *Ascl.* 1, 22; *S.H.* xi.4.

ordinate visions by which Poimandres conveys his account of God and creation reflect the emotional exaltation that colours the relationship of master and pupil at this advanced stage of initiation. And when Hermes at length attains the plenitude of divine knowledge, Poimandres sends him out 'to become a guide to the worthy, that through you human kind may be saved by God'.

And I began to proclaim to men the beauty of piety and knowledge (γνῶσις): 'O peoples, men born of the earth, you who have surrendered yourselves to drunkenness and sleep and ignorance of God, be sober, cease to be intoxicated, spellbound by senseless sleep.' And when they heard, they gathered around me with one accord. And I said: 'O men born of the earth, why have you given yourselves up to death, when you have the power to partake of immortality? Repent, fellow-travellers of error and partners with ignorance! Rid yourselves of the light which is darkness, partake of immortality, leave perdition behind you.' And some of them abused me and stood aloof, for they had given themselves up to the way of death. But the others threw themselves at my feet and asked to be taught. So, raising them up, I became a guide for mankind, teaching them the doctrine, how and in what way they might be saved. And I sowed in them words of wisdom, and they were nourished with ambrosial water. When evening came, and the light of the sun began to disappear altogether, I bade them give thanks to God. And when they had done with their thanksgiving, each betook him to his own bed.

Here, as in the very similar fragment of sermon preserved as *C.H.* VII,[13] we catch the forceful, vivid tones of the popular preacher who, himself inwardly illuminated, goes out into the world to turn his fellow-men by personal example into the way of salvation.[14] The Hermetic *paideia* proceeds by stages towards the final initiation; but the perfected adept is not left to pass his life in mystic communion. He too must now take up the teacher's burden, so that others may in time ascend the same steps by which he himself attained to truth.

From the philosophical texts there emerges, then, a picture of an inspired spiritual teacher surrounded by a small group of followers who sought a philosophical understanding of the divine realm which was not otherwise available to them even in the mystery religions. Beyond that, some at least longed for a personal illumination which would permanently transform their lives. Through study, instruction, question and answer, prayer, the singing of hymns and the enjoyment of other sorts of close fellowship with master and fellow pupils, the adept came to feel himself part of a tradition, if not, in the strict sense, of a community; and, thus strengthened, he could the more easily endure the ascetic discipline required to extract himself from the

[13] Cf. also *P. Oxy.* 1381.203–18.
[14] For parallels see Wlosok, *Laktanz* 137–9.

snares of the world. But the most striking external characteristic of this milieu was its informality, even fluidity. There was no institutional structure to provide formal limits and sanctions – all depended on the personal authority of the teacher. Likewise there was no fixed body of doctrine, and both the manner and the content of instruction will have varied widely, to an even greater extent than is reflected in the surviving texts. In particular, any attempt to describe the milieu of Hermetism must take into account the extensive common ground that has been established between the philosophical and technical aspects of the doctrine. Although the technical Hermetica are even less revealing than the philosophical texts about the circumstances in which they originated, we can assume that it will often have seemed inappropriate to make the distinction at all. However small the Hermetic circles, they will always have included people at different stages of instruction and spiritual understanding; and there is no reason why we should not imagine adepts in the techniques of astrology and alchemy sitting together with those who yearned for a more spiritual wisdom at the feet of the successor of Hermes.

Finally, the texts can by implication tell us something of the more general cultural level of their authors and audience. Although their thought will often have seemed naïve to professionals, many of the philosophical Hermetica are written in a sophisticated language and presuppose, or at least reveal, some familiarity with the classical literary and intellectual tradition.[15] This is obviously less true of the technical Hermetica; but astrological texts, for example, were used by an enormous range of people, including the leading intellectuals of the age, and required some elementary technical knowledge in order to be understood. In general terms one could say that, while virtually anyone might come into contact with the technical Hermetica, those who read the philosophical books are likely to have progressed as far as a rhetorical education – what we would call secondary school level – without necessarily having gone on to a professional or philosophical training.

So much, then, can be deduced from the texts themselves. But they, with their mythological setting, can at best offer us an idealized

---

[15] Nock, *Essays* 26–32, 642–52; Festugière 2.30–1, *Etudes d'histoire* 231–73; Schwartz, in *Hommages à Claire Préaux* 223–33 (arguing that the author of the *Korē kosmou* had read Lucian), and *R.H.Ph.R.* 62 (1982) 167–9 (on possible Latin literary references in the *Ascl.*); Mahé 2.60–1.

portrait of the milieu in which they circulated. It is time now to see what the external testimonia can add or subtract, before a more historical description is attempted at the end of this chapter.

First-century Alexandria – and beyond

For any investigation of the milieu of Hermetism, within or without Egypt, Alexandria is the natural point of departure, not just because it was there that Hellenism and Egyptianism most easily attained that fusion of which the Hermetica are products, but also because so much of what we know about the Hermetic aspects of this fusion is to be found in literary sources associated with the city. But from this latter circumstance the historian is well advised to conclude only that the literary productions of the metropolis more easily escaped oblivion than those of the provinces. After all, for archaeological and climatic reasons the exactly opposite geographical imbalance is to be observed in our papyrological sources, which make up, often vividly, for the exiguity of our literary testimonia about Upper Egypt. To compensate, then, for the capricious distribution of our materials, we must be constantly sensitive to what is typical and what is more likely to have survived because of its oddity.

Because of their wide appeal as well as their priority in time, the technical writings were the earliest vehicle of Hermes Trismegistus's reputation. Above all, Hermes was known as an astrologer, his fame such that already in the Ptolemaic period it had spread beyond the bounds of Egypt.[16] But the source of this reputation was undoubtedly Alexandria, whether in its own right or as an entrepôt. Here too our earliest hints at the Hermetic milieu are astrological. Pamphilus, an Alexandrian grammarian of the first century A.D., is scathingly denounced by Galen for having taken seriously a treatise on astrological botany attributed to Hermes.[17] We have already noticed the possible familiarity of his compatriot and approximate contemporary Chaeremon with Hermetic astrology.[18] And it was one Harpocration of Alexandria who, probably towards the middle of the second century, composed a treatise on occult properties which will have had much in common with the book used by Pamphilus. Later this work

[16] Above, 3 n. 11.
[17] Gal. 11.797–8. Cf. Wendel, *R.E.* 18 (2).344–6; Festugière 1.77–8.
[18] Above, 139–40.

was incorporated into the *Cyranides*, but many of its distinctive features are still discernible, notably its kinship with the spiritual doctrines of philosophical Hermetism.[19] As for the process by which the Hermetica were disseminated outside Egypt, Chaeremon, who became Nero's tutor, and Thrasyllus, the Alexandrian astrologer and friend of Tiberius, were no doubt distinguished only by their social prominence from many others who carried Hermetic astrological lore throughout the Mediterranean world.[20] Egypt was the height of fashion in the expanding Roman empire; her astrologers were among the most potent of her cultural exports; and Hermes Trismegistus was 'the Egyptian' *par excellence*. Until the end of antiquity, in the Greek and Latin worlds alike, the frequency of references to and plagiarism of Hermes in the astrological literature is eloquent of his fundamental and pervasive influence, which it is impossible to catalogue in detail here.[21] Taking into account as well the growing dissemination of the *Cyranides* (or at least of its constituent parts),[22] the strength of Galen's denunciation of this sort of literature, Plutarch's attestation of theological Hermetica[23] and the first datable appearances of the name 'Hermes Trismegistus' in Philo of Byblos and Athenagoras,[24] it seems safe to claim that by the mid-second century A.D. at the latest an impressive range of technical Hermetica was available throughout the Greek-speaking parts of the empire.

All this by way of preface, though, to a source of unique interest, if questionable reliability, for the sociology of first-century Hermetism: the *De virtutibus herbarum*, attributed to one Thessalus. The *De virtutibus* has survived in a confusing array of more or less fragmented Greek and Latin versions, one of which attributes it, not surprisingly in view of its affinity with the *Cyranides*, to Harpocration.[25] An autobiographical introduction, cast in the form of a letter to an emperor, takes us straight into the upwardly mobile urban world of the Graeco-Roman East, whose young men travelled restlessly in search of the education that, however little esteemed it might be for

---

[19] Above, 87–9.

[20] On Thrasyllus see above, 3 n. 11 (also on Antiochus of Athens), and below, 216 and n. 2. See also Bowie, *Y. Cl. S.* 27 (1982) 42–3, on Alexandrian scholars patronized by Rome.

[21] See the extensive assemblage of evidence in Gundel 104–274; also Festugière 1.102–6.

[22] See e.g. Lucian, *Podagra* 174 (and Festugière 1.205–6); Tert., *Cor.* vii.5 (and above, 87 n. 57); and the parallels between the *Cyr.* and Marc. Sid., *Pisc.*, noted in Heitsch's edition (and on whose significance see the discussion by Heitsch noted in the bibliography of his edition).

[23] See above, 138.   [24] See Appendix.

[25] On the background see Festugière, *Hermétisme* 141–80; Smith, *Map is not territory* 172–89. Thessalus's prefatory letter is *Virt. herb.* 1.*prooem.* 1–28.

its own sake, offered a key to the glittering prizes of imperial patronage. Thessalus, who came from a well-off family, passed through the grammatical stage of his education in Asia, and then made his way to Alexandria, where he continued his literary studies, but also 'burnt with an excessive desire' for the study of medical theory. When he found in a library one of Nechepso's treatises on astrological medicine, he got carried away and made a complete fool of himself in the eyes of his fellow-students when the cures failed to work. Smarting from the humiliation, which he thought was 'more bitter than death',[26] Thessalus abandoned both Alexandria and any immediate intention of returning home, where he had over-hastily announced by letter his new-found skills. Instead, he decided to search throughout Egypt for some alternative to Nechepso's chimerical cures.

My soul constantly foretold to me that I would speak with the gods, and I kept on stretching out my hands to heaven, beseeching the gods to grant me, through a dream-vision or a divine inspiration, some favour that would allow me to regain my self-esteem and return rejoicing to Alexandria and my native land.

It was at Thebes (Diospolis Magna; Luxor), 'the most ancient city of Egypt, endowed with many temples', that Thessalus found the direct revelation he was seeking, among 'the archpriests with their love of letters, and the old men full of diverse learning'. After frequenting the temples for some time, he was able to induce one aged priest to arrange the longed-for vision. First they fasted for three days, which seemed to the intemperate Thessalus like three years; then on the fourth day, in a chamber cleansed and properly prepared for the consultation, the priest demanded of Thessalus whether he would converse with a dead man's soul or a god. 'With Asclepius', he replied, 'and face to face, without priestly mediation.' And so it came to pass.

I was seated, and my body and soul were fainting at the incredible sight – for human speech could not convey the features of his countenance, nor the beauty of his adornment. Stretching out his right hand, [Asclepius] began to speak: 'O blessed Thessalus, you are honoured by a god, and as time goes by and your achievements become known men will worship you as a god. Ask me then whatever you wish, and I will readily reply.'

But having obtained the apparition he sought, and overcome his astonishment, Thessalus failed to rise above the mundane preoccu-

---

[26] Cf. *Anth. gr.* xi.164 (by the Neronian epigrammatist Lucillius) on one Aulus, an astrologer who, having failed to die at the hour he had himself predicted, 'was ashamed of Petosiris' (Nechepso's astrologer-twin in our sources), and hanged himself.

pations of the student-doctor. Of all the things he could have asked the god who stood before him, he chose to enquire about the book of Nechepso; and Asclepius explained that Nechepso had indeed been a very wise man, but had gone astray because he had not received any direct divine communication. At this point begins the treatise proper, an exposition by Asclepius of the curative powers inherent in different types of plants by virtue of their affinity with the stars. Its tendency is to complete Nechepso rather than to supersede, far less refute him.

Since this remarkable passage purports to narrate historical fact, its interest in the present context is obvious. Yet one group of manuscripts omits most or all of the letter, and any reference to Thessalus, and attributes the *De virtutibus* to Hermes Trismegistus.[27] There is of course nothing surprising in the attribution of this sort of work fluctuating between two such closely-related figures – in fact several even of the Hermetic group of manuscripts describe the text as addressed by Hermes 'to his pupil Asclepius'.[28] But these variations in the tradition do serve to remind us that the function of the introduction was to arouse interest in the *De virtutibus* itself, and that its contents should be judged in that light. The historian, used to an austerer diet, is bound to be disquieted at finding himself carried along by a text which is such an unashamedly good read. One is reminded of the Egyptomane novels which became so popular in the Roman empire. And Thessalus hardly bothers to disguise the fact that his main objective in interviewing Asclepius was to solicit a book-review of Nechepso, and then to see if the god could do better himself. He even smuggled pen and paper into the room where the vision was to take place, to make sure he would get a text ready for publication. So, balancing one's suspicions against one's pleasure at finding a circumstantial description of how a technical Hermeticum was written, what can one say of the historical value of Thessalus's letter?

First of all, is it possible to identify Thessalus himself? Cumont suggested dating the *De virtutibus* to the first century A.D. (not unreasonably), and proposed that Thessalus was none other than the famous doctor Thessalus of Tralles. But there are as many arguments

---

[27] See the introduction to Friedrich's edition, 13–35.
[28] Thess., *Virt. herb.* I. *tit.* The crudity with which several of the Hermetic group of manuscripts begin with the concluding passage of Thessalus's letter, without any explanation of the context, suggests that priority should be assigned to Asclepius.

against this assumption as for it,[29] not least that it may be exactly what the letter's author (or forger) wanted us to think. In fact, to assume that the letter is a fabrication may be the best way to ensure it a measure of historical respectability, since even the forger – especially the forger – has to be plausible.[30] As we have already seen, there was no shortage in the first century of young Greeks trying to turn an education into a fortune. In fact, the market was over-subscribed. For all Thessalus's easy academic successes, first in Asia, then in Alexandria, it was tempting to try to short-cut the conventional *cursus honorum* – and Nechepso seemed to offer a chance of doing just that.[31] Thessalus longed to get a head-start on his contemporaries by doing something extraordinary.[32] His Levantine lack of reserve was almost his undoing; and it was equally Levantine of him to assume that somewhere in Egypt, and probably in a temple, he really would eventually find a cure for his woes. The sternest sceptic need have no difficulty in believing, or at least finding plausible, Thessalus's narrative up to the point when the priest leaves him (conveniently) alone in the cleansed chamber where he is to see his vision. Even the vision itself one can explain, if one wishes, as a priestly deceit, not difficult to impose on a man in Thessalus's overwrought state.[33] As an account of occult researches in first-century Egypt, Thessalus's letter presents few difficulties. It seems reasonable, then, to assume that the *De virtutibus* itself was written by Thessalus or, if he is a figment, some similarly disenchanted product of the Alexandrian schools, while the excursion to Thebes is a bit of imaginative though not implausible scenery. The author may or may not have believed that Asclepius imparted to him at least some of his materials, probably in a dream.

What, though, of the part played by the temple milieu in the evolution of the Hermetic literature? When Thessalus wanted an explanation of Nechepso, he turned to the Theban priests. There is no lack of parallels in the Hermetic literature itself. What is one to make of them?

---

[29] Diller, *R.E.* 6A.181.
[30] A requirement from which the possible availability of literary models (Festugière 1.59) is no absolute dispensation.
[31] Asclepius makes the same point with regard to the *Virt. herb.* itself: II.*epil.* 2–4.
[32] *Ibid., prooem.* 1: παράδοξον ⟨καὶ ὀλίγοις γνωστόν⟩.
[33] Festugière, *Hermétisme* 175–80; *R.E.G.* 64 (1951) 483.

Hermetism in Egypt

Temples and priests

The various references made by the philosophical Hermetica to priests, conversations in temples and so forth[34] strike one, it is true, as more decorative than essential; and the genre itself is unrelated to anything we know about the Thoth literature. But the technical Hermetica are related to the Thoth literature, as was indicated in chapter 2; and their allusions to the priestly milieu compel more attention.

Just as the priesthood had been the main authority on magic in Pharaonic Egypt, so it continued under the Ptolemies and the Romans. Even in the fourth century Jerome could tell the story of how a young man of Gaza called in the priests of Asclepius at Memphis to help him seduce a girl who had failed to respond to 'touch, jokes, nods, whistlings or anything else of that sort, which are apt to be the beginning of the end of virginity (quae solent moriturae virginitatis esse principia)'.[35] A number of priestly magicians are named in the Greek magical papyri,[36] many of them no doubt less historical than others, though one's eye is caught by the *prophētēs* Pachrates of Heliopolis, who so impressed Hadrian during an imperial visit to Egypt that he earned himself a double fee.[37] He appears too in Lucian's *Philopseudes*, Hellenized as Pancrates and metamorphosed into a *hierogrammateus* of Memphis. Though Lucian cannot resist noting Pancrates's skill at crocodile-riding, he makes clear that, as well as his magical powers, he was possessed of extraordinary learning and deeply immersed in Egyptian culture – a typical pagan holy man in fact. And he is every inch a member of the native priesthood, 'clean-shaven, in white linen, always deep in thought, speaking imperfect Greek, tall, flat-nosed, with protruding lips and thinnish legs'[38] – just such a man as Thessalus had searched

---

[34] E.g. *C.H.* XVII (Tat a *prophētēs*); Ascl. 1; *N.H.C.* VI.6.61.19; *Cyr. H.* 29, Hermes's reply to a question from 'one of the temple-dwellers in Egypt' (τῶν ἐν Αἰγύπτῳ τεμενειτῶν..., on the as yet obscure meaning of which term see the epigraphical and other material discussed by Herrmann, *M.D.A.I.(I.)* 30 (1980) 223–39 (to which add *F. Gr. Th.* 179.15), though no doubt it is employed by Hermes/Cyril in a more general sense); Cyr. Al., *Jul.* 1.548b.

[35] Jer., *V. Hil.* XII.2. The Memphite priests of Asclepius were far-famed for their skill in magic and alchemy: Festugière, *Hermétisme* 158 n. 69, to which add *Alch. gr.* 26.5–6; Chadwick, *Priscillian* 21, esp. nn. 2, 4. See also below, 182–3, on late fourth-century Canopus; and the magical discourse attributed to Calasiris by Heliod. Em. III.7–8.

[36] E.g. *P. Graec. Mag.* I.42; V.96; XIII.958–9; and cf. IV.933; XII.265, 276, 401–7. See also Cumont, *Egypte* 170. [37] *P. Graec. Mag.* IV.2446–55.

[38] Lucian, *Philops.* 34 (tr. Harmon), and cf. Reitzenstein, *R.E.* 18.2071–4 (according to whom crocodiles were a less unusual means of clerical conveyance in Egypt than one might imagine).

for. Indeed it is on a boat sailing up the Nile to Thebes that Lucian has us encounter him. Here, momentarily, we touch again on the many-faceted reality of the Hermetic milieu, for Pancrates may not have written in Greek, but clearly he was one of the many points of contact between the native clergy and the Greeks of Egypt, both inhabitants and visitors.

Alchemy and astrology too were commonly associated with the temples. Apart from the priest who figures prominently in his visions, one recalls Zosimus's visit to a Memphite temple in order to see a special furnace – Memphis was well-known for its alchemy as well as its magic.[39] Zosimus's associate Theosebia was a priestess;[40] and in the Syriac fragments Zosimus several times alludes generally to the role of priests as guardians of alchemical learning, and emphasizes that, though there are many who seek to attach their own name to alchemical formulae, everybody knows they were really written by Hermes and other Egyptian writers. In support of this assertion Zosimus invokes those priests who preserve copies of alchemical books in their temples.[41] The astrological texts, Hermetic and other, likewise abound in references to priests and temples,[42] and certain of the ancient authorities, such as Petosiris and Melampous,[43] were thought to have been members of the native clergy.

Much of all this could of course be explained away in terms of the perennial Greek obsession with the Egyptian priesthood and its arcane wisdom; and one might further recall how little that interest was reciprocated. Well into the Roman period Egyptian priests enjoyed, as was remarked in chapter 1, a reputation for stand-offishness. But, as Roman rule in Egypt wore on, it became less and less uncommon for members of the native priesthood to assimilate, like Chaeremon, to the politically dominant culture. As the old priestly culture, and especially its language and literature, fell increasingly into desuetude, clerics of a learned bent found it natural to frequent the schools of the Greeks. We quite often encounter representatives of the native clergy teaching grammar or philosophy in late antique Alexandria.[44] Such men will naturally have been well

---

[39] Above, 120; 166 n. 35.   [40] Zos. Pan., fr. syr. 308.

[41] Zos. Pan., fr. syr. 222, 223–4, 226. Cf. Alch. gr. 57 (= Bidez and Cumont, Mages 2.312): 'Synesius the philosopher to Dioscorus, priest of Great Sarapis in Alexandria, greetings...'

[42] E.g. Manil. 1.46–65; and further references in Cumont, Égypte 113–51.

[43] E.g. C.C.A.G. 8 (4).105.3.

[44] E.g. Ammonius (below, 183); Orion (Marin., Proc. 8); Heraiscus and Asclepiades (below, 184–6); and cf. the family of Aurelius Petearbeschinis of Panopolis (below, 174).

disposed towards a doctrine which associated the traditions of Egypt and the magical and astrological interests of its temple-dwellers with the fashionable Platonism of the age; and we may easily imagine them among the audience and perhaps even the authors of the Hermetic books.[45] Iamblichus may have been mistaken in his belief that the Hermetica had been written by ancient Egyptian priests; but both that belief, and the fact that he himself saw fit to expound the doctrines of Hermes in the guise of a *prophētēs*, are indicative of what seemed probable and reasonable in late antiquity.

Upper Egypt

It was not, though, to just any priests, but to priests of Thebes, that Thessalus turned in his search for enlightenment; for if Alexandria was in but not really of Egypt, Thebes distilled the country's very essence and focussed the religious traditions for which the whole of Upper Egypt was renowned.[46] Here too Thessalus's story proves more than incidentally germane to our own investigation, for Hermetism had its adepts in the provinces as well as in the metropolis. Two collections of papyri which have particular importance for our search were discovered, one at Thebes itself and the other, already familiar, near Nag Hammadi, some 110 km north of modern Luxor.

The first of these two collections has hardly ever been discussed as such by scholars,[47] though its constituent parts are well known. Its relevance to the Hermetic milieu has escaped everyone. It came to light when, probably not long before 1828, the Alexandrian merchant and antiquarian Giovanni Anastasi acquired from some Egyptians a number of papyri, some of which had been divided up before sale.[48] Certain of these papyri were stated to belong to a group discovered at Thebes,[49] are listed close to each other in the catalogues

---

[45] Cf. (with reference to the technical genres only) Stegemann, *Gnomon* 18 (1942) 279; Festugière 1.117; Gundel 11.   [46] Philostr., *V. Apol.* v.24.

[47] An exception is Preisendanz, *Papyrusfunde* 91–4.

[48] Dawson, *J.E.A.* 35 (1949) 159–60; Schneider, *De laudibus Aegyptologiae* 17–23; Lagercrantz, *Papyrus graecus Holmiensis* 54. The purchase of the papyri is mentioned by Anastasi in a letter dated 18.3.1828 now in the Rijksmuseum van Oudheden, Leiden, whose director, H. D. Schneider, kindly communicated its contents to me.

[49] Lenormant, *Catalogue* 84 ('M. Anastasi, dans ses fouilles à Thèbes avait découvert la bibliothèque d'un gnostique égyptien...'); cf. Halleux, *Alchimistes grecs* 1.5–6. Dawson, *J. E. A.* 35 (1949) 159, observes that 'it is very unlikely that Anastasi himself did any field-work...[at] Sakkārah and Thebes', but concedes that 'he may have visited these localities from time to time'.

of Anastasi's various collections, and are anyway clearly related through similarities of hand, language and content.[50] To this 'Thebes cache' (as it will henceforth be called) belong, for example, the London–Leiden magical papyrus, the large Paris magical papyrus, two magical papyri now in Berlin, the Leiden alchemical papyrus and its close relative – alike in content and written in a very similar or even identical hand – the Stockholm alchemical papyrus.[51] *P. Leid.* I 395, an important magical miscellany, is another sibling on palaeographical criteria.[52] A catalogue (undoubtedly partial) of the Thebes cache would look somewhat as shown in the table. All these

Anastasi catalogue nos.		
1072	*P. Brit. Mus.* 10070 ⎫	London–Leiden demotic magical
65	*P. Leid.* I 383 ⎬	papyrus: *P. Graec. Mag.* xiv
1073	Bibl. Nat. Paris. suppl. gr. 574	*P. Graec. Mag.* iv
1074	*P. Berol.* 5025	*P. Graec. Mag.* i
1075	*P. Berol.* 5026	*P. Graec. Mag.* ii
66	*P. Leid.* x/i 397	Leiden alchemical papyrus
75 75a ⎫	*P. Leid.* v/i 384	*P. Graec. Mag.* xii
76	*P. Leid.* w/i 395	*P. Graec. Mag.* xiii
(Gift of Anastasi)	*P. Holm.*	Stockholm alchemical papyrus

papyri have been dated to the third or earlier half of the fourth century;[53] and their group-identity is further reinforced by a marked tendency towards bilingualism. The London–Leiden magical papyrus has sections in Greek as well as demotic; and its Egyptian sections also make use of the Old Coptic and hieratic scripts, and of cipher. Exactly the same is true of *P. Leid.* I 384, which further resembles the London–Leiden papyrus in grammar, spelling and content, and indeed was written by the same scribe.[54] The Paris

[50] Reuvens, *Lettres* iii (appendix).145–7; and below.
[51] Halleux, *Alchimistes grecs* 6, 9–12.
[52] *P. Graec. Mag.* 2.86.
[53] Griffith and Thompson, *Demotic magical papyrus* 1.10–13; Halleux, *op. cit.* 22–3; and the relevant prefaces in *P. Graec. Mag.* – note the uncertainty about the dating of *P. Graec. Mag.* i and ii.
[54] Johnson, *O.M.R.L.* 56 (1975) 47–53.

magical papyrus also occasionally lapses into Coptic. The demotic of the London-Leiden papyrus and of *P. Leid.* 1 384 has been argued to be in the Theban dialect.[55]

To what end, then, was this collection assembled? It may have been designed for study rather than for the practical use envisaged by the texts' authors. The two alchemical papyri both lack the stains and other signs of wear one would expect if they had ever seen the inside of an alchemist's laboratory;[56] and the recent editor of *P. Holm.* detects in it signs of the adaptation of documentary sources to a format suitable for a literary papyrus.[57] The Paris magical papyrus's size (near 3,300 lines on 70 sides of papyrus measuring up to 13 × 30.5 cm) and anthological character also savour more of the library than the workbench. But even the mere possession of such books could be dangerous in the fourth century. Ammianus records how, during the magic-trials under Valens, 'owners of books throughout the oriental provinces...burned their entire libraries, so great was the terror that had seized upon all';[58] and perhaps it was in some such circumstances that our unknown Theban occultist secreted his books, possibly in a tomb, and so preserved them.

The neglect that has been lavished on the Thebes cache is all the more surprising when one considers the dominant position that it occupies in the study of late antique magic and early alchemy, and its similarities with the Nag Hammadi library, now exposed to the opposite form of abuse. The two collections belong not only to the same part of the fourth century but to the same geographical area as well, for the Nag Hammadi library was not buried in Upper Egypt by accident – it originated there and belonged to a person or group from the region of Diospolis Parva, which is referred to in *The Ogdoad reveals the Ennead*[59] and near to which the collection was disinterred some 1,600 years later. The language of the texts is the Sahidic used

[55] Johnson, *S.A.O.C.* 39 (1976) 105–32. Satzinger, in *Graeco-Coptica* 143 n. 22, dissents.
[56] Halleux, *Alchimistes grecs* 8; cf. Lagercrantz, *Papyrus graecus Holmiensis* 87–9.
[57] Halleux, *op. cit.* 12.
[58] Amm. Marc. xxix.2.4.
[59] *N.H.C.* vi.6.61.19–20: Hermes exhorts Tat to 'write this book for the temple at Diospolis in hieroglyphic characters'. As is clear from the Coptic *Lives* of Pachomius, native Egyptians used the simple name Diospolis for Diospolis Parva, while Diospolis Magna was by Greek-speakers called either Thebes (Θῆβαι) or simply ἡ μητρόπολις (Kees, *R.E.* 5A.1557), by Copts Nē. Since Diospolis Parva is not known to have had any exceptional devotion to Thoth (though see Capart, *A.S.A.E.* 27 (1927) 44, on an ibis cemetery of the Roman period apparently connected with a Thoth-cult), the allusion in *N.H.C* vi.6 may indicate that the treatise's author had local knowledge. Local references in the papyrus fragments (cartonnage) used to bind the codices confirm that they too were written near where they were buried: Shelton, *N.H.S.* 16 (1981) 1–11.

by educated Copts throughout Egypt; but there are elements too of the Subakhmimic dialect spoken round Lycopolis (Assyut) and some way southwards, and of the Akhmimic characteristic of the Nag Hammadi region and the whole of Upper Egypt.[60] More important though even than this coincidence in time and space is the marked influence on both collections of the interaction of Greek with Egyptian, on the linguistic level as bilingualism (Thebes cache) or translation (Nag Hammadi library), and more generally through the manifestation of many of the by now familiar religious and intellectual tendencies of Graeco-Egyptianism. Especially interesting is the possibility that the Thebes cache as well as the Nag Hammadi library preserves traces of Hermetism.

It has already been pointed out that one of the most important documents in the Thebes cache, the great Paris magical papyrus, contains a ritual for immortalization which is similar to some of the initiatory *Hermetica*.[61] *P. Louvre* 2391 (= *P. Graec. Mag.* III), which includes the prayer also found at the end of the *Asclepius* and in *N.H.C.* VI, has been proposed, speculatively but not implausibly, as a further candidate for inclusion in the Thebes cache.[62] And *P. Leid.* I 395, which undoubtedly belongs to the Thebes cache, may also contain Hermetic material. Indeed it is in its entirety an instructive product of the pseudepigraphical milieu. It is entitled *A holy book, called Monas, or the eighth book of Moses*; and in its opening section it repeatedly refers to another work by Moses entitled *The key*, as well as to a 'holy book' called *The wing* by Hermes, and an untitled work by Manethos [*sic*].[63] (It is worth recalling that the *Corpus Hermeticum* also includes treatises entitled *Monas* and *The key* – *C.H.* IV and X respectively.) Embedded amidst directions for various magical procedures, the papyrus reproduces two versions of a lengthy invocation designed to secure an oracle, and itself designates the text, in a later allusion, as a *kosmopoiia* – a narration of the world's creation.[64] The title is apt, and indeed the narrative shows striking parallels with a creation account inscribed in the temple at Esna.[65] In the papyrus, the first version is introduced by one awkwardly inserted, obscurely abbreviated and

---

[60] Keizer, *Eighth reveals the Ninth* 24–34; Mahé 1.10–11, 2.465–7.

[61] On the possibility that the papyrus (*P. Graec. Mag.* IV) also refers to the Hermetist Bitys, see above, 150 n. 34.

[62] Preisendanz, *Papyruskunde* 94. Note that *P. Louvre* 2391 is another bilingual papyrus.

[63] Cf. the further accumulation of authorities in a passage near the end (933–1001).

[64] *P. Graec. Mag.* XIII.138–209, 443–564, 696–701.

[65] Above, 63 n. 65.

perhaps originally marginal word, which the papyrus's most recent editor prints as *Hermaïkos* ('Ερμαϊκός).[66] Perhaps this constitutes a claim that what follows was written by Hermes. Certainly the *kosmopoiia* has been thought by modern authorities to bear a general resemblance to some of the philosophical Hermetica;[67] and in particular its identification of Hermes with *Nous* is paralleled in the more initiatory of the philosophical treatises.[68]

Whatever weight one assigns to these Hermetic hints, there is no doubt that the owner of the Thebes cache had a range of interests that extended beyond the mere techniques of magic and alchemy. Conversely, the new philosophical Hermeticum from Nag Hammadi reveals an interest in magical procedures – as we saw in chapter 5. In short, both collections illustrate that interlocking of the technical and philosophical approaches that we have already traced in the Hermetica, with the help among others of the Upper Egyptian alchemist Zosimus. Not that the alchemical papyri in the Thebes cache show any trace of Zosiman speculations; nor are all the magical texts as eclectic as those just mentioned. The overall emphasis of the Thebes cache is technical, that of the Nag Hammadi codices philosophical and theological. But there is enough common ground to confirm that the view of Hermetism we find in Zosimus and Iamblichus reflected a broader consensus.

We have no clue at all as to who put the Thebes cache together, or in what circumstances; and as for the Nag Hammadi Hermetica we must always remember that they are a small, in many ways untypical part of an extensive library. But we can at least attach a broad label to the milieu in which the Nag Hammadi collection of Hermetica was put together. The use of the second person plural in the scribal note in *N.H.C.* VI suggests that its writer was addressing himself to, and employed by, a *group* of people, apparently, if we judge from the general contents of this and the other codices, a circle of Christian gnostics.[69] This need not surprise us. Not only were the

---

[66] The papyrus has (line 138) ερμαῖ. (I am grateful to D. R. Jordan for providing a photograph.)

[67] By e.g. Dieterich, *Abraxas* 66–7 (but cf. 71); Festugière 1.296. On parallels between some of the magical formulae and divine names in the *kosmopoiia* and *N.H.C.* VI.6, see Mahé 1.106–7, 124.

[68] *P. Graec. Mag.* XIII.172–5, 485–90; and see above, 110.

[69] The briefly fashionable theory that the codices may have been copied in or possessed by a Pachomian monastery near the find-spot has now had to be abandoned: see Shelton, *N.H.S.* 16 (1981) 5–11. The papyrus fragments contained in the cartonnage of the codex-covers are mainly accounts and other documents of the sort one might expect to

Hermetica widely read by Christians, but we are also told by Marcellus of Ancyra that many gnostics, including the famous Valentinus, who studied in Alexandria and was probably a native of Egypt,[70] drew on Hermes along with Plato and Aristotle in formulating their doctrines.[71] In a sixth-century source we even find a sect called the 'Hermaioi' associated with Valentinus.[72] As heresy became more and more an issue in an increasingly structured Church, pressure mounted on milieux of this sort; and in some such circumstances the Nag Hammadi library was tactfully disposed of, perhaps not very long after its production in the mid-fourth century.

For all the mysteriousness of their origins, these two papyrus collections are tangible products of Upper Egyptian milieux related to, though linguistically at least more native than, that of the Hermetica. The only other comparable source we have is the alchemist Zosimus. Although we have no idea whether Zosimus spent his maturity at Panopolis or somewhere else, here is as good a place as any to recall, not just his profound debt to the Hermetica both alchemical and philosophical, and his contacts with gnosticism, but also his allusions in the Syriac fragments to the small, secret circles of devotees, primarily alchemists but not lacking spiritual aspirations, founded by Theosebia.[73] This reference to a plurality of circles, and the polemical tone of Zosimus's remarks, confirms the impression one gets from the Hermetica themselves that they were the product of a highly variegated milieu. In part that was the result of geographical separation – which no doubt also explains why Zosimus and Theosebia corresponded with each other.[74] But even so this was no elite milieu, at least numerically. Zosimus is explicit about the wide circulation of alchemical Hermetica,[75] and if he is thought to be an interested party we have only to recall that Diocletian thought it

find on the municipal rubbish-heap. Only a few can be connected, and then only speculatively, with a monastic milieu. (But cf. Orlandi, *H. Th. R.* 75 (1982) 85–95, who suggests the possibility of a connection with Evagrian monasticism.)

[70] Epiph., *Pan.* xxxi.2.2–3, 7.1.

[71] Marc. Anc., *Eccl.* 7, 9; though cf. Mercati's reservations, in the introduction to his edition (89), about the probability of Valentinus's having held the doctrines here attributed to him.

[72] Tim. Const., *Haer.*, 17b; and cf. Marc. Anc., *Eccl.* 6, mentioning 'the followers of Hermes and Seleucus' in a list of gnostics and other heretics. Note also the influence of astrological Hermetism on the gnostic Peratae (Hippol., *Haer.* v.14.8, 15.1), of whose history we know nothing save that their leaders were Euphrates ὁ Περατικός (?) and Celbes of Carystus (in Euboea) (*ibid.* v.13.9).

[73] Above, 125–6.

[74] E.g. Zos. Pan., *fr. gr.* 234.2.

[75] Above, 167.

necessary to have alchemical books gathered together and burned.[76] Magical books were equally the object of suspicion, as already noticed;[77] and the conclusion to be drawn from the numerousness of the survivors is obvious. Even the philosophical Hermetica were in abundant supply, if we are to believe the scribe's note in *N.H.C.* VI.

As for Panopolis, whether or not Zosimus lived there, one can think of few places more likely to have harboured Hermetic adepts. It was a city renowned in late antiquity for its fierce allegiance to the old gods as well as its flourishing Greek literary culture.[78] A recently discovered papyrus archive from Panopolis has revealed what must surely have been fertile soil for the growth of Hermetic pre-occupations in the priest Aurelius Petearbeschinis (clearly a native Egyptian) and his family, which embraced a suggestive combination of priests of the local god Pan-Min and thoroughly Hellenized men of letters.[79] And further north lay Hermoupolis Magna itself, the ancient centre of the Thoth-cult. In Egyptian it was most commonly called *Ḥmnw* ('City of the Eight'), because of an even earlier cult of eight primeval gods; and it was the Greeks who renamed the place after the most important of its divine patrons.[80] The thick humus of legend that continued to accumulate around Greek and Roman Hermoupolis testifies to the sustained popularity of Thoth–Hermes. Before long it came to be believed that he had founded the city that bore his name,[81] though no such tradition is attested under the Pharaohs. It was commonly held too, at least in the Roman period, that Hermes Trismegistus had been both born and buried in Hermoupolis;[82] and in the *Asclepius* Trismegistus himself alludes to these traditions, though referring them to his grandfather:

Does not Hermes, the grandfather whose name I bear, reside[83] in the city where he was born (*patria*) and which is named after him, and give help and protection to all the mortal men who come to him from every part of the world?[84]

[76] Halleux, *Alchimistes grecs* 1.23–4.
[77] For further references see Parássoglou, in *Collectanea papyrologica* 1.261–74.
[78] Cameron, *Y. Cl. S.* 27 (1982) 217–21.
[79] The archive is only partially published: Browne, *I.C.S.* 2 (1977) 184–96; Willis, *I.C.S.* 3 (1978) 140–51, and *XV Cong. Pap.* 2.98–115.
[80] Sethe, *Amun* 36–40. (It is not at all certain that Ἑρμοῦ πόλις was merely a translation of *Pr-Dhwtj* ('House of Thoth'), which was anyway a rare name for the city.)
[81] Artap. (second century B.C.), *fr.* 3 (682.29–683.3); Lact., *Inst.* 1.6.3. The *Strasb. cosmog.*, *verso* 10ff., also refers to the foundation of an Egyptian city, probably Hermoupolis, by Hermes.
[82] Birth: *P. Graec. Mag.* VIII.42–3. Burial: references listed (and their role in Christian polemic discussed) by Pfister, *Reliquienkult* 390–5.
[83] The preceding reference to the grave of Asclepius shows that the allusion is to Hermes's tomb.   [84] *Ascl.* 37.

Upper Egypt

No doubt it was the tomb of Hermes that was the focus of these pilgrims' piety. Certainly Hermoupolis remained devoted to Hermes throughout the Ptolemaic and Roman periods; and this, together with the vigorous Greek cultural tradition that the city shared with Panopolis,[85] makes one wonder if it too was among the centres of literary Hermetism. The *Strasbourg cosmogony*, for example, is a poem preserved on a fourth-century papyrus, and almost certainly of Hermoupolitan origin,[86] which describes how Hermes created the world, conjuring order out of chaos at the instance of his father Zeus, and then sought out a suitable site in Egypt for the foundation of the first city – Hermoupolis, one presumes. There is no lack of parallels, some of them quite close, in the philosophical Hermetica;[87] and one can at least say that if there were Hermetists in Hermoupolis, they will have found this rather sophisticated composition, with its *mélange* of Greek and Egyptian elements, very congenial reading.

A couple of allusions to Trismegistus in Hermoupolitan papyri indicate the sort of social milieu in which such interests will have flourished. A letter from the city council congratulating a local dignitary on his safe return from a sea-voyage to Rome in the reign of Gallienus misquotes Euripides and invokes 'our ancestral god Hermes Trismegistus, who stands by you everywhere'.[88] In a Hermoupolitan context this is no doubt just convention,[89] hardly a conscious allusion to the ever-present spiritual guide of the Hermetica,[90] though it may have been understood that way. More suggestive is the early fourth-century archive of Theophanes, a government official of Hermoupolitan origin but probably resident

---

[85] Méautis, *Hermoupolis* 18–22; Moscadi, *Aegyptus* 50 (1970) 99; *P. Turner* 9 (a book-catalogue from the first half of the fourth century). The literary papyri published by Maehler, *A.P.F.* 30 (1984) 5–29, belong to the fifth and sixth centuries. Comparison of later Ptolemaic inscriptions from Hermoupolis and Memphis (Zucker, *Doppelinschrift* 41) reveals in the former city a large number of proper names compounded from the name Hermes, and in Memphis none.

[86] Keydell, *Kleine Schriften* 287–9; and Zieliński, *Scientia* (*Rivista di Scienza*) 70 (1941) 65, 117 (pointing out that the poem may be older than the papyrus).

[87] See e.g. such cosmogonical passages as *S.H.* XXIII.25–31, 43–8 (cf. N.F. 3.CL–CLVIII, esp. CLV–CLVI); *C.H.* 1.4–13; *C.H.* III. In particular compare *Strasb. cosmog.*, recto lines 6–8, on Zeus 'sitting in a place of vantage' and watching over the creative work of his son Hermes, with *Ascl.* 27 on the supreme God (called Jupiter at *ibid.* 19) who 'dwells above the summit of the highest heaven, is present everywhere and surveys all things around him', and watches over the work of the creator gods (who are treated as different aspects of Jupiter).

[88] ...ὃς παρίσταταί σοι πα[ν]ταχοῦ. The best text of the papyrus is provided by Méautis, *Hermoupolis* 175–6.

[89] Cf. *Arch. Theoph.*, *ep.* 7.11: τοῦ φυλάττοντος θε[ο]ῦ Ἑρμοῦ.

[90] Cf. *C.H.* I. 2 (σύνειμί σοι πανταχοῦ), 22 (παραγίνομαι), referring, strictly speaking, to Poimandres. The suggestion was made by Méautis, *loc. cit.*

in Alexandria, who is known to have undertaken a major business journey to Antioch at some time between 317 and 323.[91] From the Hermetist point of view the interest of his archive lies in the fact that it contains three letters written by an *archiprophētēs* called Anatolius and entrusted for delivery to Theophanes, who is about to leave on a journey to Alexandria. The names of the addressees are Sarapion, Ambrosius and Nilus.[92] Two of these letters invoke Hermes, one as 'Trismegistus'; and in the letter to Sarapion Anatolius explains that he has been prevented from travelling by the illness of his daughters and by his obligations to the cult of Hermes – as an *archiprophētēs* he was a prominent member of the Hermoupolitan priesthood.[93] Sarapion, Ambrosius and Nilus are all as pagan as their correspondent.[94] For Sarapion, Anatolius promises to pray during the rites in which he is about to participate, while Ambrosius he describes as 'all-wise' and 'champion of the wisdom of the Hellenes', that is the pagans.[95] As for Nilus, Anatolius salutes him as a fellow-priest, the glory of his profession. The sophisticated style[96] of these letters confirms the impression that we have to do with a group of learned devotees of Hermes, in which we should probably include Theophanes himself.[97]

[91] *R. Ryl.* vol. 4, pp. 104–5; Moscadi, *Aegyptus* 50 (1970) 91. Moscadi provides the most recent text of the letters from *Arch. Theoph.* The remainder of the archive is *P. Ryl.* 616–51. On the provenance see *P. Herm.* (of which nos 2–6, re-edited by Moscadi, form part of *Arch. Theoph.*) *passim*.

[92] *Arch. Theoph., epp.* 7, 8, 12. Anatolius is called *archiprophētēs* on the *verso* of 8 (= *P. Herm.* 3), but Moscadi has absent-mindedly substituted χαίρειν. Moscadi's assertion, 119, that Anatolius lived not at Hermoupolis but 'a est di Alessandria' is based on the arbitrary assumption that the letters can only have been placed in Theophanes's hands while he was returning from his journey to Antioch. Probably we have to do with a different journey, starting from Theophanes's native Hermoupolis.

[93] Cf. Bülow-Jacobsen, *XV Cong. Pap.* 4.124–31.

[94] Moscadi's tendentious arguments about supposedly Christian vocabulary (*art. cit., passim*, and most absurdly at 94 n. 2) are at their least convincing when applied to this part of the archive.

[95] Cf. Ps.-Jul., *epp.* 181.449b, and 184.419a, on Iamblichus as 'the common good of the Hellenes', and 'the saviour of Hellenic culture' (τοῦ Ἑλληνικοῦ).

[96] Cf. esp. Moscadi, *art. cit.* 118.

[97] Rees's assumption (*P. Herm.* pp. 2–12) that *P. Herm.* 4–6 = *Arch. Theoph., epp.* 9–11 derive from the same 'circle' as *Arch. Theoph., epp.* 7, 8, 12, rests only on their presence in the same cache of papyri, and the fact that they are addressed to Theophanes. But Theophanes's acquaintances were many, and *P. Herm.* 6 = *Arch. Theoph., ep.* 11, was anyway written from Alexandria, not Hermoupolis – it is subscribed (presumably by its author), but the first hand (a scribe's?) is identical to that of *Arch. Theoph., ep.* 4, written (as appears from references in lines 9 and 18 to ἡ πόλις: cf. St. Byz. 70) in Alexandria (mentioned in *P. Herm.* 6 also simply as ἡ πόλις).

Hermetism in Egypt

Late antique Alexandria

With Theophanes we re-enter the orbit of Alexandria, which we left in the company of Thessalus. Thessalus was not alone in finding that Alexandria raised more hopes than it fulfilled. An Oxyrhynchus papyrus of the first century preserves a letter from a student to his father complaining about the difficulty of finding suitable teachers;[98] but of far more interest to us are the experiences of two of the most influential philosophers of late antiquity, Plotinus and Proclus. Plotinus, twenty-eight years old and eager for wisdom, 'had been recommended to the teachers in Alexandria who had at that time the best reputation, but was coming away from their lectures dejected and full of sadness'. Then a friend introduced him to Ammonius Saccas, and he was immediately captivated, exclaiming: 'this is the man I was searching for'. For the next eleven years he remained constantly at Ammonius's side.[99] Proclus too was disillusioned by the type of instruction he received when he began his philosophical studies in Alexandria; but he found no Ammonius to redeem the inadequacy of his teachers. Eventually he remembered a dream in which Athena had directed him to study in Athens, and it was there that at last he met the two masters, Plutarch and Syrianus, who initiated him into the theurgic Platonism of Iamblichus.[100]

Like any great centre of learning, Alexandria provided an education aimed at and no doubt sufficient for the majority of students, but apt to seem stereotyped and unimaginative to those who sought a profounder wisdom. And Marinus wrote his biography of Proclus very much from an Athenian perspective, which one would scarcely expect to allow rival schools the benefit of the doubt. Perhaps Plotinus's experience brings us nearer the truth – even the most demanding student could find what he wanted in Alexandria, granted some patience. Some such realization has recently begun to change scholarly attitudes to the intellectual life of the Egyptian metropolis. Where the pagan philosophers who abounded in fifth- and sixth-century Alexandria used to be thought of as largely concerned with writing commentaries on Aristotle, and as highly conservative compared with their Athenian competitors, it is now accepted that the more adventurous doctrines associated with Iamblichus also had

---

[98] *P. Oxy.* 2190.
[99] Porph., *V. Plot.* 3.
[100] Marin., *Proc.* 9–10.

177

a following, or at least an audience.[101] It is worth bearing this in mind when one comes to evaluate the (as usual) fragmentary evidence for Hermetism in late antique Alexandria.

In view of the important technical literature that circulated under the name of Hermes, we should remember too that Alexandria had always been a major centre of scientific research. In the fourth century the city's schools had an international reputation not just in mathematics, geometry, astronomy, medicine, music and so on, but also in astrology, divination and the study of religious doctrine as revealed in the sacred books – thus at least Ammianus Marcellinus, a sober historian.[102] Among the luminaries of this fourth-century Alexandrian scene was Theon, an eminent mathematician and astrologer who is also known to have taken an interest in techniques of divination.[103] So when we learn that he 'interpreted astronomical works, and the writings of Hermes Trismegistus and Orpheus', it seems likely that astrological Hermetica are what is intended.[104] Among colleagues or at least contemporaries of Theon who shared his interest in Trismegistus one may mention, *exempli gratia*, Paul of Alexandria[105] and the so-called 'Astrologer of the year 379' who, though he wrote in Rome, was of Egyptian origin.[106] Astrology continued to be taught in Alexandria in the fifth and sixth centuries, as part of the standard curriculum, though how important it was is difficult to judge.[107] Philosophers such as Synesius, Olympiodorus and Stephanus were credited in Byzantium with a number of treatises on both alchemy and astrology which modern scholars have treated with suspicion.[108] Certainly a number of these works do look like forgeries, and bad ones too. On the other hand Olympiodorus, or someone very close to him, definitely taught astrology, since we have some of the notes that were taken at lectures he gave in the year 564;[109] and there is much else about late antique Alexandria to

---

[101] Fowden, *J.H.S.* 102 (1982) 45–8, esp. the references in n. 103.
[102] Amm. Marc. XXII.16.17–22.   [103] Suda Θ 205.
[104] Ioh. Mal. XIII.343. The *Anth. gr.* assigns part of *S.H.* XXIX, an astrological poem, to one 'Theon' – cf. N.F.'s *app. crit.*
[105] Paul Al. 93.20–94.5, 118.24–119.7.
[106] *C.C.A.G.* 5(1).204.19–20, 209.8–9. This writer was perhaps identical with Paul: *ibid.* 194–5.
[107] Westerink, *Texts and studies* 291–4.
[108] See Lacombrade, *Synésios* 64–71, on the alchemical treatise attributed to Synesius (rather than, as Lacombrade holds, written by another Synesius – note that the text's forger is careful to associate it with Alexandria by having Synesius address it to a priest there); Westerink, *Commentaries on Plato's Phaedo* 1.22–3, on Olympiodorus's *alchymicum*; and *id.*, *Anonymous prolegomena* xxv, on Stephanus. Also the lists of alchemical authorities at *Alch. gr.* 25–6, 424–5.   [109] Westerink, *Texts and studies* 279–94.

suggest that its intellectual atmosphere was more catholic than is generally realized.

Synesius, who studied science and philosophy under Theon's daughter Hypatia in the 390s, but in later life made more practical use of his skills in rhetoric, gives in his *Dion* a revealing list of men renowned for their wisdom: Ammon, Zoroaster, Hermes and Antony.[110] It is a casual list, intended only to emphasize by contrast how foolish are the critics against whom the speech is directed; but that makes it all the more revealing. Clearly Ammon, like Hermes, derives from the Hermetica. Zoroaster was a similar sort of ancient oriental sage. And Antony of course was a Christian. So what did Synesius know of the Hermetic philosophy? And did he perhaps connect it, as Lactantius had already done,[111] with the teachings of Christ, which he himself was to expound one day as a bishop? As regards the first question, the reader of Synesius's hymns will often feel himself in the presence of an *anima naturaliter Hermetica*, though there are no formal allusions to the Hermetic literature. Hymn IX presents particularly striking parallels with the initiatory treatises of Hermes.[112] And just as Synesius's hymns are an amalgam of the Christian and pagan strands of his thought, so too, no doubt, he saw in the Hermetica a doctrine capable of reconciliation with that of the Church. Certainly other Alexandrian contemporaries were interested in Hermes, as one might expect in a city whose schools had long mixed pagans and Christians, and continued to do so even in the tenser fifth century. In fact, we know far more about the Christians' use of the Hermetica at this period than we do about the pagans' – both in Alexandria and, as we shall see in the next chapter, abroad.

The first Alexandrian Christian known to have made use of the Hermetica is Didymus the Blind (*c.* 313–98), head of the Catechetical School, who invokes Hermes at several points in his *De Trinitate*, quoting word for word from *C.H.* VI and (probably) *S.H.* I, but also using other Hermetic texts, the *Discourses to Asclepius*, which have since disappeared.[113] Didymus co-opts Hermes as an ally, and

---

[110] Syn., *Dion* 10.   [111] Below, 205–8.

[112] See the notes to Terzaghi's edition of the *Hymni*, *passim*; and the remarks of Bizzochi, *Gregorianum* 32 (1951) 381–7. Vollenweider, *Synesios* 167–8, detects Hermetic inspiration in *Provid.*

[113] Did. Al., *Trin.* II.3.26–8 (Seiler) (cf. *C.H.* VI.2–3); II.27 (quoting from the λόγος τρίτος πρὸς Ἀσκληπιόν; cf. Scott 4.171–4); III.1.776a (Migne) (τοσούτῳ κρείττονος, ὅσον τὸ ἀθάνατον τοῦ θνητοῦ: cf. *S.H.* I.1). Attempts to deny Didymus the *Trin.* are currently on the ebb: *C.P.G.* no. 2570; Hönscheid, *Didymus* 5–7.

interprets – or rather deliberately misinterprets – the *Discourses to Asclepius* as containing oracles foretelling the Christian revelation. The word *logos*, for example, occurs often enough in the Hermetica, usually in the sense of 'word' or 'discourse'; but Didymus takes it to mean the Christian *Logos*, the Son of God.[114] This ploy had already been used by Lactantius; and it is also related to an even less subtle fashion, of which more shortly, for inventing 'oracles' of Hermes in which the coming of Christ and the dogmas of Christianity are foretold. Conceivably Didymus drew on an anthology of such oracles, and had no separate knowledge of the *Discourses to Asclepius*.[115]

Cyril of Alexandria (d. 444) likewise invoked Hermes frequently, and with malicious delight, in the course of refuting the famous attack on Christianity, the *Contra Galilaeos*, launched by the emperor Julian, whom Cyril regarded as one of Hermes's leading spiritual disciples in recent times.[116] Writing during the 420s and 430s,[117] Cyril quotes word for word from *C.H.* XI and XIV, the *Perfect discourse* and *S.H.* I.[118] He also knows of the *Discourses to Asclepius*,[119] perhaps from Didymus; and he is our earliest authority for the so-called *diexodikoi logoi* addressed to Tat.[120] Other texts he reproduces have no title and correspond directly to nothing in the surviving Hermetica.[121] Although Cyril may have derived much or all of this erudition from some secondary anthology,[122] he could appear, at least, to have an impressive command of Hermetic and other pagan material, which he knew well how to deploy appositely (unlike Didymus) in support of, especially, the Christian *Logos* doctrine.[123] It was in large part through Cyril's extensive quotations that Hermes Trismegistus passed into the Byzantine Greek and Syriac literary traditions, in the unaccustomed but advantageous role of a prophet of Christ.

We find Hermes playing this part with aplomb in the apologetical oracle-anthologies, already alluded to, which were in circulation by the fourth century at the latest.[124] The point of these collections was

[114] Scott 4.171 n. 6.   [115] *F. Gr. Th.* 109 n. 215; Grant, *J.Th.S.* 15 (1964) 265–9.
[116] Cyr. Al., *Jul.* II.597d.
[117] See the introduction to the edition of Burguière and Evieux, I.10–15.
[118] Cyr. Al., *Jul.* I.549bc (= *S.H.* I.1), II.580b (= *C.H.* XI.22; a rare example of a text cited by (almost) the same title as it bears in our MSS), 597d–600b (= *C.H.* XIV.6–7, 8–10), IV.701ab (an interpolated version of *Ascl.* 29; cf. N.F. 2.336).
[119] *Cyr. H.* 23–4 (and note the parallels to surviving Hermetica adduced by N.F.).
[120] *Cyr. H.* 30, 32ab, 33; cf. Scott 4.213 n. 18, and above, 99.
[121] *Cyr. H.* 25–9, 34–5.   [122] Ferguson *ap.* Scott 4.xliii.
[123] See esp. Cyr. Al., *Jul.* I.552d–553b.
[124] On the oracle-anthologies in general see Nock, *Essays* 160–8; Speyer, *Literarische Fälschung* 246–52. On similar Jewish collections see also West, *Orphic poems* 33–5.

to convince by pagan revelation pagans who were immune not only to reason but also to Christian revelation that the gospels were true. To this end fraudulent oracles foretelling the Incarnation and so on were attributed to pagan gods, heroes and sages both ancient (such as Hermes, Solon or Plato) and modern (for example Iamblichus); and to them were added certain genuine responses, for example from the oracles of Apollo at Didyma and Claros.[125] The best-known collection is the so-called *Theosophia Tubingensis*, which has been dated between 474 and 508;[126] but there were others similar.[127] That some of them circulated in Egypt is proved by the existence of Coptic translations;[128] and that others were actually composed in Egypt is hinted by the surprisingly recondite Egyptian materials they contain.[129] For their borrowings from the Hermetica the oracle-collections are largely dependent on Cyril of Alexandria,[130] though they vary the texts they inherit from him, giving way at times to sheer fantasy and attributing to Hermes pronouncements barefacedly concocted from the commonplaces of the gospels.[131] But where the words came from was not the point – in this sort of milieu texts floated freely from one attribution to another.[132] What was important was the prestige of the name they were attached to. Clearly that of Hermes

---

[125] Robert, *C.R.A.I* (1968) 568–99; (1971) 597–619.

[126] *F. Gr. Th.* 3.

[127] See those published alongside the *Theosophia* in *F. Gr. Th.*; and the Syriac collections published by Brock, *O.L.P.* 14 (1983) 203–46; *V. Chr.* 38 (1984) 77–90.

[128] Van den Broek, *V. Chr.* 32 (1978) 118–42.

[129] That the *Theosophia* originated in Egypt might be argued from: (1) its aspiration to gather 'the so-called "theologies" of the wise men among the Greeks and Egyptians' (§1); (2) its interest in Egyptian names for Helios (§8); (3) its reproduction of a series of inscribed oracles from different parts of Egypt (§§45–9). But (1) perhaps just reflects Egypt's immense reputation for wisdom everywhere in the Greek and Latin worlds; (2) is a literary borrowing (see commentary *ad loc.*); and (3) might have been extracted from one of the many oracle-collections in circulation. (Would an Egyptian have troubled to tell us of each of the provenances that it was 'in Egypt'?) Additionally, §20 (οἱ τὴν πόλιν ταύτην οἰκήσοντες) hints at a Constantinopolitan origin; and H. Chadwick, in a private communication, encourages me to doubt Erbse's assertion, *F. Gr. Th.* 3, that use of the Alexandrian recension of the LXX implies an author/editor resident in Egypt. The danger of taking seriously anything these texts tell us is illustrated by the reappearance of the allegedly Egyptian oracle at §49 in a very different guise in another collection (*F. Gr. Th.* 210.19–24).

[130] *F. Gr. Th.* 202–3, 205, 209 (with nn. *ad loc.*, and cf. *ibid.* 104–11); 218.5–6 (cf. 203.8–9, 209.17–18, and 95 n. 181); Brock, *V. Chr.* 38 (1984) 79–80.

[131] *F. Gr. Th.* 221.3–6 (and cf. 95 n. 181; 102, esp. n. 195).

[132] See above, n. 129; and the reattribution of *F. Gr. Th.* 221.13–14 ('Plato the glorious said:...."His [i.e. God's] son, Christ, will be born of the Virgin Mary, and I believe in him"') to Hermes by the time it reaches 'Mandeville', the fourteenth-century Western travelogue-compiler (*Travels* III, ed. Letts 2.237). The same oracle was also in circulation in the Byzantine world without any specific attribution: *F. Gr. Th.* 94, esp. n. 180; 102–3.

stood high among pagans. For Christians too he had his uses. We stand here at the beginning – but only the beginning – of the long process of sanitization that ended, in the post-Byzantine period, with Trismegistus being painted on church walls in eastern Europe – though not, so far as is yet known, in the Greek world – as a Christian before Christ.[133]

Whatever Hermes himself would have thought of this metamorphosis, there were certainly pagans in Alexandria who saw it for the cynical manipulation that it was. Synesian ambiguities were not to everyone's taste – if they had been, would Cyril have bothered to apply himself, three-quarters of a century after Julian's death, to so massive a refutation of the *Contra Galilaeos*? Nor could Cyril be content with merely cerebral repression: it was while he was bishop that Hypatia was torn limb from limb on the streets of Alexandria. Mute testimony to the success of this assault on the old gods is at hand in the disappearance from the Greek tradition of Hermes's *Perfect discourse*, despite a popularity which had caused it to be translated into Coptic and Latin. In the apparent twilight of the gods the *Perfect discourse* offered an assurance of their ultimate return; and just as Christians like Augustine took this passage as a reference to contemporary events, so we may be sure did many pagans. Among them perhaps was Antoninus, an early representative of a phenomenon once thought uncharacteristic of Alexandria, the Iamblichan holy man who combined with a love of Platonist philosophy a passionate sensibility for the beauty of religious cult and its centrality to a full spiritual life. Antoninus[134] was the son of the rhetor and philosopher Eustathius and Sosipatra, a brilliant theurgical philosopher in her own right. His teacher was Aedesius, a pupil of Iamblichus who later became the focal point of a major Platonist circle in Pergamon. Like many of Iamblichus's intellectual heirs, Antoninus was fascinated by the religion of the Egyptians, to the point that he removed first to the 'holy city'[135] of Alexandria, and thence to Canopus on the coast a little to the east of the metropolis, where he appears to have settled in a temple and dedicated himself to the divine ritual and an ascetic

---

[133] Grecu, *A.R.B.S.H.* 11 (1924) 29, 55, 63, 65; Howlett, in *Byzantium and the classical tradition* 172. Cf. the famous depiction of Trismegistus in the pavement of Siena Cathedral, made in the 1480s (photograph: Scott 1, frontispiece).

[134] Eun., *V. Phil.* VI.9.1, 15–17; 10.6–11.1; 11.10–12.

[135] The phrase is Julian's, *ep.* 60.379a. See also Eun., *V. Phil.* VI.10.8: ἡ δὲ Ἀλεξάνδρεια...ἱερά τις ἦν οἰκουμένη.

personal regime.[136] Soon the youth of pagan Alexandria was flocking to him, 'and the sanctuary', says Eunapius of Sardis (our only source), 'was full of young men [acting as] priests'. To his disciples and visitors Antoninus spoke with enthusiasm of the philosophy of Plato; and since Eunapius emphasizes his refusal to say anything at all about the doctrines of theurgy, we can be certain that he had inherited his mother's accomplishment in the sacred science.[137] This reticence was in part the theurgist's habitual secrecy, but also fear of Christian reprisals; and indeed it is Antoninus's prophecy of the collapse of the Sarapis cult throughout Egypt (fulfilled as far as the famous Alexandrian Sarapeum was concerned in 391) that Eunapius sees as his greatest claim to fame:

> For while still in human guise, and conversing with mortal men, he foretold to all his followers that after him the temple would be no more, and that the great and holy sanctuaries of Sarapis would likewise pass into darkness and formlessness and be transformed, while the disfiguring darkness of mythical times would hold sway over the fairest things on earth... To everybody he said that the temples would become tombs.[138]

One is struck by the resemblance of this passage to Hermes's prophecy in the *Asclepius*;[139] and even more so by Antoninus's life-style, an imitation of that attributed to Hermes and his pupils Asclepius, Tat and (H)Ammon in the same book.

Pagans of this sort were certainly much affected by the dramatic events of 391. Among a number of others who left in a hurry we hear of one Ammonius, a 'priest of the ape' (in other words Thoth) and, it would seem, a man of letters, since after fleeing from Alexandria he settled in Constantinople as a teacher of grammar.[140] Perhaps another of the refugees was the pagan poet Claudian, who certainly left Alexandria for Rome round about this time, and shows in his works a quite specialized knowledge of Egyptian religion.[141] But most stayed put, and continued to worship the old gods and even cultivate their distinctive intellectual tradition. As one might expect, living

[136] Compare the Memphite *katochoi*. On them, and on Hor of Sebennytus (second century B.C.), who may have become a *katochos* because of a dream in which Thoth appeared to him, see Ray, *Archive of Hor* 161–3.

[137] Cf. Rufin., *H.E.* xi.26, on Canopus, 'virtually a public school of magic, under the pretence of priestly learning – for that is how they call the ancient learning of the Egyptians'.

[138] The prophecy is also alluded to by Aug., *Div. daem.* 1.1.

[139] *Ascl.* 24–7, esp. 24: 'then that most holy land, a place of sanctuaries and temples, will be filled up with sepulchres and the dead'; 25: 'shadows will be preferred to the light'.

[140] Soc. v.16.9.

[141] Cameron, *Claudian* 28–9, 199–208, neglecting Derchain, *Z.Ä.S.* 81 (1956) 4–6.

under constant threat their outlook became increasingly conservative. For example Damascius, writing in the first quarter of the sixth century, mentions one Epiphanius, a well-known interpreter of the rites of Osiris and Aion who, together with Euprepius, priest of the 'Persika', succeeded in preserving many ancient traditions at a time when Alexandria was dangerous for pagans.[142] That Hermetism was a part of this culture is confirmed by the mid-fifth-century Platonist Hermias, who in his scholia on the *Phaedrus* makes a number of references to Hermes Trismegistus and his writings, and to traditions about the god's life on earth that are only mentioned indirectly in other sources.[143] Like Theon, Hermias links Hermes with Orpheus, whose theological poems were widely read in these circles, and to whom, on occasion, we find works ascribed that elsewhere are attributed to Hermes.[144] And on the last page of several manuscripts of the *scholia* on the *Phaedrus* we find some verses composed by an admiring reader, playing on the author's name:

> ὁ πρῶτος Ἑρμῆς μνημονεύσας ἐν βίῳ
> τρίτον γενέσθαι καὶ σοφὸν τοσαυτάκις
> ἐπωνομάσθη τρισμέγιστος εἰκότως·
> ὁ δεύτερος δὲ πανσόφως σαφηνίσας
> τὸν τοῦ Πλάτωνος Φαῖδρον ἐν τρισὶν βίβλοις
> τρισόλβιος καλοῖτ' ἂν οὐκ ἀπὸ τρόπου.[145]

The type of theurgical Platonism represented at Alexandria in the later fourth century by Antoninus, and apparently difficult to find there when Proclus was a student (*c.* 430), was cultivated in the mid- to late-fifth century by two native Egyptian brothers, Heraiscus and Asclepiades, about whom we know a certain amount thanks to Damascius.[146] Their father, Horapollo the elder, was a native of Phenebythis in the Panopolite nome. Like many others from that area he was a conventional, widely-travelled literary man, entirely Hellenic in culture. His son and grandson, Asclepiades's son Horapollo,

---

[142] Dam., *V. Isid. fr.* 100.
[143] Herm., *In Phdr.* 94.21–2, 168.24–5, 258.8–9; cf. Puech, *En quête de la gnose* 1.117–18, and N.F. 4.148–9.
[144] Dam., *V. Isid. fr.* 41, 287; and below, 214 n. 5.
[145] 'The first Hermes, recalling that he was three times born, and as many times wise, was rightly called Trismegistus. The second [Hermes, i.e. Hermias], having most wisely elucidated Plato's *Phaedrus* in three books, might not unreasonably be called Trisolbios [thrice-blessed].' On these verses, which may be much later, see Westerink, *Commentaries on Plato's Phaedo* 1.30–1.
[146] Dam., *V. Isid.* 107 (*E. Ph.*), *fr.* 160–4, 174, and *Pr.* 1, p. 324, to which no further separate references will be made. For the basic biographical information and references see *P.L.R.E.* 2, *s.vv.*; Fowden, *J.H.S.* 102 (1982) 46–7.

followed in his footsteps – Horapollo the younger was to speak with obvious pride of his family's long tradition of teaching literature and philosophy in the Alexandrian *mouseia*.[147] Yet this was no ordinary academic dynasty. The second and third generations immersed themselves enthusiastically in the lore of the Egyptians as well as the erudition of the Greeks, and not (unless perhaps in the case of Horapollo) out of antiquarianism but for the sake of the spiritual teachings preserved in this most ancient of traditions. Iamblichus had after all shown that the doctrines of theurgy reposed on the wisdom of the Egyptian priests, as expounded in the books of Hermes Trismegistus; and Heraiscus was determined to drink at the very sources. 'He made his soul to dwell always in sanctuaries and mystic places', Damascius tells us, 'and fostered not only the ancestral rites of Egypt, but also those of other lands, whenever he could find any remnants of them.' It seems that both he and his brother were priests. Indeed, Asclepiades was said to be even more immersed in Egyptian wisdom than Heraiscus, because he spent less time travelling abroad. He was 'nourished in the Egyptian writings', much-versed in the native theology, and wrote hymns to the Egyptian gods, a 'harmony' of all theologies and a work on ancient Egyptian history. Granted the improbability that anybody knew enough Egyptian to read the Thoth literature at this date, we must assume that Asclepiades, like Iamblichus, derived what he knew from Greek sources, and not least of course the Hermetica, technical, theological and philosophical.

The spiritual and intellectual influence of these two brothers was considerable. Proclus, who shared their catholic interest in all manifestations of the old religion, including the Egyptian,[148] and to whom Heraiscus addressed one of his books, was said to have confessed that the Egyptian was wiser than himself. Damascius's teacher Isidore was one of the brothers' more distinguished pupils, and clearly it was at their feet that he acquired his own profound knowledge of the 'Egyptian philosophy', together with the admiration he expressed for the 'astonishing subtleties' of Iamblichus.[149] On the other hand Horapollo the younger proved that he was a man of the future by writing (or so it may be assumed) the highly misleading treatise on hieroglyphs (*Hieroglyphica*) that has been preserved under his name,[150] and by eventually apostatizing to Christianity. Asclepi-

---

[147] *P. Cair. Masp.* 67295.1.13–17 = Maspero, *B.I.A.O.* 11 (1914) 165–6.
[148] Marin., *Proc.* 19.   [149] Dam., *V. Isid.* 243 (*E. Ph.*) (= *fr.* 80), 33.
[150] Between the *Hieroglyphica* and the Hermetica Sbordone, *Hori Apollinis hieroglyphica* XXVIII–XXXI, found only 'influssi e tendenze comuni'.

ades's 'harmony' of all theologies may be taken as Graeco-Egyptianism's last attempt at a coherent *speculum mentis* within the context of the old religion – the fizzling out, in other words, of that long interaction between Greek and Egyptian paganism of which the Hermetica had been so typical a product.

The milieu of Hermetism: a socio-intellectual description

We must return now to the question posed at the beginning of this chapter about the historical content of the term 'Hermetism'. The possibility was there raised that, although contemporaries clearly were aware of a complex of beliefs clustered around the name of Hermes, and which we reasonably call Hermetism, these beliefs may not have cohered enough to generate anything that deserved to be called a Hermetist milieu. And we have now seen a number of situations – in the Thebes cache and the Nag Hammadi library, for example, or among the Platonists of late antique Alexandria – where Hermetism was indeed treated as just one among several routes leading to knowledge of things divine. In fact if we judge by the external historical testimonia alone this would seem to have been the norm. The philosophical Hermetica strongly imply, as we have seen, the existence of Hermetist individuals and circles who followed a coherent spiritual 'way'. But the external testimonia afford the hypothesis of an independent Hermetist milieu pitiably little support. Does this mean, then, that we were wrong to imagine we could draw historical conclusions from the Hermetic texts? Or is the gap between our two areas of evidence, internal and external, perhaps not as significant as it seems at first glance? Since one of the more obvious functions of any Hermetist circles that did actually exist will have been precisely the production of Hermetic texts, we can perhaps learn something by reflecting on how such production came about.

The Hermetica constituted a well-known and growing body of literature, so there were naturally some (and long before Casaubon) who found themselves unable to understand its attribution to Hermes Trismegistus in a crudely literal sense. Even Iamblichus conceded that Hermes had not acquitted himself of his authorial responsibilities entirely without benefit of human assistance.[151] On the other hand

---

[151] Iam., *Myst.* I.I.I–2; and cf. VIII.4.265 ('the books which circulate under the name of Hermes'); Plut., *Is. Os.* 61 ('the so-called books of Hermes...on the sacred names').

it is perhaps unlikely that pseudepigrapha of this sort were cold-bloodedly or indiscriminately 'attributed' to just any ancient or mythical figure in order to increase their authority or circulation – though this might be alleged by a hostile critic, as when Porphyry maintained that the gnostic 'book of Zoroaster' was 'entirely spurious and modern, made up by the sectarians to convey the impression that the doctrines which they had chosen to hold in honour were those of the ancient Zoroaster'.[152] Rather one should suppose, in the Hermetic tradition as among the Pythagoreans and Orphics, some sense of a continuity of inspiration, of which each text added to the genre was seen as a new manifestation which could fairly, if not with pedantic precision, be ascribed to the eponymous founder. As Iamblichus put it, since Hermes was the source of all knowledge, it was only natural that the ancient Egyptian priests should render him homage by attributing their writings to him.[153] So we need not imagine that a spiritual teacher who was in the habit of circulating his compositions under the name of Hermes will have felt that he was perpetrating a deception, or that he needed to dissemble what he was doing as potentially scandalous. And indeed his work will have gained in weight, in the eyes of his followers, precisely because it was not merely the product of an autonomous authorial act, but reflected the sedimentary intellectual culture of his own and earlier times – in short, because it did *not* strive after originality. (Such, clearly, was the logic which, according to Zosimus of Panopolis, impelled some people to go so far as to claim for themselves the authorship of alchemical books which 'everyone knew' had been written by Hermes.[154]) And so of course we have no way of knowing how much of a given text can be attributed to whoever gave it the shape we see today; nor can we know how conscious – at least at the later stages of composition – were the literary and other allusions that adorn the texts; nor can we expect to be able to point to individual 'Hermetists' who wrote Hermetica. The milieu did not encourage either personal or literary in-dividualism – in fact, if Hermes had not existed he would have had to be invented.

If this interpretation of our texts be accepted, it follows that we should not expect to learn any more from external testimonia about Hermetic circles than we do about Orphic or (Neo-)Pythagorean

---

[152] Porph., *V. Plot.* 16.   [153] Iam., *Myst.* 1.1.2.
[154] Zos. Pan., *fr. syr.* 226.

circles. And one of the few chance allusions we do have takes us still further in our attempt to understand why the historical testimonia illuminate so little the Hermetic milieu implied by the philosophical texts. When Zosimus of Panopolis exhorts Theosebia to save souls and lead them towards the vision of the divine,[155] he seems to have in mind the circles of alchemists that Theosebia gathered around herself, and to be implying that they had, or might have, philosophical as well as technical preoccupations. Yet the reason we have this allusion is that it appears in an alchemical text; and that reflects a general bias in the historical testimonia towards telling us about the technical milieu. That no doubt in turn reflects the higher circulation of the technical Hermetica; but such works might well be used by lone operatives, and it was only those who followed the way of Hermes to its philosophical or rather spiritual culmination who had absolute need of a teacher and so generated circles.

One begins to see that what would really be surprising would be if the historical testimonia told us *more* than they do about the milieu of the philosophical Hermetists. This is in a way consoling, but does not get us much further towards positive corroboration of the sociological conclusions that were drawn from the Hermetic texts in the first section of this chapter. The only approach left is to look at what we know of the sociology of analogous religious milieux in late antiquity, to see what light they may cast, whether by analogy or contrast, on our particular problem.

There are three movements, each the object of recent sociological investigation,[156] which can usefully be compared with Hermetism, namely gnosticism and late Platonism, whose links with Hermetism need no further explanation, and Manichaeism, whose connections with Hermetism are more tenuous,[157] but whose sociological milieu was in some respects analogous. Hermetists, gnostics, Platonists and Manichees alike offered a message of salvation to the inhabitants of a world they tended to face with indifference or even hostility. And behind these resemblances of doctrine M. Weber detected a common sociological denominator as well, classifying such groups as mani-

---

[155] See above, 125–6, and the passage quoted at 122–3.
[156] Gnosticism: Rudolph, *Gnosis* 224–61, 308–15; also 315–52, and Koschorke, *N.H.S.* 17 (1981) 120–39, for indications of gnosticism's geographical spread. Manichaeism: Decret, *L'Afrique manichéenne* 1.203–10; Koenen, in *Das römisch-byzantinische Ägypten* 93–108. Platonism: Fowden, *Philosophia* 7 (1977) 359–83, and *J.H.S.* 102 (1982) 33–59. For documentation of the summary discussion that follows, reference should be made to these studies.
[157] Below, 203–4.

Milieu of Hermetism: a socio-intellectual description

festations of a typically Hellenistic and Roman 'Laienintellektualismus', a tendency, that is, for the educated, debarred from the life of action and public service, to renounce the world and proclaim a new, transcendent set of values.[158] We shall return to this interpretation, and need retain here only the obvious point about the intellectuality of all these movements. They were none of them religions of the masses, because they all taught that salvation comes through knowledge. Knowledge may be imparted suddenly, by revelation, to whomever the teacher deems worthy, as was the wont of certain gnostics; or it might be earned by long study as among the Platonists, not a few gnostics[159] and, it seems, the Hermetists. But, however acquired, it was always the possession of an elite. Hence the tendency within these milieux towards the emergence of a two-tier structure, with a small group of teachers, the 'elect' or the 'zealots', taking responsibility for the instruction of a much larger group of what the Platonists and Manichaeans appropriately called 'listeners'.

But structure is among the less striking characteristics of these circles. Except for those of the Manichees, who evolved a regular, organized Church with a self-perpetuating hierarchy, the others were completely dependent for their coming into being, their validation and their coherence on the powerful personalities of individual holy men. This we see most clearly among the Platonists, in Porphyry's biography of Plotinus and in Eunapius's lives of Iamblichus and his followers. In these texts we observe, in the first place, the at times almost hysterical devotion of pupil to teacher, and not least of the authors themselves to their respective mentors Plotinus and Chrysanthius. In Plotinus's circle it was even thought worthy of serious discussion – to Plotinus's disgust, it should be added – whether the pupil should 'in the pursuit of virtue submit himself to carnal intercourse with his teacher, if the teacher desired it'.[160] And the concomitant of such attitudes was the tendency of the circle to disintegrate on (or even before) the Master's death. In the third and fourth centuries, at least, there was little trace left of the stability in place or continuity in time of the classical philosophical Schools; and if during the fifth century something of that was recaptured in Athens

---

[158] Weber, *Wirtschaft und Gesellschaft* 1.304–10.
[159] On the amount of school-learning to be found in the *N.H.C.* see Böhlig, in *Zum Hellenismus* 9–53.
[160] Porph., *V. Plot.* 15.

and Alexandria, the reason is to be sought in the external pressure now being applied to pagan intellectuals by the Church, which forced them for safety's sake to hang together.

One of the reasons for this late antique obsession with the holy man was the wide acceptance of the Pythagorean view of philosophy as a religion and a way of life as much as an intellectual system. It was almost inconceivable that anyone might come to philosophy except through a teacher; and the teacher was expected to do much more than simply introduce the student to a learned tradition, whether written or oral. Plotinus, for example, explained in the regular gatherings of his pupils the writings of philosophers ancient and modern, expounded his own views, and tried to resolve the objections and problems of his pupils. Yet the atmosphere of the circle, as described by Porphyry, was anything but that of a university seminar. Not only was it wholly dominated by Plotinus himself, so that it ceased to exist once the effects of the Master's illness became too painfully apparent. It also had a domestic side, since it met in the house of a wealthy Roman lady. Plotinus made himself responsible for the education of young wards from leading families, who lived together with him in the same house; and he might even be called in to identify a thieving servant. He also involved himself deeply in the personal problems of his followers. Most important of all, though, few of Plotinus's pupils, at least the inner circle, will have gone to him just for intellectual instruction, as would have been the case in, for example, the Athenian schools of the period.[161] The circle had a definitely religious atmosphere, the product, needless to say, not of Amelius's religiosity or of his teacher's preparedness to consort with Egyptian priests and magicians, but of the firmly purificatory and contemplative emphasis of Plotinus's philosophy. As for the 'divine' Iamblichus and those who followed his theurgical teachings, in these circles the holy man achieved a literal apotheosis; thaumaturgy, religious devotion and philosophical study attained a perfect mingling. In the biographies of Pythagoras written by Porphyry and Iamblichus we see the ideal which these last Platonists strove towards, a life of worship, prayer and discussion shared among like-minded men in what was almost the atmosphere of a religious community. And though, among Platonists, Plotinus's circle is the nearest we get to this sort of community in late antiquity (and it is

---

[161] Cf. *ibid.* 14.19–20, quoting Plotinus's opinion of Longinus as 'a scholar...but in no way a philosopher'.

not very near), the Platonist circles were undeniably constricted, and mounting pressures on paganism encouraged an ever more in-grown mentality.

Of gnostic circles we know less, but along similar lines. The spiritual teacher was again the focus of everything, and there was the same strong sense of group-identity as with the Platonists, so long as the holy man survived. After his death, centrifugal forces soon asserted themselves. Gnostics admittedly came in many sorts; and some sects formed themselves into regular Churches, like the Manichees. But even the Manichees preserved, within the relatively formal structure of their local communities, a sense of the close personal dependence of the ordinary *auditores* on the *electi*.[162] Attitudes to cult were similarly various. Some practised, some disapproved, some gave cultic language a hidden, spiritual meaning. The range of positions.is wider, and harder to reduce to consistency, than with the Hermetists. We have gnostic hymns, prayers and sermons, evidence for worship of statues, sharing of holy meals and exchange of cultic kisses—all these have analogues in Hermetism. But other ceremonies are attested that imply a more thorough-going ritualism: baptisms, anointings, eucharists, ceremonies designed to accompany the soul's liberation from the body and experience of rebirth, and various orgiastic rites, our accounts of which would be less entertaining had they not passed through the agile imagination of heresiologists. There was also much of magic, astrology and so on to be encountered in the gnostic milieu, as in the Hermetic.

The intellectual and elitist character of all these movements – or at least the existence of such an elite within the movement – places their origin firmly within the big cities. That is not to say that they never propagated themselves in the provinces and the countryside – they may even have begun, in the later fourth century, to be pushed in these directions by the Church.[163] But we have evidence only for the Manichaeans,[164] whose structured communities could accommodate more varied social types (including workers on the land) and stand up to external pressures better than, for example, those gnostic circles that were built on nothing more durable than the holy man's personality, or the Platonist circles whose learned character made them inconceivable anywhere but in a city. The only late Platonist

---

[162] Kippenberg, *Numen* 30 (1983) 161–8.   [163] *Ibid.* 146–73.
[164] On the exiling of Manichaeans see Decret, *L'Afrique manichéenne* 2.165 nn. 39, 49; 184 n. 142.

known to have made a point of living 'among the mountains and precipices and trees' was soon hauled back, none too ceremoniously, by his students;[165] and the sages forced out of Athens by Justinian made not for the mountains but for Ctesiphon.

Among cities, it was Rome and those of Africa and the Hellenized East that best nurtured the sort of milieux that we are interested in. With Rome one associates Marcion and Valentinus as well as Plotinus; with Africa the Manichaeans combated by Augustine but also – to anticipate a little – a whole series of Christian intellectuals who were familiar with the Hermetica. Of other western provinces, the ubiquitous followers of Valentinus penetrated even Gaul (at least its southern towns); and a number of Italian cities apart from Rome had Manichaean cells – though the Manichees were anyway incomparably more numerous and further-flung than the other movements. But nothing in the West outside Rome could seriously be compared with what was happening in the East, where we see at first hand that fusing of Greek and oriental cultures from which the religious movements we are discussing first arose. Among the cities of the East one thinks, apart from Alexandria, of Syrian Apamea, Pergamon, Ephesus, Sardis, Aphrodisias and Athens for some of the better-known Platonist circles, while gnostics are encountered almost everywhere, notably in Asia Minor, Antioch and the cities of northern Syria and Mesopotamia. Within the cities there were of course great social differences; and the movements we are dealing with reflected these either more or less generously. The Alexandrian Platonists, for example, were the cream of late antique learning, part of a tightly-knit international 'set' which even in the fifth century was prominent in the schools of Greece and Asia Minor as well as Egypt; but while the gnostic and Manichaean elites sometimes derived from not-dissimilar backgrounds, many, perhaps most, of their 'listeners' came from the trading and artisan classes. Manichaeism in particular owed much of its dissemination to the busy commerce of ideas as well as goods along the trade-routes of Asia and the Mediterranean lands. No doubt bureaucrats and officials of all sorts will also have figured prominently in these milieux, men like Theophanes of Hermoupolis, of whose travels and contacts with adepts of Hermes Trismegistus we have already caught a glimpse. We have to do with men committed to making a living for themselves in the world of everyday affairs, but educated enough to read and

[165] Eun., *V. Phil.* vi.4.

enquire after something beyond what conventional religion offered. Women too played an active part among gnostics, Platonists and Manichees alike; and the allusions to Theosebia in the exceptionally important remarks about the Hermetic milieu made by Zosimus of Panopolis suggest that women were prominent there too.

It is by now, then, plain to see that our analogical approach to the milieu of Hermetism confirms to a striking extent what the texts themselves tell us of small, informal circles of the literate but not (usually) learned gathered round a holy teacher and given up to study, asceticism and pious fellowship. Even the interlocking of technical and philosophical preoccupations is paralleled in what we have seen of gnostic circles. As for our disparate collection of external testimonia, their recurrent emphasis on the role of Alexandria and the Hellenized cities along the Nile is further confirmed; and it is now easier to see why there are Hermetic books in the gnostic library from Nag Hammadi. The analogies we have drawn also highlight contrasts which can be equally instructive. For all the structural similarities of their circles, most late antique Platonists would, one suspects, have regarded the Hermetists as socially and culturally homespun. Nor did the followers of Hermes have the organizing and missionary zeal (the *Poimandrēs* notwithstanding), or the common touch, that turned the teachings of Mani into a world religion. They modestly contented themselves with creating a common mode of spiritual discourse, which they nourished within their scattered circles and propagated through their writings, personal contacts and the sort of correspondence that Zosimus enjoyed with Theosebia – a slightly haphazard existence which is reflected in the variegated quality and contents of the literary remains. If one had to say which of the three groupings we have looked at was closest to Hermetism, one would choose the gnostics, while bearing in mind of course that, as was pointed out in chapter 4, Hermetism and Christian gnosticism are, doctrinally, parallel rather than interlinked movements.

It remains to say something of the wider historical context of these movements. They were all born out of the encounter of Hellenism (and later Rome) with the East – an encounter which, despite its fruitfulness, also bred many intellectual and social tensions. They were indisposed to accept the world as it was – or at all. And they were perceived as in varying ways unfitted to become public doctrine – Hermetism and gnosticism less unfitted, that is, than

Manichaeism, which pagans and Christians alike deemed cancerous, but more so than Platonism, which played its part, however ineptly, in Julian's restoration. This is what Weber meant by 'Laienintellektualismus'; and in his opinion the other-worldliness of these doctrines was a reaction against the lay intellectual's political powerlessness in an autocratic world-empire. Weber's analysis was long neglected; but of late it has been enthusiastically resurrected by certain interpreters of gnosticism.[166] Reading between the lines, these scholars have claimed to find in the gnostic world-view an implicit condemnation of the power-structure of the Roman state, and an attempt to assert an alternative, superior scale of values. It is not difficult to believe them – indeed, they have missed striking evidence in their support provided by those passages in the Hermetica which reflect a reaction against cultural oppression,[167] despite the fact that the most important of them, the *Asclepius* prophecy, reappears in the Nag Hammadi collection and so clearly found some resonance among gnostics too. Nevertheless, the desire of Weber and his followers to find a purely sociological 'explanation' for gnosticism strikes the historian as simplistic. In the Roman empire it was perfectly possible for intellectuals, especially those from the Graecophone East, to exercise political influence; and many did. There were also those who did not wish to; and the conflict between these two points of view comes to the surface in, for example, Themistius's tirades against the 'unsocial philosophy' of the Platonists, who prefer to lurk in corners rather than face the crowd in the market-place.[168] So intellectuals did have a choice; and in fact it was the minority who chose what Weber meant by 'Laienintellektualismus'. For every man or woman who chose a life of dedication to one or other spiritual *gnōsis*, there were hundreds who became rhetors or lawyers and made their way in the world of affairs. Ultimately the historian has to make a personal judgement about the motivation, conscious or unconscious, of such decisions, since he can neither psychoanalyse nor even interview those who made them. The present study has proceeded on the assumption that there were people in the Hellenistic and Roman worlds who considered that the spiritual life had its own value, which did not

---

[166] E.g. Kippenberg, *Numen* 17 (1970) 211–31; Rudolph, *Gnosis* 284–93, 311–15. But Kippenberg, in an essay in *Max Webers Studie über das antike Judentum* 201–18, now prefers to see gnosticism as a 'Krise der Tradition', a response to the inadequacy of traditional explanations of the world, rather than as 'Entpolitisierung'.

[167] Above, 38–44.

[168] Fowden, *J.H.S.* 102 (1982) 54–9.

depend on (though it might of course determine) whether or not one participated in the political process. As a working hypothesis, this at least has the virtue of allowing for variety, which Weber's theory does not.

Such then was the milieu of Hermetism in Egypt. Our search for it has been long and at times circuitous; and it is worth reflecting in conclusion on the reasons for this. In the first place the Hermetists did not write about each other, as the Platonists did. That may have been partly out of a secretiveness extended from doctrine to persons; but may also have reflected an awareness that they simply were not as newsworthy as the Platonists. Secondly, others did not write about them because they were not thought dangerous or even just odious, as were the gnostics and the Manichees. In particular there is little Christian polemical literature directed against the Hermetists, for pagans were in general less of a threat to the Church than heretics, and Trismegistus in particular had anyway been a prophet of Christ. For that reason – and others – he was often quoted, even approvingly, by the Fathers; though since none questioned his personal authorship of the Hermetica, most of the information we are given about their historical background is mythological. But if we are to understand the Hermes of the Christians – and indeed the pagan Hermes in his fullness – we must abandon now once and for all the narrow perspective of the Nile valley, and set ourselves to scan those broader horizons with which the Alexandrians, at least, were well familiar.

[8]

Aegypti sacra deportata[1]

That Hermes Trismegistus was often referred to simply as 'the Egyptian' is a measure not only of how well established were his roots, but also of how far-flung was his fame. It is time now to ask what Hermes meant to the world outside Egypt, and to pursue to its end the line of enquiry broached in the second part of this study, about the contribution of Hermetism to the general intellectual and religious life of late antiquity.

The personal reputation of Hermes Trismegistus as an exemplar of holiness stood high among pagans everywhere. Ammianus Marcellinus, for instance, mentions him along with Apollonius of Tyana, Plotinus and others in a list of men famed for the strength of their guardian spirit.[2] And something similar is to be found in an oracle attributed to Apollo, who was asked whether it is possible to draw close to God in this life, and replied that it is exceedingly difficult for mortals to attain the divine vision, and that the only ones who achieved this goal were the Egyptian Hermes, Moses and Apollonius of Tyana.[3] This oracle is preserved in the *Theosophia Tubingensis*; and since a few of the responses contained therein can be shown to derive from the oracles of Apollo at Didyma and Clarus,[4] it is tempting to wonder whether the same may be true of this one too. In any case the prominence of Trismegistus in the *Theosophia* is a compliment (albeit backhanded) to his considerable reputation among pagans.

As for the books of Hermes, the technical literature was read throughout the Graeco-Roman world, the *astrologica* enjoying particularly wide circulation. Of this something has already been said. But the philosophical Hermetica enjoyed a more ambiguous reputation. Though they were widely known, they were oftener quoted by Christians than by pagans; and they were not always – or even

---

[1] Aur. Vic., *Caes.* XXI.4.   [2] Amm. Marc. XXI.14.5.
[3] *F. Gr. Th.* 177.19–26.   [4] Above, 181.

very often – used in the spirit intended by their authors.[5] The circulation of the philosophical texts was both facilitated and limited by its dependence on anthologies and florilegia;[6] and we are fortunate to be able to see this process at work in the *Anthologium* of Stobaeus. Iohannes of Stobi (in Macedonia) probably lived in the early fifth century, and is known solely for having composed an immense anthology of Greek poets, philosophers, historians, orators, doctors and public figures, for use in the education of his son Septimus.[7] Stobaeus excluded all Christian writers from his anthology, various of whose features, such as the inclusion of generous extracts from the Hermetica, Porphyry and Iamblichus, seem to establish its compiler's paganism. But Stobaeus was not on the other hand a theurgist – or, if he was, he hid it well. He comes across as a serious-minded man deeply committed to the classical literary tradition but open as well to the best in the paganism of his own times. It is interesting to see what sort of Hermetic texts appealed to such a person.[8] He quotes from three of the treatises that have reached us anyway in *Corpus Hermeticum* (*C.H.* II, IV, X), and from the *Perfect discourse*. Otherwise, virtually all his Hermetic material is unattested elsewhere. This material derives, according to Stobaeus's own section-headings, from *Discourses of Hermes to Tat* (perhaps related to the *diexodikoi logoi* to Tat mentioned by Cyril of Alexandria), *Discourses of Hermes to Ammon*, *Discourses of Isis to Horus* and a treatise called *Aphrodite*, as well as from texts for which Stobaeus gives us no title.[9] Though in selecting his material Stobaeus made some use of florilegia,[10] he was evidently familiar with the Hermetic literature at first hand; but it is clear that his interest was overwhelmingly in its philosophical branch, and that among the philosophical texts those of a more initiatory and explicitly religious character did not attract him. Though Stobaeus is the only non-Egyptian source who suggests that the Hermetica should be used as a means of education, even he has no conception of the systematic Hermetic *paideia* described earlier in this study. And at least he, an average albeit unusually energetic educated man, belonged to the same sort of milieu as the Egyptian Hermetists. The intellectual elite of late antiquity was even less inclined to meet Trismegistus on his own terms.

---

[5] The *testimonia* and fragments (excluding Stobaeus) are collected by Scott 4, and N.F. 4. 101–50.   [6] Above, 4.

[7] Phot., *Bibl.* 167.112a.   [8] On the following see N.F. 3.1–XII.

[9] Only *S.H.* XXIX is attested elsewhere: see N.F.'s *app. crit.*

[10] See *S.H.* XXVIII.

Outside Egypt nobody knew much about the philosophical Hermetica before the third century. Attempts to derive certain of Numenius's doctrines from them have been inconclusive.[11] Tertullian of Carthage is the first writer who indisputably quotes from the philosophical books of Hermes, in the *Adversus Valentinianos* and the *De anima*, both written in 206/207.[12] The most interesting of these references concern the transmigration of souls. Tertullian quotes 'the Egyptian Mercury' as saying that when the soul is separated from the body it does not simply merge into the universal soul, but retains its individual identity.[13] Although this doctrine is frequently attested in the surviving Hermetica,[14] the particular quotation does not come from any of them. But earlier in the *De anima* Tertullian observes that some believe the doctrine of metempsychosis to be Pythagorean, while Albinus (the mid-second-century Platonist) treats it as divine, perhaps to be attributed to the Egyptian Mercury.[15] Clearly we must consider the intriguing possibility that Tertullian's knowledge of the Hermetica was second-hand and derived from Albinus.[16]

Tertullian may have been the first but was certainly not the last African Christian to interest himself in Hermetism. So one naturally wonders whether African pagans were not also influenced by this current of thought and writing emanating from neighbouring Egypt, no doubt along the busy maritime trade-route.[17] Since educated Africans were often fluent in Greek as well as Latin,[18] there was no serious linguistic barrier to the spread of the Hermetic literature. And anyway we know that at least one Hermetic text, the *Perfect discourse*, was translated into Latin – apparently during the fourth century, since it was used by Augustine but not Lactantius; and very probably in Africa, since the Hermetica were not well-known in other Latin-speaking areas.[19] The existence of this translation could be argued to imply a receptive audience, or even a circle of adepts.

[11] Elsas, *Weltablehnung* 93, 97. Carcopino's assertion, *La Rome païenne* 258, that Aelius Aristides became acquainted with the Hermetica during his visit to Egypt is highly speculative: a common debt to Plato is more probable (see N.F. 4.36 n. 133). Cf. also Behr, *Aelius Aristides* 72 n. 44. On Reitzenstein's attempt to establish connections between the *Pastor* of Hermas and *C.H.* 1, see Festugière 1.80 n. 14.

[12] Barnes, *Tertullian* 55. Apart from the passages mentioned below, see II.3, xv.5 (cf. Waszink's edition, 228), XLIII.7 (cf. *ibid.* 466).   [13] Tert., *An.* XXXIII.2.

[14] N.F. 4.104 n. 2.   [15] Tert., *An.* XXVIII.1.

[16] See Festugière 3.1 n. 4. Tert., *Val.* xv.1, perhaps implies personal acquaintance with the Hermetica (cf. Scott 4.3 n. 3)?

[17] Rougé, *Commerce maritime* 84, 87–9, 123–4. On the perils of the land route see Apul., *Apol.* 72; Butler, *Conquest of Egypt* 9–13.   [18] Apul., *Apol.* 36; Griffiths, *Isis-Book* 61–3.

[19] Cf. Mahé 2.55–8. The mediaeval attribution of the *Ascl.* to Apuleius is probably pure coincidence.

Apuleius (fl. *c.* 160), the sophist of Madauros and author of the *Metamorphoses*, well represents the sort of milieu in which Hermetic ideas most easily took root. Apuleius fancied himself a Platonist philosopher; and his fellow-citizens knew no better, since they dedicated a statue to him, '[ph]ilosopho [Pl]atonico'.[20] But his philosophical culture was not so profound that it would have hindered him from taking the Hermetica seriously; and he also enjoyed a wide acquaintance with mystery religions and magic. His famous account of an Isiac initiation at the end of the *Metamorphoses* guarantees first-hand acquaintance with the rites of the Egyptian goddess; while his *Apologia* reveals a strong, sincere attachment to Hermes–Mercury, not merely as patron of magic and learning, but also as ruler of the whole universe – as Hermes Trismegistus (though he does not use the title).[21] Indeed, Apuleius's possession of a wooden image of the god provided the basis for one of the principal counts against him at the famous magic-trial where the *Apologia* was delivered.[22] Like Aelius Aristides, the sophist of Madauros was also an enthusiastic devotee of Asclepius,[23] who was of course an important figure in the Hermetic pantheon. Perhaps it is significant too that Apuleius was on his way to Egypt when he was accused of being a magician.[24] Whether he ever got there is not recorded.

Equally inconclusive is the testimony of Arnobius of Sicca, a pagan rhetor turned Christian polemicist who, writing in the early years of the fourth century, addressed his pagan opponents as 'you who follow after Mercury, Plato and Pythagoras, and you others who are of one

[20] Apul., *Apol.* 12, 64; *I.L. Alg.* 2115 (with commentary).

[21] Apul., *Apol.* 31, 42, 61–5. On the popularity of Mercury in Africa, see Deonna, *Mercure* 39. It is important though to note that, for all the similarity between *Apol.* 64–5 and the doctrines Lactantius later attributes to Hermes, Apuleius's source is Plato, not the Hermetica.

[22] The allegation that the image showed 'the lean, eviscerated frame of a gruesome corpse, utterly horrible and ghastly as any goblin' (63; tr. Butler) recalls the emaciated, naked figure on the early fourth-century(?) tomb-mosaic (now in the Musée National des Antiquités Classiques et Musulmanes, Algiers) of Cornelia Urbanilla from Lambiridi (near Batna), for an ingenious Hermetic interpretation of which see Carcopino, *La Rome païenne* 207–314 (but also Charles-Picard, *Religions* 230–2; Dunbabin, *Mosaics of Roman North Africa* 139–40). Note especially the Hermetic idea of Man 'stripped naked' of passions as he ascends towards the Ogdoad (e.g. *C.H.* 1.26). Perhaps Apuleius did possess some such image; and it is not impossible that it actually depicted Thoth–Hermes (see e.g. Delatte and Derchain, *Intailles magiques* 151, no. 197), though that was not specifically stated in the charge, at any rate as recounted by Apuleius himself. Apuleius would simply then have substituted something more conventional as a courtroom exhibit. Carcopino's allusion, *op. cit.* 307–8, to a third-century Carthaginian curse-tablet, which allegedly describes Thoth as 'the god of rebirth', rests on a false reading: Wünsch, *Antike Fluchtafeln* 4.17–18; *P. Graec. Mag.* 3.222, *s.v.*

[23] Apul., *Apol.* 55, *Flor.* 18.   [24] Apul., *Apol.* 72.

mind with them and march in unity of sentiments along the same ways'.[25] Does Arnobius here have in mind Hermetists with whom he was himself familiar? It has to be admitted that this is not the obvious interpretation of the passage. Pythagoras and Plato were of course the patron saints of late antique pagan intellectuals; and Plato at least was thought to have been a disciple of Hermes Trismegistus.[26] By invoking their names, Arnobius simply addresses himself with a rhetorical flourish to the dominant Platonist current in contemporary pagan thought, principally represented in his generation by Porphyry and Iamblichus; and it is to them and their followers that he applies the famous and much debated epithet, 'novi quidam viri' – 'certain upstarts'.[27] It seems improbable that, in mentioning Mercury, Arnobius did not intend to include the devotees of Hermes Trismegistus among those to whom his arguments are addressed; and it is indeed possible to demonstrate many parallelisms between the doctrines of the 'viri novi' denounced by Arnobius and the teachings contained in our Hermetica. But there are striking divergences too; and it seems quite clear that Arnobius addressed himself to the Hermetists only as part of the wider pagan intellectual community.[28] Whether he had any personal experience of either Hermetists or Hermetica we cannot know.

As for the Greek-speaking East, Cyril of Alexandria alludes, tantalizingly, to the actual composition of Hermetic books, presumably philosophical, at Athens, without saying by whom or when – though the single quotation he vouchsafes us is very Egyptian in manner, describing Hermes just like the native Thoth.[29] But few leading intellectuals, either Christian or pagan, took the philosophical Hermetica seriously as doctrinal statements. On the pagan side one might, perhaps, have expected the books of Hermes, however banal their contents, to have been accorded higher esteem in an age swept by a mania for oriental wisdoms. The uninterest of a Plotinus – though he was educated in Egypt and must have been aware of the doctrines of Hermes, technical[30] as well as philosophical – one can understand.

---

[25] Arn. ii.13. On the dating of the *Adv. nat.* see Le Bonniec's edition, 1.30–4.

[26] Tert., *An.* ii.3; Lact., *Epit.* xxxvii.4; Proc., *In Tim.* 117d.

[27] Arn. ii.15.

[28] This was Festugière's eminently sane conclusion in an essay first published in 1940: *Hermétisme* 261–312, esp. 302–7. (Note the summary of the teachings of the *viri novi*, 292–4.) All subsequent interpretations (summarized by Fortin, *O.C.A.* 195 (1973) 197–205, to which add Courcelle, *Connais-toi toi-même* 625–37; Elsas, *Weltablehnung* 41–8; Mastandrea, *Cornelio Labeone* 127–34) have unnecessarily sought to be more specific.

[29] Above, 27.   [30] Cf. Porph., *V. Plot.* 15.21–6, on Plotinus's astrological studies.

Not so easily that of a Porphyry. Porphyry always had a catholic interest in different forms of pagan belief and practice. It would have been odd if he had ignored so important a body of literature as the Hermetica. A scholar with much experience in this field has spoken of Porphyry's 'nearness of feeling' to the Hermetica;[31] and Iamblichus, in the *De mysteriis*, indicates that Porphyry had read certain Hermetic books of a philosophical character.[32] Though that cannot be proved from the surviving fragments of his attack on theurgy in the *Epistola ad Anebonem*,[33] to which the *De mysteriis* replied, we need not doubt it. And Porphyry also alludes to the Hermetica in his *De abstinentia*, invoking 'the Egyptian' as an authority for his argument that one should abstain from meat because the impure soul of animals violently done to death lingers near their bodies and may impede the human soul's progress along the mystical way to contemplation of God.[34] But there is no reason to imagine that the Hermetica figured prominently in Porphyry's thoughts.

Iamblichus, by contrast, was well familiar with the books of Hermes, and exploited them extensively in the development and explanation of his theurgical doctrines. Yet even Iamblichus treats the Hermetica as important not so much for their own sake as because they were part of the Egyptian foundations of theurgy which Porphyry had sought to undermine. Once theurgy was vindicated and accepted, there was no further need to worry about its sources. Hermetism was not thought ingenious, obscure or even in its own right interesting enough to merit the exegesis that Porphyry and his successors lavished on the *Oracula Chaldaica*. It lacked the distinctive profile that was needed if it was to survive among the plethora of late antique 'isms'. Hence its neglect by Iamblichus's successors, even by such noted theurgists as Julian and Proclus. The Hermes these last Platonists esteemed was not Trismegistus but the older, Hellenistic Hermes Logios. The highest praise they could bestow on a fellow-philosopher was to call him 'an image of Hermes the learned' ('Ερμοῦ λογίου τύπος) or something similar;[35] and they commonly

---

[31] Nock, *Essays* 448; and cf. Ioh. Lyd., *Mens.* iv.7: 'Porphyry seems to discuss fortune (περὶ τύχης) according to the doctrines of Hermes.'

[32] Iam., *Myst.* i.1.4, viii.4.265.

[33] Cf. above, 140 n. 104.

[34] Porph., *Abst.* ii.47; and cf. the introduction to the Bouffartigue–Patillon edition, 37–9, 46–7, and Mahé 2.218, 267–9, undermining an earlier theory that the source was the *P.D.*

[35] E.g. Jul., *or.* vii.237c, on Aristotle, and xii.354c, on Libanius, 'dear to Hermes...an accomplished master of eloquence'; Syn., *ep.* 101, on the philosopher Marcianus (cf. *ep.* 19); and Dam., *V. Isid.* 16 (*E. Ph.*), on Isidore. Julian undoubtedly felt a special devotion

associated themselves with the so-called 'Hermaic chain' (Ἑρμαϊκὴ σειρά), by which they seem to have meant the divine reason (λογισμός) which emanates from God.[36] This distinction between Logios and Trismegistus was known and insisted upon, even in the relatively unsophisticated milieu of the oracle-collections.[37]

Another important reason why late pagan intellectuals were reserved in their attitude to Hermetism was its association with gnosticism and Manichaeism – demonstrably pernicious doctrines. In his biography of Plotinus Porphyry tells us something about the group of gnostics who numbered themselves among his master's disciples,

> men of the schools of Adelphius and Aculinus, who possessed a great many treatises of Alexander the Libyan, Philocomus, Demostratus and Lydus, and produced revelations by Zoroaster, Zostrianus, Nicotheus, Allogenes, Messus and other people of this kind, deceiving many and deceived themselves, alleging that Plato had not penetrated to the depths of intelligible reality. So Plotinus often attacked their position in his lectures, and wrote the treatise to which we have given the title 'Against the gnostics'; and he left it to us to assess what he passed over.[38]

Now it so happens that treatises attributed or referring to (or simply entitled) Zoroaster, Zostrianus, Nicotheus, Allogenes and Messus are known to have circulated among Egyptian gnostics; and specimens of such writings – probably the selfsame ones Porphyry names – have

to Hermes, but usually this was either the Greek Hermes (*or.* vii.230c–234c; and cf. the inscription in honour of Hermes from Trier, possibly to be associated with Julian: Bidez, *A.E.H.E.G.* 2 (1938) 15–28; Schwinden, in *Trier* 280–1) or the Hermes of the Mithraists (among whom the emperor was numbered): *or.* x.336c, xi.150d (Hermes *paredros* of Helios = Mithras); Bober, *H. Th. R.* 39 (1946) 75–84; Griffiths, *Isis-Book* 282. For a single passing allusion to Trismegistus see *Gal.* 176b. There are no serious grounds for supposing Hermetic influence on *or.* xi, *pace* Lacombrade's introduction, 92. Cyr. Al., *Jul.* ii.597d, calls Hermes Julian's 'teacher'; and Soz. v.17.3, records that Julian had Hermes depicted, along with Zeus and Ares, on his public images, but perhaps of greater significance is Ammianus Marcellinus's assertion that, as Caesar in Gaul, Julian would 'secretly pray to Mercury, whom the teaching of the theologians held to be the swift intellect (sensus) of the universe, arousing the activity of men's minds (motus mentium)', and would then occupy himself during the night with philosophy and sublime speculations (xvi.5.5–6). Is the 'teaching of the theologians' that of Hermetism? – cf. above, 95 n. 2. Certainly the particular doctrine here mentioned could be Hermetic: for the dependence of 'mens' = ψυχή (N.F. 2.374 n. 153) on 'sensus' = νοῦς (*ibid.* 399 n. 347) see *Ascl.* 18, *N.H.C.* vi.6.58.4–6 (and Mahé *ad loc.*); and for the identification of Hermes with νοῦς see above, 110. The passage may of course reflect Ammianus's own acquaintance with Hermetism (cf. xxi.14.5). Proclus's only reference to philosophical Hermetism comes in a brief quotation from Iamblichus (*In Tim.* 117d = *Myst.* viii.3.265).

[36] Eun., *V. Phil.* iv.1.11, on Porphyry; Marin., *Proc.* 28, on Proclus; and cf. Glucker, *Antiochus* 309–10.

[37] *F. Gr. Th.* 174.26–7.

[38] Porph., *V. Plot.* 16 (tr. Armstrong, with adjustments); and see also Plot. ii.9.10.3–9.

been found in the Nag Hammadi codices, whose Hermetic connections are already familiar.[39] Between *Zostrianus* (*N.H.C.* VIII.1) or *Allogenes* (*N.H.C.* XI.3) on the one hand, revelations of the divine world in the form of visions, and *The Ogdoad reveals the Ennead*, the *Poimandrēs* or *C.H.* XIII on the other hand, there are clear analogies of temperament. It is significant too that writers of the period often associate Hermes with Zoroaster[40] – clearly they were widely felt to belong to the same intellectual milieu. It seems likely that Plotinus regarded the Hermetica as the product of the same suspect circles as the gnostic writings, and ignored them for that reason.

The *Revelation of Allogenēs* is also known from fourth-century Syria, where it was connected with Audi, the founder of an Edessene sect of gnostic hue.[41] Audi's teachings came in the course of time (not necessarily in Audi's own lifetime) to be associated with those of another Edessene, Bardaisan (154–222), an eclectic thinker variously classified in our sources as a Valentinian or an orthodox Christian.[42] And Bardaisan is known to have been familiar with 'books of the Egyptians in which all the different things that may befall people are described',[43] clearly astrological Hermetica; while his doctrines have something in common with those of philosophical Hermetism too.[44] Our scant knowledge of this milieu – indeed the very nature of the milieu itself – precludes the establishment of precise doctrinal filiations; but from such (undoubtedly random) facts as those just mentioned one at least acquires a sense of where the Hermetica were most likely to be known.[45] With its well-established tradition of interest in Greek philosophy, Edessa was exactly the place one would expect Hermetism to take root; and once it had, it was likely to be disseminated still further afield, in view of the city's strategic position on the north Mesopotamian routes that linked Rome with Persia. A generation after Bardaisan, in the year 240, Mani began to teach an

---

[39] Elsas, *Weltablehnung* 31–4; Puech, *En quête de la gnose* 1.110–16. Robinson, *Int. Coll. Gnosticism 1973* 132–42, argues that *The three stelae of Seth* (*N.H.C.* VII.5) also belongs to this group of texts; and a similar suggestion has been made as regards *Marsanes* (*N.H.C.* X.1) by Pearson, *N.H.S.* 15 (1981) 244, 249–50.

[40] Bidez and Cumont, *Mages* 2.34, 86, 243.

[41] Puech, *En quête de la gnose* 1.271–94.

[42] Drijvers, *Bardaiṣan*.

[43] Philippus (Bardaisan), *Book of the laws of countries* 38–40.

[44] Drijvers, *J.V.E.G.* 21 (1969–70) 190–210.

[45] Quispel, in *Textes de Nag Hammadi* 234, 259–66, has recently argued that the *Gospel of Thomas* and the *Book of Thomas the Contender* originated in Edessa and drew on Hermetic gnomologies.

eclectic new religion at Seleucia–Ctesiphon;[46] and he was certainly well familiar with Bardaisan's work.[47] According to Ephraem the Syrian (also an Edessene), Mani claimed as heralds of his message Hermes of Egypt, Plato the Greek and 'Jesus who appeared in Judaea'.[48] Perhaps then it was through Bardaisan that Mani got to know the Hermetica, though some Manichaean sources alleged direct contacts with Egypt.[49]

At any event, Manichaeism spread fast throughout the Mediterranean world; and it is quite possible that it played some role in the dissemination of Hermetic ideas too. We happen to know that the Manichaean propagandist Faustus of Mileum invoked Hermes's supposed Christological prophecies in late-fourth-century Africa – though he may have known them only at second hand ('ut fama est'), by way perhaps of Lactantius.[50] Ephraem's firm assertion that neither Hermetism nor Platonism nor Christianity had anything to do with Manichaeism deliberately misses the point, which is that Mani absorbed elements of other systems into his own. That was, one suspects, how Hermetism usually travelled, in disguise – though in this case very much at its own risk. Manichaeism encountered firm condemnation and violent suppression from the Zoroastrian establishment in Persia, the pagan establishment in Rome and the Christian Church. Zosimus of Panopolis, a firm devotee of Hermes, states his repugnance for Manichaeism.[51] Others were no doubt less able or disposed to make the distinction.

Such associations will have fuelled Christians' as well as pagans' distrust of Hermetism. But from the ecclesiastical standpoint the main count against Hermes was of course his paganism, and other objections tended to flow from that one. We have already seen Arnobius pitting himself against Hermetism in the context of an

---

[46] Rudolph, *Gnosis* 354–6, 360–1.

[47] Drijvers, *Bardaiṣan* 225–7.

[48] Ephr. Syr., *Against Mani* 208–10.

[49] Hegem. 62–3, alleging Egyptian antecedents of Mani's teachings; and 13, on Hermas (*sic*), the disciple sent by Mani to preach in Egypt: cf. Church and Stroumsa, *V. Chr.* 34 (1980) 47–55, esp. 50 ('It is possible that the name was fashioned as suitable to Egypt.') The presence of a fragment of the Christian Hermas's *Pastor* among the Manichaean manuscripts in Iranian languages found near Turfan in Chinese Turkestan (Boyce, *Reader* 178–9) is perhaps the result of a confusion with Hermas the disciple of Mani rather than (*pace* Burkitt, *Religion of the Manichees* 95–7) with Hermes Trismegistus. That the Turfan texts have a completely different version of the mission to Egypt (Boyce, *op. cit.* 2, 39–42) is no reason to assume that Hermas was not known in these parts.

[50] Aug., *Faust.* XIII.1, 15.

[51] Zos. Pan., *fr. gr.* 232.13–17; and cf. Jackson, *Zosimos* 54 n. 72.

attack on paganism generally; and a century later Arnobius's fellow-African Augustine was to return to the theme, but in much more specific terms. In the mean time, though, Arnobius's pupil Lactantius (d. *c.* 320) had tried to show that it was possible for a Christian to make constructive use of Hermetism. This unique attempt is worth looking at in some detail, both for what it tells us about the development of Christian attitudes to Hermetism, and in order to compare our knowledge of Hermetism with that of an informed contemporary, who provides frequent and extensive citations from Hermetic texts both in the original Greek and in Latin translation.[52]

The *Divinae institutiones*, written during the first decade of the fourth century,[53] mounts a comprehensive attack on paganism in order to assert the superiority of Christianity. But in this struggle Lactantius calls on Hermes to support him, casting him in the role of a prophet of the Christian dispensation.[54] Lactantius knows that Hermes was originally a man, who in remote antiquity was raised to the condition of a god.[55] He is the last of the five Mercuries listed by Cicero in the *De natura deorum*, he who killed Argus and fled to Egypt. The Egyptians called him 'Thoyth', and he gave them their laws and letters, and wrote many books on divine matters, earning in this way the title Trismegistus. These are unusual credentials for a Christian prophet; but Lactantius does not hesitate to assign Trismegistus the first place in his discussion of the 'divine testimonia' to the idea that God is One. The Christian apologist draws attention to Hermes's teaching on 'the majesty of the supreme and only God', who is 'lord' and 'father',[56] but himself 'motherless' and 'fatherless'.[57] The Hermetic God is 'the one without a name' (ἀνώνυμος), since on

[52] For a list of citations see Wlosok, *Laktanz* 261–2. See also, on the *Ira* Kutsch, *Quaestiones philologae* 66–9; and on the *De opificio Dei* Scott 1.93–4, and Wlosok, *Laktanz* 228.

[53] Barnes, *Constantine* 13.

[54] Lact., *Inst.* IV.27.20.

[55] *Ibid.* 1.6.1–4; and cf. 1.11.61 (a reminiscence of *C.H.* x.5?), VII.13.4; *Epit.* IV.4, XIV.2–3; *Ira* XI.12; and above, 24–5, on Cicero.

[56] Lact., *Inst.* 1.6.4 ('dominus', 'pater'); *Epit.* IV.4. Precise parallels at *C.H.* V.2, XIII.21; *Ascl.* 20, 22, 23, 26, 29.

[57] Lact., *Inst.* 1.7.2, IV.13.2 (ἀμήτωρ, ἀπάτωρ); IV.8.5 (αὐτοπάτωρ, αὐτομήτωρ); *Epit.* IV.4. This vocabulary is attested as Hermetic only by Lactantius and Iamblichus, *Myst.* VIII.2.262, who quotes Hermes to the effect that God is one, αὐτοπάτωρ and αὐτόγονος; but the idea is well attested in the Hermetica, e.g. *C.H.* VIII.2 (εἰ δὲ καὶ ἐγένετο (ὁ θεός), ὑφ' ἑαυτοῦ); *S.H.* XXIII.58 (God αὐτόγονος); *Ascl.* 14 ('haec ergo est, quae ex se tota est, natura dei'), 30 ('ipse...a se est'); *N.H.C.* VI.6.57.13–15, 63.22 (cf. Mahé 1.48–52). The use of this vocabulary in a theological context is characteristically late antique, and its history a useful indicator of Hermetism's intellectual analogues: Amann, *Zeusrede* 31–4, 50–3; Robert, *C.R.A.I.* (1971) 602, 612.

account of His unity He has no need of qualification.[58] No mortal mind comprehends Him; nor does mortal tongue suffice to describe Him.[59] These are all doctrines well attested in the surviving Hermetica. But when Lactantius goes on to speak of Hermetic doctrine concerning the Son of God, his approach is less straightforward. In the *Asclepius* Hermes describes the creation of the material world as if it were a second god, offspring of the One God; but Lactantius quotes this passage (in the Greek of the *Perfect discourse*) as if it referred to Christ, the Son of God.[60] Elsewhere he explains a reference, again in the *Perfect discourse*, to the One God as demiurge as an allusion to the Christian Son of God;[61] and he similarly misinterprets a reference he found in some Hermetic treatise to a secret 'teaching' or 'discourse' (λόγος).[62] Lactantius's determination to make Trismegistus a prophet of the Christian Logos had got the better of him – though understandably, for the way the Hermetists speak of the *kosmos* is indeed very close to the language that the *Gospel of John*, in particular, uses about the Son.[63]

Lactantius also drew on Hermes in his account of the daemonic and human spheres. Quoting *C.H.* XVI and, perhaps, the *Perfect discourse*, he represents Hermetic teaching as recognizing only evil daemons[64] – a simplification of the Hermetic corpus's letter, though not of its spirit.[65] As for Man, he is exposed to the incursions of the daemons by the duality of his nature.[66] On the one hand he is immortal, cast in the image of God, his body a mysterious and wonderful compound of the practical and the beautiful; but at the same time, in his mortal part, he is perpetually compromised by the inadequacy of the matter of which his body is composed.[67] Only

---

[58] Lact., *Inst.* 1.6.4–5; *Epit.* IV.4. The idea is paralleled at *C.H.* V.10, *Ascl.* 20.

[59] Lact., *Inst.* II.8.68, IV.7.3 (cf. Scott 4.16 n. 8); *Epit.* IV.5, XXXVII.8; *Ira* XI.11–12. Cf. *S.H.* I.1 (directly quoted at *Epit.* IV.5).

[60] *Ascl.* 8 (and cf. N.F. 2.365 n. 73); Lact., *Inst.* IV.6.4 (and *Epit.* XXXVII.4–5 for a Latin version of the same passage).

[61] *Ascl.* 26 (the Greek text, from the *P.D.*, is quoted by Lact., *Inst.* VII.18.4, in another context); Lact., *Inst.* IV.6.9 (and cf. Scott 4.16 n. 3). (I see no reason to treat the Greek text of *Ascl.* 26 as corrupt: cf. the critical note at N.F. 2.330.)

[62] Lact., *Inst.* IV.7.3, 9.3; cf. Scott 4.17 n. 5, 19 n. 1.

[63] Dodd, *Fourth gospel* 22 (adding *C.H.* IX.8 ('The World is the son of God') to the passages there adduced). Siniscalco, *A.A.T.* 101 (1966–7) 83–116, discusses patristic use of *Ascl.* 8.

[64] Lact., *Inst.* II.14.6 ('Trismegistus calls [the devil] leader of the daemons (daemoniarchen)'), 15.6–8 (quoting Asclepius and Hermes on 'hostile and troublesome daemons', and Hermes on 'wicked angels' – ἀγγέλους πονηρούς); cf. respectively (?) *Ascl.* 28 ('the highest daemon'), *C.H.* XVI.15–16 (why does Lactantius call this 'sermo perfectus'?), *Ascl.* 25 ('wicked angels' – 'nocentes angeli').

[65] Above, 77–8.

[66] Lact., *Inst.* II.15.6; cf. *C.H.* XVI.14–16.

[67] Lact., *Inst.* VII.13.3, perhaps a garbled quotation of *Ascl.* 8, p. 306.27 (N.F.) – see Mahé 1.15 n. 85; and cf. *Ascl.* 10, 22; *C.H.* IV.2, XIV.4. See also Lact., *Inst.* II.10.14, VII.4.3, and

through piety, which Hermes defines as knowledge of God, is it possible to acquire immunity from the activity of the evil daemons and of fate – Lactantius here quotes from the Greek text of the *Perfect discourse* and *C.H.* IX.[68] And, in acquiring this immunity, Man becomes free to look up and contemplate God – to do, in other words, the one thing that distinguishes him from the animals. To describe this Lactantius uses the characteristically Hermetic word *theoptia*.[69]

As for Hermes's doctrine of worship and sacrifice, Lactantius claimed to find it admirable, which he was able to do by ignoring important elements of it. In fact, the African Christian is the *fons et origo* of many of the misinterpretations rebutted in chapter 6. For Lactantius, sacrifice is a twofold concept, involving a right disposition of the mind ('integritas animi') and the offering of praise ('laus et hymnus'). Lactantius finds Hermes fully in accord with this point of view, and quotes in support of it the gnomic last sentence of *C.H.* XII, together with Trismegistus's shocked condemnation of incense and other material sacrifices at the end of the *Perfect discourse*.[70] Yet the piety of the few will not save the world from the destruction that is bound to overwhelm it. Just as God by His providence gave the world its being,[71] so God will eventually purify it of its wickedness and restore its original perfection.[72] In his vision of the apocalypse Lactantius draws heavily, as we have already seen, on the prophecy in the *Perfect discourse*, a fitting culmination to his extended attempt to beat the swords of paganism into the ploughshares of the Christian revelation.

It should by now be clear that the Hermes we encounter in the pages of Lactantius is easily recognizable as the patron of the more philosophical part of the Hermetic tradition. Through what for the most part are just passing allusions, the Christian polemicist allows us to build up a jigsaw image of Hermetic doctrine that suggests a

cf. *C.H.* I.12, *Ascl.* 7, 10 (on Man the image of God); Lact., *Inst.* II.10.14, and cf. *C.H.* v.6 (on the mystery of the human body). With the possible exception of *Ascl.* 8, Lactantius cannot be shown to have been quoting from our Hermetica in any of these instances. But at *Inst.* II.12.4–5, where Lactantius quotes Hermes on the four elements as constituents of the body, he follows *S.H.* IIA.2 (and cf. Scott 4.13 n. 1).

[68] Lact., *Inst.* II.15.6, quoting *Ascl.* 29 and *C.H.* IX.4 (though in neither instance precisely). Cf. also Lact., *Inst.* V.14.11.

[69] *Ibid.* VII.9.11; cf. Wlosok, *Laktanz* 133–4.

[70] Lact., *Inst.* VI.25.10–12, quoting *C.H.* XII.23 (cf. Scott 4.22 n. 2; N.F. 1.192 n. 74) and *Ascl.* 41.

[71] Lact., *Inst.* II.8.48, *Epit.* XXXVII.2. The idea is found throughout the Hermetica, e.g. *S.H.* XII.1.

[72] Lact., *Inst.* VII.18.4 = *Ascl.* 26.

reasonably wide familiarity with the literature that circulated under the name of the Graeco-Egyptian god of learning. Apart from his extensive quotations from the *Perfect discourse*, Lactantius reveals precise knowledge of *C.H.* IX, XII and XVI, and *S.H.* I and IIA.[73] He also quotes from Hermetic books that have not survived, as well as making a number of references to Hermetic doctrines that may be based on reminiscences of surviving texts, but could equally well have been derived from books since lost. Where Lactantius acquired all this erudition can only be guessed. Probably he first became familiar with the Hermetica in his native Africa, as a pupil of Arnobius; but that does not exclude the possibility that he was able to reread and check them, or even conceivably to read them for the first time, as a teacher of rhetoric in Nicomedia under Diocletian.[74]

In order to fit Trismegistus into the garb of the Christian prophet, Lactantius did of course have to pick and choose and take liberties with the texts. Like Didymus, Cyril and the compilers of the oracle-collections, who likewise sought intimations of the gospel in the words of the Hellenes,[75] Lactantius was after all an apologist. But an important difference between him and his successors was that he felt sympathy for Hermetism. He did not regard the Hermetica just as a quarry for easy debating-points. Cyril, for example, for all the approval with which he at times quotes Hermes, faces him as first and foremost a heathen, a representative of the opposition, albeit less misguided than some others of his co-religionists. The bishop of Alexandria cannot hide his surprise at finding himself so often in agreement with the pagan sage. Lactantius, by contrast, starts from a positive disposition to admit the testimony of pagan 'witnesses' to the Christian revelation, such as the philosophers and the Sybils. Of Hermes he speaks with respect, as a venerable authority, whose paganism is less significant than his anticipation of the Gospel. That sort of openness was possible when ecclesiastical dogma was still in its formative stage; but today the doctrinal soundness of Lactantius is not universally admitted.[76] For in the course of the fourth century the bounds of the permissible were drawn more firmly, and things

[73] Ogilvie, *Library of Lactantius* 35, offers a less conservative list.
[74] Barnes, *Constantine* 291, has suggested that Lactantius returned to Africa after his Nicomedia period, and that it was there that he wrote the *Inst.*
[75] See also Soz. 1.1.8.
[76] For a favourable recent view, with references to earlier discussions, see McGuckin, *V. Chr.* 36 (1982) 145–63.

once tolerable were denounced as heresy. Heresiologists had long held that there was a connection between pagan philosophers and heresy. Hippolytus was a particularly consistent exponent of this view. For Tertullian, Plato was 'omnium haereticorum condimentarius'.[77] In the fourth century Hermes too was inculpated. Marcellus of Ancyra (d. *c.* 374), a passionate defender of the Nicene arrangement, held that all heresies were inspired by the impious trio of Hermes, Plato and Aristotle, since it was impossible that they could be founded on the pure and undivided traditions of the apostolic Church.[78] Attacking the Arians, and in particular Asterius of Amasea and Eusebius of Caesarea, for teaching that the Son is a 'second god', distinct from the supreme God, Marcellus asserted that this notion was derived from Hermes Trismegistus, and adduced the passage from the *Perfect discourse* (*Ascl.* 8) about the material world being a second god, offspring of the One God, to which we have already seen Lactantius giving precisely the interpretation of which Asterius and Eusebius are here accused.[79] Marcellus might just as well have been writing against Lactantius. He also asserted that Eusebius owed the notion of the divine Logos as a second god to Hermes; and it looks as though he may here have in mind Hermetic texts concerning the divine Logos and its relationship to God similar to those later used by Cyril of Alexandria.[80] If Didymus too believed these accusations – and to brand an Alexandrian heresy as crypto–Hermetist was not implausible – one can see why he made such a point of deploying Trismegistus in the anti-Arian polemic of the *De Trinitate*.

Whereas Lactantius's motive in invoking Hermes was to bolster what he considered to be orthodoxy, Marcellus's was to discredit heresy. From the Christian point of view these are but two sides of the same coin; but the implied attitudes to Hermetism are poles apart. It was his fellow-African Augustine who, in book VIII of the *De civitate Dei*, pronounced the most crushing condemnation of Lactantius's approach. The context is an attack on pagan daemonology,[81] and in particular on Apuleius's view of the daemons

---

[77] Tert., *An.* XXIII.5.

[78] Marc. Anc., *Eccl.* (wrongly ascribed by the MSS to Anthimus of Nicomedia: Simonetti, *R.S.L.R.* 9 (1973) 314–16) 1–3, 7, 9.

[79] Marc. Anc., *Eccl.* 10–12, and cf. 14–16 (quoting an otherwise unknown Hermetic fragment), and above, 206.

[80] Eus. Caes., *Marc.* 1.4.25–6, and cf. above, 180. For a possible imitation of the Hermetica by Eusebius see N.F. 1.81 n. 2. It is strange that Eusebius made no direct use of the Hermetica in his *P.E.*

[81] Aug., *Civ. Dei* VIII.23–6, quoting *Ascl.* 23–4, 37.

as semi-divine intermediaries between gods and men. As a counter-weight to Apuleius, Augustine makes much of the *Asclepius*'s assertion that daemons are the work of human hands, but also denounces Hermes for being too well-disposed towards them, and for lamenting the impending abolition of their worship – a reference to the prophecy-section of the *Asclepius*. The bishop of Hippo concludes that

certainly he [Hermes] had much to say...about the one true God, the creator of the world – much that corresponds to the teaching of the truth. And yet in some way because of that 'darkening of the heart' [Rom. 1.21] he sank low enough to wish men to remain forever subject to gods who, on his own showing, are the creations of men, and to bewail the prospect of their extirpation at some future time, as if there were any unhappier situation than that of a man under the domination of his own inventions.[82]

In other words, Hermes is a perilously ambiguous figure from the Christian point of view. His doctrine is part divine, part diabolical, a self-contradictory mixture of truth and falsehood;[83] and to Augustine it seemed more important to refute his errors than to annex him, following Lactantius, as a prophet of Christianity. To the Manichaean Faustus of Mileum, who invoked Hermes's supposed prophecies of Christ's advent and asserted that they were of greater significance than those of the Hebrew prophets, Augustine retorted with wilful illogicality that such predictions may well refute pagan error, but prove nothing about the authority of their authors.[84]

Whether it was polemical instinct or ignorance of Greek that led Augustine to read the *Asclepius*, alone among the Hermetica,[85] there was no better way to expose the self-contradictoriness of Lactantius's dependence on so pagan authority. And if the space devoted to Hermes in the *De civitate Dei* suggests that his writings still enjoyed some popularity in the Africa of the early fifth century,[86] they did not thereafter. Elsewhere in the West they had never been much known anyway, except for some technical texts;[87] and later Latin

[82] Aug., *Civ. Dei* VIII.23.60–5 (tr. Bettenson).
[83] *Ibid.* VIII.23.98, 24.29–31. Augustine was helped towards this conclusion by a mis-understanding of the text of *Ascl.* 37, on which see Scott 4.183 n. 2.
[84] Aug., *Faust.* XIII.1, 15. For a forthright condemnation of the use of pagan prophecies in Christian polemic see Phot., *Bibl.* 170.117b.
[85] Though cf. Theiler's comparison between *C.H.* v and the beginning of Augustine's *Confessiones*: *Vorbereitung* 127–34.
[86] See also the pagan priest Longinianus's reference to 'the Trismegistan precepts' in his correspondence with Augustine on the manner in which God should be worshipped: Aug., *ep.* 233–5, esp. 234.1.
[87] Note particularly the following: (i) Mar. Vict., *In Cic. Rhet.* 1.26, p. 223: see above, 76. (2) Aus., *Griph.* 152.38–9, makes a passing reference to 'ter maximus Hermes'. (3) Filastr.

writers quote Hermes via Lactantius or Augustine, if at all.[88] Cyril of Alexandria performed a similar intermediary role in the Christian East.[89] Among pagans and Christians, Egyptians and non-Egyptians alike, direct contact with the sources of philosophical Hermetism was being lost by the later fifth century. The last writer to show apparently independent contact with the Hermetic tradition was John Lydus, under Justinian.[90]

Much, then, of what we learned or guessed from the Egyptian evidence has been confirmed by this brief survey of Hermes's reputation and fate in the wider world. Trismegistus was a revered pagan divinity under whose name circulated a useful and much-read technical literature, and philosophical books whose appeal was narrower, but might be profounder. If pagans of above-average education do not seem to have found much to excite them in philosophical Hermetism, Iamblichus was a highly influential exception to this rule – and had access to a wide range of texts covering most of the Hermetic genres. The Hermetica were also known in Christian circles, albeit usually as food for heretical thought or grist

(bishop of Brescia in the late fourth century) x alludes to a heliolatric sect in Gaul, called 'Heliognosti'/'Deinvictiaci', supposedly taught their doctrine by 'that vain pagan Hermes Trismegistus' himself. The oriental context (cf. *ibid.* ix, xi) and the reference to Trismegistus suggest the sect may have been of Egyptian origin; and Scott 4.166 n. 3 lists some Hermetic parallels to its doctrine. (The allusion to ἡλιογνῶσται by Ps.-Eus. Al. xxii.2, is probably unilluminating, since there is no proof that this writer had any connection with Alexandria: Leroy and Glorie, *S.E.J.G.* 19 (1969–70) 47.) (4) Boano, *R.F.I.C.* 26 (1948) 60–3, has drawn attention to parallels between Rutilius Namatianus and the Hermetica. See also the next note.

[88] See e.g. Ps.-Cypr., *Id.* 6, derived from Lactantius and itself quoted by Augustine and in the treatise *Contra paganos* attributed to Augustine's Arian opponent Maximinus: N.F. 4.104–5; Quodvult. (bishop of Carthage 437–9: Lippold, *R.E.* 24.1396–7), *Haer.* iii, *Lib. prom.* iii.38.45 (with Braun's nn. *ad loc.* in the C.C.S.L. edition, and *id.* in the S.C. edition, 57–8); and the *Contra phil.* (Italy, second quarter of sixth century) iv.407–19, 437–9, 472–86, 542–8, 589–95 (with Aschoff's nn. *ad loc.*; and cf. *ibid.* pp. v–vi). An insignificant exception is Fabius Planciades Fulgentius (an African littérateur of the early sixth century), *Mit.* 1.15, quoting *C.H.* 1.1; and cf. iii.9 on Hermes Trismegistus and music; *Exp. Virg.* pp. 85.21–86.1, on Hermes (the philosophical context suggests Trismegistus) and the stars; and Scott 1.28 n. 4. The fifth-century African pagan Martianus Capella provides many doctrinal parallels with the Hermetica, but nothing that proves personal acquaintance: Lenaz, *De nuptiis* 7 n. 14. Shanzer, *C.Q.* 33 (1983) 277–83, claims to identify a quotation from a lost Hermeticum in Boethius, *Consol.* iv.6.38: 'nam ut quidam me quoque excellentior: ἀνδρὸς δὴ ἱεροῦ δέμας αἰθέρες οἰκοδόμησαν' – but δέμας nowhere occurs in the philosophical Hermetica, while ἱερός is never applied to persons, and occurs only in the Stobaean fragments, overwhelmingly in *S.H.* xxiii.

[89] See e.g. Scott 4.232–42 (qualified as regards the *Artemii Passio* by Pépin, *V. Chr.* 36 (1982) 260 nn. 37, 41); *F. Gr. Th.* 104–11; Brock, *V. Chr.* 38 (1984) 79–80.

[90] Ioh. Lyd., *Mens.* iv.7 (quoting *Ascl.* 19, 39; cf. N.F. 2.350 for additions to Wuensch's text); 32, 149 (quoting *Ascl.* 28 and cf. *ibid.* 33 *ad fin.*); 53, 64 (quoting unknown theological Hermetica, one entitled κοσμοποιία). On the unreliability of Lydus's text see N.F. 2.276 n. 2.

to polemical mills. There is no proof though that the specifically Hermetist circles posited for Egypt were transplanted abroad, where Hermetism was primarily a literary influence rather than a way of life. For this reason the unity of the 'way of Hermes', in which techniques such as alchemy were fused into the more intellectual approach of the philosophical Hermetica, might be appreciated outside Egypt, as by Iamblichus, but was not so far as we know put into practice.

Conclusion

As a practical spiritual way, Hermetism was a characteristic product of the Greek-speaking milieu in Egypt described in the first part of this study – though the Coptic translations show that some at least of the literature was eventually also made available to Egyptians who did not know Greek. And yet, like Hellenistic and Roman Egypt itself, Hermetism was part of a wider Mediterranean whole, a world with its intellectual as well as its linguistic *koinē*. The books of Hermes, both philosophical and technical, enjoyed wide dissemination in the Roman empire, while their doctrine typified and combined the Roman world's literary and religious orientalism, and its yearning for revealed knowledge.

Late antique writers, when quoting the authorities for such-and-such a statement or doctrine, often make no distinction between Hermes and the great sages, legendary or historical, of the Greek tradition.[1] He belonged in the company of the universally recognized wise, so that it was not always thought worthy of remark that he was an Egyptian. On the other hand it was possible, if one wished, to refer to him as 'the Egyptian' *tout court*;[2] and close analogies to, in particular, the technical Hermetica are to be found in the Greek writings ascribed to Zoroaster, Ostanes and Hystaspes, sages of Persia, and to their Chaldaean cousins. It is not by chance that both these groups have been referred to more than once in the foregoing pages – they are not infrequently associated with Hermes by the ancient authorities too.[3] The popularity of the Eastern sages was, of course, nothing new. It had long been believed that Pythagoras, Plato and other wise men of the Greeks had travelled in the East and sat at the feet of its renowned teachers; and occasionally their visits were reciprocated, as by the 'Chaldaean' and the 'magi' who visited

---

[1] Above, 28 n. 89.   [2] Above, 24.
[3] Above, 135–6, 203.

213

the Academy of Plato while its founder was still alive.[4] Such contacts naturally multiplied in the wake of Alexander's armies. Oriental intellectuals like Manetho or the Babylonian priest Berossus were moved to describe their own religious traditions in the language of their new rulers; while among the Greeks there arose a demand for the *ipsissima verba* of the oriental sages. Hence the books of the Persians, the Chaldaeans and, of course, Hermes Trismegistus, adjusting in various degrees the wisdom of the East to the palate of the Greek. At the heart of all these genres lies the same cultural and intellectual compromise. Graeco-Roman orientalism and the occidentalism of the Eastern elites both reflected a sense of intellectual incompleteness, and a consequent readiness to adjust cultural boundaries. Greeks were attracted by the numinousness of oriental religions and the antiquity of oriental cultures, orientals by the clear-headedness of Greek philosophy. What resulted was an unevenly and idiosyncratically homogenized culture, in which it was not uncommon for the same texts to circulate indifferently under the names of both Greek and oriental sages.[5]

That oriental wisdom was often revealed wisdom was undoubtedly important. Most religions experience internal conflicts over doctrinal authority; but Graeco-Roman paganism had the additional problem of how to choose between, let alone reconcile, a primitive theology, that lacked even the external support afforded by institutional substructures and professional priesthoods, and a highly-developed body of philosophical doctrine propagated by organized Schools.[6] The traditional religion was an amorphous agglomeration of cults that had had no discernible beginning in time and which, in the absence of any authoritative statement or source of doctrine, had to make do with the utterances of the poets. He who required explanation or elaboration of the inherited wisdom could expect little help from the oracles, whose forte was guidance on practical matters – though Apollo might on occasion answer theological questions, and Porphyry was not alone among late antique thinkers in believing that

---

[4] Momigliano, *Alien wisdom* 142–3.

[5] E.g. *S.H.* xxix, variously attributed to Hermes, Manetho, Empedocles and Theon (cf. N.F.'s *app. crit.*); *Orph.-fr.* 285, 299 (Hermes and Orpheus). The ps.-Orphic *Lithica*, which were probably first attributed to Orpheus in Byzantium (see the introduction to the edition of Halleux and Schamp, 31–3), invoke the authority of Hermes – but the Greek Hermes, son of Maia. *Pace* the introduction to Friedrich's edition, 35–6, there is little reason to assume that Thessalus's *Virt. herb.*, with its strong Hermetic connections, circulated under the name of Orpheus as well: see Heeg, in *Festgabe Schanz* 159–66.

[6] The dilemma is well posed by Jul., *or.* XI.148b.

it was possible to extract philosophy from oracles.[7] With the philosophers themselves the enquiring mind would fare little better, since no two of them could agree on anything, as was well known. And since not everybody was able to follow Lucian's Menippus down to Hades in pursuit of the truths which the poets, the laws and the philosophers were so sadly unable to illuminate,[8] it was only a matter of time before somebody thought of combining the divine authority of the oracle with the systematic reasoning of the philosopher.[9] Either a philosopher safely dead could be pronounced to have taught with divine authority – the solution chosen by the later followers of Pythagoras and Plato – or a completely new literature could be produced and presented as a revelation of indisputable truth. Hence Hermetism, a typical specimen of revealed doctrine abundantly paralleled in, for example, the Jewish and Christian (especially gnostic) traditions, but, as a comprehensive divine and literary explanation of God, the World, Man and the soul's destiny, unique in the pagan sphere.[10] This neither Orpheus and Pythagoras nor the magi and Chaldaeans could provide, though quantitatively their influence may have been greater. Here we see once more the individuality of Egypt's contribution to the late pagan thought-world, an individuality bred amidst the unusually intimate cultural inter-actions that had been stimulated by the settlement of Greeks in the narrow valley of the Nile.[11]

Guaranteed then by the prestige of Trismegistus and of Egypt, the revelatory solution to the problem of authority had an undeniable attractiveness, not least for those, like Iamblichus, who hoped to rally the ranks of Christianity's opponents. But Hermetism should primarily be judged neither by the reputation of its patron, nor by the effectiveness in our eyes of its explanation of the spheres of being, nor, of course, by its ability– not great – to withstand Christian assault. At heart it was a spiritual way, the way of Hermetic *gnōsis* – a means to an end immune from the scrutiny of philologist, philosopher and historian alike.

[7] See my remarks in *J.R.S.* 71 (1981) 181.

[8] Lucian, *Nec.*, esp. 3–6.

[9] Christians liked to needle the philosophers for their lack of 'divina auctoritas': Lact., *Inst.* III.15.2–5; Aug., *Civ. Dei* XVIII. 41.

[10] The need for a revelation was clearly felt by the author of the Asclepius aretalogy in *P. Oxy.* 1381: 'For the gods alone, and not for mortals, it is possible to tell of the powers of the gods' (40–2).

[11] Cf. Nilsson, *Geschichte* 2.307.

APPENDIX:
Earliest testimonies to the name 'Hermes Trismegistus'

Outside the Hermetica themselves, which are not precisely datable, the title 'Trismegistus' is first applied to Hermes in texts of the second century A.D. Though it was presumably current in Egypt, and probably known abroad too, before the second century,[1] proof of this should not be sought in Byzantine epitomators of earlier writers, who were perfectly capable of adding 'Trismegistus' where they read only 'Hermes'.[2] The letter in which Manetho uses the title is a forgery.[3]

The first two datable occurrences of the title are, then, in Philo of Byblus fr. 2 (810.3), and Athenagoras, *Leg.* xxviii.6. Philo's reference is interesting, or at least salutary, in that it demonstrates how little there may be in a name. Although it is theoretically possible that here too we have to do with a later interpolation, Eusebius, to whom we owe most of our Philonic fragments, was a sober copyist.[4] Yet the context of the allusion – an account of the struggle between Uranus and Cronus, in which Hermes is identified as Cronus's 'secretary' – is perhaps not Trismegistus's most natural environment, and certainly gives us little encouragement to think of Philo as a reader of the Hermetica.[5] This impression is reinforced by the Phoenician scholar's further allusion to a god or early sage (it is not quite made clear which) called Taautos, otherwise unattested, but described here as 'the first of all beings under the sun..., who invented script and was the first to write books...The Egyptians called him Thouth, and the Alexandrians Thoth, and the Greeks translated his name as Hermes.'[6] Clearly we have to do here with the syncretistic Thoth–Hermes who emerged from the intercourse of Greece and Egypt.[7] To this Taautos Philo attributes a

---

[1] *I. mét Eg.* 172; Mart., *Epig.* v.24 (with the comments of Versnel, *Mnemosyne* 27 (1974) 365–405, esp. 395–6). Manilius's modern editors do not encourage the Gundels' suggestion (*Astrologumena* 10 n. 1) that *Astr.* 1.37 be also invoked in this connection.

[2] This may well be the explanation of *C.C.A.G.* 8(3).101.16–17 (the first-century A.D. astrologer Thrasyllus).

[3] *Ap.* Geo. Sync. 73; cf. Laqueur, *R.E.* 14.1100.

[4] See the introduction to the Bouffartigue – Patillon edition of Porph., *Abst.*, 1. LXXV–LXXVIII.

[5] Trismegistus refers to Uranus and Cronus as his ancestors at *C.H.* x.5, but what interests him is their vision of God, not their famous quarrel.

[6] Ph. Bybl., *fr.* 1 (804.25–805.1).

[7] Ebach, *Weltentstehung* 63–71; Baumgarten, *Philo of Byblos* 68–72.

cosmogonical treatise which, he claims, was drawn on by his own main source, the Phoenician sage Sanchouniathon;[8] and in the Philonic (or Sanchouniathonic) cosmogony it is possible to detect, along with Greek or Semitic influences, that of various Pharaonic Egyptian theologies, including the Hermoupolitan.[9] But whether we have here symptoms of Phoenicia's well-known contacts with Egypt in the Pharaonic period,[10] or of debts contracted more recently to Alexandrian scholarship (as Philo himself appears to hint in the passage quoted above), one thing is certain, namely that Philo's cosmology has nothing to do with our Greek Hermetica.[11]

[8] Ph. Bybl., *fr.* 1 (804.19–25).

[9] Ebach, *Weltentstehung* 22–59, 71–9; Baumgarten, *Philo of Byblos* 104–20, 130–1. Note also Philo's representation of Sanchouniathon as translating the hieroglyphic texts of Thoth (*fr.* 1 (805.8–11), and cf. above, 32 n. 115), and the book-titles attributed to Sanchouniathon by the *Suda*: περὶ τῆς Ἑρμοῦ φυσιολογίας and an Αἰγυπτιακὴ θεολογία (Σ 25).

[10] For an overt allusion to these, in an alchemical context, see *Alch. gr.* 54.2–4. Philo's observation, *fr.* 2 (812.15–17), that Taautos 'conceived the holy forms of the letters' by imitating the appearance of the gods, perhaps reflects Phoenician awareness that their script was originally derived from Egyptian hieroglyphs: Ebach, *Weltentstehung* 223–34.

[11] On the possibility that Philo knew theological Hermetica see above, 138 n. 100.

Bibliography

LITERARY SOURCES

Most texts accessible in the Budé, Loeb, Oxford or Teubner series have been excluded. See also the list of abbreviations.

Archive of Theophanes, epistolae, ed. A. Moscadi, *Aegyptus* 50 (1970) 88–154

Arnobius, *Adversus nationes*, ed. (1) C. Marchesi (Turin 1953²); (2) H. Le Bonniec (Paris 1982–)

Artapanus, *F. Gr. H.* 726

Athenagoras, *Legatio*, ed. W. R. Schoedel (Oxford 1972)

Augustine, *Contra Faustum*, ed. J. Zycha, *C.S.E.L.* 25 (Vienna 1891) 249–797
    De divinatione daemonum, ed. J. Zycha, *C.S.E.L.* 41 (Vienna 1900) 597–618
    epistolae, ed. A. Goldbacher, *C.S.E.L.* 34, 44, 57, 58 (Vienna 1895–1923)

Ausonius, *Griphus ternarii numeri*, ed. S. Prete, *Decimi Magni Ausonii Burdigalensis opuscula* (Leipzig 1978) 150–8

Boethius, *Philosophiae consolatio*, ed. L. Bieler (Turnhout 1957)

Book of the dead, tr. T. G. Allen, *The book of the dead, or Going forth by day: ideas of the ancient Egyptians concerning the hereafter as expressed in their own terms* (Chicago 1974)

Books of Jeu, ed. C. Schmidt, *N.H.S.* 13

Chaeremon, ed. P. van der Horst (Leiden 1984)

Cicero, *De natura deorum*, ed. A. S. Pease (Cambridge, Mass. 1955–8)

Clement of Alexandria, *Stromata*, ed. O. Stählin and L. Früchtel (Berlin 1985⁴ (1); 1970² (2))

Contra philosophos, ed. D. Aschoff, *C.C.S.L.* 58A (Turnhout 1975)

Cyranides, ed. D. Kaimakis (Meisenheim am Glan 1976) (Greek text); L. Delatte, *Textes latins et vieux français relatifs aux Cyranides* (Paris 1942) 1–206 (Latin translation)

Cyril of Alexandria, *Contra Julianum*, ed. (1) *P.G.* 76.503–1064; (2) P. Burguière and P. Evieux (Paris 1985–)

Damascius, *Dubitationes et solutiones de primis principiis*, ed. C. A. Ruelle (Paris 1889)
    In Platonis Phaedonem commentaria, ed. L. G. Westerink, *Commentaries on Plato's Phaedo* 2
    Vita Isidori, ed. C. Zintzen (Hildesheim 1967) (*E. Ph.*: *Epitoma Photiana*; *fr.*: *fragmenta* (*Suda*))

Definitions of Hermes Trismegistus to Asclepius, ed. Mahé 2.355–406

Demetrius, *De elocutione*, ed. W. R. Roberts (London 1932)

Didymus of Alexandria, *De Trinitate*, ed. (1) *P.G.* 39.269–992; (2) (1 only) J. Hönscheid (Meisenheim am Glan 1975); (3) (II.1–7 only) I. Seiler (Meisenheim am Glan 1975)

Ephraem the Syrian, *Against Mani*, ed. C. W. Mitchell, *S. Ephraim's prose refutations of Mani, Marcion, and Bardaisan* 2 (London 1921) 190–229

Bibliography

Epiphanius, *Panarion*, ed. K. Holl (Leipzig 1915–33)

Epistola Aristeae, ed. A. Pelletier (Paris 1962)

Eunapius, *Vitae philosophorum et sophistarum*, ed. J. Giangrande (Rome 1956)

Eusebius of Caesarea, *Contra Marcellum*, ed. E. Klostermann and G. C. Hansen (Berlin 1972²)

    Praeparatio evangelica, ed. (1) K. Mras (Berlin 1954–6; 1², 1982); (2) J. Sirinelli and E. des Places (Paris 1974–)

Expositio totius mundi et gentium, ed. J. Rougé (Paris 1966)

Filastrius, *Diversarum hereseon liber*, ed. F. Heylen, *C.C.S.L.* 9 (Turnhout 1957) 207–324

Fulgentius (Fabius Planciades), *Expositio Virgilianae continentiae*, ed. R. Helm, *Fabii Planciadis Fulgentii V.C. opera* (Stuttgart 1970) 81–107

    Mitologiarum libri III, ed. R. Helm, *Fabii Planciadis Fulgentii V.C. opera* (Stuttgart 1970) 1–80

Galen, ed. C. G. Kühn (Leipzig 1821–33; repr. (with additions in vol. 20 by K. Schubring) Hildesheim 1964–5)

George Syncellus, *Ecloga chronographica*, ed. A. A. Mosshammer (Leipzig 1984)

Gregory of Nazianzus, *oratio* XXVIII (*De theologia*), ed. P. Gallay and M. Jourjon, *Grégoire de Nazianze, Discours 27–31 (Discours théologiques)* (Paris 1978) 100–75

Hegemonius, *Acta Archelai*, ed. C. H. Beeson (Leipzig 1906)

Hephaestion of Thebes, *Apotelesmatica*, ed. D. Pingree (Leipzig 1973)

Hermias, *In Platonis Phaedrum scholia*, ed. P. Couvreur (Paris 1901)

Hippolytus, *Refutatio omnium haeresium*, ed. P. Wendland (Leipzig 1916)

Instruction of Amenemope, ed. H. O. Lange, *Das Weisheitsbuch des Amenemope* (Copenhagen 1925)

Instruction of Ankhsheshonq, ed. S. R. K. Glanville, *Catalogue of demotic papyri in the British Museum* 2 (London 1955)

Instruction of Any, ed. E. Suys (Rome 1935)

Instruction to King Merikare, ed. W. Helck (Wiesbaden 1977)

Iohannes Chrysostomus, *Homiliae XC in Matthaeum*, *P.G.* 57–8

Iohannes Malalas, ed. L. Dindorf (Bonn 1831)

Isidore of Narmuthis, *hymni*, *I.mét.Eg.* 175

Jerome, *Vita Hilarionis*, ed. A. A. R. Bastiaensen, in C. Mohrmann (ed.), *Vite dei santi* 4: *Vita di Martino, Vita di Ilarione, In memoria di Paola* (Milan 1975) 69–143, 291–317

Josephus, *Contra Apionem*, ed. T. Reinach (Paris 1930)

Julian, *Contra Galilaeos*, ed. C. I. Neumann (Leipzig 1880)

    epistolae, orationes, ed. J. Bidez, G. Rochefort, C. Lacombrade (Paris 1924–64)

Lactantius, *De ira Dei*, ed. C. Ingremeau (Paris 1982)

    Divinae institutiones, ed. (1) S. Brandt (Vienna 1890); (2) (v only) P. Monat (Paris 1973)

    Epitome divinarum institutionum, ed. S. Brandt, *C.S.E.L.* 19(1) (Vienna 1890) 673–761

Liber Hermetis Trismegisti, ed. W. Gundel, *Neue astrologische Texte des Hermes Trismegistos: Funde und Forschungen auf dem Gebiet der antiken Astronomie und Astrologie* (Munich 1936, repr. with corrections and additions Hildesheim 1978)

Liber sanctus Hermetis ad Asclepium, ed. C.-E. Ruelle, *R. Ph.* 32 (1908) 247–77

Mandeville, Sir John, *Travels*, ed. M. Letts (London 1953)

Bibliography

Manetho, *F. Gr. H.* 609

Marcellus of Ancyra (Ps.-Anthimus of Nicomedia), *De sancta Ecclesia*, ed. G. Mercati, *Note di letteratura biblica e cristiana antica* (Rome 1901) 95–8

Marcellus of Side, *De piscibus, Gr. D. Fr.* LXIII

Marinus, *Proclus sive de felicitate*, ed. J. F. Boissonade (Leipzig 1814)

Marius Victorinus, *In Cic. Rhet.*, ed. C. Halm, *Rhetores latini minores* (Leipzig 1863) 153–304

Michael Psellus, *Allegoria de Tantalo*, ed. J. F. Boissonade, *Tzetzae allegoriae Iliadis accedunt Pselli allegoriae* (Paris 1851) 343–54

Nag Hammadi codices:

    II.5, ed. H.-G. Bethge, *"Vom Ursprung der Welt": die fünfte Schrift aus Nag-Hammadi-Codex II* (diss. Berlin (Humboldt-Universität) 1975)

    VI, ed. (1) D. M. Parrott, *N.H.S.* 11; (2) (6–8 only) Mahé 1–2

Numenius, ed. E. des Places (Paris 1973)

Olympiodorus, *In Platonis Phaedonem commentaria*, ed. L. G. Westerink, *Commentaries on Plato's Phaedo* 1

Oracle of the Potter, ed. L. Koenen, *Z.P.E.* 2 (1968) 178–209

Origen, *Contra Celsum*, ed. M. Borret (Paris 1967–76)

Paul of Alexandria, *Eisagogika*, ed. Ae. Boer (Leipzig 1958)

Philippus (Bardaisan), *The book of the laws of countries*, ed. H. J. W. Drijvers (Assen 1965)

Philo of Alexandria, *De vita Mosis*, ed. R. Arnaldez *et al.* (Paris 1967)

    In Flaccum, ed. A. Pelletier (Paris 1967)

Philo of Byblus, *F. Gr. H.* 790

Plutarch, *De Iside et Osiride*, ed. J. G. Griffiths (Cardiff 1970)

Porphyry, *De abstinentia*, ed. J. Bouffartigue and M. Patillon (Paris 1977–)

    De imaginibus, ed. J. Bidez, *Vie de Porphyre, le philosophe néo-platonicien* (Gent 1913) 1*–23*

    De regressu animae, ed. J. Bidez, *Vie de Porphyre, le philosophe néo-platonicien* (Gent 1913) 25*–44*

    Epistola ad Anebonem, ed. A. R. Sodano (Naples 1958)

    Vita Plotini, ed. P. Henry and H.-R. Schwyzer, *Plotini opera* 1 (Paris 1951) 1–41; 1^2 (Oxford 1964) 1–38

Proclus, *De arte hieratica*, ed. J. Bidez, *C.M.A.G.* 6.139–51

Prolegomena philosophiae Platonicae, ed. L. G. Westerink, *Anonymous prolegomena*

Ps.-Cyprian, *Quod idola dii non sint*, ed. G. Hartel, *S. Thasci Caecili Cypriani opera omnia* 1 (Vienna 1868) 17–31

Ps.-Eupolemus, *F. Gr. H.* 724

Ps.-Eusebius of Alexandria, *Sermones*, *P.G.* 86.289–462

Ps.-Julian, *epistolae*, ed. J. Bidez and F. Cumont, *Imp. Caesaris Flavii Claudii Iuliani epistulae leges poematia fragmenta varia* (Paris 1922) 228–86

Ps.-Justin, *Cohortatio ad Gentiles*, ed. J. C. T. von Otto, *Iustini philosophi et martyris opera quae feruntur omnia* 2 (Jena 1879³) 18–126

Ps.-Orpheus, *Lithica*, ed. R. Halleux and J. Schamp, *Les lapidaires grecs* (Paris 1985)

Quodvultdeus, *Adversus quinque haereses*, ed. R. Braun, *C.C.S.L.* 60 (Turnhout 1976) 259–301

    Liber promissionum et praedictorum Dei, ed. R. Braun, *S.C.* 101–2 (Paris 1964) = *C.C.S.L.* 60 (Turnhout 1976) 1–223

Bibliography

Rufinus, *Historia ecclesiastica*, ed. T. Mommsen in E. Schwartz (ed.) *Eusebius Werke* 2 (Leipzig 1903–9)

Setne I, ed. W. Erichsen, *Demotische Lesestücke* 1 (Leipzig 1937) 1–40

Socrates Scholasticus, *Historia ecclesiastica*, ed. R. Hussey (Oxford 1853)

Sozomen, *Historia ecclesiastica*, ed. J. Bidez, *G.C.S.* (Berlin 1960) = *S.C.* 306 etc. (Paris 1983–)

Stephanus of Byzantium, *Ethnica*, ed. A. Meineke (Berlin 1849)

Strasbourg cosmogony, Gr. D. Fr. xxiv

Suda, ed. A. Adler (Leipzig 1928–38)

Synesius, *Calvitii encomium, Dion, De providentia* (= *Aegyptii*), ed. N. Terzaghi, *Synesii Cyrenensis opuscula* (Rome 1944)

   epistolae, ed. A. Garzya (Rome 1979)

   hymni, ed. (1) N. Terzaghi (Rome 1939); (2) C. Lacombrade (Paris 1978)

Tertullian, *Adversus Valentinianos*, ed. J.-C. Fredouille (Paris 1980–1)

   De anima, ed. J. H. Waszink (Amsterdam 1947) = *C.C.S.L.* 2 (Turnhout 1954) 779–869

   De corona, ed. A. Kroymann, *C.C.S.L.* 2 (Turnhout 1954) 1037–65

Theophrastus, *De pietate*, ed. W. Pötscher (Leiden 1964)

Thessalus, *De virtutibus herbarum*, ed. H.-V. Friedrich (Meisenheim am Glan 1968)

Timothy of Constantinople, *De receptione haereticorum*, *P.G.* 86.12–68

Zosimus of Panopolis, *fragmenta graeca*, *Alch. gr.* 107–252

   fragmenta syriaca, tr. (only) R. Duval, in M. Berthelot, *La chimie au moyen âge* 2 (Paris 1893) 203–331

SECONDARY WORKS

The following list is intended only as an explanation of references in the footnotes. Articles in encyclopaedias have been excluded.

Adler, M., 'Der Arkesilaos-Papyrus', in *Charisteria Alois Rzach zum achtzigsten Geburtstag dargebracht* (Reichenberg 1930) 5–10

Altenmüller, B., *Synkretismus in den Sargtexten* (Wiesbaden 1975)

Amann, J., *Die Zeusrede des Ailios Aristeides* (Stuttgart 1931)

Annequin, J., *Recherches sur l'action magique et ses représentations (Ier et IIème siècles après J.C.)* (Paris 1973)

Armstrong, A. H., *Plotinian and Christian studies* (London 1979)

Assmann, J., 'Königsdogma und Heilserwartung. Politische und kultische Chaosbeschreibung in ägyptischen Texten', in Hellholm, D. (ed.), *Apocalypticism in the Mediterranean world and the Near East. Proceedings of the International Colloquium on Apocalypticism, Uppsala, August 12–17, 1979* (Tübingen 1983) 345–77

Athanassiadi-Fowden, P. (tr. Campai, A.), *L'imperatore Giuliano* (Milan 1984 [with additions to first English edition])

Barnes, T. D., *Tertullian. A historical and literary study* (Oxford 1971; 1985 [corrected reprint with postscript])

   Constantine and Eusebius (Cambridge, Mass. 1981)

Bibliography

Bataille, A., 'Quelques graffites grecs de la montagne Thébaine', *B.I.A.O.* 38 (1939) 141–79

Baumgarten, A. I., *The Phoenician History of Philo of Byblos: a commentary* (Leiden 1981)

Behr, C. A., *Aelius Aristides and the Sacred Tales* (Amsterdam 1968)

Bell, H. I., 'Graeco-Egyptian religion', *M.H.* 10 (1953) 222–37

Bell, H. I., Nock, A. D., and Thompson, H., 'Magical texts from a bilingual papyrus in the British Museum', *P.B.A.* 17 (1931) 235–87

Bellet, P., 'Bibliographical glosses and grammar in Ogdoad', *Enchoria* 9 (1979) 1–4

Bergman, J., 'Beitrag zur Interpretatio Graeca: Ägyptische Götter in griechischer Übertragung', in Hartmann, S. S. (ed.), *Syncretism: based on papers read at the Symposium on Cultural Contact, Meeting of Religions, Syncretism held at Åbo on the 8th–10th of September, 1966* (Stockholm 1969) 207–27

'Ancient Egyptian theogony in a Greek magical papyrus (PGM vii, ll. 516–521)', in Voss, M. H. van *et al.* (eds.), *Studies in Egyptian religion dedicated to Professor Jan Zandee* (Leiden 1982) 28–37

'Nephthys découverte dans un papyrus magique', in *Mélanges Adolphe Gutbub* (Montpellier 1984) 1–11

Berthelot, M., 'Sur les voyages de Galien et de Zosime dans l'Archipel et en Asie, et sur la matière médicale dans l'antiquité', *J.S.* (1895) 382–7

Betz, H. D., 'The Delphic maxim ΓΝΩΘΙ ΣΑΥΤΟΝ in Hermetic interpretation', *H. Th. R.* 63 (1970) 465–84

'The Delphic maxim "Know yourself" in the Greek magical papyri', *H.R.* 21 (1981–2) 156–71

Bidez, J., 'Les écoles chaldéennes sous Alexandre et les Séleucides', *A. I. Ph. O.* 3 (1935) (= *Volume offert à Jean Capart*) 41–89

'La découverte à Trèves d'une inscription en vers grecs célébrant le dieu Hermès', *A.E.H.E.G.* 2 (1938) 15–28

Bidez, J., and Cumont, F., *Les mages hellénisés: Zoroastre, Ostanès et Hystaspe d'après la tradition grecque* (Paris 1938)

Bingen, J., 'L'Egypte gréco-romaine et la problématique des interactions culturelles', in *Proceedings of the Sixteenth International Congress of Papyrology, New York, 24–31 July 1980* (Chico, Ca. 1981) 3–18

Bizzochi, C., 'Gl'inni filosofici di Sinesio interpretati come mistiche celebrazioni', *Gregorianum* 32 (1951) 347–87

Blackman, A. M., and Fairman, H. W., 'The myth of Horus at Edfu-2', *J.E.A.* 29 (1943) 2–36

Blackman, W. S. and A. M., 'An ancient Egyptian symbol as a modern Egyptian amulet', *A.I.Ph.O.* 3 (1935) (= *Volume offert à Jean Capart*) 91–5

Blochet, E., 'Etudes sur le gnosticisme musulman', *R.S.O.* 2 (1908–9) 717–56; 3 (1910) 177–203; 4 (1911–12) 47–79, 267–300; 6 (1914–15) 5–67

Boano, G., 'Sul *De reditu suo* di Rutilio Namaziano', *R.F.I.C.* 26 (1948) 54–87

Bober, P. P., 'The Mithraic symbolism of Mercury carrying the infant Bacchus', *H. Th. R.* 39 (1946) 75–84

Böhlig, A., 'Die griechische Schule und die Bibliothek von Nag Hammadi', in Böhlig, A., and Wisse, F., *Zum Hellenismus in den Schriften von Nag Hammadi* (Wiesbaden 1975) 9–53

Bibliography

Boll, F., *Kleine Schriften zur Sternkunde des Altertums* (Leipzig 1950)

Bollók, J., 'Du problème de la datation des hymnes d'Isidore', *Stud. Aeg.* 1 (1974) 27–37

Bonner, C., *Studies in magical amulets, chiefly Graeco-Egyptian* (Ann Arbor 1950)

Bousset, W. (ed. Verheule, A. F.), *Religionsgeschichtliche Studien: Aufsätze zur Religionsgeschichte des hellenistischen Zeitalters* (Leiden 1979)

Bowie, E. L., 'The importance of sophists', *Y. Cl. S.* 27 (1982) 29–59

Boyce, M., *A reader in Manichaean Middle Persian and Parthian: texts with notes* (Leiden 1975)

Boylan, P., *Thoth the Hermes of Egypt. A study of some aspects of theological thought in ancient Egypt* (London 1922)

Brashear, W., 'Ein Berliner Zauberpapyrus', *Z.P.E.* 33 (1979) 261–78

Braun, F.-M., *Jean le Théologien* 2 (Paris 1964)

Bresciani, E., *Graffiti démotiques du Dodecaschoene* (Cairo 1969)

Brock, S., 'A Syriac collection of prophecies of the pagan philosophers', *O.L.P.* 14 (1983) 203–46

'Some Syriac excerpts from Greek collections of pagan prophecies', *V. Chr.* 38 (1984) 77–90

Broek, R. van den, 'Four Coptic fragments of a Greek Theosophy', *V. Chr.* 32 (1978) 118–42

Browne, G. M., 'Harpocration Panegyrista', *I.C.S.* 2 (1977) 184–96

Brugsch, H., *Reise nach der grossen Oase El Khargeh in der libyschen Wüste* (Leipzig 1878)

Brunner, H., et al., *Ägyptologie* 2: *Literatur* (Leiden 1952)

Bülow-Jacobsen, A., 'The archiprophetes', in *Actes du XVe Congrès International de Papyrologie* 4: *Papyrologie documentaire* (Brussels 1979) 124–31

Burkert, W., 'Zur geistesgeschichtlichen Einordnung einiger Pseudopythagorica', *E.A.C.* 18 (1972) 23–55

Burkhardt, A., 'Zu späten heidnischen Priestern in Philae', in Nagel, P. (ed.), *Graeco-Coptica. Griechen und Kopten im byzantinischen Ägypten* (Halle 1984) 77–83

Burkitt, F. C., *The religion of the Manichees* (Cambridge 1925)

Butler, A. J. (ed. Fraser, P. M.), *The Arab conquest of Egypt and the last thirty years of the Roman dominion* (Oxford 1978²)

Calderini, A., *Dizionario dei nomi geografici e topografici dell'Egitto greco-romano* (Cairo, Madrid, Milan 1935–)

Cameron, Alan, *Claudian. Poetry and propaganda at the court of Honorius* (Oxford 1970)

'The empress and the poet: paganism and politics at the court of Theodosius II', *Y. Cl. S.* 27 (1982) 217–89

Canart, P., 'Les papyri grecs de la Bibliothèque Vaticane et du Musée Egyptien du Vatican. Histoire et inventaire', in Pintaudi, R. (ed.), *Miscellanea papyrologica* (Florence 1980) 371–90

Capart, J., 'Rapport sur une fouille faite du 14 au 20 février 1927 dans la necropole de Héou', *A.S.A.E.* 27 (1927) 43–8

Carcopino, J., *Aspects mystiques de la Rome païenne* (Paris 1942)

Casarico, L., 'Note su alcune feste nell'Egitto tolemaico e romano', *Aegyptus* 61 (1981) 121–42

Chadwick, H., *Priscillian of Avila. The occult and the charismatic in the early Church* (Oxford 1976)

Bibliography

Charbonneaux, J., 'Prêtres égyptiens', in Chevallier, R. (ed.), *Mélanges d'archéologie et d'histoire offerts à André Piganiol* 1 (Paris 1966) 407–20

Charles-Picard, G., *Les religions de l'Afrique antique* (Paris 1954)

Chassinat, E., *Le temple d'Edfou* 3 (Cairo 1928)

Church, F. F., and Stroumsa, G. G., 'Mani's disciple Thomas and the Psalms of Thomas', *V. Chr.* 34 (1980) 47–55

Courcelle, P., *Connais-toi toi-même de Socrate à Saint Bernard* (Paris 1974–5)

Couroyer, B., 'Le chemin de vie en Egypte et en Israël', *R. Bi.* 56 (1949) 412–32

Crawford, D. J., *Kerkeosiris. An Egyptian village in the Ptolemaic period* (Cambridge 1971)

   'Ptolemy, Ptah and Apis in Hellenistic Memphis', in Crawford, D. J., *et al.* (eds.), *Studies on Ptolemaic Memphis* (Leuven 1980) 1–42

Cumont, F., 'Un livre nouveau sur la liturgie païenne', *R.I.P.B.* 47 (1904) 1–10

   Astrology and religion among the Greeks and Romans (New York 1912)

   (tr. Burckhardt-Brandenberg, A.), *Die orientalischen Religionen im römischen Heidentum* (Leipzig 1931³ [with additions to fourth French edition]; Stuttgart 1981⁸ [reprint])

   L'Egypte des astrologues (Brussels 1937)

Dagron, G., 'L'empire romain d'orient au IVᵉ siècle et les traditions politiques de l'hellénisme: le témoignage de Thémistios', *T. & M. Byz.* 3 (1968) 1–242

Daumas, F., 'Le fonds égyptien de l'hermétisme', in Ries, J. (ed.), *Gnosticisme et monde hellénistique: Actes du Colloque de Louvain-la-Neuve (11–14 mars 1980)* (Louvain-la-Neuve 1982) 3–25

   'L'alchimie a-t-elle une origine égyptienne?', in *Das römisch-byzantinische Ägypten. Akten des internationalen Symposions 26.–30. September 1978 in Trier* (Mainz am Rhein 1983) 109–18

Davies, N. de G. (eds. Bull, L., and Hall, L. F.), *The temple of Hibis in El Khārgeh oasis* 3: *The decoration* (New York 1953)

Dawson, W. R., 'Anastasi, Sallier, and Harris and their papyri', *J.E.A.* 35 (1949) 158–66

Decret, F., *L'Afrique manichéenne (IVᵉ–Vᵉ siècles). Etude historique et doctrinale* (Paris 1978)

Degen, R., 'Galen im Syrischen: Eine Übersicht über die syrische Überlieferung der Werke Galens', in Nutton, V. (ed.), *Galen: problems and prospects* (London 1981) 131–66

Delatte, A., and Derchain, P., *Les intailles magiques gréco-égyptiennes (Bibliothèque Nationale, Cabinet des Médailles et Antiques)* (Paris 1964)

Delatte, L., Govaerts, S., and Denooz, J., *Index du Corpus Hermeticum* (Rome 1977)

Deonna, W., *Mercure et le scorpion* (Brussels 1959)

Derchain, P., 'A propos de Claudien, Eloge de Stilichon, II, 424–436', *ZÄ.S.* 81 (1956) 4–6

   'L'authenticité de l'inspiration égyptienne dans le "Corpus Hermeticum"', *R.H.R.* 161 (1962) 175–98

   'Pseudo-Jamblique ou Abammôn? Quelques observations sur l'égyptianisme du *De Mysteriis*', *C.E.* 38 (1963) 220–6.

   Le papyrus Salt 825 (B.M. 10051), rituel pour la conservation de la vie en Egypte (Brussels 1965)

   'Miettes', *R. Egypt.* 26 (1974) 7–20

Bibliography

Derchain-Urtel, M.-T., *Thot à travers ses épithètes dans les scènes d'offrandes des temples d'époque gréco-romaine* (Brussels 1981)

Dieterich, A., *Abraxas. Studien zur Religionsgeschichte des spätern Altertums* (Leipzig 1891) (ed. Weinreich, O.), *Eine Mithrasliturgie* (Leipzig 1923³)

Dodd, C. H., *The Bible and the Greeks* (London 1935)
The interpretation of the fourth gospel (Cambridge 1953)

Dodds, E. R., *The Greeks and the irrational* (Berkeley 1951)
Pagan and Christian in an age of anxiety: some aspects of religious experience from Marcus Aurelius to Constantine (Cambridge 1965)
'New light on the "Chaldaean Oracles"', in Lewy, *Chaldaean Oracles* (*q.v.*) 693–701

Dörrie, H., *Platonica minora* (Munich 1976)

Donadoni, S., 'Il greco di un sacerdote di Narmuthis', *Acme* 8.2–3 (1955) 73–83

Dornseiff, F., *Das Alphabet in Mystik und Magie* (Leipzig 1925)

Drijvers, H. J. W., 'De hymnen van Madinet-Madi en de hellenistische Isisreligie', *Vox theologica* 32 (1962) 139–50
Bardaiṣan of Edessa (Assen 1966)
'Bardaiṣan of Edessa and the Hermetica. The Aramaic philosopher and the philosophy of his time', *J.V.E.G.* 21 (1969–70) 190–210
'Mithra at Hatra?', in *Etudes Mithriaques. Actes du 2ᵉ Congrès International Téhéran, du 1ᵉʳ au 8 septembre 1975* (Leiden 1978) 151–86

Drioton, E., 'Une sculpture copte inspirée des hiéroglyphes', in *Studi in onore di Aristide Calderini e Roberto Paribeni* 2 (Milan 1957) 471–7

Dubuisson, M., 'Remarques sur le vocabulaire grec de l'acculturation', *R. B. Ph.* 60 (1982) 5–32

Dunand, F., *Le culte d'Isis dans le bassin oriental de la méditerranée* (Leiden 1973)
'Les syncrétismes dans la religion de l'Egypte romaine', in Dunand, F., and Lévêque, P. (eds.), *Les syncrétismes dans les religions de l'antiquité: Colloque de Besançon (22–23 octobre 1973)* (Leiden 1975) 152–85
'L'Oracle du Potier et la formation de l'apocalyptique en Egypte', in *L'apocalyptique* (Paris 1977) 41–67
Religion populaire en Egypte romaine. Les terres cuites isiaques du Musée du Caire (Leiden 1979)
'Grecs et égyptiens en Egypte lagide: le problème de l'acculturation', in *Modes de contacts et processus de transformation dans les sociétés anciennes: Actes du colloque de Cortone (24–30 mai 1981)* (Pisa–Rome 1983) 45–87

Dunbabin, K. M. D., *The mosaics of Roman North Africa. Studies in iconography and patronage* (Oxford 1978)

Ebach, J., *Weltentstehung und Kulturentwicklung bei Philo von Byblos. Ein Beitrag zur Überlieferung der biblischen Urgeschichte im Rahmen des altorientalischen und antiken Schöpfungsglaubens* (Stuttgart 1979)

Eitrem, S., 'La théurgie chez les néo-platoniciens et dans les papyrus magiques', *S.O.* 22 (1942) 49–79

Elsas, C., *Neuplatonische und gnostische Weltablehnung in der Schule Plotins* (Berlin 1975)

Emery, W. B., 'Preliminary report on the excavations at North Saqqâra 1964–5', *J.E.A.* 51 (1965) 3–8

Engelmann, H., *The Delian aretalogy of Sarapis* (Leiden 1975)

Bibliography

Erman, A., 'Die Obeliskenübersetzung des Hermapion', *S.P.A* (1914) 245–73

Ferwerda, R., 'Two souls: Origen's and Augustine's attitude toward the two souls doctrine. Its place in Greek and Christian philosophy', *V. Chr.* 37 (1983) 360–78

Festugière, A.-J., *La révélation d'Hermès Trismégiste* (Paris 1944–54; 1², 1950)
'La religion grecque à l'époque romaine', *R.E.G.* 64 (1951) 472–93
Hermétisme et mystique païenne (Paris 1967)
Etudes de religion grecque et hellénistique (Paris 1972)
Etudes d'histoire et de philologie (Paris 1975)
L'idéal religieux des grecs et l'Evangile (Paris 1981²)

Filoramo, G., *Luce e gnosi. Saggio sull' illuminazione nello gnosticismo* (Rome 1980)

Fodor, A., 'The origins of the Arabic legends of the Pyramids', *A. Orient. Hung.* 23 (1970) 335–63

Forbes, R. J., *Studies in ancient technology* 1 (Leiden 1964²)

Fortin, E. L., 'The *viri novi* of Arnobius and the conflict between faith and reason in the early Christian centuries', *O.C.A* 195 (1973) 197–226

Foucault, M., 'What is an author?', in Harari, J.V. (ed.), *Textual strategies: perspectives in post-structuralist criticism* (London 1980) 141–60

Fowden, G., 'The Platonist philosopher and his circle in late antiquity', *Philosophia* 7 (1977) 359–83
'Late antique paganism reasoned and revealed', *J.R.S.* 71 (1981) 178–82
'The pagan holy man in late antique society', *J.H.S.* 102 (1982) 33–59

Franz, M. L. von, 'Die alchemistische Makrokosmos-Mikrokosmos-Idee im Lichte der Jungschen Psychologie', *Symbolon* 1 (1960) 27–38

Fraser, P. M., *Ptolemaic Alexandria* (Oxford 1972)

Führer, R., 'Noch ein Akrostichon in den Kyraniden', *Z.P.E.* 58 (1985) 270

Gallotta, B., 'Serapide a Menfi', *P.P.* 167 (1976) 129–42

Gardiner, A. H., 'The House of Life', *J.E.A.* 24 (1938) 157–79

Glucker, J., *Antiochus and the late Academy* (Göttingen 1978)

Görg, M., 'Ptolemäische Theologie in der Septuaginta', in Maehler, H., and Strocka, V. M. (eds.), *Das ptolemäische Ägypten. Akten des Internationalen Symposions 27.–29. September 1976 in Berlin* (Mainz am Rhein 1978) 177–85

González Blanco, A., 'Hermetism. A bibliographical approach', *A.N.R.W.* II.17.4 (1984) 2240–81

Grafton, A., 'Protestant versus Prophet: Isaac Casaubon on Hermes Trismegistus', *J.W.I.* 46 (1983) 78–93

Grandjean, Y., *Une nouvelle arétalogie d'Isis à Maronée* (Leiden 1975)

Grant, R. M., 'Studies in the Apologists', *H. Th. R.* 51 (1958) 123–34
'Greek literature in the treatise *De trinitate* and Cyril *Contra Julianum*', *J. Th. S.* 15 (1964) 265–79

Grecu, V., 'Darstellungen altheidnischer Denker und Schriftsteller in der Kirchen-malerei des Morgenlandes', *A.R.B.S.H.* 11 (1924) 1–68 [offprint]

Grese, W. C., *Corpus Hermeticum XIII and early Christian literature* (Leiden 1979)

Griffith, F. Ll., *Catalogue of the demotic graffiti of the Dodecashoenus* 1 (Oxford 1937)

Griffith, F. Ll., and Thompson, H., *The demotic magical papyrus of London and Leiden* (London 1904–9)

Griffiths, J. G., *Plutarch's De Iside et Osiride* (Cardiff 1970)
Apuleius of Madauros: The Isis-Book (Metamorphoses, Book XI (Leiden 1975)

Bibliography

Groningen, B. A. van, *De papyro Oxyrhynchita 1380* (Groningen 1921)

Gundel, H. G., *Weltbild und Astrologie in den griechischen Zauberpapyri* (Munich 1968)

Gundel, W. G. and H. G., *Astrologumena. Die astrologische Literatur in der Antike und ihre Geschichte* (Wiesbaden 1966)

Gutbub, A., *Textes fondamentaux de la théologie de Kom Ombo* (Cairo 1973)

Hadot, P., *Marius Victorinus. Recherches sur sa vie et ses oeuvres* (Paris 1971)
  'Bilan et perspectives sur les *Oracles Chaldaïques*', in Lewy, *Chaldaean Oracles (q.v.)* 703–20

Haenchen, E., *Gott und Mensch: gesammelte Aufsätze* (Tübingen 1965)

Halleux, R., *Les alchimistes grecs* 1 (Paris 1981)

Hani, J., *La religion égyptienne dans la pensée de Plutarque* (Paris 1976)

Harder, R., *Karpokrates von Chalkis und die memphitische Isispropaganda* (Berlin 1944)

Hauer, J. W., *Die Dhāraṇī im nördlichen Buddhismus und ihre Parallelen in der sogenannten Mithrasliturgie* (Stuttgart 1927)

Heeg, J., 'Über ein astrologisch-medizinisches Orphicum', in *Festgabe für Martin von Schanz zur 70. Geburtstagsfeier (12. Juni 1912)* (Würzburg 1912) 159–66

Heitsch, E., 'Zu den Zauberhymnen', *Philologus* 103 (1959) 215–36

Henrichs, A., 'The sophists and Hellenistic religion: Prodicus as the spiritual father of the Isis aretalogies', in Harmatta, J. (ed.), *Proceedings of the VIIth Congress of the International Federation of the Societies of Classical Studies* (Budapest 1984) 1.339–53

Herrmann, P., 'Urkunden milesischer Temenitai', *M.D.A.I.(I.)* 30 (1980) 223–39

Hönscheid, J., *Didymus der Blinde, De Trinitate, Buch I* (Meisenheim am Glan 1975)

Hopfner, T., *Griechisch-ägyptischer Offenbarungszauber* (Leipzig 1921–4; Amsterdam 1974– [reprint with alterations])

Hornung, E. (tr. Baines, J.), *Conceptions of God in ancient Egypt: the One and the many* (Ithaca, N.Y. 1982 [with additions to first German edition])

Howlett, J., 'Some classical saints in the Russian tradition', in Mullett, M., and Scott, R., (eds.), *Byzantium and the classical tradition. University of Birmingham thirteenth Spring Symposium of Byzantine Studies 1979* (Birmingham 1981) 172–8

Ḥusayn, Ṭ., *Al-ayām* (Cairo 1929), tr. Paxton, E. H., *An Egyptian childhood. The autobiography of Taha Hussein* (London 1932, 1981)

Iversen, E., *Egyptian and Hermetic doctrine* (Copenhagen 1984)

Jackson, H. M. (ed. and tr.), *Zosimos of Panopolis, On the letter omega* (Missoula, Montana 1978)

Johnson, J. H., 'The demotic magical spells of Leiden I 384', *O.M.R.L.* 56 (1975) 29–64
  'The dialect of the demotic magical papyrus of London and Leiden', *S.A.O.C.* 39 (1976) 105–32
  'Louvre E3229: a demotic magical text', *Enchoria* 7 (1977) 55–102

Jung, C. G. (tr. Hull, R. F. C.), *The collected works:*
  12: *Psychology and alchemy* (London 1953)
  13: *Alchemical studies* (London 1968)

Kákosy, L., 'Problems of the Thoth-cult in Roman Egypt', *A. Arch. Hung.* 15 (1963) 123–8
  'Decans in late-Egyptian religion', *Oikumene* 3 (1982) 163–91

Kaplony-Heckel, U., 'Neue demotische Orakelfragen', *F.B.S.M.* 14 (1972) 79–90

Bibliography

Karle, B., *Der Alchemistentraum des Zosimus* (diss. Freiburg 1925)

Keizer, L. S., *The Eighth reveals the Ninth: Tractate 6 of Nag Hammadi Codex VI* (diss. Berkeley, Ca. 1973) [Publ. as *The Eighth reveals the Ninth: a new Hermetic initiation discourse (Tractate 6, Nag Hammadi Codex VI)* (Seaside, Ca. 1974). References to earlier and fuller version.]

Keydell, R., *Kleine Schriften zur hellenistischen und spätgriechischen Dichtung (1911–1976)* (Leipzig 1982)

Kiessling, E., 'Die Götter von Memphis in griechisch-römischer Zeit', *A.P.F.* 15 (1953) 7–45

Kippenberg, H. G., 'Versuch einer soziologischen Verortung des antiken Gnostizismus', *Numen* 17 (1970) 211–31

 'Intellektualismus und antike Gnosis', in Schluchter, W. (ed.), *Max Webers Studie über das antike Judentum* (Frankfurt 1981) 201–18

 'Gnostiker zweiten Ranges: zur Institutionalisierung gnostischer Ideen als Anthropolatrie', *Numen* 30 (1983) 146–73, and in Taubes, J. (ed.), *Gnosis und Politik* (Paderborn 1984) 121–40

Koenen, L., 'Manichäische Mission und Klöster in Ägypten', in *Das römisch-byzantinische Ägypten. Akten des internationalen Symposions 26.–30. September 1978 in Trier* (Mainz am Rhein 1983) 93–108

Kolta, K. S., *Die Gleichsetzung ägyptischer und griechischer Götter bei Herodot* (diss. Tübingen 1968)

Koschorke, K., 'Patristische Materialen zur Spätgeschichte der Valentinianische Gnosis', *N.H.S.* 17 (1981) 120–39

Krause, M., 'Ägyptisches Gedankengut in der Apokalypse des Asclepius', *Z.D.M.G.* Supp. 1.1 (1969) 48–57

Kroll, J., *Die Lehren des Hermes Trismegistos* (Münster 1914; 1928² [reprint])

Kutsch, G., *In Lactanti De ira Dei librum quaestiones philologae* (Leipzig 1933)

Labhardt, A., 'Curiositas: notes sur l'histoire d'un mot et d'une notion', *M.H.* 17 (1960) 206–24

Lacombrade, C., *Synésios de Cyrène, hellène et chrétien* (Paris 1951)

Lagercrantz, O., *Papyrus graecus Holmiensis (P. Holm.). Recepte für Silber, Steine und Purpur* (Uppsala 1913)

Lange, H.-O., and Neugebauer, O., *Papyrus Carlsberg No. 1: ein hieratisch-demotischer kosmologischer Text* (Copenhagen 1940)

Lanternari, V., *Movimenti religiosi di libertà e di salvezza dei popoli oppressi* (Milan 1960)

Lauer, J. P., and Picard, C., *Les statues ptolémaïques du Sarapieion de Memphis* (Paris 1955)

Lawson, J. C., *Modern Greek folklore and ancient Greek religion: a study in survivals* (Cambridge 1910)

Leipoldt, J., 'Von Übersetzungen und Übersetzern', in Morenz, S. (ed.), *Aus Antike und Orient. Festschrift Wilhelm Schubart zum 75. Geburtstag* (Leipzig 1950) 54–63

Lenaz, L., *Martiani Capellae de nuptiis Philologiae et Mercurii liber secundus* (Padua 1975)

Lennep, H. J. van, *Travels in little-known parts of Asia minor; with illustrations of Biblical literature and researches in archaeology* (London 1870)

Lenormant, F., *Catalogue d'une collection d'antiquités égyptiennes. Cette collection rassemblée par M. d'Anastasi...* (Paris 1857)

Bibliography

Leroy, J., and Glorie, F., '"Eusèbe d'Alexandrie" source d'"Eusèbe de Gaule"', *S.E.J.G.* 19 (1969–70) 33–70

Lewy, H. (ed. Tardieu, M.), *Chaldaean Oracles and theurgy: mysticism, magic and Platonism in the later Roman empire* (Paris 1978[2])

Lexa, F., *La magie dans l'Egypte antique de l'Ancien Empire jusqu'à l'époque copte* (Paris 1925)

Lichtheim, M., *Ancient Egyptian literature: a book of readings* (Berkeley 1973–80)
  Late Egyptian wisdom literature in the international context. A study of demotic Instructions (Göttingen 1983)

Lloyd, G. E. R., *Magic, reason and experience. Studies in the origin and development of Greek science* (Cambridge 1979)

Long, A. A., 'Astrology: arguments pro and contra', in Barnes, J., *et al.* (eds.), *Science and speculation: studies in Hellenistic theory and practice* (Cambridge 1982) 165–92

Lüddeckens, E., *Ägyptische Eheverträge* (Wiesbaden 1960)

Macmullen, R., 'Nationalism in Roman Egypt', *Aegyptus* 44 (1964) 179–99

Maehler, H., 'Bruchstücke spätantiker Dramenhandschriften aus Hermupolis', *A.P.F.* 30 (1984) 5–29

Mahé, J.-P., 'Remarques d'un latiniste sur l'*Asclepius* copte de Nag Hammadi', *R.S.R.* 48 (1974) 136–55
  'Le sens et la composition du traité hermétique, "L'Ogdoade et l'Ennéade", conservé dans le Codex VI de Nag Hammadi', *R.S.R.* 48 (1974) 54–65
  'Le sens des symboles sexuels dans quelques textes hermétiques et gnostiques', *N.H.S.* 7 (1975) 123–45
  Hermès en Haute-Egypte (Quebec 1978–82)
  'Le *Discours parfait* d'après l'*Asclépius* latin: utilisation des sources et cohérence rédactionnelle', in Barc, B. (ed.), *Colloque international sur les textes de Nag Hammadi (Québec, 22–25 août 1978)* (Quebec 1981) 405–34
  'Fragments hermétiques dans les papyri Vindobonenses graecae 29456 r° et 29828 r°', in Lucchesi, E., and Saffrey, H. D. (eds.), *Mémorial André-Jean Festugière. Antiquité païenne et chrétienne* (Geneva 1984) 51–64

Makal, M. (tr. Deedes, W.), *A village in Anatolia* (London 1954)

Marcus, R., 'The name *Poimandrēs*', *J.N.E.S.* 8 (1949) 40–3

Maspero, J., 'Horapollon et la fin du paganisme égyptien', *B.I.A.O.* 11 (1914) 163–95

Mastandrea, P., *Un neoplatonico latino, Cornelio Labeone (testimonianze e frammenti)* (Leiden 1979)

Mayer, L. A., *Saracenic heraldry. A survey* (Oxford 1933)

McDowell, R. H., *Coins from Seleucia on the Tigris* (Ann Arbor 1935)

McGuckin, P., 'The non-Cyprianic scripture texts in Lactantius' *Divine Institutes*', *V. Chr.* 36 (1982) 145–63

McNeil, B., 'A note on P. Berol. 9794', *Numen* 23 (1976) 239–40

Méautis, G., *Hermoupolis-la-Grande. Une métropole égyptienne sous l'empire romain* (Lausanne 1918)

Ménard, J. E., 'Gnose païenne et gnose chrétienne: l'"Authentikos Logos" et "Les enseignements de Silvain" de Nag Hammadi', in *Mélanges offerts à Marcel Simon. Paganisme, judaïsme, christianisme: influences et affrontements dans le monde antique* (Paris 1978) 287–94

Bibliography

Merkelbach, R., 'Der Eid der Isismysten', *Z.P.E.* 1 (1967) 55–73
 'Ein ägyptischer Priestereid', *Z.P.E.* 2 (1968) 7–30
Meslin, M., 'Réalités psychiques et valeurs religieuses dans les cultes orientaux (1er–1ve siècles)', *R.H.* 252 (1974) 289–314
Momigliano, A., *Alien wisdom: the limits of Hellenization* (Cambridge 1975)
 Quinto contributo alla storia degli studi classici e del mondo antico (Rome 1975)
Moorsel, G. van, *The mysteries of Hermes Trismegistus. A phenomenologic study in the process of spiritualisation in the Corpus Hermeticum and Latin Asclepius* (Utrecht 1955)
Morenz, S., *Ägyptische Religion* (Stuttgart 1960; 1977² [reprint])
 Untersuchungen zur Rolle des Schicksals in der ägyptischen Religion (Berlin 1960)
 Religion und Geschichte des alten Ägypten. Gesammelte Aufsätze (Weimar 1975)
Moscadi, A., 'Le lettere dell'archivio di Teofane', *Aegyptus* 50 (1970) 88–154
Müller, D., *Ägypten und die griechischen Isis-Aretalogien* (Berlin 1961)
 'I am Isis', *O.L.Z.* 67 (1972) 117–30
Mussies, G., 'The interpretatio judaica of Thot–Hermes', in Voss, M. H. van *et al.* (eds.), *Studies in Egyptian religion dedicated to Professor Jan Zandee* (Leiden 1982) 89–120
Nautin, P., 'La conversion du temple de Philae en église chrétienne', *C. Arch.* 17 (1967) 1–43
Neugebauer, O., *A history of ancient mathematical astronomy* (Berlin 1975)
Neugebauer, O., and Hoesen, H. B. van, *Greek horoscopes* (Philadelphia 1959)
Neugebauer, O., and Parker, R. A., *Egyptian astronomical texts* (Providence, R.I. 1960–9)
Nilsson, M. P., *Opuscula selecta* (Lund 1951–60)
 Geschichte der griechischen Religion (Munich 1967–74³)
Noberasco, G., 'Gli dèi a Deir el Medina', *O.A.* 20 (1981) 259–75
Nock, A. D. (ed. Stewart, Z.), *Essays on religion and the ancient world* (Oxford 1972)
Norden, E., *Agnostos theos: Untersuchungen zur Formengeschichte religiöser Rede* (Leipzig 1923²; Stuttgart 1956⁴ [reprint])
Ogilvie, R. M., *The library of Lactantius* (Oxford 1978)
Olivieri, A., and Festa, N., 'Indice dei codici greci delle bibliothece Universitaria e Comunale di Bologna', *S.F.I.C.* 3 (1895) 385–495
Orlandi, T., 'A catechesis against apocryphal texts by Shenute and the gnostic texts of Nag Hammadi', *H. Th. R.* 75 (1982) 85–95
Orth, E., *Logios* (Leipzig 1926)
Otto, W., *Priester und Tempel im hellenistischen Ägypten. Ein Beitrag zur Kulturgeschichte des Hellenismus* (Leipzig 1905–8)
Parássoglou, G. M., 'Circular from a Prefect: sileat omnibus perpetuo divinandi curiositas', in Hanson, A. E. (ed.), *Collectanea papyrologica: texts published in honor of H. C. Youtie* (Bonn 1976) 261–74
Parker, R. A., 'Ancient Egyptian astronomy', in Hodson, F. R. (ed.), *The place of astronomy in the ancient world: a joint symposium of the Royal Society and the British Academy* (London 1974) 51–65
Parsons, P. J., 'Ulpius Sérenianus', *C.E.* 49 (1974) 135–57
Pearson, B. A., 'Jewish elements in *Corpus Hermeticum* I (*Poimandres*)', in Broek, R. van den, and Vermaseren, M. J. (eds.), *Studies in gnosticism and Hellenistic religions presented to Gilles Quispel on the occasion of his 65th birthday* (Leiden 1981) 336–48

Bibliography

Peek, W., *Der Isishymnus von Andros und verwandte Texte* (Berlin 1930)

Pépin, J., 'Utilisations philosophiques du mythe d'Isis et Osiris dans la tradition platonicienne', in *Sagesse et religion. Colloque de Strasbourg (octobre 1976)* (Paris 1979) 51–64

'Grégoire de Nazianze, lecteur de la littérature hermétique', *V. Chr.* 36 (1982) 251–60

Peremans, W., 'Egyptiens et étrangers dans le clergé, le notariat et les tribunaux de l'Egypte ptolémaïque', *Anc. Soc.* 4 (1973) 59–69

'Le bilinguisme dans les relations gréco-égyptiennes sous les Lagides', in Dack, E. van 't, *et al.* (eds.), *Egypt and the Hellenistic world. Proceedings of the International Colloquium, Leuven – 24–26 May 1982* (Leuven 1983) 253–80

Pestman, P. W., *Chronologie égyptienne d'après les textes démotiques (332 av. J.-C. – 453 ap. J.-C.)* (Leiden 1967)

Pestman, P. W., *et al.*, *Recueil de textes démotiques et bilingues* (Leiden 1977)

Pfister, F., *Der Reliquienkult im Altertum* (Giessen 1909–12)

Philonenko, M., 'Une allusion de l'*Asclepius* au livre d'*Henoch*', in Neusner, J. (ed.), *Christianity, Judaism and other Greco-Roman cults. Studies for Morton Smith at sixty* 2 (Leiden 1975) 161–3

'Le Poimandrès et la liturgie juive', in Dunand, F., and Lévêque, P. (eds.), *Les syncrétismes dans les religions de l'antiquité: Colloque de Besançon (22–23 octobre 1973)* (Leiden 1975) 204–11

'La plainte des âmes dans le *Koré Kosmou*', in Widengren, G. (ed.), *Proceedings of the International Colloquium on Gnosticism, Stockholm, August 20–25, 1973* (Stockholm 1977) 153–6

'Une utilisation du Shema dans le Poimandrès', *R.H.Ph.R.* 59 (1979) 369–72

Places, E. des, *Etudes platoniciennes 1929–1979* (Leiden 1981)

Pötscher, W., *Theophrastos ΠΕΡΙ ΕΥΣΕΒΕΙΑΣ* (Leiden 1964)

Ponsing, J.-P., 'L'origine égyptienne de la formule: un-et-seul', *R.H.Ph.R.* 60 (1980) 29–34

Porter, B., and Moss, R. L. B., *Topographical bibliography of ancient Egyptian hieroglyphic texts, reliefs, and paintings* 6: *Upper Egypt: chief temples (excluding Thebes)* (Oxford 1939)

Posener, G., 'A propos de la "pluie miraculeuse"', *R. Ph.* 25 (1951) 162–8

Préaux, C., 'Les égyptiens dans la civilisation hellénistique d'Egypte', *C.E.* 35 (1943) 148–60

'Les raisons de l'originalité de l'Egypte', *M.H.* 10 (1953) 203–21

Review: B. H. Stricker, *De Brief van Aristeas*, *C.E.* 33 (1958) 153–6

Preisendanz, K., *Papyrusfunde und Papyrusforschung* (Leipzig 1933)

'Zur synkretistischen Magie im römischen Ägypten', in *Akten des VIII. Internationalen Kongresses für Papyrologie, Wien 1955* (Vienna 1956) 111–25

Puech, H.-C., *En quête de la gnose* (Paris 1978)

Quaegebeur, J., 'Teëphibis, dieu oraculaire?', *Enchoria* 5 (1975) 19–24

'The genealogy of the Memphite High Priest family in the Hellenistic period', in Crawford, D. J., *et al.* (eds.), *Studies on Ptolemaic Memphis* (Leuven 1980) 43–81

'Sur la "loi sacrée" dans l'Egypte gréco-romaine', *Anc. Soc.* 11–12 (1980–1) 227–40

'Cultes égyptiens et grecs en Egypte hellénistique. L'exploitation des sources', in

Bibliography

Dack, E, van 't, *et al.* (eds.), *Egypt and the Hellenistic world. Proceedings of the International Colloquium, Leuven – 24–26 May 1982*) (Leuven 1983) 303–24

Quispel, G., 'Note sur "Basilide"', *V. Chr.* 2 (1948) 115–16

'The *Gospel of Thomas* revisited', in Barc, B. (ed.), *Colloque international sur les textes de Nag Hammadi (Québec, 22–25 août 1978)* (Quebec 1981) 218–66

Ray, J. D., *The archive of Ḥor* (London 1976)

'The world of North Saqqâra', *W.A.* 10 (1978) 149–57

Reitzenstein, R., *Poimandres: Studien zur griechisch-ägyptischen und frühchristlichen Literatur* (Leipzig 1904)

'Zur Geschichte der Alchemie und des Mystizismus', *N.G.G* (1919) 1–37

Die hellenistischen Mysterienreligionen nach ihren Grundgedanken und Wirkungen (Leipzig 1927³)

Rémondon, R., 'Problèmes du bilinguisme dans l'Egypte lagide (U.P.Z.I, 148)', *C.E.* 39 (1964) 126–46

Reuvens, C. J. C., *Lettres à M. Letronne sur les papyrus bilingues et grecs, et sur quelques autres monumens gréco-égyptiens du Musée d'Antiquités de l'Université de Leide* (Leiden 1830)

Reymond, E. A. E. (ed.), *From the contents of the libraries of the Suchos temples in the Fayyum 2: From ancient Egyptian Hermetic writings* (Vienna 1977)

Riesenfeld, H., 'Remarques sur les hymnes magiques', *Eranos* 44 (1946) 153–60

Rinsveld, B. van, 'La version copte de l'Asclépius et la ville de l'âge d'or. A propos de Nag Hammadi VI, 75, 22–76, 1', in Pestman, P. W. (ed.), *Textes et études de papyrologie grecque, démotique et copte* (Leiden 1985) 233–42

Robert, L., *Etudes épigraphiques et philologiques* (Paris 1938)

'Trois oracles de la Théosophie et un prophète d'Apollon', *C.R.A.I.* (1968) 568–99

'Un oracle gravé à Oinoanda', *C.R.A.I.* (1971) 597–619

'Malédictions funéraires grecques', *C.R.A.I.* (1978) 241–89

Robinson, J. M., 'The Three Steles of Seth and the Gnostics of Plotinus', in Widengren, G. (ed.), *Proceedings of the International Colloquium on Gnosticism, Stockholm, August 20–25, 1973* (Stockholm 1977) 132–42

'From the cliff to Cairo. The story of the discoverers and the middlemen of the Nag Hammadi codices', in Barc, B. (ed.), *Colloque international sur les textes de Nag Hammadi (Québec, 22–25 août 1978)* (Quebec 1981) 21–58

'Preface', in *The facsimile edition of the Nag Hammadi codices: introduction* (Leiden 1984) 3–14

Rochberg-Halton, F., 'New evidence for the history of astrology', *J.N.E.S.* 43 (1984) 115–40

Roeder, G., *Urkunden zur Religion des alten Ägypten* (Jena 1923)

'Zwei hieroglyphische Inschriften aus Hermopolis (Ober-Ägypten)', *A.S.A.E.* 52 (1952–4) 315–442

Rougé, J., *Recherches sur l'organisation du commerce maritime en Méditerranée sous l'empire romain* (Paris 1966)

Rudolph, K., *Die Gnosis. Wesen und Geschichte einer spätantiken Religion* (Göttingen 1980²)

Rübsam, W. J. R., *Götter und Kulte in Faijum während der griechisch–römisch–byzantinischen Zeit* (Bonn 1974)

Ruppel, W., *Die griechischen und lateinischen Inschriften von Dakke (Les temples immergés de la Nubie. Der Tempel von Dakke 3)* (Cairo 1930)

Bibliography

Saffrey, H. D., 'Le Père André-Jean Festugière, O. P. (1898–1982): portrait', in Lucchesi, E., and Saffrey, H. D. (eds.), *Mémorial André-Jean Festugière. Antiquité païenne et chrétienne* (Geneva 1984) VII–XV

Samuel, A. E., *From Athens to Alexandria: Hellenism and social goals in Ptolemaic Egypt* (Leuven 1983)

Samuel, D. H., 'Greeks and Romans at Socnopaiou Nesos', in *Proceedings of the Sixteenth International Congress of Papyrology, New York, 24–31 July 1980* (Chico, Ca. 1981) 389–404

Satzinger, H., 'Die altkoptischen Texte als Zeugnisse der Beziehungen zwischen Ägyptern und Griechen', in Nagel, P. (ed.), *Graeco-Coptica. Griechen und Kopten im byzantinischen Ägypten* (Halle 1984) 137–46

Sauneron, S., *Quatre campagnes à Esna (Esna* 1) (Cairo 1959)

'La légende des sept propos de Méthyer au temple d'Esna', *B.S.F.E.* 32 (1961) 43–8

'Les conditions d'accès à la fonction sacerdotale à l'époque gréco-romaine', *B.I.A.O.* 61 (1962) 55–7

Les fêtes religieuses d'Esna aux derniers siècles du paganisme (Esna 5) (Cairo 1962)

'Le monde du magicien égyptien', *S. Or.* 7 (1966) 27–65

Sauneron, S., and Stierlin, H., *Derniers temples d'Egypte: Edfou et Philae* (Paris 1975)

Sbordone, F., *Hori Apollinis hieroglyphica* (Naples 1940)

Schamp, J., 'Entre Hermès et Zoroastre. Observations sur la datation traditionelle du lapidaire orphique', *A.C.* 50 (1981) 721–32

Schenke, H. M., *Der Gott "Mensch" in der Gnosis. Ein religionsgeschichtlicher Beitrag zur Diskussion über die paulinische Anschauung von der Kirche als Leib Christi* (Göttingen 1962)

Schneider, H. D., *De laudibus Aegyptologiae. C. J. C. Reuvens als verzamelaar van Aegyptiaca* (Leiden 1985)

Schönborn, H.-B., *Die Pastophoren im Kult der ägyptischen Götter* (Meisenheim am Glan 1976)

Scholem, G. G., *Major trends in Jewish mysticism* (New York 1954[3])

Schott, S., 'Symbol und Zauber als Grundform altägyptischen Denkens', *Studium generale* 6 (1953) 278–88

'Thoth als Verfasser heiliger Schriften', *Z.Ä.S.* 99 (1972) 20–5

Schwartz, J., 'La Koré Kosmou et Lucien de Samosate (à propos de Momus et de la création de l'homme)', in Bingen, J., *et al.* (eds.), *Le monde grec...Hommages à Claire Préaux* (Brussels 1975) 223–33

'Héphestion de Thèbes', in *Institut Français d'Archéologie Orientale du Caire: Livre du Centenaire 1880–1980* (Cairo 1980) 311–21

'Note sur la "petite apocalypse" de l'*Asclépius*', *R.H.Ph.R.* 62 (1982) 165–9

Schwinden, L., 'Gedicht zu einer Weihung an Hermes', in *Trier: Kaiserresidenz und Bischofssitz. Die Stadt in spätantiker und frühchristlicher Zeit* (Mainz am Rhein 1984[2]) 280–1

Schwyzer, H.-R., *Chairemon* (Leipzig 1932)

Scott, W., *Hermetica. The ancient Greek and Latin writings which contain religious or philosophic teachings ascribed to Hermes Trismegistus* (Oxford 1924–36)

Sethe, K., *Imhotep, der Asklepios der Aegypter. Ein vergötterter Mensch aus der Zeit des Königs Doser* (Leipzig 1902)

Bibliography

Amun und die acht Urgötter von Hermopolis. Eine Untersuchung über Ursprung und Wesen des ägyptischen Götterkönigs (Berlin 1929)

Sfameni Gasparro, G., 'La gnosi ermetica come iniziazione e mistero', *S.M.S.R.* 36 (1965) 43–61

Shanzer, D. R., '"Me quoque excellentior"': Boethius, *De consolatione* 4.6.38', *C.Q.* 33 (1983) 277–83

Shelton, J. C., 'Introduction', *N.H.S.* 16 (1981) 1–11

Shore, A. F., 'Votive objects from Dendera of the Graeco-Roman period', in Ruffle, J., *et al.* (eds.), *Glimpses of ancient Egypt: studies in honour of H. W. Fairman* (Warminster 1979) 138–60

Shorter, A. W., 'The statute of Khā 'emuas in the British Museum', in *Studies presented to F. Ll. Griffith* (London 1932) 128–32

Sijpesteijn, P. J., 'The historian Apollonides alias Horapios', *Mnemosyne* 33 (1980) 364–6

Simonetti, M., 'Su alcune opere attribute di recente a Marcello d'Ancira', *R.S.L.R.* 9 (1973) 313–29

Siniscalco, P., 'Ermete Trismegisto, profeta pagano della rivelazione cristiana. La fortuna di un passo ermetico (*Asclepius* 8) nell'interpretazione di scrittori cristiani', *A.A.T.* 101 (1966–7) 83–116

Smith, A., *Porphyry's place in the Neoplatonic tradition. A study in post-Plotinian Neoplatonism* (The Hague 1974)

Smith, J. Z., *Map is not territory. Studies in the history of religions* (Leiden 1978)

Smith, M., *Clement of Alexandria and a secret gospel of Mark* (Cambridge, Mass. 1973)

Sodano, A. R., *Porfirio, Lettera ad Anebo* (Naples 1958)

Sokolowski, F., *Lois sacrées des cités grecques* (Paris 1969)

Speyer, W., 'Religiöse Pseudepigraphie und literarische Fälschung im Altertum', *Jb. A.C.* 8–9 (1965–6) 88–125

Die literarische Fälschung im heidnischen und christlichen Altertum: ein Versuch ihrer Deutung (Munich 1971)

Stegemann, V., Review: W. Gundel, *Dekane und Dekansternbilder*, *Gnomon* 18 (1942) 271–83

Stricker, B. H., *De Brief van Aristeas: de hellenistische codificaties der praehelleense godsdiensten* (Amsterdam 1956)

Stroumsa, G. A. G., *Another seed: studies in gnostic mythology* (Leiden 1984)

Świderek, A., 'Sarapis et les Hellénomemphites', in Bingen, J. *et al.* (eds.), *Le monde grec...Hommages à Claire Préaux* (Brussels 1975) 670–5

Tardieu, M., *Trois mythes gnostiques: Adam, Eros et les animaux d'Egypte dans un écrit de Nag Hammadi (II, 5)* (Paris 1974)

'Aberamenthō', in Broek, R. van den, and Vermaseren, M. J. (eds.), *Studies in gnosticism and Hellenistic religions presented to Gilles Quispel on the occasion of his 65th birthday* (Leiden 1981) 412–18

Terian, A., 'The Hellenizing School: its time, place, and scope of activities reconsidered', in Garsoïan, N. G., *et al.* (eds.), *East of Byzantium: Syria and Armenia in the formative period* (Washington, D.C. 1982) 175–86

Thausing, G., 'Jamblichus und das alte Ägypten', *Kairos* 4 (1962) 91–105

Theiler, W., *Die Vorbereitung des Neuplatonismus* (Berlin 1964²)

Thelamon, F., *Païens et chrétiens au IVᵉ siècle. L'apport de l'"Histoire ecclésiastique" de Rufin d'Aquilée* (Paris 1981)

Bibliography

Thompson, R. C., *Semitic magic: its origins and developments* (London 1908)

Tröger, K.-W., *Mysterienglaube und Gnosis in Corpus Hermeticum XIII* (Berlin 1971)

Vanderlip, V. F., *The four Greek hymns of Isidorus and the cult of Isis* (Toronto 1972)

Velde, H. te, 'The god Heka in Egyptian theology', *J.V.E.G* 21 (1969–70) 175–86

Vergote, J., 'Clément d'Alexandrie et l'écriture égyptienne. Essai d'interprétation de *Stromates*, v, iv, 20–21', *C.E.* 31 (1941) 21–38

Versnel, H. S., 'Mercurius amongst the *Magni Dei*', *Mnemosyne* 27 (1974) 144–51

'A parody on hymns in Martial v 24 and some trinitarian problems', *Mnemosyne* 27 (1974) 365–405

'Destruction, *devotio* and despair in a situation of anomy: the mourning for Germanicus in triple perspective', in *Perennitas. Studi in onore di Angelo Brelich* (Rome 1980) 541–618

Viaud, G., *Magie et coutumes populaires chez les Coptes d'Egypte* (Saint-Vincent-sur-Jabron 1978)

Vogel, C. J. de, *Greek philosophy: a collection of texts, [selected and supplied] with [some] notes and explanations* (Leiden 1950–9)

Vollenweider, S., *Neuplatonische und christliche Theologie bei Synesios von Kyrene* (Göttingen 1985)

Volten, A., *Demotische Traumdeutung (Pap. Carlsberg XIII und XIV verso)* (Copenhagen 1942)

Wachtel, N., *La vision des vaincus: les Indiens du Pérou devant la conquête espagnole 1530–1570* (Paris 1971)

Waelkens, M., 'Privatdeifikation in Kleinasien und in der griechisch-römischen Welt: zu einer neuen Grabinschrift aus Phrygien', in Donceel, R., and Lebrun, R. (eds.), *Archéologie et religions de l'Anatolie ancienne. Mélanges en l'honneur du professeur Paul Naster* (Louvain-la-Neuve 1983) 259–307

Wagner, G., 'Inscriptions grecques du temple de Karnak (1)', *B.I.A.O.* 70 (1971) 1–38

Weber, M., *Wirtschaft und Gesellschaft: Grundriss der verstehenden Soziologie* (Tübingen 1976[5])

Weber, M., *Beiträge zur Kenntnis des Schrift= und Buchwesens der alten Ägypter* (diss. Cologne 1969)

Weinreich, O., *Antike Heilungswunder: Untersuchungen zum Wunderglauben der Griechen und Römer* (Giessen 1909)

West, M. L., 'Magnus and Marcellinus: unnoticed acrostics in the *Cyranides*', *C.Q.* 32 (1982) 480–1

The Orphic poems (Oxford 1983)

Westerink, L. G., *Anonymous prolegomena to Platonic philosophy* (Amsterdam 1962)

The Greek commentaries on Plato's Phaedo (Amsterdam 1976–7)

Texts and studies in Neoplatonism and Byzantine literature: collected papers (Amsterdam 1980)

Whittaker, J., 'Harpocration and Serenus in a Paris manuscript', *Scriptorium* 33 (1979) 59–62

Wigtil, D. N., 'Incorrect apocalyptic: the Hermetic 'Asclepius' as an improvement on the Greek original', *A.N.R.W.* II.17.4 (1984) 2282–97

Wildung, D., *Imhotep und Amenhotep: Gottwerdung im alten Ägypten* (Munich 1977)

Williams, R. J., 'The sages of ancient Egypt in the light of recent scholarship', *J.A.O.S.* 101 (1981–2) 1–19

Willis, W. H., 'Two literary papyri in an archive from Panopolis', *I.C.S.* 3 (1978) 140–51

'The letter of Ammon of Panopolis to his mother', in *Actes du XVᵉ Congrès International de Papyrologie* 2: *Papyrus inédits* (Brussels 1979) 98–115

Wilson, R. McL., 'From gnosis to Gnosticism', in *Mélanges d'histoire offerts à Henri-Charles Puech* (Paris 1974) 423–9

Wlosok, A., *Laktanz und die philosophische Gnosis. Untersuchungen zu Geschichte und Terminologie der gnostischen Erlösungsvorstellung* (Heidelberg 1960)

Wortmann, D., 'Kosmogonie und Nilflut. Studien zu einigen Typen magischer Gemmen griechisch-römischer Zeit aus Ägypten', *B.J.* 166 (1966) 62–112

Wünsch, R., *Antike Fluchtafeln* (Bonn 1912²)

Yates, F. A., *Giordano Bruno and the Hermetic tradition* (London 1964)

Youtie, H. C., '"Because they do not know letters"', *Z.P.E.* 19 (1975) 101–8

Yoyotte, J., 'Bakhthis: religion égyptienne et culture grecque à Edfou', in *Religions en Egypte hellénistique et romaine. Colloque de Strasbourg 16–18 mai 1967* (Paris 1969) 127–41

Žabkar, L. V., 'Adaptation of ancient Egyptian texts to the temple ritual at Philae', *J.E.A.* 66 (1980) 127–36

Zandee, J., 'Das Schöpferwort in alten Ägypten', in *Verbum: essays on some aspects of the religious function of words, dedicated to Dr. H. W. Obbink* (Utrecht 1964) 33–66

Zauzich, K.-T., 'Demotische Texte römischer Zeit', in *Das römisch-byzantinische Ägypten. Akten des internationalen Symposions 26.–30. September 1978 in Trier* (Mainz am Rhein 1983) 77–80

Zieliński, T., *Iresione* (Lvov 1931–6)

'La cosmogonie de Strasbourg', *Scientia (Rivista di scienza)* 70 (1941) 63–9, 113–21

Zintzen, C., 'Bemerkungen zum Aufstiegsweg der Seele in Jamblich's De mysteriis', in Blume, H.-D., and Mann, F. (eds.), *Platonismus und Christentum. Festschrift für Heinrich Dörrie* (Münster 1983) 312–28

Zucker, F., *Doppelinschrift spätptolemäischer Zeit aus der Garnison von Hermopolis Magna* (Berlin 1938)

Zuntz, G., *Opuscula selecta: classica, hellenistica, christiana* (Manchester 1972)

Index

Index

Egypt: demise prophesied, 38–41, 43; foreign attitudes to, 14–17, 162, 181 n. 129; holiness, 13, 14, 15, 39–40, 77 n. 9; mixed culture in Greek and Roman period, 17–22, 171, 186; 'mother of magicians', 66; nationalistic sentiment, 15–16, 37–44, 55; uniqueness, 13–14, 17; Upper, 13, 168–76

Egyptian language and script (hieroglyphic, hieratic, demotic), 54, 61, 63–5, 185, 217 n. 10; survival after antiquity, 64 n. 75

Egyptian priesthood: and alchemy, 166 n. 35, 167; and astrology, 30 n. 106, 167; crocodile-riders, 166; hereditary character, 61; ignorance, 63; international prestige, 14–15; knowledge of Greek, 16, 167–8; and magic, 66, 166, 183 n. 137; relations with Greeks, 15–16, 52–6, 167–8; role in Hermetica, 166–8; sacred literature, 22, 53, 57–68; and theurgy, 135; training, 61; translators of Egyptian texts into Greek, 16, 30, 54; way of life, 54–6

Egyptian religion/theology: account of by Iamblichus, 137–41; alien to Greeks, 17, 51; condition in late antiquity, 63, 185; cosmogony, 23, 62, 217; henotheist tendency, 18; and magic, 80–1; materialism of, 139–40; symbolism, 55, 56 n. 34, 74; syncretism with Greek religion, 18–22, 32, 185–6

Eleusis, 48, 149 n. 28

energies, see sympathy, cosmic

Ennead, 5, 97, 110

Ephraem the Syrian, 204

Epiphanius, priest, 184

Esmet, priest, 65

Esna, temple of Chnum, 63, 64, 171

Essenes, 37 n. 139

Etruscan divination, 144

Euphantus, Egyptian translator of religious texts, 16 n. 18

Euphrates, gnostic, 173 n. 72

Euprepius, priest, 184

Eusebius of Caesarea, 209; reliability of his quotations, 216

fate, 78, 91–4, 109, 119, 123–4, 143, 145, 151, 152, 153 n. 43, 207

Faustus of Mileum, Manichaean, 204, 210

Festugière, A.-J., xxii–xxiii, 72–3, 104 n. 38, 116 n. 1, 156–7

Filastrius, bishop, 210 n. 87

Fulgentius, Fabius Planciades, writer, 211 n.88

Galen, 120 n. 15, 125, 161, 162

General discourses of Hermes, 4, 11 n. 53, 97–9, 100, 106 n. 55, 108

Genesis, Book of, 36

gnomologies, 71–2, 203 n. 45

gnōsis, 101–3, 104–15, 159

gnosticism, Christian, 85 n. 49, 113–15, 118, 145 n. 12, 172–3, 188–9, 191–5, 202–3; geographical diffusion, 192; influence on Zosimus of Panopolis, 120

gnosticism, pagan, 113–15, 187

God: as creator, 77, 107, 207; in Egyptian theology, 137–9; Man's knowledge/vision of, 70, 83–4, 99, 101–3, 104–15, 124, 148, 207; mercy of, 104 n. 41; nature of, 32 n. 115, 70, 102–4, 205–6; see also Man

gods: made by Man, 143; names, 138; self-identification of Man with, 25–6, 71 n. 103, 84, 87 n. 54

Graeco-Egyptianism, see Egypt

Hamra Dum, 4

Harpocrates, 48 n. 10

Harpocration of Alexandria, occultist, 87–9, 161–2

Hecataeus of Abdera, 52

heka, magical power in Egyptian thought, 76

Heliognosti, sect, 210 n. 87

Heliopolis, 66 n. 84; obelisk, 51 n. 19; priesthood, 63

Helios, 83, 84, 181 n. 129, 201 n. 35

Heraiscus, philosopher, 167 n. 44, 184–5

Hermaea, festival, 26

'Hermaic chain', 202

Hermaioi, (?)gnostic sect, 173

Hermanubis, Graeco-Egyptian god, 20

Hermapion, translator of Egyptian inscriptions, 51 n. 19

Hermas, Manichaean missionary, 204

Hermas, *Pastor*, 198 n. 11, 204 n. 49

Hermes: archangel, 27 n. 84; character and legend, 23–4, 24–5, 205; divided by Hermetists into homonymous grandfather and grandson, 29–31; identified with Thoth, 23–4, 25 n. 68, 26–7; Logios, 24, 201–2; in magical papyri, 26, 172; original humanity, 24–5, 27–31; in *Strasbourg cosmogony*, 175; see also Hermes Trismegistus; Michael

Hermes Paotnouphis, 27

Hermes the Theban, 27 n. 86

Hermes Trismegistus: in alchemical texts, 123 n. 27; associated with Isis, 32, 35; called 'the Egyptian', 24, 95 n. 2, 196, 213, a 'theologian', 95; character and legend, 94, 179, 184, 205; consulted by Chaldaeans, 136; depicted in Christian churches, 182; emergence of title, 26, 27, 162, 216–17; evolution from Thoth and Hermes, 22–31, 76, 216; herald of Mani,

Index